943.085   M877we   86-22484
Morris, Warren Bayard
The Weimar Republic and Nazi
  Germany

STARK COUNTY
DISTRICT LIBRARY
CANTON, OHIO 44702

AUG 0 5 1986

The Weimar Republic and Nazi Germany

Warren B. Morris, Jr.

943.085
M877we

The Weimar Republic and Nazi Germany

Nelson-Hall nh Chicago

To my wife, for helping so much
and to my professors
James Caster and W. A. Owings
for introducing me to history

LIBRARY OF CONGRESS CATALOGING IN PUBLICATION DATA

Morris, Warren Bayard, 1948-
  The Weimar Republic and Nazi Germany.

  Bibliography: p.
  Includes index.
  1. Germany—History—20th century.   I. Title.
DD232.M58   943.085   81-14179
ISBN 0-88229-336-2(Cloth)   AACR2
ISBN 0-88229-797-x(Paper)

Copyright © 1982 by Warren Bayard Morris

All rights reserved. No part of this book may be reproduced in any form without permission in writing from the publisher, except by a reviewer who wishes to quote brief passages in connection with a review written for broadcast or for inclusion in a magazine or newspaper. For information address Nelson-Hall Inc., Publishers, 111 North Canal Street, Chicago, Illinois 60606.

Manufactured in the United States of America

10 9 8 7 6 5 4 3 2 1

The paper in this book is pH neutral (acid-free).

Contents

Preface	vii
1 Germany before the First World War	1
2 The First World War and German Politics	19
3 The "Stab in the Back"	33
4 The Revolution of 1918–1919	47
5 Constitution and Treaty	61
6 The Years of Instability	73
7 The Youth of a Dictator	89
8 The Beer Hall Putsch	109
9 The Stresemann Era	125
10 Society and Culture in Weimar Germany	139
11 The Depression	155
12 The Birth of the Third Reich	171
13 The Nazi Dictatorship	191
14 Culture in the Third Reich	217
15 Nazi Foreign Policy 1933–1936	233
16 The Road to War	249
17 Blitzkrieg	279
18 The Fall of Fortress Europe	297
19 The New Order in Europe	325
20 The Twilight of the Gods	347
Notes	363
Selected Bibliography	375
Index	385

Preface

Several years ago, while teaching a course on Weimar and Nazi Germany at Southwestern University in Georgetown, Texas, I discovered that, although there are many excellent studies of various aspects of the history of Germany during this important period, it is very difficult to find a basic survey history of Germany from 1914 to 1945. This book is an effort to fill this gap and to discuss the political, social, economic, and intellectual history of Germany during this tragic period. It is also an attempt to place the terrible events of this era in their proper historical perspective.

Because this is a survey history designed to provide both an introduction to, and an original interpretation of, the subject, I have adopted an abbreviated method of documentation. The notes were designed to enable the reader to find the major primary and secondary sources for each topic discussed. In this way, it is hoped that the work will be well documented without being overly burdened with long and involved notes. Naturally, much of the information contained in this work is the result of research in hundreds of documents and other primary sources. However, if every document were cited, the result would be almost as many pages of notes as there are of text.

I would like to express my gratitude to the persons who helped me with this book. Dr. Douglas D. Hale of Oklahoma State University, Dr. Virgil D. Medlin of Oklahoma City University, Dr. William A. Owings of the University of Arkansas at Little Rock, and Dr. Gaines Post, Jr., of the University of Texas at Austin offered many useful suggestions concerning the content and organization of the manuscript. Professor Katherine Wildermuth of Southwest Texas State

University and David Wildermuth and Richard Wells of the University of Texas at Austin provided many valuable criticisms of the manuscript. I would also like to express deep gratitude for the invaluable assistance of Dr. Douglas Hooker of Southwestern University in the study of the psychological development of Hitler. Finally, I would like to thank my wife, Dr. Cheryl Haun Morris, for assisting me with every aspect of the research and writing of this work.

1

Germany before the First World War

At eleven on the morning of the eleventh of November 1918, silence descended on the battle-scarred landscape of northern France. At last the war had ended, leaving over ten million dead and twenty million wounded. At first the quiet startled the men who had spent the last several years of their lives dodging enemy shells as they lived like animals in the filthy trenches. Slowly they realized that peace had finally come, and a few cautiously peered over the edge of their earthen fortress, testing whether or not the war had actually ended. When enemy fire did not meet them, they grew bolder and climbed out into the sun of the cool autumn morning. As they stood gazing clearly for the first time at their former enemies, they began to cheer, and shouts of joy spread along the four hundred mile front. The war to end all wars and to make the world safe for democracy, as it had been designated by Woodrow Wilson, the idealistic president of the United States, had been won. The hated German kaiser and his followers had been discredited, and the former ruler had been forced to flee Germany for the quiet life of a Dutch farmer. The old German Empire had been transformed into a republic, and it seemed that a new era of peace and democracy had begun.

However, within a few years all the dreams had been turned to despair, for Germany fell into chaos; a fanatical dictator seized power, and once again democracy became the dream of a few, as a new tyranny more terrible than any other in modern history descended on Europe. Within twenty years the sons of the soldiers of the First World War would be forced to take up arms in a war that would kill millions and leave much of Europe a smoking heap of rubble in place of the once proud cities and majestic cathedrals. How had all the good intentions and hopes that engulfed mankind with the end of the First World War ended in such utter failure? How could a people that produced a Goethe, a Schiller, a Beethoven, an Einstein, and dozens of other great men and women allow themselves to become enslaved by a mad dictator and his fanatical followers? The answers to these questions lie partially in the history of the German people before the fateful year of 1914.

The German people, descended from the Teutonic peoples first described by Julius Caesar in his *Gallic Wars* and Tacitus in *Germania,* had built a mighty empire on the ruins of the Roman Empire. On Christmas Day, 800, Charles the Great, or Charlemagne, having inherited the Frankish kingship from Pepin the Short, was crowned Holy Roman Emperor by Pope Leo III. This marked the founding of the Holy Roman Empire, a state that would rule the German people for the next several hundred years. To Charlemagne's glittering court at Aachen came the greatest minds of the day. But a period of division and disorder followed the emperor's death, and it was not until the crowning of Otto I, the Great, in 962 that stability was restored. Yet the successors of Otto were more interested in conquering Italy or crusading against the Moslems than in providing their subjects with effective leadership. Once again Germany sank to a level of anarchy as rival dynasties fought to carve out small states for themselves. Despite the effective leadership of the descendants of Rudolf of Habsburg, elected emperor in 1273, the Holy Roman Empire became an empty title, and more than three hundred separate states arose in Germany.

The disintegration continued and gained momentum in the aftermath of the Protestant Reformation, which began when an obscure monk, Martin Luther, dared to challenge the might and power of the Roman Catholic Church. Seeing an opportunity to enhance their own position while gaining the riches that belonged to the Popes, many German princes rallied to Luther's support, while others followed him out of genuine religious conviction. Germany became a battleground as each warring religious faction fought to destroy the other. First in the War of the Schmalkaldic League and in the disastrous Thirty Years War between 1618 and 1648, armies swept across Germany spreading death and destruction. Even French, Swedish, and Spanish troops, hungry for power and plunder, marched across Germany destroying what little power the empire had wielded. In the Peace of Westphalia, the treaty ending the Thirty Years War, hundreds of princes and cities won the basic rights of sovereignty, completing the disintegration of the Holy Roman Empire.

Although the office of emperor continued to exist until 1806, it was but a hollow title with little more than ceremonial functions. Into the vacuum came two powerful states to contest the leadership of Germany. The first, Austria, founded by the Habsburg dynasty on the ruins of the Holy Roman Empire, grew into a vast state ruling not only Germans, but also Czechs, Rumanians, Hungarians, Croats, Serbs, and several other ethnic groups. Under the rule of such giants as Charles IV, whose troops marched through the debris of the collapsing Ottoman Empire, or Maria Theresa and Joseph II, who both introduced many badly needed reforms and patronized the Enlightenment, Austria became the dominant power in southern Germany. Vienna, its capital, became a glittering center of culture and learning that sheltered great composers such as Haydn, Mozart, and Beethoven.

Meanwhile, in the north, the Hohenzollern dynasty of Brandenburg also was building a great state. Before the outbreak of the Thirty Years War, Brandenburg became one of the largest states of Germany through the inheritance of John Sigismund of the Duchy of Prussia and lands on the Rhine. After the devastation of the religious wars, Frederick William the great Elector rebuilt his lands and established one of the strongest armies in Europe. This military stronghold, controlled by the arrogant landed aristocracy, or Junkers, became the major focus of the Hohenzollern realm. The armed forces controlled almost every aspect of society and politics, and the chief function of government was to provide for their needs. As a result the military unified the scattered peoples governed by Berlin into a body dedicated to the service of their ruler, and it also set the pace of life while it indoctrinated the youth in the principles of discipline and duty to higher authority. A cult of order and rigidity resulted and has persisted to this day. The leaders of the army, organized into the general staff, became an elite corps, subject to the monarch alone and contemptuous of civilian authority. Its power was so great that it survived the fall of the monarchy in 1918 and continued to exist as a body yielding only lip service to the principles of the Weimar Republic. Although the military would play a major role in setting the stage for the victory of National Socialism, it would refuse to yield its ancient prerogatives to Hitler and his accomplices and would become one of the centers of opposition to Nazism.[1]

After the death of the great elector in 1688, three great rulers added to his accomplishments to make Prussia the dominant power in northern Germany. Frederick I elevated the Hohenzollern lands to the level of a kingdom and attempted to turn Berlin from a provincial town into a city worthy of ruling a mighty kingdom. His son, Frederick William I, earned the title "Soldier King" by his dedication to the army and by the reorganization of the Prussian government to support his military establishment. Finally, Frederick II led his troops against the most powerful nations of Europe to challenge the Habsburg hegemony over Germany. In the War of the Austrian Succession, 1740–1748, he wrested Silesia from the Habsburgs, announcing to the world the new position of the Hohenzollern kingdom. The Prussian challenge so threatened Vienna that Maria Theresa ended the centuries old rivalry with France to form a new alliance directed against her new foe. A few years later, the Prussian monarch earned the fear and respect of all of Europe by daringly preserving his kingdom against overwhelming odds during the Seven Years War. Throughout the next century the conflict between Prussia and Austria would continue to smolder, reaching its climax at the battle of Königgrätz in 1866.

The eighteenth century was also a period of great intellectual activity. The age of science and reason dominated all aspects of society. In Austria, Maria Theresa and her son Joseph II supported education and reformed legal codes, while Frederick II accomplished much the same in Prussia. The Enlightenment led to a golden age of German literature. Gotthold Lessing called for a rejection of French models and the creation of a new literature based on the new learning. Johann Wolfgang von Goethe and his contemporary Friedrich Schiller championed Storm and Stress, which was a literary movement that rejected the rigidity and anti-emotional tone of the old literature. It produced such masterpieces as *Götz von Berlichingen,* the story of a leader of the Peasant's Revolt of 1524; *The Sorrows of Young Werther,* the tale of an emotion-filled youth who takes his own life when rejected by a woman; and the *Robbers,* glorifying the struggle of a freedom-loving bandit against an oppressive society. As the century neared an end, the excesses of Storm and Stress led to a reaction normally called German Classicism. Inspired by Johann Winckelmann's cry for a literature of noble simplicity and quiet greatness, Goethe and his fellow authors turned away from the cult of emotion to create refined works like *Iphigenia* and Schiller's great historical dramas. However, despite the elegant nature of German Classicism, new winds blew across German culture and swept away the last remnants of the cult of reason. In Königsberg, near the icy waters of the Baltic, Immanuel Kant preached to his students that man cannot understand the universe through pure reason but must rely also on his perception and understanding. The publication of Kant's *Critique of Pure Reason* in 1781 was the final block in the foundation of the Romantic movement, which would dominate German culture for the next hundred years and provide inspiration for the founders of the philosophy that led to National Socialism.

Outside of Germany, other events were bringing the eighteenth century to a dramatic conclusion. After centuries of oppression by greedy rulers who built lavish palaces while their subjects starved in their primitive huts, the French people revolted and established a constitutional monarchy. When the horrified monarchs of the rest of Europe openly opposed the revolution, a group of radicals swept into power and executed the unlucky Louis XVI and thousands of others suspected of disloyalty to the new French republic. The zealous leaders of France also decided that the only way to preserve their power was to export revolution, and Europe was plunged into almost twenty years of bloody warfare. The French armies, fired by the patriotism of their leaders, swept across Germany, quickly subduing the armies of the Habsburgs and Hohenzollerns. At the same time, a new leader arose from the midst of the fighting, Napoleon Bonaparte, a name that would terrorize all foes of France for the next decade. Napoleon quickly defeated the Austrians, forcing them to sign the Treaty of Campo Formio in 1797, thereby recognizing French domination of the Rhineland. After snatching a crown from Pope Pius VII and crowning himself emperor in 1804, Napoleon once again set out to conquer Germany, defeating the combined armies of Austria and Russia at the Battle of Austerlitz in 1805 and the army of Prussia two years later at Jena.

Napoleon's conquest ended the fragmentation that had afflicted Germany since the disintegration of the Holy Roman Empire. To consolidate his holdings, the French emperor wiped from the map the majority of the principalities, ecclesiastical states, and free cities that had claimed sovereignty since the Peace of Westphalia. He allowed the rulers of Württemberg and Bavaria to assume the royal title and carved out a kingdom in Westphalia for his brother Jerome. However, Napoleon overreached his power by trying to conquer Russia in 1812. After the French army began its trek back from the frozen fields of the Slavic empire, the German people rose up to drive the invader from their fatherland. At Leipzig, in October 1813, the once-mighty armies of Napoleon, retaining only a shadow of the power they possessed before the debacle in Russia, met with defeat, and the Napoleonic threat vanished, never again to jeopardize seriously the freedom of the German people.

The era of the French Revolution and the crusade against Napoleon coincided with the birth and growth of Romanticism. A new generation of authors, nursed in the works of Goethe and Schiller, strove to rid themselves of the last restraints of the cult of reason to create a new art based on feeling and inspiration. In the same year that the people of Paris stormed the Bastille, Ludwig Tieck and the brothers August Wilhelm and Friedrich Schlegel founded *Athenaeum,* a new periodical dedicated to the principles of Romanticism. Others soon followed. Friedrich von Hardenberg, known to his devoted readers as Novalis, praised the poet as the priest of the true religion and wrote of the quest for the unobtainable, symbolized by the blue flower in his *Heinrich von Ofterdingen.* Wilhelm Wackenroder exhorted his followers to recapture the glory of art as divine revelation and glorified the Middle Ages as a time not of darkness but of greatness and achievement.

The same soil that produced Romanticism also produced nationalism. As the German people increasingly grew to resent their powerlessness in the face of the unified French, men arose to preach the new gospel of German nationalism. Even before the outbreak of the French Revolution, Johann Gottfried von Herder, a Lutheran clergyman, argued that each people sharing a common language and history possessed a unique culture rooted in the common people or folk. As the Germans gathered their forces to drive the French from their fatherland, Johann Gottlieb Fichte, a philosopher and rector of the University of Berlin, stood before his students to deliver *Fourteen Addresses to the German Nation.* These messages captured the imagination of the German youth and served as the foundation for a new religion of nationalism. Fichte argued that the German people possessed a special genius lacking in the culture of other peoples. He pleaded with his audience to find true freedom by becoming a part of the German nation and joining the fight to drive the French from their homeland and create a new united Germany on the ruins of the old separate states.

The growth of patriotism during the War of Liberation led to the rediscovery of the German past and a new interest in the culture of the common people. Building on the work of Schiller, who had turned to history for the inspiration of his last works, the authors of the patriotic romanticism loaded their pages with tales glorifying the heroes of the past. Heinrich von Kleist filled the stage with dramas praising men like the brave Teutonic warriors who had defeated the Romans at Tutenberger Forest and the hero of *Prince Friedrich von Homburg*, who found redemption from a sentence of death by accepting his duty to obey the commands of his sovereign, Frederick William, the great elector. Kleist preached to the German youth in his *Catechism for the Germans* about the superiority of the German people and about the need for a new united nation to replace the multitude of states. Some turned to the culture of the common people for inspiration. Achim von Arnim and Clemens Brentano captured the songs of the folk in *The Youth's Cornucopia*, and Jacob and Wilhelm Grimm traveled from village to village collecting stories for their famous edition of *Fairy Tales*. Others combed the libraries for medieval manuscripts, rediscovering the saga of Siegfried's death and the revenge of Kriemhilde in the *Lay of the Nibelung*. Patriotic literature continued to proliferate during the nineteenth century, laying the foundation for the cult of the folk, which would prepare the way for national socialism.

Despite the fervor of the movement for German unification under a liberal constitution, the powers of Europe met in Vienna and refused to give the German people the united nation they so longed to obtain. Instead, led by the Austrian foreign minister, Prince Klemens von Metternich, the Congress of Vienna created a loose confederation of thirty-nine semi-independent states united only by membership in a powerless diet. The failure to achieve national unification and constitutional government led to a rebirth of radicalism. The students of Germany flocked to join the Burschenschaft, a nationalistic fraternity founded in 1815 at the University of Jena. They spread nationalistic propaganda and defied their elders through a massive demonstration at the Wartburg Castle, the place where almost three hundred years earlier Martin Luther had translated the Bible into German. Metternich was horrified, and after Karl Sand, a fanatical student, assassinated the reactionary author August von Kotzebue, he pressured the German rulers meeting in Karlsbad to enforce a set of repressive measures to force the rebellious students into submission. Nevertheless, the demand for German unification continued to grow. In several southern states, the liberals gained power and forced their rulers to accept constitutional forms of government. At the same time, Prussia stimulated the movement for national unification by forming a customs union, which by 1853 included all the states except Austria and Liechtenstein.

Meanwhile, the authors continued to produce nationalistic works. From exile in Paris, the great poet Heinrich Heine called for national unification and bemoaned his forced separation from his homeland. In the 1840s, after a group of extreme nationalists took control of the government of France, an event that seemed to threaten the German Rhineland, a new generation of poets lent their support to the nationalistic crusade. Nicholas Becker wrote his famous song of the Rhine, and a generation of Germans sang, "They shall not have it, the free German Rhine!" Max Schneckenburger exhorted his fellow patriots to vigilantly "Watch on the Rhine." From the British-dominated island of Elba, Heinrich von Fallersleben pleaded for devotion to "Germany, Germany over all." Deprived of a unified nation, the German people developed an exaggerated nationalism that would later lead to dangerous excesses.

The crusade for German unification reached a climax in the Revolution of 1848. Inspired by the example of the French, who had forced Louis Philippe to flee and had established a republic, the German people rose up in March 1848 to demand national unity under a constitutional government. Unable to quell the revolt, the princes yielded to the demands of the rebels. In the south, the rulers appointed liberal "March Ministers," who proclaimed the end of the separate states by calling for election of a national parliament to decide the new shape of the fatherland. Even Frederick William IV of Prussia submitted to the revolution and withdrew all troops from Berlin rather than order them to storm the barricades.[2]

On March 18, 1848, the first nationally elected parliament in German history met in St. Paul's Church in Frankfurt am Main. There, the would-be leaders of the new Germany spent more than a year debating every aspect of the new constitution. After rejecting the demands of the *Grossdeutsch* ("Large Germany") party to include the Habsburg lands in the Reich, they elected King Frederick William IV of Prussia emperor of Germany. They also designed a national government, to be headed by the Hohenzollern kaiser, with a legislative branch consisting of a bicameral Reichstag and a national judicial system. Finally, the Frankfurt National Assembly adopted a set of constitutional guarantees of basic civil rights.

Frederick William IV refused, however, to accept an imperial crown from a body that lacked the might to enforce its will on the princes. Instead, he favored a proposal, made by his old friend Joseph Maria von Radowitz, that the Revolution of 1848 be used as a means to establish Prussian hegemony over Germany by sponsoring national unification under a revised form of the new constitution. The revision would substitute, for the office of kaiser, a college of princes headed by the king of Prussia. Although the majority of the local rulers supported the Prussian Plan of Union, the Austrians, led by Prince Felix von Schwarzenburg, refused to allow themselves to be driven from Germany. Instead, they used a conflict between the elector of Hesse-Kassel and his people to challenge the Prussians and finally, after Tsar Nicholas II threatened to send troops, forced the Prussians to agree to the rebirth of the old German confederation.[3]

Although the Revolution of 1848 failed, it had an important impact on German history. After 1848 the champions of German unification dropped their demand for constitutional government to concentrate on the drive for the creation of a united nation-state. They began to turn to Prussia for leadership, seeing the Plan of Union as a sign that any future unification movement must depend on the Hohenzollerns to challenge the Habsburgs, who sought to prevent unification at all costs. By accepting Prussian leadership, they unknowingly accepted the future domination of Prussian militarism. Finally, the failure of the revolutionaries to achieve their goals led to the birth of a new politics that rejected the idealism of the past in favor of a more realistic approach.

It was such an atmosphere that prepared the way for Otto von Bismarck. Born in 1815 of Junker parents, Bismarck violently rejected the liberalism of 1848, proclaiming instead the old virtues of duty to authority and discipline. After a successful career as Prussian minister to the Diet of the German Confederation, St. Petersburg, and Paris, the future leader of Germany was prepared to assume power in Prussia. When King William I and his advisers failed to win the support of the Prussian diet for desperately needed military reforms, Bismarck stepped in to break the deadlock by demanding the obedience of the Prussian liberals to a new politics dedicated not to the principles of majority votes, but to the concept of rule through "Iron and Blood." Bismarck defied the diet, reformed the army, and collected taxes to pay for the new expense, while the liberals looked on, powerless to take action.[4]

Bismarck, like the German nationalists, realized that until a unified nation had replaced the multitude of semi-independent states, Germany would never be a major power. He took advantage of the conflict between the nationalists and the king of Denmark, who wanted to incorporate into his kingdom Schleswig-Holstein, two duchies ruled by the Danish kings since medieval times, to place Prussia in the forefront of the movement for national unification. When the Germans in the duchies revolted in the fall of 1863, several rulers of smaller states sent troops to defend them from the attempted violation of their rights. Realizing that if Prussia did not intervene it would lose influence over an important issue, Bismarck concluded an agreement with Vienna; and a joint Austro-Prussian army invaded Denmark in early 1864. The Danes were no match for the combined might of the two great German powers and swiftly yielded. At Gastein, the victors divided the spoils; Prussia occupied Schleswig, and Austria administered Holstein, until a more permanent solution could be reached.

The conflict that developed over the future of the newly liberated duchies set the stage for the final scene in the long struggle between the Habsburgs and the Hohenzollerns and the victory of Prussian militarism. The crafty Prussian minister-president won a promise of neutrality from Napoleon III of France by vaguely promising land in the Rhineland and began to marshal his forces for the coming battle. In the summer of 1866, the Austrians gave Bismarck the excuse he was looking for by attempting to call a meeting of the local diet of Holstein to discuss the fate of the duchies. He accused Vienna of violating the Treaty of Gastein and sent the Prussian army to occupy Holstein. The furious Austrians appealed to the Diet of the German Confederation, which voted to condemn the Prussian action and to mobilize its troops. Following the fateful vote, the Hohenzollern delegate, on Bismarck's instructions, stood up to announce Prussian withdrawal from the German confederation and invited the other states to join Berlin in forming a new union that would reflect the true situation in Germany. After a short war, climaxing in the defeat of the Austrians at the Battle of Königgrätz, or Sadowa, on July 3, 1866, Prussia emerged the undisputed master of northern Germany. Bismarck then organized the North German confederation and annexed large areas of northern Germany, including the duchies and the Kingdom of Hanover. After more than a century of dispute, the Habsburgs stood vanquished by the Hohenzollerns.

With Prussian hegemony over the north achieved, Bismarck next set out to win the allegiance of the southern states. He sought to soothe the wounded feelings of the Austrians by refusing to allow the Prussian army to flaunt their victory by marching through the streets of Vienna. Meanwhile, the greedy French emperor, Napoleon III, demanded the right to annex portions of the Rhineland as a reward for his neutrality. Bismarck wrapped himself in the banner of German patriotism and announced that he would not stand by and allow the French to occupy the Rhineland. His declaration won the friendship of the southern states; yet he still had not persuaded them to accept Prussian hegemony. Bismarck found an opportunity to accomplish his last goal when the Spanish, who had forced their queen to abdicate, offered their crown to Prince Leopold of Hohenzollern-Sigmaringen. The French were terrified and used every possible means to prevent a member of a branch of the ruling house of the strongest state in Germany from coming to power in Madrid. King William, who had been skeptical about the idea of Hohenzollern rule in Spain, yielded to pressure and forced Leopold to reject the offer. However, the fanatical nationalists in control of Paris demanded a guarantee that a Hohenzollern would never accept the Spanish throne. William refused this demand and, after a stormy scene in Bad Ems, where he was taking the waters, dismissed the persistent French minister.

The additional French ultimatum played into Bismarck's hands. He issued a statement to the press about the incident at Bad Ems that so inflamed the French that they declared war on Prussia on July 19, 1870. Once again the Hohenzollern minister appealed to the nationalism of the southern states, and they flocked to defend the fatherland from the French threat. Despite the belief that their forces would march through the Brandenburg Gate within a few weeks, the French army crumbled before the German armies at Sedan on September 1, and the victorious troops marched to Paris. After a long siege, during which the starving Parisians were reduced to eating dog meat or anything else they could find, the Germans marched into the French capital on January 28, 1871. The defeated French accepted the German demand for an indemnity of six billion francs and allowed the victors to annex the primarily German-speaking portions of the Alsace-Lorraine, a territory torn from the Holy Roman Empire by Louis XIV. The people of France never forgot the humiliation of 1870. Their demand for revenge helped lay a foundation for the First World War and the Treaty of Versailles that followed.

By humiliating the French, Bismarck emerged as the champion of German nationalism. Delirious with victory, the southern states yielded to his persuasion and agreed to join the north German confederation. On January 18, 1871, the princes assembled in the magnificent Hall of Mirrors of the Sun King at Versailles to proclaim William I as kaiser of Germany. At last, after almost a century of struggle, the German people had a united nation. Although the old states continued to exist, they were now part of a greater Reich that would take its rightful place as a major European power. The new empire was not, however, the creation of the German people as a whole; rather, it was the result of the victory of Prussian militarism. The Reichstag had little real power and could not even force unpopular officials to resign. Actual authority rested in the hands of the kaiser, who appointed the ministry and controlled the military. Significantly, Bismarck, unlike more traditional conservatives, had no fear of the German people. He believed that they would support his kind of government; so he provided for elections to the Reichstag through universal manhood suffrage. Thus, Bismarck united Germany under Prussian hegemony.

The drive for German unification produced in its wake an intellectual movement that would have dire consequences. Influenced by patriotic romanticism and the emphasis on the common people, some authors began to develop a cult of the folk that went to great extremes.[5] In 1857 Wilhelm Heinrich Riehl wrote a book, *Land and People*, that had a major impact on German thought. Riehl condemned the new industrial society, with its ugly cities and rootless middle and working classes, and called for a return to the land, whence came all that was pure and genuine. It was the folk, unstained by the smoke and grime of the industrial centers, who had produced the true German culture, and only those who returned to the folk were civilized. Riehl condemned all who lacked ties with the soil, especially the Jews, as inferiors without a genuine culture.

Riehl's work was only the first of many works reflecting the impact of the cult of the folk. During the period after the establishment of the Reich, a group of authors glorified the life of the peasant. Berthold Auerbach told his readers of the mystical tie between the farmer and nature and of the purity of rural life. Conrad Ferdinand Mayer, one of the greatest creators of short stories, glorified the heroic peasants who led the struggle for Swiss independence. Hermann Löns published "Der Wehrwolf" in 1910, a story of the peasants who braved the destruction of the Thirty Years War. Through these and other works, many Germans elevated the simple people of the country to the level of saints who lived their lives uncorrupted by the materialism of the impersonal, mechanical world of capitalism.

Some became so enraptured by the cult of the folk that they built a new religion based on its myths and customs. In 1878 Paul de Lagarde published a series of essays entitled *German Writings*. In these he argued that the German people had a special sense of the spiritual that made them superior to other ethnic groups. This prophet of Germanic religion rejected traditional Christianity as the product of the Jewish legalism of St. Paul and called for the rebirth of the ancient faith of the German folk. Others took up Lagarde's ideas, leading to a new paganism. Julius Langbehn made a creed of race, asserting that a true people must remain pure and avoid contamination by "inferior" groups. In Langbehn's works, the racially pure people took the place of Christ as the true reflection of divinity; the author himself would later reject these ideas and end his life as a Roman Catholic monk. Another spokesman for the religion of the folk was Eugene Diedrichs. From the pages of his journal, *The Deed ("Die Tat")* Diedrichs preached for the development of a science dedicated to the study of the origins of the Germanic folk and for a "New Romanticism" that would emphasize the *Geist* ("Spirit") of the world as found in the feelings of the folk.

The cult of the folk also led to a rebirth of the ancient religion of the Germanic tribes. Enthusiastic Germans studied Tacitus's *Germania,* a work written to glorify the primitive Teutonic peoples as examples for the Romans to follow. Others read and reread the *Edda,* an ancient collection of Germanic mythology. Guido von List published several scholarly works describing in detail the legends and customs of the Teutonic tribesmen. In Schabing, the artistic section of Munich, Alfred Schuler preached the new gospel that race and blood determined the fate of a people to adoring crowds that included Adolf Hitler. Some even tried to rekindle devotion to the sun, the center of much of ancient Germanic religion. In Leipzig a man calling himself Tarnhari, the reborn leader of the Völsungen, one of the Teutonic tribes, called for the worship of the sun, symbolized by the hooked cross, or swastika, and gained many followers.

It was only natural that a cult glorifying the Germanic tribes and their religion would provide fertile ground for the growth of racism. As the followers of the cult of the folk fell under the influence of

Charles Darwin's theories on evolution and survival of the fittest, some began to look upon the blonde blue-eyed Nordic, or Aryan, people as superior to the other peoples of the world. Ironically, the first proponent of Aryan superiority was not a German, but a Frenchman named Arthur de Gobineau, who argued that pollution of the blood of the Aryans by "inferior" races would lead to ruin as a culture and nation. In 1894 Ludwig Schemann organized a society in Germany dedicated to Gobineau's ideas. Another important foreigner who had great impact on the development of racism in Germany was Houston Stewart Chamberlain, who left his native England to spend most of his life in Germany. In 1900 he published his major work, *The Foundation of the XIX Century,* in which he praised the pure-blooded Aryan as the perfect human being, whose looks were the standard of beauty, and denounced the Jews as an inferior people, whose dark features formed the opposite to the beauty of the Aryan. He believed that a person's outer appearance, including the size and shape of his skull, determined his inner nature. Chamberlain saw history as a life-and-death struggle between the pure-blooded Aryans and their Jewish foes, who used every means to debase and enslave the Germanic peoples. His work had a major impact on the thinking of some Germans and paved the way for national socialism, which he supported until his death in 1927.

The anti-Semitism of Chamberlain and others became one of the major articles in the creed of the cult of the folk. Fanatical enthusiasts of the new faith considered the Jews an inferior Asiatic people lacking the roots in the soil necessary for racial and cultural growth. Anti-Semites characterized the Jews as a greedy people using unethical means to attempt to dominate all aspects of German political and economic life. Otto Böckel's anti-Jewish tirades won him a large following and a seat in the Reichstag in 1880. Two years later, Hermann Ahlwardt published a fiery tract, *The Desperate Struggle Between the Aryan Peoples and the Jews,* in which he openly advocated violence to drive the Jews from Germany. He argued that they must be declared foreigners and deprived of all rights of citizenship. Thus the basic ideology of national socialism and its hatred for the Jews had been formulated long before Hitler began to gain a following.

The cult of the folk became a national movement and began to influence the education of a whole generation of German youth. German schools introduced a new type of social studies that indoctrinated pupils with the basic ideas of the movement. In 1898 Hermann Leitz founded a school in Iisenburg, Saxony, dedicated to bringing up his young charges in the proper "Aryan" atmosphere. Three years later, thousands of boys flocked to join the *Wandervögel,* a hiking society organized in Steglitz, a suburb in Berlin. The adult leaders of this forerunner of the Hitler youth used camping and hiking through the woods to instruct their followers in the cult of nature and the folk. They made physical fitness and the glorification of the human body into a religion and taught their pupils to dedicate their lives to following a strong leader. Through the influence of the cult of the folk on education and on the *Wandervögel* and similar groups for girls, a whole generation of German youth was prepared for Hitler's message.

The cult of the folk was not the only aspect of late nineteenth-century German culture that laid a foundation for the Nazi movement. The growth of Romantic opera provided a musical expression of the nationalism that gripped the German people. Building on the work of men like Carl Maria von Weber, who produced *Der Freischütz ("The Marksman")* in 1821, Richard Wagner brought forth a revolutionary form of art that combined the best of music and drama. Wagner, who had joined the Russian anarchist Bakunin in a revolt in Dresden in 1849, found a supporter in the mad king of Bavaria, Louis II, and built a theater in Bayreuth, where his devoted followers could come to worship. He boldly rejected the old division of opera into chorus, aria, and recitative to create a new musical drama of continuous melody that burst forth on the stage with force seldom heard in opera. Wagner, greatly influenced by the cult of the folk, chose themes from Germanic mythology for his greatest works. In his four-part *Ring of the Nibelung,* Siegfried, Brunhilde, and others pound the audience with the sheer might of their voices while the orchestra sends forth shattering crescendos of sound. Wagner was, above all, a German and has the chorus in the last act of the *Mastersingers of Nuremburg* close the opera with a hymn to German art. He was also anti-Semitic and wrote several works denouncing the Jews. Some see *Parsifal,* his last opera, as an allegory of the need to keep the German race free from the contamination of Jewish blood. Young Adolf Hitler was enraptured by Wagner's operas, and they became the inspiration for the semipagan nazi ceremony that had such an important impact on the Third Reich.[6]

Another intellectual who had a major influence on German thought and played a role in preparing the ground for the growth of national socialism was the philosopher Friedrich Nietzsche. As professor of classics at the University of Basel and as author of such works as *Thus Spake Zarathustra*,[7] Nietzsche outlined a philosophy of force and power that has influenced several generations of intellectuals. He exhorted his followers to dedicate themselves to a future dominated by a new kind of man who would live by the will to power and become a magnificent beast of prey, crushing the weak with sheer force. Nietzsche called upon man to liberate himself from the shackles of Christianity, which he considered a slave's religion that had suppressed mankind with a false moral code. Although he spoke of rearing and training a race of supermen, he was not a German nationalist and strongly condemned anti-Semitism. While Nietzsche was not a Nazi, and his influence on Hitler cannot be definitely proven, he sowed seeds in the minds of many German intellectuals that enabled them to turn to national socialism in the 1920s and 1930s.

It would be a serious oversimplification to interpret all nineteenth-century German culture as preparing the way for the advent of Hitler. The writings of Lessing, who violently denounces anti-Semitism in his masterpiece, *Nathan the Wise,* and of Goethe, whose *Faust* is one of the greatest works of world literature and stresses the importance of continual striving, continued to have great influence. Even romanticism tended to turn away from the nationalism of the War of Liberation to favor fairy tales or fantastic works like those of Ernst T. A. Hoffmann. Some, like Heinrich Heine, realized the dangers of extreme nationalism and prophesied disaster unless the primitive emotions of the Germanic tribes could be curbed. After the failure of the Revolution of 1848, romanticism gave way to the new literature of realism. Gottfried Keller wrote *Green Henry,* about a youth who ended his life in obscure disappointment after failing to become an artist. Gerhardt Hauptmann criticized the unjust industrial society in works like his *Weavers,* the story of the suffering and unsuccessful revolt of the Silesian weavers. Even Wagner was not typical of nineteenth-century German music, which produced such giants as Ludwig von Beethoven and Johannes Brahms. Most Germans preferred to waltz to the music of Johann Strauss and his family rather than to emerge exhausted from one of Wagner's massive works.

Nineteenth-century Germany also produced Marxism, the philosophy of Karl Marx and Friedrich Engels.[8] Marx rejected nationalism to preach for the liberation of the workingman from the chains of capitalistic exploitation. He argued that history consisted of class struggle and that the state had actually been created by the ruling classes to keep others in submission. Marx gained a wide following in Germany, where a party dedicated to socialistic revolution was organized in Eisenach on August 7, 1869. The German Marxists, led by August Bebel and Wilhelm Liebknecht, joined the followers of Ferdinand Lassalle, an evolutionary socialist, on May 22, 1875, to form the Socialist Labor party. As World War I approached, many socialists like Eduard Bernstein rejected Marx's concept of revolution to emphasize social reform to better the lot of the workingman. Despite Bismarck's frantic efforts to crush the socialists, they had become the largest party in the Reichstag by 1914.

It would be a serious error to neglect to consider the growth of fanatical nationalism and anti-Semitism in other countries. The persecution of Alfred Dreyfus, a Jewish officer in the French army, caused a scandal that rocked the whole world. Tsarist Russia was the scene of violent anti-Jewish pogroms. Racism was also rampant in much of the United States, as thousands of blacks found themselves the target of the violence of groups like the Ku Klux Klan. As we shall see, it was an historical accident that allowed the extremists to take control of the destiny of the German people. Had the First World War ended in a different manner, or had the Weimar Republic had a real chance at success without the constant demands for excessive reparation payments, Hitler and his followers might have ended their lives as a mere footnote to history.

German history before the First World War had been dominated by the struggle for hegemony between the Hohenzollerns and the Habsburgs and by the movement to replace the multitude of separate states with a united nation. This left an indelible mark on German culture. Prussia built its power on the army and created a cult of order and discipline that reached to the lowest element of society. The struggle for national self-determination, first against the French and then against the rulers of the most powerful German states, created an exaggerated sense of nationalism that would turn to chauvinism of the worst kind. Deprived of a united nation, some Germans turned to Romanticism and developed a cult of the folk that led to racism and anti-Semitism. It would be the terrible fate of the German people to allow these currents to become a mighty tidal wave that would sweep all the positive elements of German culture into an orgy of national socialism.

2

The First World War and German Politics

The tranquility and security that the German people thought had been achieved in 1871 were only illusions. Although Bismarck tried desperately to preserve the peace by constructing a complex system of alliances and counteralliances designed to isolate the French, his work was in vain. William II, the headstrong kaiser, who finally forced Bismarck to retire, made no effort to preserve his policies. Instead, he supported the Habsburg aspirations in the Balkans, driving St. Petersburg into the waiting arms of Paris. When an obscure fanatic assassinated the heir to the Austro-Hungarian throne, the world plunged into one of the bloodiest and most senseless wars in history. When the conflict began in 1914, the German people and their political leaders united behind their ruler in a patriotic frenzy. However, as the war stretched from year to year and millions died in the trenches, the best efforts of the military masters of Germany to keep the horrible truth from their people failed, and many became disenchanted, vowing to end the insane conflict.

Politically, the later part of the nineteenth century was a period of autocratic government. Bismarck, the real power in Germany, dominated William I. He unsuccessfully fought the Roman Catholic Church during the cultural struggle of the 1870s. The father of German unification also sought to crush the infant socialist movement through a series of repressive measures. When these failed to stem the growth of social democracy, Bismarck tried to win the support of the workingman through a farsighted program of legislation to provide health and accident insurance and pensions for all. However, this too met with failure, and between 1878 and 1890 the number of Social

Democrats in the Reichstag increased from nine to thirty-five. By 1912 the Socialists were the largest single party in Germany.

Bismarck, aware that renewed war could destroy the Germany he had created, based his foreign policy on isolating the French. He sought and won an alliance with Austria and Russia by forming the League of Three Emperors in 1872. However, as both Vienna and St. Petersburg scrambled to increase their influence in the Balkans, they fell into an irreconcilable conflict that shattered the fragile alliance. Bismarck was determined to prevent war between the two great powers of eastern Europe and showed his genius by negotiating a pact with Vienna and then turning to Russia to form the Reinsurance Treaty that guaranteed the friendship of the Slavic empire.

Although the crafty chancellor had dominated William I and had kept Frederick II from challenging his position, he had much less success with William II, who ascended the throne in 1888. The headstrong young emperor, who made up for his crippled left arm with personal vanity, was determined to resist any challenge to his power. In 1890 he forced the resentful Bismarck to resign. Free of the influence of the Iron Chancellor, William radically changed the direction of German foreign policy. Rejecting Bismarck's frantic advice, he refused to renew the Reinsurance Treaty with Russia, instead insisting on supporting the Austrian drive into the Balkans. This serious mistake cost Berlin the friendship of St. Petersburg and drove Russia to seek agreement with France. William turned a deaf ear to the British attempt to form an alliance and insulted the English by openly expressing sympathy with the Boers in their effort to resist British domination in South Africa. Finally, London sought the friendship of Paris and St. Petersburg. Thus, William II had undone the painstaking diplomacy of Bismarck and had enabled the French to emerge from the isolation Bismarck had tried so hard to enforce on them.

During the first years of the new century, a series of crises increased international tensions to the breaking point. William insisted on showing his power by meddling in Morocco. On March 31, 1915, he visited Tangiers to express his support of the effort of the Moroccans to resist French domination. Although an international conference at Algeciras in 1906 sided with Paris, the German kaiser refused to yield and in 1911 sent the gunboat *Panther* to Morocco to show his determination to play a role in North African politics. In the Balkans, William II stood solidly behind Austria when the Habsburg Empire annexed Bosnia and Herzegovina, despite violent opposition from Serbia and Russia.[1]

Finally, in 1911 and 1912, the decaying Ottoman Empire fell victim to Italy and then to Bulgaria, Serbia, and Greece. In September 1911 Rome took advantage of the preoccupation of the powers with Morocco to seize Tripoli from the Turks. This showed the weakness of the Ottoman Empire and led Serbia, Greece, and Bulgaria to capture Macedonia in the First Balkan War of 1912. However, the victors found themselves in conflict over the division of their spoils, causing Greece and Serbia to form an alliance to take the disputed area for themselves in the Second Balkan War. In the same conflict Rumania attacked Bulgaria from the north, winning Dobruja. Since Russia had failed to exert influence during both the Bosnian crisis and the Balkan Wars, many in St. Petersburg believed that the Slavic empire must take a strong stand in any future conflicts in southeast Europe or forever lose the ability to control this strategic area.

Thus, by the fateful year of 1914, Europe consisted of two hostile camps: the German-Austrian Alliance and the British, French, and Russians. The beginning of the year was deceptively peaceful; for a while it appeared that the tension of the past would die away and that war would be averted. Then on June 28 in the Bosnian city of Sarajevo, Gavrilo Princip, a dedicated Serbian nationalist, shattered the calm by assassinating Archduke Francis Ferdinand. The murder was the result of a plot hatched in Belgrade by the chief of Serbian military intelligence, Colonel Dragutin Dimitrijevich, a member of the radical Black Hand. Immediately on hearing the tragic news, many in Vienna demanded vengeance. However, the Austrian chancellor, Count Leopold Berchtold, persuaded the ministry to seek German support before responding. On July 5 the Austrian ambassador to Berlin, Count Szögyeny, met with William II and his chancellor, Theobald von Bethmann-Hollweg. The emperor and his minister told their delighted guest that Vienna could count on the approval of Germany for any action against Serbia that it might take to revenge the assassination. The kaiser's statement is the famous German "blank check" that would later form the major evidence for the argument that Germany and its allies were responsible for the First World War. However, it must be remembered that Berlin approved action against only Serbia, not against Russia or France. It should be kept in mind that an agent of the Serbian government was directly involved in the assassination conspiracy through the work of Colonel Dimitrijevich and that the Serbian prime minister, Nikola Pashich, failed to take adequate steps to warn Vienna after he learned of the conspiracy. Therefore, Belgrade must share the blame for the outbreak of the First World War.

With assurance of support from Berlin, Vienna demanded an immediate end to all Serbian-sponsored anti-Austrian activity and the right to send officials to the Slavic kingdom to participate in the investigation of the conspiracy. In the meantime, the president of France, Raymond Poincaré, arrived in St. Petersburg to urge the Russians to stand firm behind Serbia, lest the Slavic empire suffer another loss of face in the Balkans. Aware of the attitude of the Allies and unwilling to sacrifice its sovereignty, Serbia rejected the Austrian demands on July 25, 1914. It is symbolic of the state of affairs during that confused month that the Serbian reply was handwritten because the only typewriter in the foreign office broke down while the message was being typed. Three days later, without prior consultation with Berlin, Vienna declared war on Serbia.

During the next few days, note after note flew between the capitals of Europe, as minister and ruler alike frantically sought to prevent the conflict between Serbia and Austria from leading to a major war. William II tried in vain to persuade Vienna to limit the invasion of Serbia to the occupation of Belgrade, hoping to isolate the conflict, and he sent several telegrams to Tsar Nicholas II in a desperate effort to prevent war between the two empires. Nevertheless, with French support, Serge Sazanov, the Russian foreign minister, persuaded the Tsar to order a general mobilization. This led to a serious debate in Berlin between General Helmuth von Moltke, the chief of the general staff, who favored immediate action lest Russia catch Germany unprepared, and Bethmann-Holweg, who favored waiting to allow Vienna an opportunity to negotiate with St. Petersburg. William sided with the military. On July 31 Berlin sent a note to the Russians demanding an immediate end to mobilization. That same day, the Germans requested a pledge of neutrality from Paris. The French replied by mobilizing their army, and the Russians simply refused to answer the German ultimatum. Therefore, on August 1, 1914, Germany declared war on Russia. The German plan of battle developed in 1905 by General Alfred von Schlieffen proposed to defeat France by a thrust through Belgium and then to swiftly transport the army to Russia by rail. Since the Schlieffen Plan made movements through Belgium necessary, Berlin demanded the right to send troops through the neutral country. On August 3, Brussels rejected the German request, and the German army crossed into Belgium, thereby evoking a British declaration of war.

Although the victorious Allies forced the Germans to accept complete responsibility for the outbreak of the First World War, such a verdict is not justified by the facts. It is clear that Serbia must shoulder a part of the blame because of the assassination of Archduke Francis Ferdinand and that Austria was guilty of refusing to consider negotiations and of failing to confide fully in its German ally. Berlin was really more guilty of a failure to realize the consequences of unquestioning support for Vienna than of trying to start a war. William actually believed that the conflict could be isolated and failed to realize the determination of the Russians. When the Germans realized that war with the Slavic empire was a possibility, they made the terrible mistake of considering military matters more important than continued diplomacy. Thus, the Germans declared war and violated the neutrality of Belgium, making a major war a certainty. St. Petersburg also played a role in bringing on the war by its support of Serbia and its refusal to consider the consequences of the decision to mobilize. Finally, the French urged the Russians and Serbians to offer stiff resistance to the Habsburg demands. Therefore, the view that Germany alone was responsible for the war is false, for all the powers were at least partially to blame. The truth is that in July 1914, most leaders gave up all hope of peace and, assuming that war was inevitable, began to think solely in terms of obtaining a military advantage.

The peoples of Europe greeted the news of the outbreak of the war with great enthusiasm. In every German city, crowds of ecstatic men and women gathered to hear the announcement and to pledge their loyalty to the fatherland. In their patriotic fury, most Germans accepted their government's claim that the war was a glorious crusade to defend their homes from the "barbaric" Slavs, who had deliberately caused the war. The German people shared the frenzy with their foes. In Paris, crowds shouted their support for the struggle, as they dreamed of revenge for the humiliation of 1871. Some French soldiers painted the words "To Berlin" on the railcars that would carry them to battle. In Russia, millions swore their allegiance to their Tsar with a religious devotion. Bearded priests clad in golden vestments stood amid altar boys carrying glittering icons, blessing the marching troops as clouds of incense mingled with the hymns. Even the normally sober British received word of war with enthusiasm. Thousands crowded outside Buckingham Palace to cheer and sing patriotic songs, backed by the ringing of church bells, while inside Prime Minister Herbert Asquith informed King George V of the decision to enter the war. All sides believed that the war would end with a quick victory, and some predicted that the troops would be home by Christmas.

Thus began the First World War. For the next four years a reign of fire and death would engulf Europe, leaving the once fertile fields of France and Belgium covered with the corpses of millions of soldiers. When the smoke cleared and the carnage ceased, amid the ruins would be the once mighty Habsburg Empire, the vast realm of the Tsars, and the Hohenzollern Reich and its member principalities. Europe closed the door on the past in 1914 and entered a new era, in which the pomp and circumstance of the monarchies would yield to the thunder of marching squads clad in brown or black shirts and the cries of fanatical mobs shouting devotion to their dictators.

When the war came, groups in the German Reichstag that had traditionally opposed military spending rallied to the cause. The Social Democrats, who had fought every pfennig voted by the legislature for the military, clamored for war. At their party caucus only fourteen of the ninety-two present dared speak against support for the war credits. The majority, however, justified their stand by arguing that the war was really a struggle against the reactionary government of Tsar Nicholas II. When the Reichstag voted to support the war credits, the Socialists voted as a bloc. Even the well-known radical Karl Liebknecht chose to disregard his antiwar beliefs and to cast his vote with his party. The academic community joined the chorus of nationalism, as the leading thinkers of Germany rushed to sign the declarations against the enemy. Ninety-three of the most distinguished scholars in Germany signed a manifesto defending the invasion of Belgium as necessary for the defense of the fatherland from possible French aggression. The trade unions called upon workers to support the war and agreed to a ban on strikes. The government responded to the expressions of loyalty by the left by repealing laws designed to halt the growth of socialism, and on September 2, 1914, even lifted the ban on the distribution of socialistic literature in military installations.[2]

Of course, the resounding support for the war was not universal, and a few brave individuals dared to raise their voices to oppose the war on the grounds that the real cause was imperialism rather than self-defense. The revolutionaries Karl Liebknecht and Rosa Luxemburg finally joined pacifist authors like Herman Hesse and a small group of university professors to form the Society of the New Fatherland in early 1915. This small core of dedicated workers believed that the war must be ended in a compromise peace that would satisfy both sides without leaving one the victor and one the vanquished. Helmuth von Gerlach, who established the newspaper *Die Welt am Montag,* carried the group's message to the men and women on the streets. In the pages of his newspaper, Gerlach criticized German foreign policy and called for an early end to the war.

The hope of an early victory vanished abruptly during the First Battle of the Marne, September 5 through 12, 1914. After the German army had crushed the Belgian resistance, it moved into northern France. There the French, led by General Joseph Joffre, with British support, threw their full force into a desperate attempt to stop the Germans before they reached Paris. The combined French and British armies fought strongly against the advancing Germans, forcing General Alexander von Kluck to order reinforcements from his left wing to his right wing, causing the German advance to stop. Kluck's action opened a gap between the First and Second German armies that the Allies quickly filled. The bloody battle continued for several days, until the Germans had to retreat behind the Aisne River. Paris had been saved, and the Schlieffen Plan had been defeated. In their new position, the Germans dug trenches to protect themselves and began the deadly trench warfare that would curse the war. Millions of men would spend their days and nights amid the mud and stench of their "forts," only to be cut down by machine gun fire as they climbed over the top to struggle for a few feet.

In the East the Germans were more successful. An ineffective and corrupt government strangled the once-proud empire of the Romanovs, and Russia, with its poor railway network and weak economy, was unable to challenge the combined might of Germany and Austria. To divert the Germans from the attack on the French, the Russians invaded East Prussia from the east and south in September 1914. At first the Slavic Empire met with victory. At the Battle of Gumbinnen, from August 9 through 20, reinforced with troops drawn from the fighting in the West, they drove the Germans to the Vistula River. But their victory was short-lived. William removed Prittwitz and replaced him with two of the most brutal commanders in German military history, General Paul von Hindenburg and his chief of staff, General Erich von Ludendorff. Hindenburg lost no time in flinging his army on the enemy, devastating them at the Battle of Tannenberg from August 26 through 30. When the smoke cleared from the field, the Germans had taken over 100,000 prisoners, and the Russian commander, General Alexander Samsonov, had so disgraced himself that he took his own life rather than face the censure of his superiors. From Tannenberg the German advance on the Slavs continued, with victories at the Battle of Masurian Lakes from September 6 through 15, the battles of Warsaw and Ivangorod from October 9 through 20, and the battles of Lodz and Lowicz on November 16 and 25. By the beginning of the winter of 1914, the Germans had entered Russian Poland and forced the Russian army into retreat.

Success againt the Russians notwithstanding, by the fall of 1914 German setbacks in France had ended hope for peace by Christmas. William dismissed Helmuth von Moltke and appointed General Eric von Falkhayn commander of the German army. The emperor set up headquarters in the field and prepared to direct the war effort himself. Unfortunately, he lived in a fool's paradise, as his aides falsified reports to make it appear that a victory was a certainty, in the belief that the real state of affairs would only lead to a mental breakdown of the headstrong monarch. When officials tried to inform him of the true situation, his advisers intervened to prevent pessimistic reports from reaching his royal ears.

As the war continued, the power of the military crept into all aspects of German life. With the emperor deluded by his aides into believing that things were better than they actually were, the military began to take German domestic policy into its own hands, so that the supreme command, headed after August 29, 1916, by Hindenburg and Ludendorff, became the real ruler of the empire. This body intervened in every facet of government, including labor policies, food distribution, usage of raw materials, and the composition of the ministry. The leaders of the military continued to deceive the German people into believing in the inevitability of victory by censoring news reports and by forbidding the publication of any item that might indicate to the German people that they were not winning the war. All daily reports spoke of great victories, and accounts of defeats were either underplayed or simply not reported. This caused most Germans to believe that victory was theirs. When they finally learned the truth, many would refuse to accept the fact that the mighty German army had been defeated. The unrealistic reporting of the war laid the foundation for the "stab in the back" theory.

The military control of German society especially tightened in economic matters. The German empire had entered the war unprepared for a long conflict and dependent on foreign imports of food, fats, and oils, as well as strategic chemicals such as nitrates. Immediately after the outbreak of the war, the British established a blockade of German ports that the small navy under Admiral Alfred von Tirpitz could not break. To solve the serious economic crisis and alleviate the shortage of essential raw materials, William appointed Walter Rathenau, former head of the *Allgemeine-Elektrizitäts-Gesellschaft* ("General Electric Company"), chief of the war materials office on August 9, 1914. Rathenau effectively organized the economy, basing his policy on regulation, synthetic manufacture, and substitute products. He placed all industry under strict governmental control and organized new firms of mixed private and public ownership to administer raw materials, which he secured from individual concerns for the war effort. He sponsored a program to keep the greatest scientists of Germany busy developing artificial substitutes for materials formerly imported from abroad. Fritz Haber of Berlin invented the nitrogen fixation process to manufacture explosives, ending the dependence on nitrates from Chile. Others developed a process to make synthetic ammonia and to use cellulose as a substitute for the cotton used in the manufacture of explosives.

The warlords of Germany established a war foodstuffs office to ease the serious food shortage caused by the blockade. This body supervised the raising and distribution of food to insure that the troops would be fed and that starvation would not spread on the home front. Nutritionists developed a special "war bread" made from a mixture of flour, turnips, and potatoes, thereby stretching the small supply of grain. The office decreed that Germans would abstain from meat two days a week. Finally, the government resorted to rationing and introduced bread cards on January 25, 1915.

Another serious problem caused by the war was a severe labor shortage. With the best of the youth away at the front, many important factories faced shutdowns because of the shortage of skilled workers. On December 5, 1916, the masters of Germany introduced the Hindenburg Program, or the National Service Law. This resulted from the work of Karl Helfferich and General Wilhelm Gröner and from negotiations between the military and the leadership of the trade unions. Every male between seventeen and sixty who was not in the army became a member of the auxiliary services under the authority of the Ministry of War. The law provided for the establishment of committees of workers in every factory to administer the law and to help regulate industry. Compulsory arbitration would settle all labor disputes. The growth of regulation and control over every facet of German life and the effective organization of the economy had far-reaching consequences. It served as an example for other nations during the war and the Great Depression and accustomed the German people to regulation. Once accustomed to governmental interference in economic and social matters, the German people were prepared for the strict control to be established by the National Socialists, who learned much from the example of the First World War organization of German domestic affairs.

The feverish nationalism that made the military takeover of German domestic life possible also affected the discussion of war aims. One group of Germans saw the war as purely defensive and looked for an outcome that would restore and guarantee a return to affairs as they had been before the outbreak of hostilities. Another considered the war Germany's chance to carve an empire from the defeated countries. Their ideas grew from the nationalism of the past, which portrayed history as preparing Germany to play a special role as the new dominant power in the world. They traced their spiritual ancestry back to the Large Germany faction of 1848 and wanted to redraw the boundaries of the Reich to include all German-speaking peoples. Of course, the majority of Germans stood between the two extremes, shifting their opinions toward restoration of the prewar order as German fortunes waned on the battlefield, and toward annexation as it seemed that the fatherland would win a glorious victory.[3]

The supporters of the imperialistic war aims came from several different groups. Heinrich Class's Pan Germans dreamed of the day when all Germans would unite in one Reich. They were joined by the Association of Industrialists, members of the Supreme Command, and members of all political parties except the Social Democrats to campaign for a war of conquest. When the war began, Class met with several other ultra-nationalists to prepare a resolution on war aims. According to the plan, postwar Europe would be reorganized to reflect the new German hegemony. Belgium would become a military and economic satellite of the Reich, and France would lose its coastal districts as far as the mouth of the Somme, the important coal area of the north, and the fortresses of Verdun, Longwy, and Belfort. Class and his fellow annexationists also demanded a new colonial empire, corresponding to Germany's greatness, and valuable agricultural territory from Russia to provide a new source of food for the fatherland.

The program of the annexationists contained much that Hitler would later adopt in his plan for conquest.

Since the real power in wartime Germany was the military, its attitude toward the question of war aims would be decisive. Yet the warlords of the Reich never outlined a clear program for the reorganization of Europe after a German victory. The few official utterances of the military tended to favor the position of the annexationists. The major concern of the generals was creating a new Europe that would guarantee the security of the fatherland. Ludendorff openly favored placing Belgium under German economic, military, and political hegemony. Some, such as General Hans von Seeckt and Hindenburg, suggested large annexations along the Baltic Sea to provide room to maneuver in any future conflict with Russia. Others looked to the fertile Ukraine as a possible source of food and advocated extending German influence over this rich agricultural area.

The civilian government, powerless to shape the course of German policy, never clearly defined its position on war goals. Chancellor Theobald von Bethmann-Hollweg denounced the annexationists and tended to favor a more conciliatory policy after the predicted victory. However, like so many others, he fell under the spell of the ultranationalists and spoke vaguely about increased influence in postwar Belgium. Since Germany lost the war, it is impossible to predict what sort of Europe would have resulted had the kaiser's troops vanquished their enemies, but it is clear that the magnitude of the victory would have greatly influenced the shape of the final peace. Had the Reich completely shattered its foes, the masters of Germany would have demanded a much more severe peace than they would have, had they only won a slight victory. Naturally, the Peace of Brest-Litovsk, to be discussed later, shows the influence of the radical nationalists and is a good indication of what the Allies might have expected at the hands of their conquerors. It would be a major oversimplification, however, to consider every ultra-nationalist speech an indication of official German policy. It would also be a mistake to fail to consider the atmosphere of the war and the frenzy of patriotism that generated the extreme position of the annexationists. Finally, it is very important to remember that many spokesmen for Germany's foes were equally fanatical in demanding a peace with revenge.

The discussion of war aims and the continuation of the war led to the rapid growth of the pacifist element of the Social Democrats. Although the party achieved a shaky unity to vote as a block in support of the war credits on August 4, 1914, as the fighting stretched from month to month without a foreseeable end, many began to change their position. On December 2, 1914, Karl Liebknecht broke party ranks to vote against renewed war expenditures, beginning a campaign that would split the Socialists into warring factions. Others followed his lead. On June 9, 1915, a group of opponents to the war published a pamphlet denouncing the political truce that had resulted from the wave of patriotism that had swept Germany the year before; they called upon their fellow Social Democrats to demand an immediate peace. In August 1915, twenty-nine Socialists left the Reichstag chamber rather than join their party in supporting the war.

Tension between the opponents of the conflict and its supporters within the party continued to grow. On September 8, 1915, ten Germans attended an international conference of Socialists in Zimmerwald, Switzerland, which passed resolutions condemning the war as imperialistic and demanding an immediate peace without annexations by either side.[4] On October 29 and November 5, 1915, Karl Kautsky, the leading Marxist theorist within the party, wrote two articles in *Neue Zeit* calling for the formation of a new party dedicated to peace. Eighteen Social Democrats responded to Kautsky's summons by forming the Independent Social Democratic party. The division between independents and loyalists cut across old party lines and included such former political foes as the orthodox Marxist Kautsky and Eduard Bernstein, the father of revisionism. On December 21, 1915, the Independent Socialists joined two loyalists to oppose the war credits.

The Independent Socialists were not the only group to break with the Social Democratic party. The uneasy truce between revolutionary and nonrevolutionary broke under the strain of the war. Karl Liebknecht and Rosa Luxemburg rallied their followers to form the International Group. This faction, dedicated to a socialist victory through violent revolution, would serve as the basis for the Sparticist Society, which would lead a bloody revolt in the early months of the Weimar Republic. While the Internationalists favored socialism through the spontaneous action of the people, a third faction, led by Karl Radek, endorsed the elitist ideas of V. I. Lenin. Thus, the First World War led to a serious struggle within the Social Democrats that split the party into four rival factions. The loyalists, free of the influence of the radical left, would continue to move toward the center until they would become the dominant faction of the Weimar Republic.[5]

As the deadly war dragged on without a victory, non-Socialists joined the opposition to the continued fighting. After the fall of Tsar Nicholas II in March 1917, many believed that the chief cause of the war, the aggressive policy of the reactionary Russian government, had been removed and that peace was now possible. At the same time, many Germans began to doubt the devotion of the Habsburg Empire to the alliance. On November 21, 1916, Emperor Francis Joseph died after a reign of sixty-eight years. His successor, Charles, believed that the war must be ended or disaster would result. He used family ties to France through his wife, Zita, of Bourbon Parma, to attempt negotiations. In May 1917 the Austrian foreign minister, Count Ottokar Czerin, went to Berlin to discuss the possibility of reaching a negotiated end to the bloody conflict. He found the Germans more interested in discussing the annexation of Poland than in contemplating peace. Nevertheless, while in the Hohenzollern capital the Austrian official visited Matthias Erzberger, a member of the Center party. He told the former schoolteacher that the prospects of victory were not as bright as the picture painted by the military. At the same time, Erzberger fell under the influence of the Socialists and decided to make a personal inspection of the front to discover the true state of affairs.

On July 6, 1917, Erzberger shattered the optimism of the majority of the Reichstag through a secret speech. He scolded his fellow deputies for allowing the military to deceive them about the military situation. The brave critic of the warlords of Germany courageously pointed out the high cost of the war in money and human lives and the serious food shortages it had caused. He denounced as pure fantasy the popular belief that unrestricted submarine warfare would lead to the folding of the Allied effort in the West. Finally, he sarcastically condemned the annexationists, arguing that it would be cheaper to build asylums for them than to prolong the war until their aims had been won. Erzberger's declarations shook the membership of the Reichstag. Many realized for the first time the futility of continuing the war. During the days that followed, members of the Majority Socialists joined members of the Progressive party and the Center party to form a coalition dedicated to ending the carnage. Together they mustered enough support to push the Peace Resolution of July 19, 1917, through the Reichstag. This challenge to the military masters of Germany reaffirmed the defensive nature of the war, denounced the annexation of any enemy territory, and demanded freedom of the seas. It further opposed any plan that would lead to economic isolation and hostility after the war and called for the formation of an international organization of all nations to keep the peace after the conflict had ended. The Peace Resolution also reaffirmed the unity of the German people and the commitment of the Reichstag to the security of the fatherland. It is significant that Woodrow Wilson would include several of the demands of the Peace Resolution in his Fourteen Points.[6]

The action of the Reichstag had far-reaching consequences. Once the leaders of the Majority Socialists, the Progressives, and the Center party had learned to work together closely, they continued their cooperation and eventually formed the coalition that established the Weimar Republic. The Peace Resolution also brought the fall of Bethmann-Hollweg, who had been chancellor in name only since the beginning of the war. After he failed to defeat the proposal, Hindenburg and Ludendorff threatened to resign unless William dismissed him. The kaiser yielded and on July 12, 1917, appointed an obscure official of the interior administration, George Michaelis, as the new chancellor. Michaelis, who had won the favor of the military through his work in grain and bread rationing, proved to be even weaker than Bethmann-Hollweg, and the dictatorship of the army over civilian life became absolute. Another important consequence of the resolution was the alienation of many Germans who still believed that victory was at hand and saw the effort to win peace as a betrayal of the brave soldiers at the front.

The First World War began amid a burst of patriotism. The people of all countries rallied to their leaders' calls for support and marched to the field of battle confident in eventual victory. But the troops of both sides dug trenches in the wake of the First Battle of the Marne, transforming the conflict from a crusade for the mother country into a nightmare of death and destruction unparalleled in modern memory. As millions died in the putrefaction of the trenches and the war continued without any hope of peace, many Germans began to split with their leaders and demand an end to the senseless killing. The war shattered the unity of the Social Democrats and left the party split into four rival factions. Finally, others realized the futility of continued fighting and supported Erzberger's call for peace.

3
The "Stab in the Back"

The Peace Resolution of July 19, 1917, expressed the disillusionment with the seemingly endless war shared by many on both sides of the conflict. Yet the leaders of the fighting nations still mistrusted each other, and many looked for deliverance to a man across the Atlantic who posed as a champion of justice and virtue. This man, Woodrow Wilson, president of the United States, stood above the petty conflicts that had embroiled Europe in the disastrous blood bath. Wilson, born in Staunton, Virginia, in 1856, the son of a Presbyterian minister, had distinguished himself as a leading scholar and statesman. He had received a Doctor of Philosophy degree from Johns Hopkins University at a time when few aspired to the highest academic achievements. He had taught history, jurisprudence, and political economics at Bryn Mawr, Wesleyan, and Princeton and in 1902 had become the first nonclerical president of Princeton. In 1911 Wilson left the academic world to become the reform-minded governor of New Jersey, and by the next year he had been elected president of the United States.

Wilson was a man of lofty ideals, who promised to bring the world into a new era of international cooperation and peace. Yet he also had an exalted opinion of himself and refused to consider that he might not have all the answers to the problems of mankind. The Calvinism of his father had heavily influenced the young Wilson and at times had led him to see himself as chosen by God to lead the world out of the darkness of the past into a new era of light. Yet his sense of mission proved to be his downfall, for he refused to consider alternatives to his programs and finally sacrificed his ideals to win British and French approval for his pet project, the ill-fated and ineffective

League of Nations. He uttered statements and made promises during the war without consulting his allies, and by so doing he gave the Germans a false view of the terms they would receive from the victors after surrender. When the Allies gave the Germans not the just peace spoken of by Wilson, but the harsh Treaty of Versailles and the reparations that followed, they felt deceived. This sense of betrayal was one of the major factors that led many Germans to seek revenge for the war and made them susceptible to the ravings of Adolf Hitler.[1]

Wilson and the American people stood above the controversies that had led to the outbreak of the war and promptly declared their neutrality upon hearing of the opening of the conflict. Yet the idealistic president, never really impartial, admired the British. In January 1916 Wilson sent his chief representative in Europe, Colonel Edward M. House, to inform Bethmann-Hollweg, still German chancellor, that England would consider peace if Berlin would agree to evacuate France, Belgium, and Poland. The German leader, realizing that the military would never accept such conditions, refused to accept Wilson's terms, and the effort met with failure. However, knowing of the president's sympathy for the British cause, the Germans decided to attempt negotiations on their own to prevent the American from playing the role of mediator. On December 5, 1916, they called for a peace conference, but the Allies rejected the offer.

Wilson, afraid that allowing Berlin's peaceful mood to pass would increase hostility and eventually draw the United States into the war, decided to act. He asked all sides on December 18, 1916, to openly declare their war aims. The American chief executive hoped that once each side had stated its goals, he would be able to act as mediator and bring about a compromise that would end the war. The British, however, suspected Wilson of collusion with the Germans and made severe demands that the enemy evacuate the occupied areas of Belgium, Serbia, Montenegro, France, and Russia and that Berlin and Vienna accept full blame for the war and agree to pay reparations. The Allies required, in addition, the liberation of Italians, Slavs, and Rumanians living under Habsburg rule, a proposal that would spell the destruction of the Austro-Hungarian Empire. Berlin and Vienna refused to reply to Wilson's request, and 1916 ended without hope of peace.

The failure of the peace efforts of December, 1916, to end the war led to a renewal of the demand of the German military to be allowed to use unlimited submarine warfare to starve the British into submission. Many believed that the submarine would prove to be the decisive weapon that would halt shipping to England, causing the island kingdom to agree to peace on German terms. However, the attitude of the United States was the chief obstacle to unlimited submarine warfare. Wilson, reflecting the traditional American stand for absolute freedom of the seas for nonbelligerents, had forced the Germans to abandon undersea warfare on May 4, 1916, by threatening to break diplomatic relations over the issue. Notwithstanding, as the war dragged on without victory, many military leaders believed that fear of earning the president's wrath had robbed Germany of one of its most effective weapons. Bethmann-Hollweg and his civilian advisers had argued successfully against submarine warfare as long as hope of peace existed, but after this vanished they were unable to counter the influence of the military. At a conference at Hindenburg's headquarters at Pless on January 8 and 9, 1917, Ludendorff convinced the reluctant civilians to agree to undersea attacks on British shipping. The Germans knew that such a radical action would almost certainly bring the United States into the war on the side of the British, but they hoped that the new weapon would be so effective that victory would be won before the Americans had time to mobilize their forces. On January 31 the German ambassador to Washington, Count Johann von Bernstorff, informed Secretary of State Robert Lansing of the opening of unrestricted submarine warfare on February 1. Wilson was furious and broke diplomatic relations with Berlin three days later.

War might have come between the United States and Germany on the basis of the battle at sea alone, but on March 1 the American people learned of the Zimmerman Note, making war a certainty. Alfred Zimmermann, the German foreign minister, telegraphed the German ambassador in Mexico on January 19 with instructions to seek the aid of the Latin American country should the United States enter the war on the side of the Allies. To win Mexican support, Berlin offered to assist them to regain the territories in Texas, New Mexico, and Arizona that had been lost to the Americans after the Mexican War in 1848. Although the Mexicans were angry with the United States because of an invasion in 1916, they refused to consider the German offer, choosing neutrality instead. Zimmermann made the mistake of sending his offer by a telegraph wire, which the British had intercepted. Since the English had deciphered the enemy code, they passed a copy of the incriminating correspondence to the American State

Department, which released it to the press. The shocking revelation of German attempts to threaten the American Southwest caused a wave of anti-German indignation to sweep through the United States. On April 2, 1917, Wilson stood before the Congress to ask for a declaration of war against Germany and its allies. On April 6, 1917, America joined the war. The fresh and eager "Yanks" broke the stalemate on the Western Front and insured victory for the Allies.

While Germany had sowed the seeds of its own defeat by causing the Americans to enter the war in the West, German fortunes fared much better in the East. On March 8, 1917, the Russian people revolted against the incompetent government of Nicholas II; the revolt led to his abdication on March 15 and the creation of a provisional government. Thus, centuries of autocratic rule had ended. Although the new rulers of Russia yielded to the frantic appeals of the Allies to continue the war, the Russian people had grown tired of the carnage and destruction and longed for peace. Their army fled in disorder rather than fight the advancing Germans, and the anarchy and starvation undermined the ability of the provisional government to hold power. Seeing an opportunity to take advantage of the disorder that crippled the former empire, the German leaders allowed the leader of the radical Marxists, Vladimir Ilyich Lenin, to travel through Germany to St. Petersburg. When he arrived in the Russian capital, he called for an immediate end of the war and of the provisional government. Lenin's faction of the Russian Social Democratic party, the Bolsheviks, believed in a revolution controlled by an elite corps of professionals and refused to participate in the elections called by the provisional government. On November 7, 1917, Lenin and his followers seized power from Alexander Kerensky, the leader of the provisional government.

The new masters of Russia lost no time in fulfilling their pledge to end the war. On December 20, 1917, Lenin sent Adolf Joffe to meet with a German team of negotiators headed by General Max von Hoffmann and Richard von Kühlmann. The Germans, realizing that the bolshevik government was too weak to resist, demanded the surrender of all territories occupied by German forces. In addition, the representatives of Berlin supported a revolt in the Ukraine, where the people sought to rid themselves of centuries of Great Russian domination by establishing a state of their own. Joffe vainly attempted to persuade the Germans to reconsider their harsh terms. Lenin replaced him with his commissar for foreign affairs, Leon Trotsky. Trotsky also failed, returning home in desperation to consult the leadership of the Bolshevik party.

The severe German demands caused a serious split among the new masters of Russia. Lenin, favoring peace at all costs, demanded acceptance on the grounds that a successful revolution would soon spread to Berlin, and then a new peace could be negotiated with the German Marxists. Trotsky refused to allow Lenin's arguments to sway him and proposed that the Russians reject the German demands while refusing to fight, creating a situation of "no peace, no war." After a stormy debate, the majority of the party sided with Trotsky on January 21, 1918, and sent him back to Brest-Litovsk to resume negotiations. However, the Russian foreign commissar returned to find a changed situation. The Ukrainians had successfully overthrown their former masters and signed a peace with Hoffmann on February 9 that allowed Berlin to exercise considerable influence in the new state. The next day Trotsky formally refused to accept the German terms and announced his formula of "No peace, no war." Berlin replied swiftly and brutally. German armies moved even deeper into Russian territory, sweeping aside the remnants of the Russian army. This turn of events caused renewed discussions among the leadership of the Bolshevik party. Lenin repeated his demand for peace at any price, and the success of the German army persuaded the party leadership to accept the enemy terms. Discredited by his failure, Trotsky resigned, and on March 3, 1918, a new Russian delegation signed the Treaty of Brest-Litovsk. This pact left Russia only a fraction of its former size, as the Ukraine, Finland, and the Baltic States won their independence, and the victorious Germans took Poland and much of White Russia. The severe terms of the Treaty of Brest-Litovsk show the power of the ultra-nationalists in Germany and give some indication of the type of peace the West could have expected if the warlords of Berlin had been able to dictate to the British and French as they did to the Russians. However, this was not to be so, and the Treaty of Brest-Litovsk was soon to be abandoned in the wake of the German defeat.[2]

In the West, the bloody conflict continued for almost a year after the peace between Russia and Germany. The Bolshevik condemnation of the war as imperialism had a major impact on the West, where Wilson countered the Communist charges by issuing his famous Fourteen Points. The American president promised an end to the war that would be fair to all sides and that would be reached through open and just negotiations. He also pledged freedom of the seas and the removal, as far as possible, of all barriers to international trade. Wilson guaranteed that all colonial claims would be fairly adjusted and that the occupied territories of Belgium, France, including Alsace-Lorraine, and Russia would be restored to their rightful owners. Further, the chief executive proclaimed the principle of self-determination for the peoples of the Habsburg and Ottoman empires and promised free access to the sea for Serbia and Poland. Finally, he proposed mutual disarmament after the conclusion of the war and the formation of an international organization to insure peace and justice for all. Wilson's Fourteen Points were similar to the Peace Resolution of the German Reichstag and caused many Germans to hope that the victorious Allies would not inflict a severe settlement in case of defeat. However, the American president issued his program without bothering to consult his allies, who had other ideas about the terms of a German surrender. When Wilson failed to fulfill his promises, many Germans felt betrayed and vowed revenge. Had Wilson not made promises he could not fulfill and had the Germans approached negotiations without preconceived notions, the fate of Europe might have been radically different.[3]

After almost four years of fruitless fighting, Ludendorff and his military friends decided to attempt a bold attack that would break the stalemate and insure a German victory. On May 21, 1918, the thunder of over six thousand German guns broke the silence of the French dawn, shattering the Allied defenses. When the bombardment ended, the Teutonic forces unleashed clouds of choking gas and, covered by a thick fog, began the advance on their surprised enemies near St. Quentin. The startled British and French troops were unable to resist the pounding of their enemy. After a few days the Allies fell back, and the Germans advanced almost forty miles into Allied territory. At last it seemed that victory was within the grasp of the Germans, as their enemies struggled to halt the march. The French could do little but rush reinforcements to the front in a valiant effort to hold the line against the Teutonic onslaught. Finally, after days of bloody fighting, the fresh troops stood their ground and halted the enemy advance at Aimes on April 1. Having won time to regroup and reorganize their forces, the Allies appointed a French general, Ferdinand Foch, commander in chief and began to prepare for the next attack. On April 9 Ludendorff threw his forces into battle south of Ypres. Once again the swift German action caught the Allies unprepared, breaking through the British lines at Armentières. However, the success surprised even the Germans, and lack of reinforcements forced them to halt without taking full advantage of the gap in the defenses of the battle-weary British.

Nevertheless, Ludendorff opened a surprise attack against the French on the Aisne on May 27. Once again the Germans pounded their weak enemy and broke through the lines, taking Soissons two days later. The next day the Germans reached the Marne River, only thirty miles from the French capital. German victory seemed a certainty, but Ludendorff underestimated the will of the French to save their capital, and most important, the impact of the fresh American troops who arrived in France eager to face the enemy. On June 4, at Chateau-Thierry, the zealous "Yanks" met the Germans and turned the tide of battle in favor of the Allies by beating the weary Germans until their attack stopped. However, the determined Ludendorff decided to make one more attempt to break through the Allied lines and ordered his men to attack near Rheims. The ground of the famous champagne area thundered as the opposing armies fought, leaving the rich countryside in ruins and the great Gothic cathedral of Rheims in rubble. On July 18 Foch mustered his forces and ordered a counterattack. Reinforced by the Americans, the Allies hit the Germans hard on all fronts, driving them back inch by inch. When the smoke cleared on August 2, the French stood once again at Soissons, and the mighty German army faced retreat. From that point on, the Allied effort advanced without letting up, as the tired, outnumbered Germans fought futilely to stem the Allied tide of victory. On August 8 the British attacked at Amiens with over four hundred tanks. These new monsters of battle proved able to withstand the feeble German machine guns and moved out of the trenches and across the field against the enemy lines. Throughout the month of August and into September, the relentless Allies pulverized the straining German lines, regaining inch by inch and foot by foot the territory lost in Ludendorff's spring offensive. The brave Americans fought through the dense Argonne Woods, stumbling over the trees and brush, as enemy guns cut through their numbers. Some would have shunned such a dangerous route, but the relentless Americans refused to turn back, gradually winning ground and forcing the Germans to retreat. At the same time, the British moved to the east toward Cambrai and then north to Lille. Although the German forces fought with all their might and the carnage increased as the terrible days went by, the

Allies were victorious, and by October the Germans had lost the initiative and had been flung back to their positions of the summer of 1914.

Ludendorff realized that his effort had failed and that the Germans had spent all their strength in their disastrous effort to achieve a breakthrough. On September 29 he informed the shocked government that the war had been lost and that peace was an immediate necessity. The commander advised that immediate contact be established with Wilson and an attempt be made to win an armistice on the basis of the Fourteen Points. To win the sympathy of the American leader, Ludendorff suggested that the emperor appoint a new government based on broad popular support. The next day the other military leaders endorsed Ludendorff's request. The announcement of defeat struck the civilian leaders like a tidal wave. For four years they had believed the reports of impending victory; now they learned to their dismay that Germany had lost the war. When pressed for an explanation, Ludendorff, regaining his composure after the panic of a few days earlier, calmly told them that he was just a simple soldier and not a politician. The arrogant commander even criticized Chancellor Hertling for failing to warn the members of the Reichstag of the seriousness of the situation. Unable to cope with the responsibility of telling a nation that their sacrifice had been in vain, Hertling resigned, leaving Germany without a government.[4]

William and his advisers decided to choose a chancellor that would meet with the approval of the Allies. He named Prince Max, heir to the throne of the grand duchy of Baden, the new leader of the government. The prince was well known for his liberal views and had earned the respect of the enemy through his work with the International Red Cross on behalf of prisoners of war. Max arrived in Berlin on October 1 and heard for the first time of the military defeat of the fatherland. His first inclination was to refuse to become involved and return home; but Hindenburg, upon hearing of the prince's reluctance to accept office, rushed to the German imperial city to beg him to reconsider. Max yielded to pressure and accepted the chancellorship. On October 3, 1918, the new head of the German government sent a formal note to Wilson requesting his aid in opening negotiations for the end of the war that had gripped Europe for over four years. Two days later, the new chancellor stood before the Reichstag to announce his program. While the liberals cheered, he promised that all future chancellors would serve only with the support of the majority of the

Reichstag, not only at the pleasure of the kaiser, as in the past. He also pledged himself to electoral reform and to an end of military control over German life. At last, in its dying hours, the German empire had transformed itself into a parliamentary democracy; but the change had come too late to have any real meaning, for within a few days the empire itself would come crashing down. Prince Max completed his speech by informing the shocked members of the Reichstag that he had asked the American president to begin peace talks as soon as possible.

Although most Germans welcomed liberalization of their government, they were shocked by the announcement that the war had been lost. The warlords had told them for four years that the army stood invincible and victorious, and now, for the first time, every German had to face the fact that he had been deceived. Even the liberals refused to accept defeat. Many liberal leaders believed that the reform of the government made possible a new people's war and called for the enlistment of every able-bodied German to fight any attempt of the Allies to dictate the terms of the peace. *Vorwärts,* a leading liberal newspaper, praised the new parliamentary government and called for a display of national solidarity to bring about a German victory. Walter Rathenau stated in the *Vossische Zeitung* that the new form of government would only strengthen the will to fight and that a premature peace would only place the Germans in a position to be unable to resist the dictates of the Allies.

After the end of the war, the military refused to accept the blame for the defeat, claiming that the army stood unvanquished in the field and that peace had been negotiated by the liberals who lacked the will to continue the fight to a victorious conclusion. Ludendorff gave this account to a British officer, who asked if he meant that the German army had been stabbed in the back. The general and his friends took up this phrase and proclaimed that the liberals had actually stabbed the victorious army in the back by losing courage and insisting on peace at any cost. It is clear that, although many Germans believed this and turned against the progressives, the military itself had insisted that the war was lost and had forced the civilian government to open negotiations. Therefore, it was the army that lost its nerve, not the liberals, who had loyally supported the fatherland and even wanted to continue the fight after the military had given up all hope of success.

On October 8 Prince Max received the long-awaited American

reply to his proposal for negotiations. President Wilson demanded that the Germans evacuate all occupied territory as a precondition to peace talks. He also attempted to use the German desire for peace to force them to adopt his concept of democratic government, stating that the most important issue was the political future of Germany and whether or not the forces that had controlled the Reich would remain in power. The American leader's attempts to force the Germans to reject their past and accept the former professor's textbook theories of government would prove to be one of the most disastrous chapters in German history. The war continued as Prince Max and his advisers scrambled to please Wilson, believing that once they had done so he would live up to the promises of the Fourteen Points and negotiate a liberal peace.

The day after receiving Wilson's reply, the ministry met with Ludendorff to discuss the reply to his demands. The general opened the session with a complete report on the military situation. In response to a call for mass conscription to strengthen the army to continue the fight, he replied that such a step would probably do more harm than good and that there was little chance that additional troops could reverse the debacle. He did, however, assure the ministry that the army could defend Germany from an Allied invasion should talks prove fruitless, provided that they won two or three months to regroup the shattered forces and to prepare for the defense. Several additional meetings followed, during which the ministry decided, over the objections of some members who opposed the evacuation of northern France and Belgium, to reply to Wilson's note on October 12, 1918. The new German communication invoked the Fourteen Points as the basis for peace and assured the American president that the ministry had the support of the vast majority of the Reichstag.

Wilson chose to forget the promises of the Fourteen Points in his reply on October 16. Instead, he informed the Germans that no armistice could be considered that did not leave the Allies militarily superior to the Germans. He also escalated his attempts to remake the German government by demanding that the rulers of Germany rid themselves of the influence of the military and those who had ruled the Reich in the past. Wilson's latest ultimatum led to much discussion in the government. Many interpreted the president as demanding the abdication of the kaiser and urged the immediate rejection of his terms. However, other members of the ministry argued that peace must be won regardless of the price. The decisive factor in determining the response to the American president was the ability of the military to withstand Allied attacks. On October 17 Prince Max summoned Ludendorff to appear before the ministry. One by one the ministers asked him detailed questions on the capacity of the army to hold the lines long enough to place Germany in a better bargaining position. The general, recovered from the panic that had led him to demand peace talks, refused to give clear answers. The ministry had to be satisfied with a statement that the military could possibly hold the line against renewed attacks.

Unable to force Ludendorff to give a clear statement on the ability of the army to resist the enemy, Prince Max decided to meet Wilson's demands. On October 21 the chancellor sent his third note to Washington, stating that he had ordered all submarine commanders to cease attacks against passenger vessels. He assured the American president that the new government had been formed with the approval of the people and contained the leaders of the major political parties. Finally, Prince Max promised that no future German ministry would be organized without the consent of the majority of the Reichstag. The next day the chancellor attempted to demonstrate the good intentions of the ministry by introducing a constitutional amendment that would give the Reichstag sole power to declare war and to make peace. Another proposal would make the minister of war responsible to the will of the Reichstag and not to the kaiser alone, as in the past. Thus, the transformation of Germany from an absolutist monarchy to a constitutional monarchy had been completed without violence.

However, the stubborn American president refused to accept Max's reforms and pressed his campaign to force the Germans to adopt his theories of government. On October 23 he stated that if the Allies had to deal with the military masters and monarchial autocrats of Germany, the only acceptable peace would be on the basis of unconditional surrender. Had Wilson been content to accept the German response to his initial demands and the genuine progress toward democratic government, the war would have ended several weeks earlier and Germany might have been spared the bloodshed of the next few months. But Wilson's vision of himself as divinely ordained to bring about changes in Germany that would fit his ideas, rather than German traditions, was so strong that disaster resulted. His refusal to deal with the military forced the civilian government to accept blame for the defeat and discredited it in the eyes of many patriotic Germans. Had

Wilson dealt with Kaiser William and the army in such a manner as to make it clear that these forces, rather than the civilian government, had led Germany to defeat, the republic that followed might have had more support from the people and might have succeeded. Wilson's efforts to remake Germany in his image only allowed the military to escape blame and prepared the way for the failure of the republic and the rise of Adolf Hitler.

Wilson's severe demands caused the army to regain its lost courage and to attempt to prevent its humiliation and the abdication of the emperor. On October 24 the Supreme Command issued a proclamation signed by Ludendorff in Hindenburg's name rejecting Wilson's ultimatum and pledging an all-out fight to avoid acceptance. Although this statement was meant for circulation among the military alone and was to remain secret from the people and the civilian government, a telegraph operator, who was an Independent Socialist, copied it down as it was being transmitted to the eastern headquarters. He then sent a copy to an Independent Socialist deputy, who read it to the stunned membership of the Reichstag. Prince Max was furious and telephoned the Supreme Command headquarters to demand an explanation. Much to his surprise, he learned that Ludendorff and Hindenburg had defied his orders and were on their way to Berlin. The chancellor then demanded that the kaiser choose between the wishes of the government and those of the military. On October 25 the two crafty officers met with the emperor to tell him that they had only demanded an armistice to show the German people that Wilson would fail to fulfill the promises of the Fourteen Points and would demand a humiliating peace. They then demanded that William order the government to break off negotiations with the American president. However, the confused ruler refused to intervene in the debate and ordered Ludendorff and Hindenburg to speak with the ministry. Since Prince Max was ill, the pair held a stormy session with Vice-Chancellor Friedrich von Payer that accomplished nothing. On October 26 the kaiser regained his determination and summoned Ludendorff and Hindenburg to Bellevue Palace in Berlin. After the angry emperor scolded Ludendorff for attempting to interfere in the affairs of the ministry, the officer could do little but submit his resignation.

The inability of the military to withstand a possible Allied attack and Wilson's refusal to modify his demands led to the cry for William's abdication. On November 1 the minister of the interior, Dr. Wilhelm Drews, went to William's headquarters at Spa to cautiously suggest that he resign. However, the stubborn Hohenzollern ruler refused to even consider the proposal. At the same time General Wilhelm Gröner, Ludendorff's successor, recommended that the kaiser seek a death of glory by going to the front and dying while personally leading the troops. Gröner hoped that this would redeem William from the disgrace of a lost war, but the emperor was not interested in the idea. Although Wilson's fourth and final note of November 5 failed to mention the matter, the demand for the kaiser's abdication continued to gain momentum. The leaders of Germany hoped that the resignation of William would prevent any delay in the formal signing of the armistice and would insure that the victors would not demand a severe peace treaty. On November 7 the socialist members of the Reichstag demanded that Prince Max force the ruler to abdicate. The chancellor, who had also become convinced of the necessity of William's resignation, telephoned the kaiser on November 8 to suggest that he surrender the crown. However, the obstinate monarch refused to yield and even stated that he would turn to the army for support. The next day, Gröner coldly told William that the military would not fight to allow him to retain his throne. William then announced that he would abdicate as kaiser but not as king of Prussia. Finally, Prince Max decided that further discussions with the Hohenzollern ruler were pointless and on his own authority issued a press release announcing William's abdication as emperor and king of Prussia. Realizing that he had lost all support, the former kaiser boarded a train to take him to exile in Doorn, Holland. Had William realized the true situation and laid down his crown several weeks earlier, the position of the ministry might not have deteriorated, and the bloody revolution and civil war that followed might have been averted.

On November 11, 1918, in Marshall Foch's railroad car at Compiègne France, Matthias Erzberger, the representative of Germany, signed the armistice that ended the bloodshed of the past four years. The agreement provided that German troops would evacuate all occupied territories and return all Allied prisoners of war, and that Berlin would renounce the Treaty of Brest-Litovsk and accept an army of occupation on the Rhine. Thus, the long and bloody war ended with a German defeat. However, the authors of the disaster escaped without the humiliation of having to sign the surrender. Instead, an obscure politician, the representative of the coalition that would create the Weimar Republic, the one element that could have saved Germany from the unfortunate events of the next twenty years, signed the agreement. This led many Germans to believe that the civilian leadership had stabbed the army in the back and betrayed the fatherland by submitting to the dictates of the American president. Had Wilson demanded that Ludendorff and Hindenburg sign the armistice and surrender their swords in the traditional manner, the credibility of the civilian government might have been spared and the true defeat of Germany would have been an inescapable fact. Wilson's apparent demand for the end of the monarchy in his note of October 26 robbed the Reich of a degree of stability. Had William or his heir been allowed to remain the ceremonial head of state, Germany might have had an equilibrium that it lacked and might have been spared some of the unrest of the future. Instead, a wave of anarchy engulfed Germany and destroyed all hope of success by the civilian leadership. The First World War had ended, but the real tragedy of German history had just begun.

4

The Revolution of 1918-1919

While the politicians debated the terms of the armistice and the future of the Reich, many Germans grew dissatisfied with the slowness of the discussions and took to the streets in an effort to influence the future shape of the fatherland. This led to a series of violent clashes between the right, left, and middle and to the development of military bands on all sides. The spread of anarchy weakened the already feeble republic and enabled the old military class to utilize the fears of the coalition government to win back much of its old prestige and to guarantee its independence from civilian control in the years to come. In the end, it would be the army that would act almost as a state within the state, that would decisively force the destruction of the republic and the coming of the Nazi dictatorship.

The revolution began at the northern port city of Kiel, the home of the German navy. Although prewar Germany had spent great sums to build a large navy, this powerful fighting machine gathered rust during most of the war, only venturing out of port to face the British at the Battle of Jutland on May 31, 1916. This engagement proved a disaster for the overconfident Germans, who failed to overcome the more experienced and better-equipped British. The Germans fled to the safety of their home port, not daring to leave throughout the rest of the conflict. The sailors, idled by this failure, became restless as they passed their days in fruitless drills and maintenance activities. Soon, rumors began that the admirals planned to save face by ordering the fleet to make a surprise attack on the British. Although the sailors had tired of the routine of in-port activities, they had no desire to face death from the English, and many became determined to resist any effort to force them to enter battle. On October 28, 1918, the command ordered the fleet to leave port and to gather in the North Sea. The next day, Admiral Franz von Hipper met with the squadron commanders and told them that the object of the mission was to relieve the German army in Flanders and to engage the British fleet in battle. The leaders of the navy hoped that this would lead to a decisive victory that would strengthen the government's hand in the peace negotiations and prevent Wilson from dictating his terms to the German leaders. However, this last-ditch effort to save the Reich from defeat was not popular with the sailors, who, aware of the opening of negotiations, desired only a chance to return to their families and not an almost certain death in battle with the superior British.[1]

As rumors of the intentions of the officers spread among the sailors, some of the crews rose up in mutiny and refused to sail farther, extinguishing the fires in the boilers to force the ships to return to port. Faced with a major revolt, the officers could do little but order the fleet to return to Kiel and abandon the enterprise. However, after the return to Germany the officials rounded up the leaders of the mutiny and threw more than six hundred men in prison. Instead of forcing the remaining sailors to submit, the arrests made them more determined than ever to resist any attempt to send them into battle. They planned a meeting in the Trade Union Hall to protest the arrests. Word of the proposed demonstration traveled swiftly to Admiral Wilhelm Souchon, the commander of the fleet, who ordered the shore patrol to close the building. Despite this action, the determined sailors assembled in the exercise field outside the city and called for a meeting, to be held on Sunday, November 3, of sailors and workers to discuss the situation. Faced with such defiance, the admiral decided to make no effort to halt the assembly, relying instead on the loyalty of the sailors by sounding the alarm signal during the meeting. Souchon believed that the clanging of the signal would awaken the discipline in his men and that they would return to their ships ready for orders.

On the appointed day, nearly 20,000 men gathered in the exercise field to hear impassioned speeches by Karl Altelt, a stoker, and Arthur Popp, the leader of the Independent Socialists in Kiel. Amid the calls for resistance the alarm rang out, but the sailors refused to obey and remained at the meeting. Thus, hundreds of years of built-in discipline came crashing down as the rank and file of the navy for the first time in German military history defied the authority of their officers, beginning the Revolution of 1918–1919. The emotions of the crowd grew as Popp called for a march on the prison to free the captives and for the organization of a council of workers and sailors to govern the port city. Carrying torches and singing the "International," the determined mob marched through the streets of the city toward their goal. Frantically, the officers ordered the shore patrols to resist the onslaught and to restore order. However, most of the patrols, caught up in the sway of the mob, refused to fire on their fellow sailors, joining the throng instead. As thousands paraded toward the prison, one lone patrol led by Lieutenant Steinhauser stood its ground. Passions ran high when the wall of humanity approached the few loyal troops. As the advancing hoard came nearer, the nervous officer ordered his man to fire a volley above their heads. The startled mob hesitated momentarily and then continued to pour toward the small patrol. In desperation, Steinhauser commanded his men to fire directly into the marchers. When the smoke cleared, eight lifeless bodies lay on the blood-stained pavement; twenty-eight more had been wounded. Suddenly, horror spread among the marching hoard, and thousands of men who had fearlessly joined the revolt panicked, running for safety. Now the small patrol stood alone, surrounded only by a strange stillness in the streets, where just seconds before the light of the torches had blazed and the sounds of the singing mob had echoed. The officers had their victory, but at the price of ordering German troops to fire on their comrades.

The next day the rebels regained their courage, and the once quiet city rumbled with violent street fighting, as sailors and workers united to force the authorities to give power to a council of workers and soldiers. This revolutionary body demanded the immediate freeing of the prisoners and the right of the sailors to veto any further action of the fleet. The council also requested the officials to take immediate steps to improve the food and the living conditions of the seamen. The officers and civilian rulers of the embattled city failed to resist the popular uprising, and by the end of the day the red flag of revolution fluttered above all the ships in the harbor except the *König,* on which the imperial flag waved defiantly.

When news of the mutiny reached Berlin, a startled government decided to send Gustav Noske, a leading Majority Socialist, to bring order to the troubled port. The tall mustachioed man arrived in Kiel by train on November 4. News of his coming had preceded him, and he found the station filled with a throng of revolutionaries expecting him to announce his support for the revolution. After some nervous hesitation, the reluctant politician climbed out of the train. At this moment, thousands began to chant "Noske! Noske!" in unison, as they ran to greet Berlin's representative. A few sailors lifted the shaken man to their shoulders and carried him through the mob to a waiting automobile, where he took a seat next to Karl Altelt. As they drove through the streets surrounded by a sea of red, the revolutionary stoker waved a red flag shouting, "Long live freedom." When the procession reached Wilhelmplatz, first Altelt and then Noske greeted the throng. Someone handed the politician a sword, which he nervously returned while trying to calm the crowd with promises of a favorable action from the new government in Berlin.

Although Noske succeeded in bringing an uneasy peace to the troubled port of Kiel by releasing the prisoners and by negotiating with both sides, the spark ignited in the north quickly spread to other cities. Soon revolutionary mobs marched through the streets of Lübeck, Hamburg, Bremen, Hanover, Magdeburg, Brunswick, Oldenburg, Schwerin, Rostock, Cologne, Dresden, and Leipzig, demanding peace and the abdication of the kaiser. On October 7 the Spartacists Society, an organization of revolutionary Marxists, issued a manifesto demanding the nationalization of banks, heavy industry, and large estates by a revolution led by councils of workers and soldiers on the Soviet model. On October 23 the government proclaimed a general amnesty that enabled Karl Liebknecht to join the developing revolt. In Berlin, Richard Müller led a group calling itself the revolutionary shop stewards, which held a series of meetings addressed by Liebknecht to gather support for a general strike on November 11.

In the meantime, the leaders of the Majority Socialists realized that they must act or lose the support of the workers. Led by Friedrich Ebert and Philip Scheidemann, they forced the cabinet to issue a proclamation on November 5, pledging the transformation of the Reich into a people's state. The next day the Majority Socialists presented an ultimatum to Prince Max demanding freedom of assembly, the relaxation of military and police regulations, the abdication of William, and greater power for the Socialists in the government. By November 8, the stubborn emperor had refused to give up the throne, so the Majority Socialists resigned from the government in protest. The next day the leaders of the party met with the heads of the Greater Berlin Trade Union Council to endorse the call for a general strike on November 9. The revolutionaries formed the Worker's and Soldier's Council and began to win the troops stationed in the capital city to their cause. When the fatal day for the strike arrived, Ebert, Scheidemann, and other representatives of the Socialists met with Prince Max to demand the immediate abdication of the kaiser. After this session, the chancellor issued the press release that William had yielded, and he announced his own resignation in favor of a new government headed by Ebert.

Friedrich Ebert, the new head of the German government, had been born in 1871, the son of a tailor. Ebert had left his profession as a saddler to become an active Social Democrat and trade unionist. In 1915 he accepted the post of secretary general of the party, and in 1913 he succeeded August Bebel as party chairman. He loyally supported the war effort and worked with Prince Max's government. Ebert issued a proclamation pleading with the people for support and pledging a new government of the people that would work for peace and would seek to relieve the serious starvation that had been stalking the fatherland. The new chancellor hoped that some form of the monarchy could be saved from amid the revolutionary agitation of the mobs and the demands of the victorious Allies.

However, even Ebert was unable to withstand the cry of the masses as they engulfed the capital city. The various revolutionary organizations planned a mass demonstration that wound its way through the streets toward the Reichstag building. Inside, Philip Scheidemann sat eating his lunch, a bowl of potato soup. Upon hearing of the arrival of the throng, he boldly decided to counter the agitated radicals, who had been excited by speakers like Liebknecht and by the news from Munich of Kurt Eisner's proclamation of a republic. Laying down his spoon, he went upstairs to the reading room, flung open the window, and leaned out over the swarming mass. Acting on his own authority, the leading Social Democrat announced the resignation of Prince Max and the formation of a new government under Ebert. Then, almost as an afterthought, Scheidemann proclaimed the German Republic. With that, he closed the window and returned to his soup. Thus, Germany became a republic, and the mighty Hohenzollern monarchy came crashing down.[2]

Meanwhile, Ebert arrived at the Reichstag and waited for Scheidemann in the restaurant, unaware of what had taken place. Suddenly, a breathless man burst into the room to announce Scheidemann's proclamation. His face red with rage, the new chancellor turned to Scheidemann to ask if the report were true. When he meekly replied that it was, Ebert hammered his fist on the table and angrily demanded to know by what authority he had taken such a drastic step, shouting that only a constituent assembly had the authority to determine the future form of the German government. Unable to undo Scheidemann's deed, Ebert began to seek support for his government by arranging a meeting with the leaders of the other socialist factions. However, Liebknecht and Richard Müller of the left wing of the Independent Socialists opposed any compromise with the Majority Socialists, seriously splitting the party. The remainder of the Socialists decided to join Ebert's government, demanding that only Socialists be allowed to participate and that all political power be given to councils of workers and soldiers. The Independent Socialists forced Ebert to agree to postpone the meeting of the constituent assembly until the revolution could be consolidated. After some negotiation, Ebert accepted these conditions and formed the Council of People's Representatives, with himself and Hugo Haase, leader of the Independent Socialists, serving as cochairmen.[3]

While Ebert tried to win the support of the radical left, he also approached the military. On November 10 the chancellor placed a fateful telephone call to the army general headquarters at Spa. He spoke with General Wilhelm Gröner, Ludendorff's successor. The crafty officer, realizing the weakness of the government in the face of increasing revolutionary agitation from the left, forced Ebert to pay a high price for military support. Hindenburg would remain in office and the general staff would retain all control of the military. Gröner also demanded Ebert's promise not to destroy the general staff. This meant that the fortunes of Ebert's government were tied to those of the military and that the continued life and independence of the general staff was guaranteed. Ebert's telephone call on November 10 was one of the turning points in German history. Through Ebert's agreement, the historic position of the officer corps had been saved and would withstand all attempts to place the army under civilian control.

With the support of the left and the military assured, Ebert and his fellow People's Representatives faced the serious problems of a defeated nation. First the new government consolidated the revolution by abolishing censorship of the press and by guaranteeing freedom of expression and assembly. The government also decreed that all citizens over twenty would have the right to participate in equal, secret, and direct elections of all officials. The war had left the German economy in weak shape, made worse as thousands of former soldiers returned home to seek work. In the face of the economic crisis, the factory owners turned to organized labor for cooperation. In the Ruhr, the owners recognized the right of the workers to strike. On November 15, 1918, the captains of German industry joined with the leaders of the trade unions to form the Central Cooperative Union. The entrepreneurs recognized the rights of the workers, and both agreed to negotiate pacts regulating wages and working conditions as collective agreements, binding on whole industries. The owners also consented to allow the laborers to form shop councils to protect their privileges and to guarantee the proper administration of the collective agreements. The government complemented the Central Cooperative Union by establishing a national office with regional commissars and district officers to manage the economy during demobilization. The national office introduced the eight-hour day and required former employers to take back workers who had left to fight in the war.

With progress toward the solution of the economic crisis and the support of a large faction of the left, the government turned to the state governments for support. Ebert invited the heads of the local administrations to attend a conference of states in Berlin on November 25. This body issued a proclamation favoring German unity and calling for the early election of the promised constituent assembly.

On December 16 the Congress of Workers' and Soldiers' Councils, the legislative branch of the new government, which was chosen by local councils, met in Berlin. Of the 450 delegates, the government coalition held a majority of 350 votes. After much debate, the congress voted on December 19 to hold elections for the National Assembly on January 19, 1919. The congress also voted to give legislative and executive power to the Council of People's Representatives until the Assembly could take power. It established a general council of the representatives of the local workers' and soldiers' councils to supervise the activities of the People's Representatives, with power to remove and appoint the members of the government. The radicals in the congress fought to give the central council more authority, but the coalition of Majority and Independent Socialists thwarted their efforts. Thus, for a time at least, Germany had the promise of an effective government and economic recovery. However, this seeming order was short-lived, for the radicals set out to destroy the government and seize power for themselves.

The leaders of the radical cause were the Spartacists, led by Rosa

Luxemburg and Karl Liebknecht. The Spartacists were radical Marxists, who opposed all compromise with the Majority Socialists. They favored a socialist revolution that would give all authority to the workers and violently opposed allowing the middle classes or the factory owners to exercise any power in the new government. They favored violent revolution as the only means to crush the capitalistic system and transform Germany into a socialistic state.

The second phase of the Revolution of 1918 was opened by the action of the sailors. After the abdication of the kaiser, a group of seamen from Kiel marched to Berlin. There they set up headquarters in the royal stables, as they undertook their task as self-proclaimed protectors of the many art treasures in the royal palace. They soon became an irritant to the government. Ebert decided to dismiss them and send them home. However, the sailors refused to leave until they received their back pay. The financially unstable government rejected their demand, whereupon some of the sailors arrested Ebert and held him prisoner for several hours on December 23. They also seized Otto Wels, one of the leading Majority Socialists, and threatened to kill him unless they received their money. After the sailors released him, Ebert immediately telephoned General Gröner and appealed for military assistance. The general ordered General Leuqis to attack the next morning to drive the sailors from their fortress in the stables. However, as his troops approached the sailors' position, many realized that they were not being asked to fire on French or British soldiers, but on fellow Germans and they refused to press the attack. After some of Leuqis's troops joined the rebels, the general called off the attack and withdrew from the city, leaving the revolutionaries in control.

The attack on the sailors caused further radicalization of the left. The Independent Socialists resigned in protest on December 29. The next day the Spartacists sponsored a convention that formed the Communist party of Germany. Rosa Luxemburg drafted the party platform, which pledged a revolutionary war against the capitalist classes that would end in the creation of a worker's state and the establishment of communism. The new group also announced its opposition to the planned elections for the National Assembly.

With the loyalist troops removed from Berlin, the sailors firmly entrenched around the palace, and the formation of the Communist party, all had been prepared for the outbreak of a bloody revolt. The spark came from Emil Eichhorn, the Independent Socialist president of the Berlin police, who had refused to resign his post on December

29 when his fellow party members had left the government. On January 4, 1919, the ministry, now firmly in the hands of Ebert and his supporters, demanded Eichhorn's resignation. The obstinate radical refused, declaring that the executive committee of the Workers' and Soldiers' Councils had placed him in office and only it could remove him. He became a hero of the radical socialists, and both the Communists and the Independent Socialists began active cooperation to bring about the downfall of the Majority Socialists.

The radicals organized a massive demonstration in Alexander Square on January 6, 1919. There, in the historic center of Berlin, over 200,000 workers waved red flags and cheered, as Eichhorn and Liebknecht exhorted them to support the revolution, denouncing the Majority Socialists as traitors to the cause of the working class. Whipped into a frenzy by the speeches and the climate of revolt, mobs streamed out of the square, determined to attack the symbols of the opposition. One group seized the *Vorwärts* building, the headquarters of the Majority Socialist newspaper, while others occupied the government printing office, where great amounts of freshly printed money had been stored; another group fell upon the Silesian Railroad Station. Soon Berlin became a battleground, as supporters of both sides fought.

The government, startled by the initial success of the radicals, issued a desperate call for support. When the hoard of protesters reached the government quarter, they found it guarded by an equally determined human wall of Ebert's supporters. The revolutionaries, faced with the difficult decision of fighting with fellow members of the working class, halted rather than fire upon the very class they claimed to favor. Even the sailors, safe in their stable fortress, announced their refusal to take sides in the fight, as the rival mobs swarmed outside. Others, such as Müller, the head of the Revolutionary Shop Stewards, and Independent Socialists declared their opposition to the revolt and offered to serve as negotiators. Even the revolutionary leaders, Rosa Luxemburg and Karl Liebknecht, felt the revolt was premature.

Unable to control the city, Ebert fled and turned once again to Gustav Noske, who had become a hero for his handling of the Kiel affair. Muttering, "Someone must be the bloodhound, I do not fear the responsibility," the foe of revolution accepted Ebert's challenge. In his effort to gather forces for the drive to liberate Berlin from the grasp of the radicals, Noske turned to the Free Corps that had sprung up throughout Germany. The prewar youth movement had trained a generation of young men in the principles of duty to a charismatic leader and the cult of the folk. During the war, these men developed a sense of comradeship as they faced death together. They had also fallen under the influence of the Shock Troops, elite groups of men united under the leadership of daring officers, who were thrown into battle at important moments to break through the enemy lines. The Shock Troops, with their special uniforms and devotion to their leader, served as a pattern for the Free Corps movement. The men in the trenches developed a suspicion of the people at home, who had not shared their experiences. They fell easy prey to the myth of the "stab in the back" And upon returning to Germany to find their fatherland swept by revolution, they banded together to fight against the new foe. General Ludwig Märcker organized the first Free Corps on December 12, 1918. With the approval of his military superiors, he gathered a few thousand men into several units under the command of young officers. Soon between 200,000 and 400,000 men flocked to join the Free Corps, motivated by their desire to regain the comradeship of the trenches and daily pay of thirty to fifty marks, plus a food allowance and benefits for their families. Many former officers, deprived of their elite position by the close of the war, gathered Free Corps of their own. Even Sergeant Suppe of Berlin, an enlisted man, led a Free Corps. Many members of these squads would later become Nazi Storm Troopers. By January 1919, sixty-eight Free Corps stood ready for the fight.[4]

From his headquarters in a convent school in the fashionable suburb of Dalhem, Noske concentrated on planning the recapture of Berlin. He organized a force of three thousand dedicated followers and planned the attack for January 11. The day before the operation, a group of Free Corps men ruthlessly retook the *Vorwärts* building from the radicals, who proved powerless to withstand the superior arms and flame throwers of their enemy. On the appointed day, Noske's forces marched into the city, and the revolutionary "army" vanished as quickly as it had arisen. A small group of Sparticists made their stand in the police headquarters, which the government took after bloody fighting on January 12. The victorious troops seized Luxemburg and Liebknecht and brutally murdered them while transporting them to jail to await trial. The government established a military tribunal to try the leaders of the revolt; however, most were freed, and the rest received only light sentences.

The Communists, having lost the leadership of Luxemburg and Liebknecht, refused to give up the fight and used the elections for the national assembly and its opening on February 6, 1919, as the occasion for a series of strikes in all industrial regions of the Reich. The Marxists planned a massive general strike in Berlin for March 3, in a renewed attempt to overthrow the government of the Majority Socialists. Before the appointed day the Communists issued a manifesto demanding the election of workers' councils to take control of all factories and the transfer of all police power from the government to local councils of workers. The Communists further ordered the dissolution of the officer corps and the formation of a Red Guard, consisting solely of revolutionary workers, to act as the new army of the people's state. After the proletarian victory, the Marxists announced that a revolutionary court would try Ebert, Scheidemann, Noske, and the other leaders of the government as enemies of the people. The executive council of the Workers' and Soldiers' Councils joined the Communist call for a general strike, but they rejected the demand for the trial of Ebert and his supporters.[5]

On March 3, as planned, the workers of Berlin once more took to the streets. At first the effort succeeded, and anarchy reigned in the crippled city. When the strike committee decided further to paralyze Berlin by shutting off all water, light, and power, once again their radicalism caused many to reject the revolution and rally in support of the government. Even the leaders of the trade union deserted the strike. Ebert again summoned Noske to restore order. The determined foe of revolution proclaimed martial law and called upon the military and the Free Corps to join the fight. For five days the streets of Berlin flowed with blood, as the loyal forces ruthlessly put down the revolt. On March 8 the strike leaders realized their defeat and surrendered. However, the Spartacists refused to give up the fight, and sporadic fighting rocked the city until March 17, when Noske's forces finally regained complete control, leaving twelve hundred workers dead in the bitter fighting. Thus, the Communist effort to capture Berlin met with bloody failure.

To the south, in Bavaria, the fighting continued. The normally placid city of Munich had been rocked with revolution ever since word had arrived of the sailors' revolt in Kiel. The leader of the Bavarian revolution was Kurt Eisner, son of a Jewish merchant and former editor of *Vorwärts*. After the split within the Social Democrats, Eisner joined the Independent Socialists and busied himself as a free-lance writer for the *Münchner Post,* the leading southern German socialist newspaper. On November 4, 1918, a large group of workers met to demand the abdication of the kaiser and peace, thus beginning the Bavarian revolution. For the next several days, revolutionary fever continued to grow, fed by radical speeches in the many beer halls of the Bavarian capital. On the sunny fall afternoon of November 7, thousands gathered in the Theresian Meadow, amid banners demanding bread and peace, to listen to impassioned speeches denouncing the war and the emperor. Carried by the mood of the mass demonstration, Eisner and the Independent Socialists met the next day to organize the Soldiers', Workers', and Peasants' Council and to announce the establishment of the Bavarian Democratic and Socialist Republic.[6]

Headed by Eisner and a cabinet consisting of members of the Majority and Independent Socialist parties, the new provisional government seized control without bloodshed. It called for peace, a constitutional convention, the security of property and person, and the maintenance of order. Eisner refused to purge the civil service of questionable officials, proclaiming that all government workers would retain their positions. On November 15 the government issued its official program. This envisioned the formation of a United States of Germany by a national constituent assembly that would include the German-speaking people of the defunct Habsburg Empire. Eisner pledged religious freedom for all and placed first priority on the restoration of the economy and on socialization.

Although the Bavarian revolt had achieved a victory without violent fighting, unlike the revolt that had left rivers of blood in the streets of Berlin, Eisner failed to win the support of the majority of the normally conservative Bavarians. In elections held on January 12 and February 2, Eisner's opponents won control of the Bavarian Diet. The Majority Socialists then demanded Eisner's immediate resignation. However, the revolutionary leader refused to yield to pressure, claiming that only the full Diet could make a decision on such an important matter. Eisner, trying to win popular support, then began a series of speeches pledging to fight any attempt to take control from the Workers', Soldiers', and Peasants' Council.

Tension continued to grow as the long-awaited opening session of the Diet neared and as both sides campaigned for approval from the masses. On February 21, the appointed day, Eisner left his office in the Foreign Ministry accompanied by two aides to walk to the first meeting of the Diet. Suddenly, as Eisner turned a corner, Count

Anton von Arco-Valley, a member of a local right-wing organization called the Thule Society, burst out of the shadows of the stately buildings on Promenade Square and fired two shots into the head of the radical leader. Eisner fell to the pavement, covered with blood, and died instantly. Eisner's guards shot the assassin, dragged him from the reach of an angry mob, and threw him into prison. News of the murder caused a wave of violence to rock the Bavarian capital, as Eisner's supporters sought revenge for his death. The announcement caused the Diet to break up amid chaos, as Alois Lidner, an apprentice butcher, marched into the hall and shot Erhard Auer, a leading Majority Socialist who was speaking to the deputies. Although the bullet knocked Auer from his chair and left him seriously wounded, it failed to take his life. After Lidner killed a soldier trying to capture him, the Diet broke up in confusion. Outside, the people of Munich greeted the death of Eisner with the ringing of church bells, the flying of flags at half mast, and the formation of a revolutionary Red Guard. Eisner's funeral on February 26 turned into a popular demonstration. The workers proclaimed a three-day general strike, and thousands of workers and peasants formed a procession behind the body of their fallen leader, as others threatened frightened priests with death if they refused to ring the bells of their churches.

Faced with the spread of anarchy, the Majority Socialists fled to the more quiet city of Nuremberg to the north and formed a new cabinet under Johannes Hoffmann. Throughout March, daily battles took place between leftists and armed bands of the upper class and nobility. A group of Red Guards set up an honor guard on the spot of Eisner's assassination that members of the radical right-wing Thule Society broke up by throwing bags of flour permeated with the scent of female dogs in heat. Groups of male dogs invaded the site, turning it into utter chaos. The Thule Society had been formed in 1918 by a group of fanatical followers of the cult of the folk. Its symbol was the swastika. On April 7 the Independent Socialists seized control of Munich and proclaimed the establishment of a soviet republic. However, the Communists, refusing to recognize the leadership of the Independents, shook the solidarity of the revolution two days later by proclaiming a rival soviet republic of their own and preparing for battle.

Meanwhile, the exiled Bavarian government called on the military and the Free Corps to converge on Munich to restore its control. Nationalist officers from all over Germany and groups of Free Corps harkened to the call and marched on Munich to drive the radicals from power. The bloody scene of Berlin was repeated, as savage fighting between the rival groups turned the once quiet city into a bloody battleground from April 30 to May 8. The nationalists fought from street to street and from building to building against the radicals who tried in vain to save the revolution. After almost six hundred persons had lost their lives in the battle, the military and the Free Corps defeated the last pockets of resistance. The victorious nationalists established a reign of terror and gathered hundreds of suspected revolutionaries and shot them while others were cast into prison. On May 13 Hoffmann's government returned to Munich, and the Bavarian Revolution ended.

The first stormy months of the German Republic left an indelible mark on the history of Germany for the next fourteen years. The Majority Socialists had been forced to turn to the very powers they had opposed to establish their government. In so doing, Ebert and his followers alienated the radicals and many workingmen, placing the party on the side of the military and representatives of the old order by rejecting radical socialism. The army had won a new position by placing the government in its debt. From then on, any attempt to restrict its privileges would meet with failure. The government feared doing anything that would deprive it of the necessary support of the army. Thousands of returning soldiers reacted to the radicalism of the left and their sense of betrayal by flocking to the radical right. Such groups as the Free Corps prepared the way for the rise of Hitler and national socialism.

5

Constitution and Treaty

Even as revolutionary violence swirled around them, the leaders of Germany attempted to solve the serious problems that faced the defeated nation: the drafting of a new constitution and the final negotiations with the Allies. In the first task they proved more successful, at least for the moment, than in the second; for the vengeful victors rejected Wilson's lenient Fourteen Points and sought to inflict a severe peace on the powerless losers. The ill-conceived Treaty of Versailles would poison relations between Germany and the rest of the world and cause many Germans to reject the politicians who had signed the humiliating peace. The Weimar Republic would never be able to escape from under the shadow of Versailles, and in the end the treaty and the reparations that followed would be major reasons for the fall of the Weimar Republic and the birth of the Nazi dictatorship.

On November 15, 1918, the People's Representatives asked Hugo Preuss, professor of constitutional law at the University of Berlin and the new secretary of the interior, to propose a draft constitution. The scholar invited a group of experienced government officials and academicians to the capital city to lend their advice to the undertaking. After much thought and discussion, Preuss proposed the creation of a centralized democratic parliamentary republic to take the place of the old empire. He also recommended the drastic reduction of the power and number of the old states to sixteen administrative units. The head of state would be a president, elected by a nationwide vote, with the power to initiate plebiscites on laws passed by the Parliament over his objections. According to Preuss, the highest organ of the state should be the legislative branch, consisting of a reichstag chosen by all Germans over twenty, and a House of the States selected by the governments of the provinces.[1]

Naturally the state governments strongly objected to the proposed reduction of their jealously guarded power. On December 27 the governments of Bavaria, Württemberg, and Hesse met to discuss the professor's draft and demanded its rejection. Instead they favored the establishment of a federal state that would guarantee the privileges of the individual states. The serious conflict about the position of the provinces in the new Germany was only a continuation of the centuries-old struggle between centralization and particularism. Since the time of the Holy Roman Empire, local rulers had resisted every effort to create a strong central government at their expense. The victory of the petty princes had been one of the major reasons for the downfall of the empire. Throughout the nineteenth century, the conflict had continued between the advocates of national unification and the local rulers who guarded their semi-independent status. Although Otto von Bismarck had successfully forced the states to accept Prussian hegemony and to yield to the centralized empire, he had failed to destroy the old particularism, and it once again reasserted itself in 1918.

While the debate over the status of the states raged, the political parties that had grown during the nineteenth century revised their programs to fit the new situation of German politics. There were eight major parties and several minor ones. The Center party, consisting of representatives of all classes, occupied the middle of the political spectrum. It rejected a rigid program in an effort to appeal to as many voters as possible. The organization had been formed in the middle of the nineteenth century as the chief representative of the German Roman Catholics, but it had enlarged its base during the war to attract Protestants and had even begun to nominate them for office. In the south, the Bavarian People's party also represented the moderate cause. Unlike the Center party, with which it had originally developed close ties, the Bavarian group strongly championed the preservation of the historic rights of the states and reflected the primarily rural character of its homeland by fighting for the rights of the farmer. The third group of the middle was the Democratic party, formed on November 16, 1918. It was a basically middle-class organization that rejected the socialism of the left while supporting the formation of a democratic republic.

There were two major right-wing parties. The members of the old National Liberal party, which had originally supported Bismarck, formed the German People's party on a largely conservative middle-class base. It opposed socialism and consisted of many who longed for the return of the monarchy. The radical rightists united to form the German Nationalists People's party as the bastion of the ultra-conservatives and monarchists. The two parties of the right represented a serious source of disloyalty to the new German Republic, as their members made no effort to hide their disdain for the republic or their desire to restore the monarchy.

As we have seen, the war and revolution caused a serious split in the German left. The Independent Socialists and the Communists left the more moderate Social Democratic party to work for radical socialism. Together, these two leftist groups opposed the constitution as the creation of the middle-class masters of the workers, and they proved to be a major source of opposition to the republic. The Social Democrats, or Majority Socialists, responded to the disorder that marked the birth of the German Republic by appealing to the military for support and by rejecting the revolutionary ideology of the past. They would be the strongest supporters of the government they had created, but they would rapidly lose influence as the German people sought someone to blame for the fate that had befallen them at the hands of the victorious Allies.[2]

After months of waiting, over 80 percent of the German men and women went to the polls on January 19, 1919, to elect 435 members of the National Assembly, each member representing 150,000 persons. In this election the German people rejected radicalism, casting 76.2 percent of their votes for the moderate parties, 37.9 percent for the Social Democrats, 19.7 percent for the Center, and 18.6 percent for the Democrats. Together these parties, which had supported the Peace Resolution of 1917, formed the Weimar Coalition, which would dominate the Assembly and write the new constitution. The radical left-wing Independent Socialists won only 7.6 percent of the vote, and the right gained only 14.7 percent, of which 4.4 percent was for the German People's party and 10.3 percent was for the Nationalists. The Communists boycotted the elections in protest of the failure of the revolution to create a Communist state.

On February 6, 1919, Friedrich Ebert opened the national assembly with a speech praising the accomplishments of the provisional government and proclaiming a new era of freedom and prosperity for the German people, who were free at last from the despotic rule of the monarchs. Ebert also asked for the loyal support of the people, stating that the day of the necessity of illegal acts had passed and called upon them to unite behind the new republic. The head of the provisional government sharply condemned any attempt by the Allies meeting in Paris to force the new republic to accept a repressive peace.

Instead of meeting in Berlin, a city full of unrest and associations with an imperial past that they were striving to forget, the leaders of Germany gathered in the peaceful city of Weimar, the home of Goethe. The National Assembly had three important tasks before it: the creation of a legal government, the making of peace, and the writing of a constitution. The Central Council of the Workers' and Soldiers' Councils immediately resigned, granting its political authority to the Assembly, which became the new temporary government of Germany. On February 11, 1919, the delegates elected Ebert head of state with the title "President of the Reich" and authorized him to form a cabinet. Ebert and his fellow Social Democrats offered the Independent Socialists a place in the ministry in return for their recognition of the National Assembly as the legitimate government and a denunciation of the use of force to seize power. However, the radical left valued their revolutionary ideology more than power and rejected Ebert's overtures. The president next turned to the Center and the Democratic parties, which agreed to form a ministry, with Philip Scheidemann as chancellor. With the first task accomplished, the new government began the difficult chore of negotiating with the Allies and of writing a new constitution.

While the representatives of the German people occupied themselves at Weimar, the representatives of the Allies met in Paris to discuss the terms of the peace treaty. Unlike the Congress of Vienna, which rebuilt Europe after the Napoleonic wars, the Paris Peace Conference refused to allow the vanquished to participate in its deliberations. Although the twenty-seven victorious nations sent seventy men to discuss the shape of Europe after the disastrous war, the real power lay in the hands of the "Big Four," Georges Clemenceau, David Lloyd George, Vittorio Orlando, and Wilson. Clemenceau, the premier of France, hoped to negotiate a peace that would leave Germany too weak ever to threaten his people again. He also sought approval for French annexation of the left bank of the Rhine, the coal-rich Saar Valley, and the former German colonies. Lloyd George, recently reaffirmed as the British prime minister by a smashing victory at the polls, had promised the English that he would make the Germans pay for the war and place the former kaiser on trial for war crimes. The English leader had no intention of supporting a settlement that would allow Germany to ever again menace the stability of the world. Vittorio Orlando, the prime minister of Italy, planned to win territory for his country by annexing the Italian-speaking areas of South Tyrol, Trieste, and Fiume.[3]

Woodrow Wilson, the idealistic president of the United States, arrived in Europe amid the cheers of thousands, who saw him as a deliverer from the injustices and wars of the past and the father of a new era of peace. Wilson responded to the praise by seeing himself as a man unfettered by the greed of his fellow statesman and as the representative not of one nation, but of all the oppressed peoples of Europe. He entered the negotiations with an air of moral superiority, as he condemned the old diplomacy and spoke of a foreign policy under the control of the people, through their parliaments, and of treaties achieved through open discussion rather than behind closed doors, as in the past. Wilson spoke loudly of self-determination for all and of a future when all nations would unite in an international organization that would achieve the solutions of problems through democratic procedures, making war obsolete. In the end, Wilson lost much of his glamour, as he abandoned his principles one after another under the influence of Clemenceau, Lloyd George, and, to a lesser extent, Orlando.

Although the American president had pledged himself to the principle of open discussions of the peace terms in his speeches and in the famous Fourteen Points, he made no effort to fulfill this promise during the conference. Even the victorious nations had no real influence over the negotiations, as the "Big Four" met behind closed doors to hammer out the agreements. Wilson and his fellow delegates refused to follow the example of the more successful Congress of Vienna, which had allowed the defeated French to participate in its sessions, and they barred the Germans and their allies from even discussing the peace terms. Instead, the victors presented their demands to the defeated nations and demanded acceptance under threat of renewed fighting. The failure of Wilson to carry out his promise of open negotiations gave the Germans still another reason to feel betrayed.

When the sessions opened, Clemenceau immediately demanded a vengeful peace that would tear the left bank of the Rhine from Germany and give France the Saar Valley with its rich coal deposits. The French premier further demanded the occupation of the Rhineland by Allied troops for thirty years. Wilson, striving to fulfill at least part of his promises, insisted that the period of occupation be cut in half, to fifteen years, and that the Saar Valley be placed under the League of Nations for the same time, after which a plebiscite would be held to determine its future. Wilson, however, sought to placate the French by granting them title to the coal mines in the Saar as compensation for the French mines destroyed during the war. The French also demanded that the new Polish state receive the city of Danzig and the surrounding area as an outlet to the Baltic Sea. Lloyd George resisted this, arguing that the contested city should be placed under the mandate of the League of Nations. Although Poland would not receive the former German city, it would be given an outlet to the sea through the Vistula Valley and a guarantee of the right to trade through Danzig. Finally, Wilson sided with the British leader, thus ending the dispute. The "Big Four" also decided that the people of Upper Silesia, an area of mixed German and Polish population, would decide their fate through a plebiscite.

Wilson had yielded much to the French premier, but he hoped that the League of Nations would act to preserve the peace and bring about international understanding, thus achieving some of the promises of the rejected Fourteen Points. The new body would consist of two branches: an assembly in which each member state would have one vote and a council of nine members, five of which, France, England, the United States, Italy, and Japan, would be permanent; and four of which would be elected by the assembly. The League would sponsor the World Court and the International Labor Office. The Allies chose Geneva, in neutral Switzerland, as the site for the headquarters of the League. The assembly was to meet once a year and the council four times a year. All members would be required by the charter to submit all international disputes to arbitration or to the council for review. Finally, all decisions of the international body would have to be unanimous to take effect. Despite Wilson's dreams, the League of Nations would prove to be a weak organization, unable to save the world from the consequences of the failure of the Paris Peace Conference to solve the tensions that had led to the First World War.

On May 7, 1919, the shocked Germans received the terms of the peace treaty. The Reich would lose large areas, including Alsace-Lorraine, a few towns to Belgium, most of Posen and West Prussia, and all of the former colonial possessions. Furthermore, both the Saarland and Upper Silesia would be detached from Germany and their futures determined by plebiscites to be held under the supervision of the League of Nations. While many of the territorial losses of Germany could be justified, Wilson and his colleagues failed to allow many Germans living in the lost areas the right of self-determination, which he had once so loudly promised. The Germans were especially angry over the creation of the Polish Corridor in former German areas, separating East Prussia from the rest of the Reich. Many Germans resented the territorial arrangements, and they would do much to shatter the peace and stability of Europe by providing fertile ground for the propaganda of the extreme nationalists.

The treaty also called for the destruction of the German military. In the future, the German army could consist of no more than 100,000 men. It was forbidden to possess large guns and was allowed only a limited number of smaller ones. Since the American president had been especially opposed to German submarine warfare, the treaty forbade the Germans to possess even one submarine. The navy, in deference to the British, who feared any threat to their command of the seas, could have only six warships and a corresponding number of smaller craft. Wilson, afraid that the Germans might use conscription to build a large army of trained men, to be called up at a moment's notice, as the Prussians had done under Napoleon's rule, insisted that Germany be forbidden to introduce conscription. This was a major mistake, for it insured that the German army would remain an elite corps of professionals, loyal only to their commanders and their interpretation of nationalism. This served to further strengthen the power of the officer corps and prevented any attempt to replace the professional force with a more democratic army, as the German liberals had hoped would happen for more than 100 years.

Perhaps the most severe aspects of the peace treaty were the provisions designed to fulfill Wilson's demand for compensation for the destruction of the war. The victors required the Germans to accept full guilt for the outbreak of the war and to pay for all civilian damage and the cost of the armies of occupation. First the Allies forced the Germans to turn over to them all German merchant ships over 1,600 tons, half of those between 800 tons and 1,600 tons, and a quarter of the fishing fleet. The winners of the war also demanded that the Germans build 200,000 tons of shipping annually, to be given to the Allies without payment. Not only did the losers have to deplete their shipping fleet, but they also had to deliver large quantities of coal to France, Belgium, and Italy during the next ten years. All German property in the Allied countries was to be sold, with the proceeds going to the victors. Finally, the Germans had to internationalize all their rivers and to allow Allied warships to pass through the Kiel Canal. All in all, the Germans had to agree to deliver 20 billion gold marks worth of goods to the Allies by March 1, 1921. However, this would only be the beginning of the reparations, for the Allies reserved the right to set the total bill at a later date. The economic aspects of the treaty proved to be its most severe section. The Germans ended the First World War with a national debt of 144 billion gold marks. The burden of reparations in material and money harmed the already weak German economy, helping cause a serious inflation and leaving thousands of workers without jobs to earn the money to feed their starving families. The "War Guilt Clause" was clearly based on a total misrepresentation of the facts and unjustly made the Germans accept full blame for causing a war they did not cause. The Germans were certainly to blame for bloodshed, but so were the Serbs, the Russians, and the French.

The publication of the terms of the peace treaty struck the Germans like a thunderbolt. They had surrendered believing that the peace would be based on Wilson's Fourteen Points, only to receive a demand that they sign a treaty that rejected the spirit, if not the specific details, of Wilson's promises. The National Assembly met in special session in Berlin on May 12 to discuss the document. One by one the political leaders of all the parties, including the Independent Socialists, rose to strongly denounce the treaty and demand its revision. After the stormy session ended, the angry delegates stood to sing the German national anthem, "Deutschland über Alles." Ebert frantically asked the Allies to reconsider and open negotiations, only to be told that Germany must sign the treaty by June 23 or else face even more severe action. The treaty led to a major political crisis, as no German politician wanted to be saddled with the blame for accepting its harsh terms. On June 19 the entire ministry resigned in protest. Ebert desperately turned to General Gröner in hopes that the army could protect the fatherland from a possible attack. However, the head of the military informed the somber president that his forces were in no position to resist the stronger Allies. Gröner also told Ebert that Germany had no choice but to sign the hated document and hope that in time its terms could be revised. A new coalition cabinet headed by Gustav Bauer finally accepted office and yielded to fate by recommending that the National Assembly approve the treaty. On June 23, only four hours before the Allied ultimatum expired, the Assembly voted 237 to 138, with 5 abstentions, to sign the treaty. A number of delegates refused to attend and to participate in the humiliation of the land they loved.[4]

On June 28, 1919, the victors assembled in the Hall of Mirrors, where almost half a century before the German princes had proclaimed William I their emperor, to accept the German signatures. There amid the faded splendor of Louis XIV, as the sunlight danced between the mirrors and gilt of this monument to the era of baroque, Wilson and Clemenceau presided as thousands filled the room to watch the ceremony. The two German representatives, Dr. Müller and Dr. Bell, one who played second violin in a Brunswick orchestra and the other a university instructor, but both obscure politicians because no man with hope of a future in German government would ruin his career by signing the treaty, entered, pale and nervous, more like prisoners than diplomats. Clemenceau made a short statement. The tense Germans jumped up to sign, but they were told to sit down as it was not yet time. Finally, they put their shaky signatures on the fateful document and left the hall. Outside, fountains played amid the vast gardens, and the victors celebrated their triumph with toasts of the finest French champagne. Perhaps the best comment on the whole affair was made by Sir Harold Nicolson, a member of the British delegation, who wrote in his diary for that day, "To bed, sick of life."[5]

The joyous Allies had little to celebrate because the treaty they had forced the Germans to accept proved to be the undoing of the peace. Within twenty years, Europe once again entered a war. The Second World War, in reality a conclusion of the First World War, left millions dead and much of Europe in rubble. The Treaty of Versailles, named for the place of its signing, more than any other factor led to the destruction of the Weimar Republic and the rise to power of a dictator. It left most Germans feeling that they had been tricked into surrender by Wilson's false promises. Had the American leader not made pledges he could not keep, much of the dissatisfaction of those who felt betrayed by the American president and the politicians who signed the armistice would not have developed. When the full impact of the treaty and the reparations were felt by the German nation, disillusionment with Wilson's broken word and the harsh terms of the Treaty of Versailles grew. Many vowed to revenge the disgrace and overthrow the leaders and the republic that had accepted its devastating terms. If the Allies had realized that the treaty would cripple the

German economy and destroy any chance the Reich had of developing into a genuine democratic republic and had adopted more realistic terms, history might have been drastically changed, and the holocaust of the Nazi tyranny and the Second World War might have been avoided.

In the meantime, the National Assembly completed work on the constitution and formally approved it on July 31, 1919, by a vote of 262 to 75. The Weimar Constitution went into effect on August 14, 1919. It was a democratic document with long sections guaranteeing civil rights. The Parliament consisted of two houses: the Reichstag, representing the people and elected by universal, equal, direct, and secret ballot every four years; and the Upper House, representing the states. The delegates to the Reichstag would not be chosen by majority vote, but rather by a complicated system designed to give a political party the same percentage in the lower house as it received at the polls. This proved to be one of the major flaws in the document because it made possible the entry into the Reichstag of many small groups that were unable to win a majority but could get enough votes to qualify. The multitude of political parties was one of the most serious problems of Weimar Germany. It made it very difficult for a ministry to be formed with the support of the majority of the Lower House, thereby causing a great deal of instability.

The states, which had been reduced from the prewar twenty-five to eighteen by the unification of eight small central states to form Thuringia, retained many of their old rights and chose representatives for the Upper House of the Parliament. However, the central government retained all executive, judicial, legislative, and financial power over matters of national concern and was superior to that of the provinces. Thus, the National Assembly rejected Preuss's proposal in favor of a form more acceptable to the state governments, which, like the royal governments they replaced, jealously guarded their rights.

The president was elected in direct popular election for a term of seven years and served as head of state of the new Germany. However, in an effort to prevent the president from becoming a republican kaiser, the constitution required that each action of the chief executive be countersigned by the chancellor or the cabinet officer concerned before it could take effect. The charter also gave the Reichstag the right to remove the president by a two-third's vote, subject to approval by a national referendum. The president's chief duty was to appoint the chancellor and the ministry, with the requirement that the cabinet enjoy the support of the majority of the Reichstag. Despite the limitations placed on the power of the president by the constitution, he received great privileges under Article 48. This section permitted the chief executive to use the military to force state governments to obey orders from the national government. He also had the right to suspend the civil rights guaranteed by the constitution and to use the military to restore order in times of serious crisis. Article 48 became the most dangerous provision of the new constitution, for it allowed the president to make himself a dictator and rule by decree. During the Weimar Republic, the various presidents used it over 200 times, thereby paving the way for Hitler's autocratic rule. Had the national assembly not made the fatal mistake of placing Article 48 in the constitution, Hitler's seizure of power would not have been as easy.[6]

In 1919 the German people elected a constitutional assembly that provided them with a new frame of government and negotiated the final peace with the victorious Allies. However, the Treaty of Versailles did not successfully end the tensions that had erupted in war in 1914, but only laid the foundation for new conflicts that would plunge the world into a new and more terrible war in 1939. By insisting on vengeance instead of the justice and understanding promised by Woodrow Wilson, the Allies fed the resentment of the defeated Germans and crippled their already weak economy. During the next few years, the war reparations would prevent a full recovery from the chaos of the past and hamper any effort to restore economic stability. The Allies rejected self-determination for many Germans, placing them under foreign rule and driving a wedge between the bulk of the Reich and its eastern portion through the hated Polish Corridor. The German leaders, gathered in Weimar, did little to preserve the democratic republic they tried so hard to create. They allowed the many political factions to make their influence felt through the method of electing the Reichstag, dooming any possibility of stable government. They also gave the head of state such broad powers to meet emergencies through Article 48 that it took very little effort to turn the democratic government into a dictatorship. In truth, the mistakes of both the Allies and the Weimar National Assembly doomed the republic to failure before it even had a chance to obtain a foothold.

6

The Years of Instability

Just as the Weimar Republic was born in the tempest of a tumbling down monarchy and a lost war, so was its history marred by violence and instability, as political factions fought for power and extremists worked for its downfall. Between 1919 and 1931, seventeen different ministries tried in vain to bring order to the strife-torn nation. At the same time, international conflict beset Germany because the Allies sought every last pfennig of reparation payment. This helped cause the already weak economy to sink even further amid a crippling inflation that wiped away the savings of thousands and left still more jobless. Finally, the French occupied the industry-rich Ruhr, charging that the enfeebled Reich had failed to meet its obligations for payment of the reparations. As the condition of Germany continued to grow worse, many sought deliverance by flocking to the cause of extremists such as Adolf Hitler, the leader of the infant national socialist movement.[1]

Although the young Weimar Republic had successfully withstood the attack from the left in 1918 and early 1919, it faced an even greater threat from the right in 1920. The extreme nationalists, still loyal to the exiled kaiser, vowed revenge against the men who had humiliated Germany by accepting the hated Treaty of Versailles. Many officers of the army believed that Germany's many problems could only be solved through a military coup that would overthrow the republic and establish military rule. Some even talked about bringing back the fallen emperor. Colonel Max Bauer, who was an associate of Ludendorff and had played a major role in the fall of Bethmann-Hollweg during the war, and Major Waldemar Papst, a former staff officer and

Free Corps organizer, led a conspiracy to overthrow the government and to give power to Dr. Wolfgang Kapp. Kapp, the son of Friedrich Kapp, a revolutionary in 1848, an exile to America, and a liberal member of the Reichstag, had become an extreme nationalist. Upon learning of the Treaty of Versailles, Kapp even suggested war against Poland to regain the lost honor of the fatherland. Realizing that such a dangerous undertaking as the overthrow of the republic would require expert leadership, the conspirators approached Gustav Noske, then minister of war. Although the conqueror of the Spartacists had supported the Free Corps in their mutual campaign against the leftist revolutionaries, he loyally supported the republic and refused to associate himself with any attempt to destroy it. He sternly informed Major Papst of his position and sharply rebuked him for attempting to involve the military in civilian affairs. Noske also ordered the dissolution of the major's division and dismissed the conspirator from the service.

Noske's reprimand only strengthened the determination of the plotters. They organized the National Union to carry on an active propaganda campaign designed to appeal to the growing hostility toward the republic and the Treaty of Versailles and to prepare the way for a military takeover. The movement began to grow, as more and more officers and extreme rightists joined. One of the most important recruits was General Walter von Lüttwitz, the commander of the Berlin garrison and well-known critic of the government. The growing tension between the ultra-right faction and the political leaders of Germany reached a breaking point when Noske, yielding to pressure from the Allies to observe the troop limitations of the Treaty of Versailles, ordered the dissolution of two marine brigades stationed in Döberitz, near Berlin, under the command of Captain Hermann Ehrhardt, a monarchist and veteran of the Free Corps. Since the units formed part of Lüttwitz's force, the general violently objected to their destruction. He angrily informed Noske on February 20, 1920, that he would never accept such an order. A few days later, during an inspection, he pledged to the enthusiastic men that he would reject any command to destroy the two units. Upon hearing of Lüttwitz's disloyal behavior, the furious Noske immediately removed the forces from his command. The irate officer then requested a meeting with President Ebert, during which he demanded more power in the government for the military and a new election of president and Reichstag. The head of state calmly rejected Lüttwitz's ultimatum and attempted, without

The Years of Instability

success, to reason with the determined general. Finally, Noske, who was present at the fateful confrontation, intervened and denounced the general for forgetting his duty to obey the orders of the government and attempting to interfere in civilian affairs. Lüttwitz then left, more determined than ever to bring down the republic and the men who had created it.

For the next few days, rumors flew around Berlin about sinister plots against the government. On March 11 Noske decided to take action to prevent any attempt to destroy the republic. He ordered the arrest of Kapp and relieved Lüttwitz of his command. However, the police proved too slow to capture the fleeing leaders of the conspiracy, and they escaped to continue their treason. As the day went on, the tension continued to mount; the press reported stories of a coming insurrection. Early the next morning, Noske sent Admiral von Trotha to Döberitz to find out what was happening. However, the seaman, no true friend of the republic, warned Ehrhardt of his approach. That evening Trotha reported to Noske that he found nothing unusual during his mission. A reassured minister of war telephoned the editor of *Vörwarts* to immediately inform him that the reports of an impending military revolt had been greatly exaggerated, unaware that even as he spoke, Erhardt and his fellow traitors were busy making last minute preparations for the march on the German capital.

Late on the evening of March 12, 1920, the stillness of the Berlin night was shattered when five thousand rebellious troops led by Captain Ehrhardt marched through the Brandenburg Gate. Despite weeks of rumors, the government was totally unprepared for the events that followed. Ebert and Noske did not learn of the invasion through their agents, but received news by a call from a newspaper reporter. The president frantically appealed to the army for support, but only General Walter Reinhardt, chief of the army command, and Major von Gilsa, Noske's chief of staff, affirmed their willingness to fight for the government. The other officers coldly informed the minister of war that they would never order their men to fire on fellow German soldiers. General Hans von Seeckt replied that the unity of the officer corps must be preserved at all costs and would be shattered by forcing the military to fight its own members. Faced with lack of support from the leaders of the army and with an invasion of Berlin, Ebert could do little but flee the city for Dresden. The rebel troops occupied the capital unchallenged and quickly took over the government office buildings. The victors then proclaimed the formation of a new government, headed by Kapp, and the end of the hated republic. However, once they had taken power, the temporary masters of Germany were unable to govern effectively because they had neglected to plan their next step. While Kapp and his followers pondered what to do next, the supporters of the republic took action.

Before the socialist members of the ministry resigned Berlin to the rebels, they called upon the workers of Germany to save the republic through a general strike. The trade unions at once endorsed the idea, and within a few hours all railroads, newspapers, communications, and all industrial activities were at a standstill, leaving the great city paralyzed. At the same time, instead of greeting Kapp and his friends as liberators, the people of Berlin joined the opposition. Hans von Seeckt, who had refused to oppose the insurrection actively, refused to support the revolt and simply left office. Unprepared to face a general strike and popular opposition, Kapp and Lüttwitz were unable to act. Some of the troops that had joined the revolt in the beginning deserted to the republic. Some brave men even arrested their officers for participation in the plot.

For several days, Kapp and Lüttwitz tried to hang onto power, as their supporters left them one by one. The traitors had spent so much time plotting to seize the capital city that they had neglected to plan what to do with it once they had it under their control. They had made no provisions for finances or even for issuing a new constitution to replace the one they had destroyed. Fräulein Kapp, who had been working on a manifesto to announce the new government, was unable to finish it in time for the newspapers because she could not find a typewriter in the chancellory. Thus, the rebels could not even find an effective way to announce their victory to the people of Germany. In the meantime, the general strike had effectively spread, leaving Berlin in chaos. The officers finally realized that Kapp was incapable of ruling and decided to end his reign as quickly as possible. On March 17 the officers at the Ministry of Defense sent Colonel General Wilhelm Heyne to Lüttwitz and Kapp to demand that they admit defeat and turn control of the army over to Seeckt. The arrogant general rejected Heyne's ultimatum, and a bitter argument followed, during which Lüttwitz pulled his sword and drove the representative of the officers from his presence. However, after he regained his composure, Lüttwitz, too, realized that the revolt had been a failure and convinced Kapp that they should begin planning their escape. After burning their papers, Kapp fled by air to Sweden and Lüttwitz to Hungary.

Thus, the Kapp Putsch fell apart almost as quickly as it had begun.[2]

President Ebert, upon returning to Berlin, named Hans von Seeckt the new commander of the military but took no further step to purge the army of those who had refused to defend the republic during the abortive revolt. This was one of the most serious mistakes in the history of the Weimar Republic. A large number of officers and men had proved themselves potential traitors and should have been removed. By failing to cleanse the army of antirepublican sentiment and placing it completely under civilian domination, Ebert allowed it to continue to hold a privileged position and remain a potential threat to the stability of Germany.

The troubles had not ended, for the rightist attempt at revolt and the successful general strike awoke the Communist movement from the slumber that had overtaken it since the fall of the Soviet Republic of Bavaria. Throughout 1919 and 1920, the industrial Ruhr had been teeming with unrest, as workers tried to feed their families in the midst of growing economic problems. Mobilized by the general strike, many workers fell under communist influence. With the support of the Marxist Red Army, consisting of 50,000 men, many workers took arms during the strike. Once Kapp fell, they refused to disband, hoping that they could begin a Communist revolution. Barely recovered from the impact of the Kapp Putsch, the startled government sent Carl Severing to the troubled region to attempt negotiations with the leftist rebels. Severing offered the members of the Red Army amnesty if they would surrender their weapons, but the determined Reds refused to consider this offer and seized control of the entire Ruhr district.

Faced with a new threat to the republic, the ministry of Gustav Bayer proved unable to cope with the situation and resigned on March 27, after less than a year in power. Ebert called on Hermann Müller to form a new cabinet, consisting of Social Democrats, Centrists, and Democrats. Müller was more decisive than his predecessor and called upon the military to march into the troubled area to suppress the revolt on April 2, 1920. The army, quite willing to fight the Communists, responded to the government's call for aid with bloody vengeance. Bitter fighting shook the Ruhr for several weeks as the army moved to eliminate the Red threat, killing all prisoners, even the wounded. By the end of the month the government had crushed the revolt and once more controlled the important industrial region. However, the abortive insurrection in the Ruhr inspired other Marxists to arise. Led by Max Hölz and aided by Moscow, armed bands of Communists roamed the countryside of Saxon Vogtland throughout April attacking anti-Red forces. Once again Berlin called on the military to restore order. Supported by local rightist vigilante groups called Home Guards, the army once more moved with full force to suppress the leftists. By the end of the month, the supporters of the government had defeated the Communists, and peace had returned to Saxony.[3]

The military occupation of the Ruhr during the communist revolt had violated provisions of the Treaty of Versailles, which banned the German army from the eastern bank of the Rhine. Fearing any buildup of German forces that might threaten their homeland, the French, without consulting their allies, occupied Frankfurt, Darmstadt, and the surrounding area on April 6. The British, more concerned about the possibility of a communist revolt in Germany than the peace agreement, resented the refusal of Paris to discuss the matter. London protested and by the middle of May had persuaded the French to withdraw. The conflict between the two former partners over their policy toward the Reich marked the beginning of a serious split, as the English began to doubt the validity of the French fears of a revived Germany.

With calm finally restored, the government turned to the knotty problem of the army. Noske had lost much support by advocating a strong officer corps and by his refusal to take action during the Kapp Putsch. Although Ebert still supported his minister of war, others in his party were determined to remove the untrustworthy official. After Noske's critics won control of the Social Democratic party, they forced him to resign. The president then appointed Dr. Otto Gessler, the son of a Bavarian noncommissioned officer, as the new head of the military. The removal of Noske was only a hollow victory because Gessler was at best a nominal supporter of the republic. The real power in the German military passed not to Gessler, but to Hans von Seeckt, the chief of staff of the army between 1920 and 1926. Coming from a Pomeranian Junker family with ancient ties to the officer corps, the new warlord of Germany had served in the First World War as the chief of staff of the Austro-German army and as an adviser to the Turkish forces. Seeckt's first and foremost loyalty was to the army. He considered the republic a temporary government and longed for the restoration of the monarchy. The haughty chief of staff held politicians and parliamentary governments in contempt, believing that the state must rely on a strong army as the only source of stability and hope of a rebirth of the fatherland as a great power. Seeckt looked to Russia, which had not been a party to the hated Treaty of Versailles, as a potential ally in the Reich's struggle to evade the terms of the treaty.[4]

Seeckt was a strong commander who ruled the officers and his subordinates with a masterful hand. He craftily used the limitations of the Treaty of Versailles to build a professional military, loyal to his supporters, and to purge the army of republicans. Although he refused to allow his men to become involved in the squabbles of the many political parties, he ordered local commanders to indoctrinate the troops with rightist ideas and removed all officers who resisted. He insisted on committing the army to no specific political system, except loyalty to a greater German Reich. Under Seeckt's strong leadership, the army continued to occupy a privileged position as a state within the state, with little contact with the civilian government and its bureaucracy. The new warlord did, however, involve the military in the making of foreign policy by initiating secret talks with the Russians. He also worked to build an even more aristocratic military than the old imperial army. Under the kaiser, every fourth officer was the son of an officer. Under Seeckt's administration, every second officer was the son of an officer; in 1920 one-fifth of the officer corps came from the nobility; by 1932 this proportion had been increased to one-fourth. Thus, instead of creating the democratic army envisaged by the founders of the republic, the Weimar era saw a transformation of the army into an even more aristocratic body than it had been.[5]

Although Seeckt refused to allow his men to become tied to one political party, he did encourage support for nonpartisan patriotic organizations. The army developed very close ties with the rightist veteran organization, the Stahlhelm ("Steel Helmet"). Founded by Franz Seldte, a reserve officer, in Magdeburg on December 25, 1918, the Stahlhelm grew rapidly to a membership of more than one million by 1927. Like the Free Corps, the organization appealed to the frustration and nationalism of the returning troops who sought to preserve the old soldierly virtues and revive the comradeship of the trenches. The Stahlhelm campaigned to free the German people from the chains of the Treaty of Versailles. Eventually, it developed a close connection with the German People's party.

Another rightist group with good relations with the military was the Frontier Guard Units. In May 1921, Wojciech Korfanty, the former leader of the Polish members of the German Reichstag, organized a force of Polish nationalists to campaign in Upper Silesia. The Germans in the plebiscite area responded by appealing for help from the fatherland, and irregular groups of German soldiers drifted into the disputed area to battle Korfanty's forces. After several weeks of heavy fighting between the two rival groups, the Allies intervened to bring peace. Meanwhile, across the border, under the protection of the army, which organized a permanent guard on the German-Polish frontier, a group of men formed the Frontier Guard units on large estates. Officers of the regular army in each frontier county kept lists of men in the units for use in case of emergencies. Operating without the restraints that a legal basis would have imposed, the units became centers of radical nationalism as the members made no efforts to hide their antirepublican feelings. The regular army officers, who functioned as quasi-leaders of the Frontier Guard units, kept its membership and activities secret. Anyone who revealed the true nature of its activities met a violent death. Although Seeckt tried to keep the guard units out of politics, the lax discipline caused his efforts to fail.

Faced with the threat of various veteran's organizations on the right and the Red Army on the left, the Social Democrats finally decided to form their own veteran's organization, the Reichsbanner, Black, Red, and Gold, in 1924. Like the others, it attempted to appeal to the former soldier's frustration with civilian life, but unlike its counterparts, the Reichsbanner was dedicated to the Weimar Republic. It was a success and consisted of several million men. Although its leadership tried to appeal to the military as a counter to the Stahlhelm, the officers refused to endorse it because of its "suspect" republican sentiments. The formation by the various political groups of quasi-military groups, such as the Reichsbanner and the Stahlhelm, reveals a particularly sinister aspect of the politics of Weimar Germany. It would not be long until the various organizations began to fight, reducing the political process to the level of gang warfare and crippling any chance the republic had for survival.

The results of the first election for the Reichstag under the new constitution revealed yet another serious weakness of the still young republic. The election of June 16, 1920, was a major defeat for the parties that had formed the Weimar coalition and written the constitution. Although they had won a two-thirds majority in 1919, they failed to win even a simple majority the next year. The Social Democrats won only 21.7 percent, compared to 37.9 percent the year before. The Center party's representation fell from 19.7 percent to 13.6 percent, and the Democrats from 18.6 percent to 8.3 percent. At the same time, the parties hostile to the republic radically increased their appeal. The German People's party jumped from 4.4 percent the year before to 13.9 percent, and the German Nationalists party grew from 10.3 percent to 15 percent to form the rightist faction in the Reichstag. The Independent Socialists grew from 7.6 percent to 17.8 percent, and the Communists, who had refused to participate in the election of 1919, emerged with 2.1 percent. Thus, the supporters of the republic had a mere 43.6 percent, while its enemies had combined representation of 48.8 percent, 28.9 percent for the right and 19.9 percent for the left. Therefore, less than a year after the creation of the Weimar Republic, only a minority of the German people were willing to cast their vote for its founders.

The election revealed that the middle classes had begun to turn away from democracy. Many had supported the republic in the hope that if Germany could prove to the Allies that the old autocratic government was a thing of the past, they would grant the fatherland a lenient peace. But after the victors forced the Germans to accept the harsh terms of the Treaty of Versailles, many felt betrayed and turned from the parties that had created the republic and had accepted the hated settlement. Many solid middle-class Germans were terrified by the threat that the fatherland would become another Soviet Russia and longed for the peaceful days of the empire. In their fear, they turned to the parties of the right because they represented the forces that had defeated the communist uprisings. Many Ruhr industrialists, alarmed by the unsuccessful revolts, gave large sums of money to the German People's party. Under the effective leadership of Gustav Stresemann, the People's party campaigned against the left and even announced its intention to exclude the Social Democrats from the ministry. The German Nationalist party became even more radical as the membership removed the more moderate leaders and gave control to radicals who blamed the republic for the Treaty of Versailles and the strength of the radical left. Even the Center party began to move to the right in reaction to the treaty and the communist-incited violence. Thus, the republic began to lose support as the German people searched for a reason for the unrest and the harsh terms of the Treaty of Versailles.

The election also had a major impact on the Independent party, which split between the right and left wings. The majority, led by

Ernst Däuming, sympathized with the Communists and favored joining the Soviet-sponsored Third International. The minority right wing, led by Rudolf Hilfdering and Wilhelm Dittmann, rejected the radicalism of the left and moved closer to the Social Democrats. After several months of interparty strife, the Independent Socialists divided into two groups at a convention held at Halle in October 1920. Influenced by the presence of Gregory Zinoviev, a member of the Politburo of the Soviet Union and head of the Communist Third International, or Comintern, the left wing formally left the party and merged with the Communists.

Meanwhile, the political leaders of Germany were trying to put together a government that would have the support of the majority of the Reichstag. The Social Democrats demanded that the right wing of the Independent Socialists be invited to join the ministry. When the Center and Democrats refused to agree, the Socialists withdrew from discussions. Finally, Konstantin Fehrenbach of the Center party put together a coalition of the Center, the Democrats, and the People's party to form a new cabinet. Thus, the government of Germany fell into the hands of moderate rightists and included members of a political party that only mildly supported the constitution and contained many who dreamed of the restoration of the monarchy. Although the Social Democrats continued to be the largest party in the Reichstag until 1932, after 1920 they never again were able to dominate the German government.

Although excluded from the national government by their insistence on the participation of the Independent Socialists, the Social Democrats continued to control the government of Prussia, where Otto Braun was prime minister until 1932, except for short periods in 1921 and 1925. Braun, a former agricultural worker in East Prussia, had come to power in the wake of the Kapp Putsch. He was a good politician, who built his government on the basis of the old Weimar coalition. When this team lost control of the Prussian Diet in 1921, Bauer returned to power by inviting the People's party to join the government. Thus, although the Center and Democratic parties allied themselves with the parties of the right, they remained loyal to their alliance with the Social Democrats in the former Hohenzollern kingdom. Under Braun's enlightened leadership, the largest state of Germany became a model of efficient democratic government that set an example for the other states. Braun's minister of the interior, Carl Severing, sought to destroy the old autocratic Prussian police and create a new, democratic force.

As 1920 passed, it seemed that the Germans had at last achieved some measure of domestic peace. However, the demands of the victorious Allies shattered this momentary calm. Through the "War Guilt Clause" of the Treaty of Versailles, the Germans had agreed to pay the cost of the war. Although the treaty stipulated that the Reich must pay 20 billion gold marks by May 1, 1921, it left the decision of the final sum at the discretion of the Allies. In January 1921, the chief of the commercial division of the French foreign office, Seydoux, proposed that the Germans pay 3 billion gold marks yearly for a period of five years. At first, Berlin accepted this demand. However, within a few days after Seydoux had suggested his program, Aristide Briand assumed office and appointed Paul Doumer minister of finance. The new French government, remembering the massive destruction and loss of life caused by the war, proved less tolerant of the German plight, and at an Allied conference on January 24 demanded higher reparation payments. David Lloyd George of England at first rejected the French demands as excessive. However, after discussion the Allies agreed that Germany must make payments for forty-two years, beginning with 2 billion gold marks annually and increasing to 6 billion gold marks for a total of 132 billion gold marks (thirty-three billion dollars). The victors also demanded that Berlin turn over 12 percent of all exports. They finally agreed that France would receive 25 percent of the payment, England 22 percent, and Italy, Belgium, and the other nations the remaining 26 percent. The United States was more interested in collecting the more than 4 billion dollars owed by Britain, the more than 3 billion owed by France, and the several billion owed by the other Allies than in sharing in the reparations from Germany, and it demanded nothing.

Upon receiving the schedule of payments, the Germans, believing that such large payments would destroy the already weak economy, vowed to resist. The politicians made speeches denouncing the reparations to cheering crowds, and Karl Bergmann, the German representative to the Allied Reparations Commission, tried in vain to negotiate with the victors. Finally, the Allies decided to use force to persuade the reluctant Germans to pay; agree so they occupied Düsseldorf, Duisburg, and the Ruhr Valley. Dr. Walter Simons, the German foreign minister, then appealed to President Warren G. Harding of the United States to intervene in the dispute and to act as referee between the two sides. However, the Americans, having rejected the Treaty of Versailles, had no desire to become involved in Europe's squabbles and refused to interfere. Having failed to persuade the Allies to reconsider their demands, Fehrenbach and his cabinet resigned, leaving Germany once again without a government.

On May 10, Dr. Joseph Wirt, a member of the Center party and former minister of finance, formed a new ministry on the basis of the Weimar coalition, allowing the Social Democrats to enter the government again. Wirt appointed Walter Rathenau, the effective chief of the War Materials Office during the war, minister of reconstruction and placed him in charge of negotiations with the Allies. Rathenau realized that the Germans could not resist the victors of the war and quickly began discussions with them. He accepted the reparation terms and arranged to borrow 250 million gold dollars from London to make the first payment. In addition to the cash, the Germans agreed to make annual deliveries of coal, chemicals, timber, ships, railroad equipment, machinery, and other items demanded by the Allies.

At the same time that the Allies forced the Germans to accept the reparation agreement, they imposed their own solution to the problem of Upper Silesia. This area of mixed German-Polish population had been racked with fighting between the two national groups since the end of the war. The Allies decided to hold a plebiscite to decide whether the disputed land would become a part of Germany or Poland. On March 20, 1921, the people of Upper Silesia voted 60 percent in favor of unification with Germany. However, the British and French refused to respect the results of the election and asked the Council of the League of Nations to decide the future of the contested area. On October 20, 1921, the council assigned about 40 percent of the district to Poland, giving the rest to the Reich. Although the majority of the people in the section awarded to the Slavic state were Poles, there was a substantial German minority that would become a constant source of tension as they demanded unification with their fatherland. Many Germans also objected to the decision of the League because the section awarded to Poland was the richest part of Upper Silesia.

The reparations and the loss of much of a former portion of Germany, despite the expressed wish of the majority of its people, only strengthened the appeal of the extremists. The German economy sank to new lows as the draining of money and goods to satisfy the Allies helped bring about a serious inflation that wiped out the savings of thousands of middle-class Germans and left others jobless. Some ultra-nationalists began to murder politicians who they believed had betrayed the German people into the hands of the French and British. On August 29, two former members of the Ehrhardt Brigade killed Matthias Erzberger. The death of the author of the Peace Resolution of July 19, 1917, caused panic to spread among other leaders of the republic. A terrified President Ebert invoked Article 48 of the constitution to ban antirepublican publications, meetings, and organizations. However, this failed to halt the extremists. On June 14, 1922, as Walter Rathenau rode to his office in the Foreign Ministry, two former members of the Ehrhardt Brigade drove beside his open car. A shower of bullets from a submachine gun tore into Rathenau's body. After he collapsed, a grenade explosion tore the last breath of life from the dying man. Rathenau's assassination caused Chancellor Wirt to attempt sterner measures to halt the growth of the radical right. He pushed the Law for the Protection of the Republic through the stunned Reichstag, creating a special court in Leipzig to try cases involving attempts from the right and left to overthrow the government or to spread subversive ideas.

However, the efforts of the national government to meet the serious threat from the right failed, largely because the radicals found a sanctuary in Bavaria under the control of the conservative Bavarian People's party. The head of the government in Munich, Gustav von Kahr, refused to enforce Ebert's emergency decrees, and the German president was unable, or unwilling, to force him to do so, for fear that he might bring on an even more serious crisis. Thus, protected by the Bavarian People's party, the right continued to flourish in the south.

Although the Germans had failed in their attempts to negotiate with the West, they were much more successful in developing relations with the communist government of Soviet Russia. Representatives of the two "outlaw" nations met at an international conference called by the French at Lloyd George's urging in Genoa, Italy, on April 10, 1922. The organizers of the meetings, who assembled the nations to relieve international tensions, invited the Germans and Russians to participate, but they refused to accord them the same respect given the representatives of other nations. Offended by the treatment they had received, the Russian and German delegations met at the nearby resort of Rapallo to discuss common problems. On April 16, 1922, they signed the Treaty of Rapallo. In this important pact, both sides agreed to drop all claims against each other resulting from the war. The Germans consented to waive all demands for compensation for German-owned properties nationalized by the Communists in return for a trade agreement granting both sides "most favored nation" status. The news of the accord between the Germans and the Russians shook the conference and caused it to break up without accomplishing anything.

The Treaty of Rapallo caused the growth of important trade between Moscow and Berlin and paved the way for further cooperation. Seeckt, who had long favored close ties with the Soviets, used the spirit of concord to establish military agreements with Moscow. Even before the treaty had been signed, the Ministry of War had established the Society for the Development of Weaponry, with offices in Berlin and Moscow. The Russians, eager for military assistance, allowed this organization to build a Junker aircraft factory near Moscow, a poison gas plant at Samara, and munition works under Krupp administration at Tula, Leningrad, and Schlüsselberg. Thus, under the cover of a trade pact with the Soviet Union, the German army began to evade the military provisions of the Treaty of Versailles that specifically forbade the Germans to build military aircraft and placed severe limitations on the growth of German munitions.

Despite the new trade with the Soviet Union, the German economy continued to plunge under the pressure of the reparations. Alarmed by the growing distress and the inability of the Germans to buy British goods, thus harming the English economy, London offered to cancel all war debts and withdraw all demands for reparations from the Reich if the other Allies would agree to do the same. However, the conservative president of the United States, Calvin Coolidge, refused to consider this, demanding that the British and French repay the large sums of money borrowed from the Americans during the war. Since London planned to use the German reparation payments to repay the Americans, the proposal died.

As the year went on, the crushing burden of the reparations continued to harm the German economy. In December 1922, Raymond Poincaré, the president of France, charged that Berlin had failed to deliver promised shipments of coal and timber. When the Germans rejected his demand for the goods, he sent five French divisions and one Belgian division, on January 11, 1923, to occupy the Ruhr and seize control of the industry in this rich area. The Germans then halted all reparation payments and called upon all government officials and employees, including those working on the railroad, to refuse to cooperate with the French invaders. Faced with the passive resistance of the German officials, frequent clashes between workers and their overlords, and a wave of sabotage as radicals from the left and right destroyed machinery and placed bombs on railroad bridges, the French adopted a policy of force. They executed one saboteur, Albert Leo Schlageter, a former Free Corps member who had been delivered into the hands of the French by a fellow worker in Düsseldorf on May 6, 1923, making him a national hero. The French also expelled over 100,000 German officials and railway workers and their families and ordered their own soldiers to occupy and work the factories, mines, and railroads.

The French occupation of the Ruhr and the reparations crisis sent the already floundering German economy to new depths. The government began to print money without backing in an effort to meet its obligations and support the unemployed workers. By the end of 1932, the government had 133 printing offices, with 1,783 presses, turning out paper money night and day. But the rapid increase in currency only fed the already serious inflation. The money became worthless as soon as it came off the presses, and the mark sank to a value of 25 billion to one American dollar. This led the government to print even more money. To fill the demand for currency, the printing offices stamped new denominations in red ink on old bills. Even this did not meet the growing demand, and the government allowed private firms, as well, to set up presses to print new values on old money. Some cities began to issue their own tender, using silk, leather, linen, or whatever could be found.

The inflation continued to worsen. Prices rose ten, or even one hundred, times in a single day. At one time the cost of butter increased from 100,000 marks a pound in the morning to 500,000 marks by afternoon. Factories paid their workers twice a day, with time off to buy food for their families before prices went even higher. People bought two beers at a time and drank the second warm because, if they waited, the price would double or triple while they enjoyed the first. Housewives went to the bakery with bushel baskets full of paper money to buy a loaf of bread. By November a subscription to a Berlin newspaper for one week cost 500 billion marks. As the value of the currency continued to plunge, many turned to a primitive system of barter to obtain goods. Starving mobs began to attack trucks carrying food to market because they had no money to buy even the basic necessities of life.

The inflation of 1923 was one of the greatest disasters in German history. Helpless middle-class Germans watched as the crisis destroyed their hard-earned savings. A few crafty men profited by speculating in bankrupt stores and industries, but most Germans suffered from the growing chaos. Many turned to the radical left in desperation, and the communist movement experienced a new power. Bands of workers attacked capitalists. In Saxony and Thuringia the radical wing of the Social Democrats joined the Communists to form Marxist governments, and Berlin responded by sending federal troops. On October 22 radical workers joined the Reds in a bloody uprising that ended two days later when the local police relentlessly restored order. In this atmosphere, with the Reich on its knees before the Allies and a crippling inflation, a relatively obscure former corporal began to speak to crowds in the beer halls of Munich, spreading the message of national socialism.

7

The Youth of a Dictator

Amid the political and economic chaos of the first years of the Weimar Republic, the voice of an obscure young former corporal arose. This tall lean man with a small toothbrush moustache spoke to cheering crowds in the smoky Munich beer halls, telling them that their troubles were not the fault of the good loyal Germans but of betrayal by the Allies and the treason of the political leaders. Adolf Hitler's simple answers appealed to many who groped for a reason for their problems. His followers would continue to multiply until one day thousands of them would march through the streets of the Reich, singing, carrying banners, and lighting the dark nights with their torches. Yet, for all that is known about him during his rise to power and after, mystery shrouds his early life. Historians have filled thousands of pages trying to sort out the meager details of his youth and explain his origins. Many myths and misunderstandings have grown with the elaborate theories based on little concrete evidence. However, despite the falsehoods and gaps in his life, there is ample information to sketch the youth of this elusive figure in history.[1]

Perhaps the greatest unsolved mystery about Hitler's life is the identity of his grandfather. His grandmother was Maria Anna Schicklgruber, the daughter of Johann Schicklgruber, a peasant living in Strones, Austria, a small village located in that portion of the Habsburg territory lying between Linz and the Czech border. She was born in April 1795 and spent the first forty-two years of her life in obscurity, tending the family farm and earning extra money as a maid in local houses. On June 17, 1837, while employed in the home of Johann Trummelschlager, she gave birth to a son, whom she named Alois. Although her employer stood as godfather at her son's baptism, she failed to give the name of the father; so the priest wrote in the space provided for the father's name the word "illegitimate."

In 1842 Maria Anna Schicklgruber married Georg Johann Hiedler, or Hüttler, according to one spelling, the son of Martin Hiedler, a peasant from Spital, a village northwest of Strones. Hiedler was a mill worker who spent much of his life moving from place to place. He had lived in Hohensich in 1823, where he married the daughter of a local peasant. Apparently she died, because he did not take her with him when he moved the next year. After living in several places, he moved to Strones, where he lived with his new wife and her aged father. He continued to work in a local mill and supplemented their income with his wife's inheritance from her deceased mother. A few years later the family moved to the village of Klein-Motten, where Maria Anna died on January 7, 1847.

After his wife's death, Georg Johann Hiedler left Klein-Motten and was unheard of until his death on February 9, 1857. Significantly, he never made an effort to adopt or legitimize his wife's child. Young Alois went to live in Spital with Johann Nepomuk Hiedler, Georg Johann's younger brother. After completing his education and serving as an apprentice to a local shoemaker named Ledermüller, Alois went to Vienna, the bustling capital of the Habsburg empire, to earn his fortune. He worked for a while as a shoemaker but entered the Austrian customs service in 1855. He rose rapidly in his new career. In 1860, after service as a noncommissioned officer in the frontier guard in Wels, a town southwest of Linz, he went to Vienna for further training. The next year Alois Schicklgruber passed his examinations and became a superviser. Two years later his superiors transferred him to Saalfelden near Salzburg. In 1864 he again received a promotion and became provisional assistant in the customs service. After serving in Linz and Mariahilf, he moved to Braunau in 1871 as assistant inspector. In 1875 he became chief inspector of customs for this town on the Austro-German border.

Alois Schicklgruber was a man of little morality. He had a son in the 1860s but failed to marry the mother. In 1873 he married Anna Glassl, the daughter of a local official. She became ill soon after the marriage, and his romantic interests turned to other women. He had an affair with a local barmaid named Franziska Matzelberger, and when she failed to occupy all his sexual energies, invited Klara Pölzl, the granddaughter of Johann Nepomuk Hiedler, to live in his home as a maid. Thus, Alois was married to one woman and had affairs with two others.

The Youth of a Dictator

On June 4, 1876, Alois went to the Reverend Josef Zahnschirm, the priest who kept the records of Dollersheim, the area including Strones, the place of his birth, to officially change his name and claim legitimization. The customs official persuaded four men to testify that Georg Johann Hiedler had told them that Alois was his son and that he wanted the baptismal record changed accordingly. The priest agreed and entered the change in the parish register. However, instead of spelling the family name Hiedler or Hüttler, the priest wrote Hitler, apparently in deference to Alois's wishes. Since the four witnesses were illiterate, they could not know that the spelling had been changed. Father Zahnschirm then informed the office of the district commissioner in Mistelbach, from which the application for legitimization was sent to the bishop of St. Pölten and the proper officials in Vienna. On November 25 Bishop Matheus Joseph sent his approval, and five days later the governor's office ratified the change. Thus, Alois Schicklgruber became Alois Hitler.

There is no evidence as to the real reason Alois had his name changed to Hitler. He did not seem motivated by embarrassment over his illegitimacy or affection for Georg Johann Hiedler. One possible explanation is that Johann Nepomuk Hiedler, who may have promised Alois a small inheritance, influenced his decision. Shortly after Hiedler's death on September 17, 1888, Alois suddenly came into some money, which he used to buy a farm on March 16, 1889. Perhaps Hiedler, who had produced three daughters but no son, wanted the family name to continue, or perhaps he had developed a genuine affection for Alois during the years he had lived with him.

Besides the affidavit sworn before the priest, there is no actual proof that Georg Johann Hiedler was actually Alois's father. Certainly neither he nor his wife made any such claim. When he married Alois's mother, he took no steps to adopt the boy or to have the record of his baptism changed. By leaving Alois in the care of his brother after the death of his wife, Georg Johann certainly did not show the concern expected from a father for his son. Throughout his life, Adolf Hitler was plagued with doubts about his ancestry. He made several attempts to discover the true name of his grandfather, but each time he met with failure. It is ironic that the leader of a state that placed so much emphasis on pedigree could never produce one of his own and legally would not have been considered a true member of the "master" race.

Historians and others have written much to illuminate the many theories as to the true identity of Adolf Hitler's grandfather. At least one historian has maintained that Johann Nepomuk Hiedler was Alois's real father and that he could not acknowledge this because of his jealous wife, Eva Maria. Although Alois did live with his "uncle" after the death of his mother, there is no real evidence to support this claim. Others have identified Johann Trummelschlager as Alois's true father, because his mother lived in the Trummelschlager home when he was born and he agreed to serve as godfather to the boy at his baptism. There is no proof to substantiate this, either. Maria Anna Schicklgruber had the baby in the Trummelschalager house because she worked there as a maid.

The most fantastic theory about the identity of Adolf Hitler's grandfather was told by Hans Frank, the former Nazi legal expert and governor-general of occupied Poland, while awaiting sentence at Nuremberg. Frank claimed that in 1930 Hitler sent him to investigate a press report that the Nazi leader was of Jewish ancestry. Frank claims that he found evidence in Graz that Maria Anna Schicklgruber had become pregnant by the youngest son of the Jewish Frankenberger family while working as a cook. He also maintained that they sent money for the support of young Alois. If this were true, it would mean that the greatest anti-Semite of modern history was himself part Jewish. However, a list of the inhabitants of Graz shows that no family named Frankenberger lived there in 1837 or 1838. Since Maximilian I had decreed on March 19, 1496, that no Jew could live in Styria, a regulation in force until the early 1860s, it would have been impossible for a Jewish family to have lived in the southern Austrian city. Neither does the population directory reveal that Maria Anna Schicklgruber resided in Graz or ever served as a maid there. The records of her inheritance from her mother in the office of the orphan's fund reveal no change of address during 1837 and 1838. Instead they show that she remained in Strones during these years. Therefore, Frank's account has no solid historical basis and is easily disproved by an investigation of the facts. Since there is no concrete support for any theory, the true identity of Hitler's grandfather must remain a mystery.[2]

After changing his name to Hitler, Alois returned to his wife in Braunau. Anna quickly grew tired of his extramarital activities and on November 7, 1880, won a legal separation from her unfaithful husband. Alois continued his affair with Franziska Matzelberger, who had a son in January 1882, whom she named Alois. Because strong Roman Catholic influence made it impossible for him to remarry as long as his first wife remained alive, Alois could not wed his mistress.

However, on April 6, 1883, Anna Hitler died of consumption. Alois married Franziska on May 22, 1883, and legitimized his son as Alois Hitler, Jr. One month after the marriage, Franziska gave birth to a daughter, Angela. Just as Alois's first wife became ill with respiratory problems, his second spouse was stricken one year after their marriage. She moved outside of Braunau to the village of Ranshofen, where it was hoped the fresh air would aid her recovery. Since she left her two children with her husband, he invited Klara Pölzl to come and live with him in his lodgings above the Pommer Inn. There she took care of the children and resumed her affair with her uncle. On August 18, 1884, the ailing Franziska died, leaving Alois free once more to remarry.

About the same time that Franziska died, Klara became pregnant. However, by changing his name, Alois had made Klara his niece and could not marry her without obtaining a dispensation from the law of the church that forbade unions between close relatives. On October 27, 1884, Alois applied to Rome for permission to marry, claiming that Klara was poor and would probably not have another chance to marry. After receiving a positive reply, the couple married on January 7, 1885. The customs inspector dominated his wife so completely that she continued to address him as uncle for many years after their marriage. On May 17, 1885, they had a son named Gustav, and on April 20, 1889, Adolf Hitler came into the world.

Adolf Hitler's early years are important, for they shaped many attitudes he would have throughout his whole life. As an infant he was rather sickly and became the center of his mother's attention. He rarely saw his father, who spent his leisure hours following his hobby of beekeeping or drinking beer with his friends in the local tavern. In 1894 the customs service promoted Alois Hitler to the office of higher collector of customs and, since there was no place for a person of his new rank in Braunau, reassigned him to the city of Passau. Two years later, the elder Hitler received a post in Linz.

On March 24, 1894, one week after Alois Hitler learned of his new assignment, Klara gave birth to a boy, whom they named Edmond. Since the infant was too young to travel, Klara stayed in Passau with the children. With his mother busy caring for the new member of the family and his father living in Linz, the five-year-old Adolf was relatively free of parental interference. He spent his days playing war and cowboys and Indians with the other children of the area. Even as an adult, Hitler never lost his fascination with the great American West.

He devoured the writings of James Fenimore Cooper and Karl May, a German who told exciting tales of cowboys, bad men, and Indians in gory detail although he had never been to America. Even after becoming chancellor, Hitler continued to reread the works of May and to discuss his stories with his acquaintances.

Young Adolf Hitler's brief period of absolute freedom was shattered in April of the next year when the family joined their father. On June 25, 1895, Alois retired and moved his family to a small farm that he had bought at Hafeld, near Lambach, where he fulfilled his dream of becoming a full-time beekeeper. Alois Hitler was a stern father who dominated his family completely. He attempted to force Adolf to respect him by liberal use of corporal punishment. He also instilled a rigid sense of the importance of the status he enjoyed as a high official in the bureaucracy and a disdain for men of lesser station. Alois taught his son to hold the priesthood and the church in contempt. The brutality with which Alois handled his son and the sympathy of his mother had a major impact on the development of the future dictator of the Third Reich. Although Hitler would later speak of respect for his father, he never had the same affection for him that he had for his mother. Clearly the harsh punishment dealt by his autocratic father laid the foundation for severe mental problems that explain many of his later actions.

During the same year that he moved to Hafeld and came under his father's heavy hand, young Hitler also began to feel the strict discipline of the schools of the period. He entered the school at Lambach run by the local Benedictine abbey. At first he was a good student and earned high grades. He became an altar boy and sang in the children's choir of the abbey. The magnificent worship of the church, with its colorful vestments, clouds of fragrant incense, and impressive music, fascinated the youth, who even dreamed of becoming a priest. It is significant that Abbot Hagen's coat of arms and the church were decorated with swastikas. This symbol, which would later signify the hate and violence of national socialism, had been employed by Christians as a sign for Christ, the "sun" of righteousness.

Alois's hopes of success as a gentleman farmer and beekeeper met with failure. In 1898 he sold his lands and moved his family to a large house in Löding, near Linz, after spending six months in Lambach. Frustrated by his vain attempt at beekeeping, the elder Hitler became even more domineering. He spent his days with friends in the local tavern, returning home to abuse his terrified family. Adolf, unable to cope with his violent father, retreated into a world of fantasy populated by cowboys and Indians. He led his friends in games based on the plots of Cooper and May or pretended that they were Boers fighting the British in South Africa.

In 1900 Adolf Hitler completed his elementary education and had to decide whether to pursue classical studies as preparation for higher education or to receive a technical training as a prelude for the profession of his father. Alois, whose autocratic manners had driven his first son, Alois Hitler, Jr., from the home, wanted his second son to follow in his footsteps and enter the civil service of the Habsburg Empire. However, Adolf wanted to become an artist and strongly resisted pressure from his father. After violent arguments between the father and son, Adolf entered the technical secondary school in Linz. The struggle with his father about his career was a major turning point in Hitler's life. The once active boy, who had spent so much time playing with his friends, suddenly became ill. The exact nature of his affliction is not known. Some historians maintain that he was stricken with epidemic encephalitis. This dreaded disease begins as a severe attack of influenza or a head cold in young persons and emerges later in life as Parkinson's disease, which also may produce major personality alterations. While it is true that Hitler did exhibit some symptoms of Parkinson's disease in his last years, there is absolutely no evidence that he ever had epidemic encephalitis. As we shall see, he was under much stress, did not eat well, and underwent the care of a physician who filled his system with dangerous drugs. A more plausible explanation for Hitler's sudden illness and personality change was the serious conflict with his father and the youthful rebellion against Alois's attempt to force his son to enter the Habsburg civil service. It is clear that Hitler resented his father. Significantly, he constantly referred to Germany as the "motherland," not the "fatherland," as most German nationalists did.[3]

Adolf Hitler's years in secondary school were very unhappy. He had to walk an hour and a half to school or take the train into town. He was smaller than the rest of the class and matured slowly, continuing to play schoolboy pranks at an age when most of his fellow pupils had become more serious. His relations with girls were strained and childish, perhaps the result of his unhappy home life. He satisfied his adolescent curiosity about sex by visiting the adult section of a local wax museum. Throughout his life, Adolf Hitler would have serious trouble in developing normal relations with women.

Hitler, who had earned good marks in elementary school, proved to be a poor secondary school pupil. He seemed lazy and uninterested in his subjects and earned such poor grades that he had to repeat his first year. Influenced by the anticlericalism of his father, he rebelled against the compulsory religious training. He heckled his religious teacher, Father Schwarz, with difficult questions about the Bible. Once he stole the filthy handkerchief the priest kept in his cassock and returned it to the embarrassed cleric in front of the other teachers, holding it by the corner. Another time, before Easter confession, the youth sneaked into the classroom to write on the blackboard. When the priest entered, Hitler quickly turned the slate around. Several weeks later, the teacher ran out of blackboard space and turned it to reveal the words, "I have indulged in an unnatural act." Father Schwarz told Hitler's mother that her son was damned, although he later changed his judgment after seeing the youth come out of the cathedral where he had been busy studying its architecture. Hitler's experiences with his religious teacher illustrate his attitude toward his studies.

Despite his failure as a pupil, his years in Linz made a major impression on his developing mind. The northern Austrian city was a center of Pan-Germanism, an important movement of German-speaking inhabitants of the Habsburg Empire, who looked on the non-German peoples of the monarchy as inferior and resented their growing influence in Vienna. The Pan-Germans sought inspiration from the Hohenzollern Empire and openly campaigned for separation from the Austro-Hungarian Empire to join the German Reich. Hitler's history instructor, Leopold Pötsch, was a passionate German nationalist who taught his young charges to hate the Slavs and other non-Germans of the empire. He spent long hours lecturing about the glory of the German people and praising the Hohenzollern Empire while presenting his somewhat warped view of history. From Pötsch and the Pan-Germans, Hitler learned the extreme nationalism that would become one of the major aspects of the national socialist movement.

On January 3, 1903, Alois Hitler collapsed while drinking his usual glass of wine in a local tavern. His companions carried him home, where he died before a physician could arrive. That spring Adolf's mother placed him in a home for school boys in Linz so he could be closer to his school. However, even though his hated father was gone, leaving him to enter the career of his choice, Adolf never recovered his ability to study. He hated French, the only language he formally studied, and failed his examination. To remain in school he had to pass French. He retook the examination and finally passed. However, in order to receive a passing mark from his French teacher, Dr. Eduard Hümer, he had to agree to enter another school. Although Hitler had barely passed his test, he was able to use the language during the First World War and could read French newspapers and books.

Unable to return to school in Linz, Adolf Hitler entered the secondary school in Steyr in September 1904, where he lived in a room rented from Conrad Edler von Cichini. As at Linz, Hitler was a poor scholar and had no real friends. He finally graduated in the fall of 1905, but because of poor grades he was unable to advance to the senior secondary school. After receiving his certificate, Hitler decided to celebrate with a group of fellow graduates. He stayed out all night and returned home drunk the next morning. When he recovered from the effects of the quart of wine he had drunk, he discovered that he could not find his diploma. Realizing that his mother would be furious, he considered telling her that he had lost it when it blew out of the window of the train as he rode home. But he soon decided that she would not believe this story. Trembling with fear, he went to see the headmaster to request a duplicate. After waiting what seemed like hours, he finally entered the office of the director of the school. He told him that he had lost his certificate and asked for a new one. At that point, the stern educator gave the scared youth four dirty pieces of paper. Horrified, Hitler realized that during the previous night's escapade he had used the important document as toilet paper while in a drunken stupor. Thus ended the formal education of the future warlord of Europe.

After leaving Steyr, Adolf Hitler returned to his family in Linz, where he lived on the inheritance of his father. Finally free from the regimentation of the school, the young man devoted his time to his interest in art. He dreamed of becoming an artist or architect and spent his days reading books on these subjects and designing buildings, bridges, churches, and a new opera house for Linz. He spent many evenings at the local opera. Having seen his first Wagnerian opera while in secondary school, young Hitler became a devoted follower of this great German composer. He was enraptured by the heroic music and by the glorification of the German people and their heritage, a theme that forms the basis for much of Wagner's work. He would remain a devotee of Wagner's powerful operas, which would provide an example for much of the ceremony of the Third Reich. It was at the opera that he met the only close friend of his youth, and perhaps of his whole life, August Kubizek, a music student and son of a local furniture manufacturer.

Hitler's relationship with Kubizek reveals a great deal about his personality. He dominated his friend to such an extent that Kubizek had no time for other acquaintances. Even then the future leader of Nazi Germany had the ability to spellbind his listeners with his piercing eyes. Hitler spent hours lecturing his friend about art and politics, demanding complete agreement. Kubizek later wrote that his willingness to listen to Hitler's tirades was the basis for their friendship. Interestingly enough, the man who would later head a movement that glorified exercise and the healthy body refused to accompany his companion to sporting events and displayed a disdain for those who participated in such things. Although he had rebelled against entering his father's profession and had contempt for bureaucrats, he never let Kubizek forget that his father had held an important post in the civil service and spoke often of his scorn for men of lesser station than his father.[4]

It was during these years that Adolf Hitler first experienced love. One day Kubizek and the future führer were standing on one of the major streets of Linz when Hitler noticed a tall, slim, fair-haired girl. She was Stefanie, the daughter of a high government official who had died shortly before. Hitler fell deeply in love with this girl and waited on the street near her house for her to pass by. He spent long hours writing poems to her and spoke to Kubizek of his plans to build a large Renaissance house for her. When he saw her with other men, he was downcast and once even contemplated suicide. However, despite his passion for the young girl, he could not bring himself to speak with her and had to confine himself to smiling at her as she strolled down the street with her mother. Sometimes she smiled back and he was in ecstasy for days. Once during a flower festival, she rode in a carriage covered with blossoms. As she passed her secret lover, she tossed him a flower. Hitler was delirious with joy, for he believed that she shared his love, but he still refused to speak to her or to her mother. Eventually, Hitler forgot her as he turned his attention to other things.

After living in Linz for a year, Hitler realized that to fulfill his hope of becoming an artist, he would have to leave his home and seek training in the capital of the empire, Vienna. In May 1906, he persuaded his mother to allow him to visit the city. Vienna was quite different from Linz, which was only a large provincial village. Even today, long after the fall of the mighty Habsburg monarchy, one is struck by the beauty of its wide Ring Street, lined by such magnificent buildings as the Renaissance university, the neo-Gothic city hall, the neoclassical parliament, the Square of the Heroes, which is bordered on one side by a large flower-filled park and on the other by the rising columns of the new portion of the imperial palace, and finally the opera house. Vienna is also filled with awe-inspiring baroque palaces and churches and is crowned by the Gothic towers of St. Stephen's Cathedral. Hitler spent hours filled with admiration as he studied the monuments of the dying empire. After a few weeks amid the splendor of one of the most beautiful cities of the world, Hitler returned to Linz.

After seeing Vienna his beloved home seemed dull in comparison, and Hitler vowed to return to the capital. He was delayed by the illness of his mother, who was stricken by cancer of the breast in January 1907. After she had seemingly recovered from an operation, Hitler felt able to resume his studies of the art of Vienna. In September 1907, he moved to Vienna and rented a room near the West Train Station. His goal was to become a student in the celebrated Academy of Fine Arts. Immediately after finding lodgings, he went to the academy to take the yearly admissions examination. He passed the first section and was asked to submit some samples of his work. The officials judged these of poor quality, for Hitler's art, some of which still exists, consisted largely of drawings of buildings that resembled photographs more than the work of a talented artist. Significantly, he could not portray the human figure with any degree of skill, perhaps a sign of his inability to relate to others. The officials, therefore, refused to admit him to the school. The determined youth then sought and obtained an audience with Siegmund L'Allemand, rector of the Academy of Fine Arts, to plead for permission to study at the institute. The director told the saddened youth that his works were not of sufficient quality to justify entrance, but he suggested that he try to become a student of architecture. Hitler then applied to the architectural school, but he was denied admission because he had failed to graduate from senior secondary school. Thus ended Hitler's hope of receiving a formal education in his chosen profession. Perhaps his frustration over his failure laid a foundation for the irrational hate that would motivate many of his later actions.[5]

The dedicated young artist refused to return home in defeat and continued to live in Vienna. He spent his days studying every book on art and architecture he could find and memorizing every detail in them. He also wandered about the city gazing at the many magnificent monuments to the Habsburg Empire, making minute drawings of them on his return home. He saved his money and took advantage of every opportunity to attend the productions of Wagner at the state opera. However, the sudden death of his mother on December 21, 1907, after a painful illness, shattered the dream world in which he lived. He returned to Linz and stood crying at her grave three days later. Although Hitler expressed his gratitude to Dr. Edmund Bloch, the Jewish physician who cared for his dying mother, one cannot help but wonder if his failure to save her life played a subconscious role in the development of Hitler's fanatical anti-Semitism. Hitler truly loved his mother and would speak of her with a fondness lacking in his accounts of his father. After her funeral, several members of his family tried to persuade him to apprentice himself to a local artisan and learn a trade. But the aspiring youth angrily replied that he was an artist and a student and would not lower himself to do menial work, revealing yet another aspect of his complex personality.

While in Linz, Hitler persuaded Kubizek, who wanted to study music, to join him in Vienna. Arriving in the city in February 1908, Kubizek had no problem being admitted to the celebrated Viennese Music School and spent his time in class or practicing on the piano in the rented room he shared with Hitler. The future dictator continued his self-designed program of study. He was an avid reader and had subscribed to three libraries in his native city to satisfy his huge appetite for books. In Vienna he frequented the magnificent Court Library and continued to study the great buildings of the city until he knew every detail by heart. He also designed buildings of his own and designed huge projects to turn Linz into a magnificent city. He even decided to rebuild Vienna and planned to destroy the imperial palace to make room for an even larger and more splendid structure that he hoped to cover with marble.

Since Vienna contained an opera house unparalleled for the quality of its productions, Hitler and Kubizek saved every penny to buy tickets to the standing-room section. The future master of Nazi Germany continued his devotion to Wagner, whose *Lohengrin* was his favorite opera. Besides the story of the swan knight, Hitler enjoyed the *Mastersingers of Nuremberg* and Wolfgang Mozart's *The Marriage of Figaro*. He allowed Kubizek to persuade him to see several productions of works by Giuseppe Verdi, but he considered the work of the Italian master trivial and inferior to the Germanic Wagner, although he did like *Aida*. Hitler held the works of Charles Gounod, Peter

Tchaikovsky, and Bedrich Smetana in contempt. Hitler's fascination with opera was such that he once decided to write his own, based on the legend of Wieland the Smith. He spent several weeks playing his composition on the piano while Kubizek tried to write the notes down on paper. However, since Hitler had had little training in music, the work was weak and very crude. Eventually he became interested in other things and abandoned the project.

Although Hitler often spoke of his time in Vienna as a period of poverty, he was not really in financial trouble. He had a steady of income of fifty-eight kronen a month from his father's estate and an additional twenty-five kronen from the orphan's fund. Since beginning attorneys earned seventy kronen a month, teachers sixty-six, and postmen sixty, Hitler's income was more than adequate. Despite his relative financial security, Hitler lived very frugally. He ate simply and neither drank nor smoked. He did not have an elaborate wardrobe, but he dressed neatly, putting his trousers carefully under his mattress every night so that in the morning he would have a freshly pressed pair to wear.

Vienna was a city filled with beautiful girls, but Hitler continued to dream of his Stefanie. Although Kubizek claims that many women were openly attracted to the self-taught artist, Hitler never returned their interest. Neither did he display signs of strong sexual desires. He adamantly condemned the many prostitutes of the city. Once, after attending a performance of Frank Wedekind's *The Awakening of Spring* at the Court Theater, Hitler decided to explore the city's red light district, dragging Kubizek along with him. As they walked down the street watching the scantily clad girls lure men into their rooms, Hitler became enraged and finally fled to avoid contamination. Upon returning home, he spent hours lecturing his friend on the evils of prostitution.

While Hitler showed little signs of the normal youthful desire for relationships with women, he was not a practicing homosexual. Once a gentleman treated the future führer and his friend to supper at a fashionable hotel and invited them to visit him. Once away from the man, Hitler turned to Kubizek and proclaimed that their benefactor had been a homosexual attempting to seduce them. He then launched into a tirade against homosexuality. Hitler was repulsed by homosexuality and refused to associate with anyone he suspected of being a homosexual, perhaps a manifestation of doubts about his own normality.

Hitler's studies included politics, and he formulated many ideas while in Vienna that later became basic principles of the national socialist movement. He visited the neoclassical parliament building to study its architecture but became interested in the sessions of the Austrian Parliament that he witnessed while examining the chamber. He was horrified by the disorder of the legislative body of the Austrian half of the empire, which often degenerated into anarchy as members shouted at each other in their native languages while the speaker desperately rang his bell in a vain attempt to restore order. Hitler became a strong critic of parliamentary government, which he considered mob rule dominated by self-seeking politicians. He was also shocked by the working-class slums of the city and spoke of destroying them to build new, clean, and comfortable homes for the workers.[6]

During his years in the imperial city, he was greatly influenced by the mayor of Vienna, Karl Lüger, the leader of the Christian Social Party. Lüger was a demagogue who appealed to the concerns of the middle class. He condemned big business and championed the small shopowner. He was a German nationalist who spoke fondly of the Hohenzollern Empire and denounced the non-German peoples of the multinational Danubian monarchy, especially the Hungarians. Although he campaigned against the Marxism of the Social Democrats, he favored welfare programs to protect the workingman from exploitation by his employer. Under his administration, the city undertook to gain control of utility companies and to place them under public ownership. Lüger's combination of nationalism with programs to benefit the workers and middle class appealed greatly to Hitler, and many of his later programs reflected this influence.

In July 1908, Kubizek returned to Linz to visit his family. Although Hitler sent him several postcards, the music student returned to find that Hitler had moved without leaving an address. At first Kubizek tried to find his lost friend, but eventually he gave up without contacting him. Hitler had taken a room only a few blocks away. He would see Kubizek thirty years later and offer to help him find a position as conductor of an orchestra, but he never explained the reason for his sudden departure. Thus ended the first and probably only real friendship Adolf Hitler ever had.

The next few years of Hitler's life are obscure; the "student" lost himself amid the masses of the Austrian capital. He tried once again to pass the entrance examination of the Academy of Fine Arts, but the officials refused to allow him even to take the test, pronouncing his work inferior. Unable to receive a formal education in art, Hitler returned to his self-designed studies. In August 1909, he ran out of the money left him by his family and took a job as a laborer on a construction project. Hitler soon found himself involved in political controversy with his fellow workers. When they asked him to join a trade union, he refused, and when they discussed politics during lunch hour, he argued with them. Many of the workers were members of the Social Democratic party of Austria and had been heavily influenced by Marxism. They strongly condemned the capitalist classes and some spoke of the state as the creation of the bourgeoisie to protect its interests. This directly conflicted with Hitler's intense nationalism, and he found himself in violent debates with the radical laborers. At one point the controversy became so fiery that Hitler was almost physically thrown off the project. Hitler's experiences with the Marxist workers turned him against social democracy. He was first and foremost a dedicated German nationalist and rejected the internationalist aspect of Marxism. However, he was no supporter of the bourgeoisie, which he considered an oppressive class that had blocked needed reforms and had driven the workers into the arms of the Socialists.

Hitler's hostility to social democracy fed the extreme German nationalism that he had learned in Linz. He began to hate the multinational Habsburg Empire and its rulers. As he walked among the streets of Vienna, the many non-Germans living and working there repulsed him. He decided that no loyal German could support the Austro-Hungarian Empire and dreamed of the day when the German subjects of Vienna would be liberated and be able to unite themselves with the German Reich. As he grew more and more into a fanatical German nationalist and anti-Marxist, Hitler began to search for the cause of all the evils he found. He bought and studied the social democratic press and decided that the many Jews living in Vienna were the real directors of the conspiracy against nationalism. The appearance of the many eastern Jews, who walked the streets clad in long caftans and flowing locks angered him. He looked at them and saw not a German, but a foreigner who he believed was seeking to destroy the pure German race. He began to blame them for all ills of society, including poverty, slums, and prostitution.

Hitler's intense nationalism turned to racism as he began to consider all non-Germans, and especially Jews, as inferior peoples. In this development, probably begun while a schoolboy in Linz, Hitler was greatly influenced by the philosophy of a magazine he happened to pick up one day, *Ostara,* published by Lanz von Liebenfels. Liebenfels, whose real name was Adolf Josef Lanz, was the son of a school teacher. He had become a Cistercian monk but left the monastery to spread his hateful philosophy. He forged papers of nobility and assumed the name Lanz von Liebenfels. He founded *Ostara* in 1905 to spread his racist ideas. Heavily influenced by the cult of the folk, he told his readers of the natural superiority of the blond, blue-eyed Aryan and wrote of the dark, hairy non-Aryans, whom he considered little better than apes. When Adolf Hitler read *Ostara,* he found much with which he agreed and sought out the editor to learn more and to obtain back copies of the hate-filled publication.

Hitler's newfound political studies and inability to get along with his fellow workers kept him from finding a job, and in 1909 he had to move out of his rented room. He sank to utter poverty, sleeping on park benches and on lawns. Finally, in December 1909, he swallowed his pride and sought lodging in a charity home near the South Train Station. Here he lived in a dormitory and was able to bathe. Since the home did not provide food, he joined other men outside St. Catherine's convent where the good sisters distributed free food. One day he met Reinhold Hanisch, a German who spent hours telling Hitler about life in the Hohenzollern Empire. At first they spent their days begging for food and earning a few coins carrying the baggage of the passengers at the South Train Station. Then Hanisch enabled Hitler to escape the utter poverty of the charity home by encouraging him to use his artistic abilities to earn extra money. The German persuaded Hitler to write his sister for money to buy a new overcoat and art supplies. With the tools of his chosen trade, Hitler was once again able to paint. Hanisch took Hitler's works and found shops to sell them, earning enough money to seek lodgings elsewhere.

On February 9, 1910, they moved into the hostel for men, where Hitler rented a small room. He spent his days in a corner of the lounge painting pictures for Hanisch to sell. There was a ready market for Hitler's works because many people bought hand-painted postcards, and sofas with small picture frames in the back were popular. Through his art and Hanisch's efforts, Hitler was able to earn a small living and even to attend the opera occasionally. He lived an austere, almost monklike existence, wearing simple but neat clothing and cooking his own meals. As before, Hitler never squandered his money on drink and rarely smoked a cigarette. However, Hitler's friendship with Hanisch was short-lived. One day he went to the police to charge his friend with pocketing the money gained by selling a picture Hitler had painted of the Austrian parliament. Although the judge sentenced Hanisch to a few days in jail, Hitler never recovered his lost money. He found a new friend in Josef Greiner, a former lamplighter. Together the two men discussed ways to get rich, including developing a hair restorer and a cream to prevent windows from breaking.

Hitler continued his political development at the men's hostel. One day he saw a film by Bernhard Kellermann entitled *The Tunnel.* This work told the story of a successful demagogue who was able to use his ability with words to sway the masses. The idea fascinated Hitler, who began to believe in the power of speech. Influenced as well by the campaign methods of Lüger, he decided that great men who stirred the passions of the common man through bombast led all successful movements. Hitler began to try his ability as a speaker. Occasionally he would throw down his brush and pencil to stand up in the lounge to deliver a violent harangue against Jews, Communists, or foes of German nationalism to all who would listen. Perhaps more than any other factor, Hitler's ability to appeal to the emotions of a crowd and to make them believe what he was saying, as he looked at them with his piercing eyes, was the key to his rise from obscurity to the leadership of the Third Reich.

In early 1913 Hitler decided to leave the multinational Habsburg Empire that he hated so much and move to the German Reich. He packed his meager belongings and set out for Munich, the capital of the Kingdom of Bavaria. There is a strong possibility that other factors than his desire to live in the Hohenzollern Empire motivated Hitler. Austrian law required him to have registered for military service in 1909, but he had failed to do so. His failure to register caused him some legal problems, and he may have fled to avoid service in the army of a state that he considered corrupted by non-German influence. However, he could not escape the Austrian authorities. On December 29, 1913, the Austrian police asked the German officials if Hitler had registered with them. A few days later the police of Munich sought out Hitler and told him that he must return to Linz and enlist in the Austro-Hungarian army by January 20, 1914. Since Hitler made no effort to comply with the summons, the police arrested him and took him to the Austrian consulate the day before he was required to appear in Linz. Although he was able to convince the Austrian officials that he was too ill and poor to afford a journey to his former home, they required him to report to Salzburg, which was closer to Munich. On February 5, 1914, he presented himself to the officials in the city of Mozart's birth, and they rejected him as unfit for military service because of ill health.

In Munich Hitler found lodgings in the home of Josef Popp. Once again he earned a modest living selling his paintings and spent his time reading and arguing politics in cafes and beer halls. Although Hitler's education had ended in failure, his passion for reading made him a self-educated man. He studied every aspect of politics and political philosophy. He read many works on Judaism and even attempted to learn Hebrew to confirm his anti-Semitism. He also read the works of Karl von Clausewitz on war and military strategy, which would later influence his methods during the Second World War. Hitler studied the works of Friedrich Nietzsche, which strengthened his belief in the importance of the demagogue and the politics of brute force. He became a passionate student of the past and studied the lives of the great men, whom he considered the prime movers of world history.

Suddenly, on June 28, 1914, an event occurred that would tear Hitler from a comfortable life in Munich and would throw him on the path to a new life. An obscure Serbian radical assassinated Archduke Franz Ferdinand in Sarajevo. Hitler was at first pleased because he hated the heir to the Austro-Hungarian throne, who held a well-known sympathy for the Slavic peoples, and believed that at last the Habsburg Empire would be destroyed. However, when Germany entered the conflict, he changed his position. He believed that at last the war had come that would make Germany the master of Europe and destroy the old multinational Danubian monarchy. On August 1, the first day of the war, Hitler joined a cheering and singing crowd on Odeon Square to listen to the formal declaration of war. A picture of the mob shows him standing toward the front, his eyes blazing with excitement, as he joined the people of Munich in pledging their loyalty to their king.

Although Hitler had been unwilling to join the Austro-Hungarian army, he passionately wanted to join Germany in its fight against the French and Russians. He petitioned King Ludwig III of Bavaria for permission to join the Bavarian army, although he was a subject of the Habsburg emperor. On August 3, with shaking hands, he opened a letter from the officials. His heart filled with joy as he read that his request had been granted and that he would be allowed to join the

First Company of the Bavarian Reserve Infantry, known as the List Regiment after its commander, Colonel Wilhelm von List. Significantly enough, another member of the company was Rudolf Hess, and the clerk was Sergeant Major Max Amann, who would become the business manager of the nazi press. Hitler and his fellow soldiers spent a few weeks receiving training and then left for the front on October 21, 1914.

Hitler threw himself completely into the German war effort. He and his comrades reached Lille on October 23 and immediately joined the fighting as reinforcements for the Sixth Bavarian Division of the Sixth Army, under Bavaria's Crown Prince Rupprecht. As the Germans tried to break through to the English Channel amid bloody fighting, Hitler and his comrades fought with every ounce of strength. Even after a bullet tore his right sleeve from his shirt as it whistled by, Hitler continued to press forward. However, the battle ended without a German victory, and 349 of Hitler's fellow soldiers of the List Regiment, including their commander, lay dead on the battlefield. After his first taste of combat, Hitler was assigned to the dangerous task of carrying messages between regimental headquarters and his company. It was hazardous duty, and many men were killed as they ran between the trenches attempting to dodge enemy fire. Hitler was a dedicated soldier and was so brave in the face of almost certain death that his commander recommended him for the Iron Cross Second Class, which he received on December 2, 1914. He was also promoted to the rank of lance corporal. During the next few months, the future warlord of Nazi Germany spent his free time reading and discussing politics with his fellow soldiers as they huddled in the trenches waiting for the shooting to start once again. The next year Hitler's company took part in the Battle of the Somme, and on October 7 an enemy bullet hit him in the knee, forcing him to return to Germany for recovery.

In March 1917 Hitler once again returned to the fighting, and in the spring of 1918 he participated in the last major German offensive. On August 4, 1918, the commander awarded him the Iron Cross First Class. There is no official record of what he did to earn the honor, and some of his political opponents charged that he did not deserve it. Another account claims that he single-handedly captured a group of French soldiers. After receiving the exalted decoration, Hitler continued to fight, and on the night of October 13/14, 1918, he was blinded by a cloud of deadly mustard gas launched by the British as he ran up a hill near Werwick, south of Ypres. Unable to continue in the fighting, Hitler was sent to a hospital at Pasewalk, in Pomerania, not far from the city of Stetten. It was here that he learned of the abdication of the kaiser. He was shocked as he realized that all the sacrifices had been in vain and that his beloved fatherland had lost the war. He returned to his room and threw himself on his cot crying for the first time since his mother's funeral. After several sleepless nights spent pondering the war and the bloodshed, trying desperately to find a reason for Germany's failure, Hitler decided that the Jews and politicians had betrayed the German people and led them to defeat. At that moment, according to his testimony in *Mein Kampf,* Hitler vowed to enter politics and begin a career that would carry him to the height of power.

Hitler's first twenty-nine years provided the basis for his later work. The brutality of his father created the unbalanced mind that would send millions to their deaths and then turn to a discussion of art or a film. The young Hitler fell under the spell of the ultra-nationalistic teaching of Pötsch and the Pan-Germans while still in school. Later, while wandering the streets of Vienna contemplating the reasons for his failure to become an art student, he rejected Marxism and became a fanatical anti-Semite. He developed his idea of the politics of bombast and mass movements through watching Lüger and an obscure film, and he learned of his ability to sway others while earning a meager living in the hostel for men. Finally, the future warlord of Europe developed, during the First World War, the concept of comradeship that would play such an important part in the nazi movement. In 1918, a frustrated, mentally unbalanced artist swore to enter politics to restore the Reich to the position it had lost in the First World War.

8

The Beer Hall Putsch

The month of November 1918 was a major turning point in German history and in the life of Adolf Hitler. The kaiser and his empire had fallen, and a revolutionary tide had engulfed the fatherland. Thousands of soldiers returning from the field tried to reconstruct their shattered lives. They had spent four years dodging bullets as they watched their friends and relatives become cannon fodder. As they groped for the reason for the useless slaughter, many lost all faith in the leadership of the new Germany. They saw their homeland turned into a battleground as various groups fought for the right to determine the future of the Reich. The disorder repulsed many who longed for a return to the principles of discipline that they had experienced in the trenches. Adolf Hitler, who left Pasewalk Hospital on November 21, 1918, would speak to these men and provide simple answers to their complex questions. He and his followers would offer order in the midst of chaos and call for loyalty to the old soldierly virtues. His movement continued to grow until it overthrew the hated republic.

After his release from the hospital, Hitler, like so many men in 1918, returned to the life that he had known for the last four years—the military. He hurried to rejoin his old unit, now in Munich. At first he took no part in the political drama taking place around him. Instead, he busied himself by helping sort out the mountains of unused war supplies and spent some time guarding French prisoners of war as they prepared to return to their homeland. During the bloody Communist revolt and its suppression, Hitler remained in the safety of his barracks, refusing to aid either side.

However, Hitler's inactivity soon came to an abrupt end. On June

5, 1919, his superiors sent him to a special school designed to prepare soldiers for the transition to civilian life. Hitler and his comrades spent a week listening to such men as Professor Karl Alexander von Müller and Dr. Michael Horlacher lecture on history and politics, lectures designed to indoctrinate the men in rightist political ideas. Gottfried Feber, an engineer, spoke on economics, condemning the parties that had created the November Revolution and calling for the formation of a new revolutionary party to lead Germany. Hitler, who had already become a radical nationalist, listened with great enthusiasm and spent long sessions discussing his opinions with his comrades. His tirades soon caught the attention of the authorities, and he became a political instructor at the Lechfeld demobilization center west of Munich. Here, Hitler once again discovered his ability to sway others with his voice. Later he joined the press and news bureau of the political department of the Seventh District Command of the German army in Munich under Captain Karl Mayr. On September 10, 1919, his superiors sent him to investigate the attitude of the Bavarian Socialists toward the Jews. Two days later he received orders to attend a meeting of the German Worker's party.

The German Worker's party grew from the work of members of the Thule Society, an organization dedicated to the cult of the folk and organized in 1918 by ultra-nationalists dedicated to the memory of Wotan, the ancient Teutonic god of war. Baron Rudolf von Sebottendorff brought the Thule Society to Munich. Sebottendorff, whose real name was Alfred Rudolf Glauer, was born in Saxony of lower-middle-class parents. He had left Germany for the Middle East, where he served as head of the Turkish Red Crescent during the Balkan Wars. He returned to Germany as a Magnus of the Society of Rosicrucians in 1917, and the next summer he founded the Bavarian branch of the Thule Society. The following year he once again left Germany to return to Turkey. The Thule Society played a major role in support of the rightist cause during the Bavarian Revolution of 1918–1919 and would serve as the nucleus of the German Worker's party.

The actual organization of the German Worker's party was the work of Anton Drexler, a locksmith, and Karl Harrer, a sportswriter. On March 7, 1918, Drexler formed a committee to fight profiteering and the peace movement. In October 1918, as Germany neared defeat, Drexler met with Harrer and Michael Lotter, a locomotive engineer, to discuss the formation of a new political party. On January 5, 1919, they inaugurated the German Worker's party. At first they had no real program but held meetings in beer halls to spread antidemocratic, anti-Semitic, and nationalistic propaganda.[1]

On September 12, on instructions from his superiors, Hitler went to a meeting of the party in the Sterneckerbräu Tavern in Munich. To obscure his true purpose as a spy for the army, he wore civilian clothes. Hitler found a group of about twenty-five people listening to a speech by Gottfried Feder, whom he had met during his political indoctrination several months before. At first Hitler was bored, and he decided to leave; but Professor Baumann stood to deliver an address advocating that Bavaria secede from the German Reich to unite with Austria. Unable to contain his feelings, Hitler jumped up and delivered a violent harangue denouncing Baumann, as the members of the party listened in great interest. When he left the hall, someone gave him a pamphlet written by Drexler, entitled "My Political Awakening."

Hitler's first reaction was to dismiss the German Worker's party as an organization of no consequence. However, that evening, as was so often the case, no matter how hard he tried, he could not get to sleep. As he lay on his cot that mild summer night, he began to think about what he had seen and the effort of those few men to change the shape of German history. He looked among his papers and found Drexler's pamphlet. As he read, Hitler's spirits rose, for he discovered that he was not alone in his thoughts. At last he had found someone who agreed with him that Germany had been betrayed by Jewish-dominated politicians. Nonetheless, he might have forgotten the party if he had not received a postcard a few days later informing him that he had been accepted for membership in the German Worker's party and inviting him to the next meeting.

At first Hitler was greatly offended by the arrogance of the small organization that made him a member without his approval. On September 16, 1919, he went to the meeting with the intention of rejecting their overture. As he entered the site of the meeting, the Altes Rosenbad, he found a rather dingy empty room. He went into a side room and found four men sitting under a simple gas lamp. He sat unnoticed and listened to the treasurer report that the party that hoped to overthrow the German Republic had the total sum of seven marks and fifty pfennig. Finally, he gained the attention of the presiding officer and asked a few questions. Then, instead of declining membership in the small group, Adolf Hitler accepted and became member number 555 of the German Worker's party. Since the organization had begun counting members at 500, Hitler was the fifty-fifth person to join the party. He changed his mind because he was caught up in the spirit of the small movement. He knew that reason would have told him to refuse to associate himself with this insignificant band of men, but he had found an organization he believed he could shape according to his political principles.[2]

Hitler injected new life into the German Worker's party. He believed in vigorous action and used his power as a speaker to win the support of his listeners. Hitler also realized the value of publicity and began to advertise the meetings in the local press. The attendance continued to grow as more people fell under the sway of Hitler's eloquence. On February 24, 1920, the party was large enough to hold a meeting in the mammoth Hofbräuhaus, where over two thousand people eagerly listened to the Nazi message. The meeting began with a rather unimpressive speech by a Dr. Dingfelder. Then Hitler stood up to address the crowd. Speaking amid loud catcalls, while a group of leftists stood outside singing the "International," Hitler summoned all his ability as an orator. After he finished his violent denunciation of the Jews and of the republic, the awed crowd leaped to their feet and cheered for thirty minutes.

That evening, on Hitler's suggestion, the party changed its name to the National Socialist German Worker's party and adopted a platform of twenty-five points. The program reflected the ultranationalism of the membership by calling for the unification of all German-speaking people under one Reich and for the repudiation of the hated Treaty of Versailles. It also called for the restriction of German citizenship to pure-blooded Germans. All others, including the Jews, would be considered only guests of the Reich and would not enjoy the same civil and economic rights as Germans. The platform emphasized the socialistic aspects of the movement by demanding an end to high interest rates and the domination of the retail market by large chain stores. It called for land reform to protect the interests of the farmers and profit sharing to benefit the workers. It even endorsed the nationalization of all large trusts. The platform strongly condemned usurers, racketeers, and profiteers, calling for their arrests and executions. While affirming the obligation of all to work, it opposed child labor. The Nazi program also called for measures to protect the health and welfare of all Germans. Showing the influence of the cult of the folk, it demanded the replacement of Roman law with Germanic law and the transformation of all education, art, literature, and journalism to reflect the racial ideas of Nazism. The party promised to respect religious freedom as long as the churches supported the Germanic race. Finally, the Nazi platform called for the strengthening of the powers of the national government as a means of accomplishing its goals. The terrible movement that would bring tyranny to Germany and death and destruction to Europe had begun.

Through his powerful speeches and organizational ability, Hitler emerged as the leader of the party. On January 5, 1920, Karl Harrar, one of the founders of the movement, resigned as chief of party propaganda, and the leadership named Hitler to the post. He accepted his new office with enthusiasm and threw himself into party activities, having resigned from the army to devote full time to the growing nazi movement. When the Kapp Putsch erupted in March 1920, Hitler hurried to Berlin, disguising himself to avoid detection by the authorities. In the late spring and summer he toured southern Germany, enthralling crowds of eager listeners with his bombastic oratory. In August he spoke to a meeting of German nationalists from the Reich and Austria and continued his speaking tour to Vienna, Innsbruck, and Braunau. Hitler's triumphant tour won many adherents to the nazi cause, and by 1921 the party had grown to a membership of two thousand. The new success of the movement was symbolized by a meeting on February 3 at Krone's Circus, which six thousand five hundred supporters attended.

However, not all fell victim to Hitler's speeches. Many older members of the party resented the swift rise of the newcomer and formed a circle around Anton Drexler to prevent Hitler from becoming the leader of the party. Taking advantage of a trip by their foe to Berlin in July 1921, Drexler and his followers decided to merge the party with a nationalistic group in Hanover. When he heard of this, Hitler immediately returned to Munich to fight what he considered the subversion of the movement by uniting it with an organization that was only mildly anti-Semitic. Unable to tolerate even the slightest deviation from party doctrine and any challenge to his leadership, Hitler officially resigned from the party on July 11. Three days later he sent a letter to the central committee stating that he would reconsider only if the merger plan were abandoned and he received complete control over the party. Realizing that Hitler's ability had enabled the association to grow to such importance, Drexler and his friends finally relented and agreed to give Hitler unquestioned obedience.

Other Nazis were not quite as ready as Drexler to make Hitler dictator of the party. Some of them circulated an anonymous letter calling him a petty demagogue who was trying to lead the movement astray. Another plastered the walls of the beer halls frequented by members of the party with posters charging that Hitler had become a tyrant, whose goal was to become "King of Munich." With the warring factions fighting for control, the growing controversy threatened to cripple the party. On July 29 the central committee called a special meeting to discuss the problem. Hitler addressed the membership and discussed the reasons for the split, ending by inviting anyone who disagreed with the decision to make him leader to resign the party. Then Drexler stood up and moved that the meeting give Hitler a vote of confidence, which passed by a vote of 543 to one. Thus, by thirty-two, Adolf Hitler had grown from an obscure soldier to the absolute dictator of a political party with over three thousand members.

With complete control of the national socialist movement firmly won, Hitler set out to transform the party into an effective fighting force. In December the party bought the *Völkischer Beobachter,* which appeared twice weekly until 1923, and thereafter daily. Through this hate-filled newspaper, the party reached thousands who had been unable to hear the nazi leader in person. He developed an ideology influenced by the Romanticists who had looked to the common folk as the center of all culture. However, Hitler, like others before him, warped the ideas of men like the Grimm brothers, turning them into the basis for a fanatical brand of racism. Hitler violently denounced all attempts to mix the blood of the "superior" German people with that of "inferior" races. He believed that this mixing would lower the level of the superior people to that of the inferior and, in the process, destroy the indigeneous German national culture. Like the followers of the cult of the folk, he spoke of the Nordic Aryans as a race of supermen who were destined to lead the world into a new era of greatness. Hitler proclaimed that the cause of the destruction of all great cultures of history had not been economic or political but the pollution of the blood of the master race with that of foreign and inferior peoples. Thus, racism was the foundation upon which the nazi ideology had been built and would become the new religion of millions of Germans.

Hitler complemented the party ideology by adopting the hooked cross, or swastika. No one knows the origins of this sign, the name of which means fortune in Sanskrit. It apparently was associated with the worship of the sun in ancient times. Forms of it can be found in such diverse places as thousand-year-old Hindu and Buddhist temples and sculpture, and even on the artifacts of the American Indian. The early Christians used the hooked cross as a symbol for Christ, the sun of righteousness. Hitler probably first saw the swastika on the coat of arms of the Abbey school that he attended as a child in Lambach. As the cult of the folk developed, many adopted the hooked cross as the symbol of Aryan superiority. *Ostara,* the violently anti-Semitic and nationalistic newspaper that Hitler read in Vienna, prominently bore a swastika on its masthead. The Austrian German Worker's party also adopted the hooked cross. Thus, despite its association with Christian and ancient religions, the swastika had become a symbol of extreme German nationalism and racism by the 1920s. Hitler and his followers placed it on a red background for socialism, and inside a white circle for nationalism, to create the nazi flag.[3]

The secret of Hitler's rapid rise to leadership of the infant nazi movement was his ability to spellbind large groups of people with his fanatical speeches. In Vienna, through watching the politician Lüger, and Kellermann's film *The Tunnel,* Hitler had learned of the importance of the demagogue. He never wrote out his speeches, relying instead on a few key words or phrases scribbled on a piece of paper. He began every speech slowly, with stiff movements, while he attempted to gain a feel of his audience. Then, as he relaxed, he began to shout louder and louder, and he hammered in his points with his right arm. He expressed one thought and then abruptly shifted his arguments to another aspect of his doctrine of hate. Time and time again he drove home his points, his high-pitched voice reaching higher and higher levels. While he spoke, his intense stare pierced his audience. Hitler drove his listeners into a frenzy bordering on hysteria; more and more fell under the influence of the growing nazi movement.

By March 1922, even the right-wing Bavarian government was concerned about the growth of the Nazi party, which had over six thousand members. Franz Schweyer, the Bavarian minister of the interior, decided that Hitler was dangerous and must be stopped before he caused real trouble. He looked into the nazi leader's background and, discovering that he was still a citizen of Austria, tried to have him deported. However, the future master of the Third Reich had many friends in high places, and Schweyer's effort failed; even the leader of the Bavarian Socialists, Erhard Auer, disapproved of the plan. Yet Schweyer had Hitler imprisoned from June 24 to July 27, 1922, on charges growing out his participation in the violent breaking up of an anti-Prussian separatist meeting the year before.

Despite Schweyer's efforts, Hitler continued to gather new supporters with the web of words he was so capable of throwing over a crowd. A typical example of his ability to sway the masses occurred on August 16, 1922, when a large delegation of Nazis, carrying flags adorned with the swastika, joined a large outdoor demonstration against the new Law for the Protection of the Republic. A turbulent fight between leftists and Nazis followed, and amid the turmoil Hitler stood up and angrily addressed the crowd of 50,000. As he played on the emotions of the gathering to win support and to prevent a riot, his words were like magic. On November 3, at a large meeting in the famous Hofbräuhaus, one hysterical member named Hermann Esser called on the Nazis to copy the example of Benito Mussolini, who had taken control of Italy by his successful March on Rome of October 28, 1922. The nazi fever mounted, and when the Socialists announced five meetings for December 13, Hitler's men held twice as many.

Hitler's success in avoiding legal troubles in Bavaria was not duplicated in the rest of Germany. The Law for the Protection of the Republic had authorized the banning of radical groups, and on July 4, 1922, the state of Baden, long a center of German liberalism, forbade the Nazi party to carry on its activities. Other states, alarmed by the appeal of the moustachioed demagogue, followed the example of Baden. Thuringia banned the Nazi party on July 15, Prussia on November 15, and later Hamburg, Schaumburg-Lippe, Hesse, and Brunswick joined in passing laws designed to destroy the nazi movement. To counter these laws, Hitler's apostles in these states simply changed the name of the organization and carried on their propaganda campaign.

As the party continued to gain adherents, it won the support of several men who would play very important roles in the history of the Third Reich. One of the first was Julius Streicher, an elementary school teacher from Nuremberg. Born on February 12, 1885, Streicher served in the Bavarian infantry during the war, won the Iron Cross, and formed his own political party in 1920. The next year he and his followers joined the national socialist movement. Streicher was a radical anti-Semite and a dedicated Nazi. After he forced his pupils to greet him with cries of "Heil Hitler" and took sick leave to march in a nazi parade in Munich, his superiors dismissed him from his teaching duties. Able to devote full time to the service of

Hitler, Streicher founded a weekly newspaper, *The Stormer,* in April 1923, which was filled with often obscene invectives against the Jews. Streicher became one of the crudest anti-Semites in the growing nazi movement.[4]

One of the most important early supporters of Hitler's message of hate was Alfred Rosenberg. This leading Nazi represented the German-speaking minority in the Baltic states, having been born in Revel in Estonia, then a part of the Russian empire, on January 12, 1893. He, like his leader, had intended to become an architect. Before the outbreak of the First World War he entered the technical institute at Riga. When German troops marched into Russia and threatened the Estonian capital, Rosenberg and his fellow students sought safety in Moscow. He spent the war years engaged in his studies and with his wife in Crimea, where she had gone to recuperate from an attack of tuberculosis. While there he read works by Nietzsche and Houston Stuart Chamberlain, as well as the most important works of Russian literature. After the war he returned to Riga to practice his profession and would have been an architect had not the outbreak of the Bolshevik Revolution driven him into exile in Munich in 1918. Unable to practice his trade, Rosenberg returned to the ideas he had read during the war years and became a raging anti-Semite. He joined the Thule Society and became a member of the German Worker's party even before Hitler.

Rosenberg became one of the chief theorists of national socialism; although he never held a high office in the Third Reich. In 1920 he wrote *The Trail of the Jews in the Course of Time* and *The Immorality of the Talmud.* Three years later he produced *The Protocols of Zion and Jewish World Politics.* In these works Rosenberg charged that the Jews were engaging in an international conspiracy to enslave mankind and to destroy the superior Aryan race. His most important work was *The Myth of the Twentieth Century,* published in 1930. Influenced by Chamberlain and the cult of the folk, Rosenberg describes world history as the struggle between races for domination. He argues in true Nazi fashion that the pure-blooded Nordic possesses a special genius that other groups lack and that all that is great in world culture can be traced to Germanic influence. Rosenberg denounced Christianity as a false religion that teaches original sin and love instead of the natural superiority and comradeship of the Aryan peoples. The nazi theorist also wrote of the need to capture living space to provide a source of food and raw materials for the German fatherland. In 1929 he organized the Fighting League for German Culture to put his ideas of "pure art" into practice. This society laid the foundation for much of the culture of the Third Reich.

Another nazi leader born outside the fatherland was Rudolf Hess, who came into the world in Alexandria, Egypt, on April 26, 1894. Like Hitler, young Hess struggled with his father, who wanted his son to become a businessman like himself. He refused to allow him to prepare for the university and sent him to Germany at the age of nine to study a trade instead. Like so many other young men in 1914, Hess escaped his plight by joining the army, serving in the same company as Hitler. When peace finally came, Hess defied his father's wishes and enrolled in the University of Munich. There he listened with rapture to the lectures of Karl Haushofer. Haushofer, the chief German theorist of geopolitics, taught his students that a nation must control the living space needed to provide its people with a secure source of food and raw materials. Hess became an ultra-nationalist and joined the Free Corps. In June 1920 he became a member of the National Socialist party. He served as the leader of the nazi student organization at the University of Munich and joined the Brown Shirts. Hess became a devoted follower of Hitler, whom he introduced to the ideas of Haushofer. He became a member of the nazi leader's inner circle, giving him the love and devotion he could not give his own father. It was to Hess that Hitler would later dictate much of *Mein Kampf,* the nazi bible. In 1933 the dictator would show his gratitude by appointing Hess his deputy. Later, Hess would lose his mind, as he contemplated the theology of the new religion of national socialism.[5]

One of the most brutal of Hitler's early followers was Ernst Röhm, born in Munich on November 28, 1887. Forsaking the traditions of his family, which had provided the kings of the south German monarchy with several generations of bureaucrats, Röhm entered the army, rising to the rank of captain during the First World War. After the armistice he joined the staff of the army district command in the Bavarian capital. When revolution swept through Munich, he joined the Free Corps unit led by Franz von Epp and participated in the bloody repression of the Communists in 1919. Röhm became a Nazi shortly after Hitler and assisted in founding the Storm Troopers, using his influence with the military and rightist circles to provide Hitler's private army with needed supplies. Unlike many Nazis, Röhm took the word *socialist* in the party name very seriously. He hoped that the movement would appeal to the lower classes and overthrow the oppression of the republic and the upper classes. He would emerge as the leader of the Brown Shirts and would finally meet his death for daring to challenge the authority of the führer himself. Röhm was a brutal man, who believed in the utilization of force and terror to intimidate the enemies of national socialism into submission.

The most important early Nazi, however, was Hermann Göring. Unlike many of Hitler's comrades, who came largely from middle-class backgrounds, Göring was an aristocrat, born in 1893 in Rosenheim, the son of Heinrich Ernst Göring, the first governor of German Southwest Africa. He studied at the military academies in Karlsruhe and Gross Lichterfeld and became a member of the elite Royal Prussian Cadet Corps through the intervention of his mother's lover, Hermann von Epenstein, a minor nobleman of Jewish ancestry. He became a national hero during the First World War, serving as a fighter pilot and leader of the famed Richtofen squadron. He shot down twenty-two enemy planes and earned the highest decorations the fatherland had to offer. After the war he traveled to Denmark and Sweden as the representative of the Fokker Aircraft Company, earning extra money by giving flying exhibitions. While in Sweden he fell under the spell of the cult of Nordic superiority, which had grown popular with the aristocracy of the Scandinavian kingdom. In 1923 he would marry a Swedish noblewoman, Carin von Kantzow, the wife of Captain Nils von Kantzow, after an adulterous love affair. In 1921 he returned to his homeland to study history at the University of Munich, unable to earn a living as a flyer.

Göring, like so many Germans, had become disenchanted with the republic and the Treaty of Versailles. In November 1922 he attended an open air meeting to protest the Allied demand that Germany surrender men charged with war crimes for trial. There he heard Hitler speak for the first time and fell under his verbal spell. After the rally he sought out the nazi leader to learn more of his ideas. As he listened, he knew that he had found a man who believed the same as he did, that the republic had betrayed the German people by falling under the influence of Jews and Socialists and must be overthrown by a new nationalist crusade. He immediately joined the Nazi party, which was glad to count a man of fame among its members, and he supervised the training of the Storm Troopers. Göring was one of the most arrogant members of Hitler's band of fanatics. He would rise to great heights in the party and for a while would be the second most powerful man in the nazi hierarchy. He would also use his position to gather great wealth and to live in luxury.[6]

Göring's first major contribution to the nazi movement was the transformation of the Brown Shirts into an effective fighting force. The Storm Troopers, named from the elite corps of fighters during the First World War, had been organized as Hitler's bodyguard in October 1921 under the command of Johann Ulrich Klintzsch, a lieutenant in the navy. The Storm Troopers showed their "worth" for the first time at a party rally in the Hofbräuhaus on November 4, 1921, by severely beating seven hundred Communists who attempted to break up the meeting. Shortly after joining the party, Göring took over leadership of this band of streetfighters. He drilled the ragtag army of students, workers, former soldiers, and Free Corps members, instilling in them a sense of discipline and devotion to national socialism. The Storm Troopers, which had grown to a membership of between five and six thousand by early 1923, used clubs, knives, and bare fists to terrorize Communists and other foes of national socialism, breaking up rival meetings and beating participants. They had special motorized units that could rush to the scene of a rival rally and provide instant protection for Hitler. Soon every village and town in Bavaria had brown-shirted bands of Storm Troopers who marched through the streets every weekend spreading the nazi message.

Under Hitler's effective leadership, the nazi movement developed from an obscure group of men to a huge national organization with thousands of members and a core of dedicated leaders. It was only a matter of time before Hitler would try to use his great power to overthrow the hated republic and to put his theories into effect. He found that opportunity in 1923. That year the French invaded the Ruhr, causing a wave of nationalism and resentment to spread among the German people. At the same time, the economy was destroyed by a crippling inflation, and thousands groped for a way out of their misery. Hitler held a series of meetings to denounce the French and to preach the nazi message, and he announced a massive rally for January 27 through 29. Realizing the danger of thousands of fanatical Nazis being driven to a frenzy by their leader's passionate speeches, the Bavarian government immediately declared a state of emergency and banned the meeting. However, Röhm and others persuaded General Otto von Lossow, commander of the district headquarters of the army, that Hitler's plans would not threaten the peace, and the government lifted the ban. The rally took place without violence.

The Beer Hall Putsch

After effectively challenging the authority of the government, the nazi leaders felt strong enough to face the Communists, who had planned a parade in Munich on May 1. Upon learning that red flags and marching leftists would fill the streets of the Bavarian capital, Hitler announced the decision of the Nazis to hold a rival demonstration. On the cool spring morning of May 1, 1923, Hitler, Göring, Hess, Streicher, and other Nazis gathered on the outskirts of the city to await a signal from Röhm, who had gotten some weapons from nazi sympathizers in the army. The violence that would almost certainly have followed after the two rival processions met, however, did not materialize. Hitler and his aides waited impatiently for Röhm the whole morning. Finally, at one in the afternoon, he arrived with a military escort and told the disappointed rightists that Lossow had learned of their plans and had demanded the immediate return of the weapons. Unwilling to face an open confrontation with the leftists, the führer told his disappointed comrades that the demonstration had been canceled, and left.

Despite the failure of May 1, the Nazis continued to agitate against the French and the republic. On September 1 and 2, Hitler addressed 100,000 enthusiastic nationalists who had gathered in Nuremberg to celebrate the anniversary of the German victory over the French at Sedan in 1870. The success of the rally frightened the national government, and President Ebert attempted to ban further publication of the *Völkischer Beobachter,* the nazi newspaper. However, Lossow refused to enforce Ebert's command, and the newspaper continued to circulate its message of anti-Semitism and extreme nationalism. Throughout the next few months, Hitler whipped mobs into frenzy and gained new supporters.

After the government proved powerless to drive the French from the Ruhr, Hitler decided that the time had come for a nazi march on Berlin in imitation of Mussolini's famous march on Rome the year before. He chose November 8, the fifth anniversary of the leftist revolution in Bavaria, to launch his crusade to overthrow the republic and to seize control of the Reich. That evening Gustav von Kahr, the state commissar for Bavaria, was scheduled to address a nationalist meeting at the Burgerbräu Celler in Munich. After the official had spoken for half an hour, Hitler entered the crowded room with his Iron Cross prominently displayed and waved a revolver. As a policeman tried in vain to stop him, Hitler jumped on a beer-stained table and shot his weapon at the ceiling. The explosion echoed through the hall, causing the speaker to stop in the middle of his speech, and all eyes in the room focused on the strange figure in a frock coat. His eyes blazing, Hitler cried that the revolution had begun and announced the deposition of the Bavarian and the national governments. He told the shocked crowd that the Storm Troopers had occupied the army and police headquarters and had sent six hundred men to surround the hall.

At this point Göring calmed the crowd with jokes about Bavarian beer, while Hitler led the startled Kahr, Lossow, and Hans von Seisser, the head of the police, into an adjoining room, after sending for Field Marshal von Ludendorff. In the small room he brandished his smoking weapon at the frightened men and told them that a new government had been formed with Ludendorff's support and that they had no choice but to join it. In a dramatic gesture, he threateningly informed his captives that he had four bullets in his gun, three for them and one for himself. As the three prisoners pondered their next step, the nazi leader calmly pointed the revolver at his own head, stating that if he failed in his effort, he would be dead the next morning. History would have been radically different had Hitler lived up to his promise. Intimidated by a madman waving a gun at them, the three terrified men had no choice but to agree to his terms. Later they claimed that as they left the hall, Lossow had whispered to them that they should humor Hitler until they could get away from him.

Assured of support from his captives, Hitler returned to the hall to triumphantly announce the formation of a new Bavarian government under Kahr and a new national government led by himself, with Ludendorff as head of a new nationalistic army. Lossow would serve as minister of war, and Seisser as head of the national police. Leaving his comrades to speak to the crowd, Hitler then returned to the small room. By this time Ludendorff, who had joined the Nazi movement because of the influence of his girlfriend, Mathilde Kemnits, had arrived. The field marshal first denounced Hitler for acting without consulting him and then announced to the startled company his decision to join the revolt. Excited, Hitler once again returned to the hall where, amid the cheering of the people, he made a short speech, after which all present stood up and sang "Deutschland über Alles." However, at this crucial moment Hitler had to leave the scene of his triumph to settle a quarrel among the Brown Shirts on the best method for seizing the engineer's barracks. While he was gone the hall emptied, and Kahr, Lossow, and Seisser left. Once free of Hitler's intimidation, they immediately denounced the revolt and began planning a counterattack.

It appeared that at last the radical right had won and overthrown the hated republic, but by allowing the crowd and his prisoners to leave, the would-be head of the Reich made a serious mistake that would spell his defeat. Kahr, free of Hitler's threats, moved the Bavarian government to Regensburg and issued a proclamation denouncing the promises he had made in the beer hall and dissolving the National Socialist party. Upon receiving word of the outbreak of the Nazi revolt, Seeckt telegraphed Lossow that he must immediately suppress the National Socialists or he would send federal troops to occupy Munich. Prince Rupprecht, the pretender to the Bavarian throne, whose support Hitler had hoped to win, issued a statement condemning the Nazis and calling on the government to use force if necessary to restore order. Thus, even before it had begun, Hitler's march on Berlin was doomed to failure.

Outside the empty hall the Storm Troopers were carrying out their part of the revolution. By morning over three thousand brown-shirted men stood ready to march. Storm Troopers seized the *Munich Post,* a social democratic newspaper, smashing the presses. Across the city, Röhm led a force that captured the offices of the War Ministry and surrounded the building with machine gunners and a wall of barbed wire. But when a group of Nazis tried to occupy the police headquarters, the officers refused to join the revolt and promptly arrested the attacking force.

After hesitating until dawn because his captives had been allowed to escape, Hitler decided to march on Lossow's headquarters with Ludendorff, believing that the people of Munich would join the nazi throng as it passed through the city. At 11:00 A.M. on November 9, Hitler and between two and three thousand followers left the Bürgerbräu Celler on the south bank of the Isar River on their way to the center of the city. As the horde proceeded, the streets echoed with the sound of marching men passionately singing patriotic songs. At the head of the procession walked a man carrying a large swastika-adorned flag, followed by Hitler and the tall Ludendorff. The parade reached the square outside the Gothic city hall and turned down Residence Street toward Odeon Square. However, a lone company of police stood at the place where the street opened into the picturesque square, which was bordered on one side by the palace, on another by the Hall of Soldiers, and on the third by the towering baroque

Theathina Church. Although the approaching mob outnumbered the police, the small street had forced the Nazis to form a narrow column. It was a dramatic scene as the breathless police waited for the revolutionaries to approach. At a crucial moment one of the Nazis, Ulrich Graf, ran forward calling on the opposing force not to shoot because Ludendorff and Hitler were coming. Hitler shouted a demand for the police to surrender, but the brave defenders of the republic stood their ground. Suddenly a shot rang out, and a shower of bullets filled the air. To this day no one knows who fired first, the police or the Nazis. Hitler fell or was pulled down by one of his followers, as the panic-stricken mob ran for cover. Only the aging field marshal kept his nerve amid the stampede. He believed that no one would dare fire on his exalted person. When the smoke cleared, the mob that seconds before had filled the street with their songs as they marched had vanished. The lifeless bodies of sixteen Nazis and three police lay on the blood-stained pavement. Hitler, who the night before had pledged his life to his cause, was filled with terror and joined his fleeing men, escaping in a yellow car. Göring, wounded severely in the groin, was smuggled across the nearby Austrian border by his wife. Thus, the first nazi attempt at revolution ended just as quickly as it had begun.[7]

On November 11 the police arrested Hitler at Uffing, where he hid in the home of Ernst Hanfstängl. On February 26, 1924, the government put the nazi leader, Röhm, Wilhelm Frick, who was a pro-nazi official of the Munich police, and Ludendorff on trial for treason. In a sensational trial covered by the world press, Hitler defended his actions, turning the sessions into a political platform and gaining for the first time an international audience. On April 1 the court sentenced Hitler to five years in prison. The other defendants received their freedom. Thus, a man who had led a movement to overthrow the Weimar Republic by force received a penalty that would enable him to live to fight another day. Despite the failure of the Beer Hall Putsch, the national socialist movement had become a major factor in German politics. Led by a fanatical demagogue, the Nazis appealed to many disillusioned Germans who sought an explanation for the economic and political ruin that had followed the First World War. With the help of effective organizers like Göring, Röhm, and others, Hitler had created a movement, complete with its own private army, that would eventually triumph and bring the downfall of the attempt to turn Germany from an autocratic monarchy into a liberal democracy.

9

The Stresemann Era

In 1923 the Weimar Republic seemed ready to fall under the weight of many unsolvable problems. The French had entrenched themselves in the Ruhr and refused to discuss a compromise. The mark had become worthless in the wake of an inflation that had destroyed the possibility of prosperity. The pressure of the economic crisis and seeming inability of the government to deal with the Allies led many Germans to join the extremist parties that threatened the existence of the republic. The news of Hitler's Beer Hall Putsch further shook the German people, and many began to wonder when, not if, the republic would fall. To solve the many problems that faced the Reich, a strong leader was needed, someone with the courage to take whatever steps necessary to save the government and to restore economic order. Such a man was Gustav Stresemann.

Gustav Stresemann, a short man with a small moustache and thinning hair, dominated the history of Germany from 1923 to 1929 through decisive action that brought an era of relative stability. Stresemann was born on May 10, 1878, the son of a Berlin innkeeper and beer distributor. After completing his secondary education, he entered the Universities of Berlin and Leipzig, where he studied history, economics, and literature. In 1900 he received his doctorate for his dissertation on the growth of the bottled beer industry in Berlin. Young Stresemann then took a position as administrative assistant to the German Chocolate Maker's Association, beginning his career in business. Successful in this venture, he became an officer in the national organization of light industry. However, his attention turned to politics, and he joined the National Liberal party in 1903. He succeeded in politics as he had in business. In 1907, after serving on the city council of Dresden, he became at twenty-eight the youngest member of the Reichstag. Through his vast knowledge of economics, he rose to national prominence and became one of the founders of the German People's party in 1918. On August 13, 1923, he became chancellor of the Reich. For the next six years, first as chancellor then as foreign minister, Stresemann was the most important man in the Weimar Republic. His policy was directed toward restoring economic stability through negotiating a reduction of the reparation payments and attempting to persuade the Allies to revise the harsh terms of the Treaty of Versailles. In this effort, he forged an alliance with the powerful German military that followed a policy of close cooperation with the foreign office in its effort to lay the foundation for a rebirth of German power. Stresemann also convinced the army to acknowledge the supremacy of the executive branch of the government in the area of foreign affairs, although the generals would never accept the superiority of the Reichstag.[1]

His first task in his new position was to deal with the French in the Ruhr. The Germans had failed in the policy of passive resistance because Paris simply brought in Frenchmen to work the mines and the railroads. On September 26, 1923, Stresemann ended passive resistance and attempted to open negotiations with Paris. However, the French refused to discuss the issue and once again demanded guarantees that the Germans would make the reparation payments. Unable to deal directly with the stubborn French, Stresemann adopted a new plan. He instructed the individual businessmen in the Ruhr to negotiate with the French themselves, promising that the German government would repay any special expenses incurred while delivering the reparations. This policy worked, and by November 23 the situation had cooled considerably.

With a method found to deal with the French, Stresemann turned to the complex economic crisis. On November 12, 1923, he appointed Hjalmar Schacht special currency commissioner under Hans Luther, the minister of finance. Schacht introduced a drastic and successful scheme to deal with the inflation. On November 16 he announced that all real estate and industrial equipment in the Reich would be mortgaged. A new bank called the Rentenbank would be established to hold these mortgages and to issue a new currency backed by them called the Rentenmark. Furthermore, the Rentenbank would give the government 1.2 million Rentenmarks with which to buy the old Reichmarks at a rate of one Rentenmark to one trillion old marks. At the same time, the government began a program of austerity by balancing the budget and removing all unnecessary officials and workers from the federal payroll. Schacht's bold policy succeeded. The currency stabilized at last, and some form of economic stability came to Germany for the first time since the end of the First World War.

The inflation had several drastic effects on the German people. It destroyed the hard-earned savings of the middle class, causing many to lose faith in republican government and to look back with fondness to the reign of William II, when times had been better. Speculators took advantage of the situation by buying up lands, factories, and industrial equipment with inflated currency. The inflation enabled the German government to pay completely the national debt. Thus, although the decisive policies of Stresemann and Schacht had brought an end to the economic chaos, they would never be able to undo the harm that the inflation had done to the German people.

Stresemann and Schacht's program was not without its drawbacks, for fiscal restraint severely curbed payments to the unemployed, and many resented the introduction of the Rentenmark. The Rhineland, where the workers had been without work since the French invasion, was the center of resistance to the new economic policy. The businessmen of the region resented the abandonment of the old currency, and several bankers in Cologne announced that they would not accept the Rentenmark. Louis Hagen, president of the chamber of commerce of Cologne, proposed the establishment of a new Rhenish currency to be backed solely by gold and suggested that the people of the Rhineland look to Paris for support in their opposition to the economic policies of Berlin. Naturally, the French and their Belgian allies took every opportunity to encourage dissatisfaction with Berlin, in hopes that the German Reich could be weakened and a French satellite could be established in the occupied regions. On October 21 an armed band supported by the French and Belgians occupied the city hall of Aachen and announced the foundation of a new separate Rhenish state. Armed uprisings followed in Koblenz, Bonn, Trier, Mainz, and Wiesbaden. Dr. Adam Dorten proclaimed the birth of a Republic of the Rhine, while a farmer named Heinz Orbis founded the Republic of the Palatinate.

However, the people of the Rhineland and the Palatinate had no desire to accept the puppet government of Paris and rallied to the support of Berlin. They refused to obey orders from Dorten's government, and in November farmers near Bonn killed one hundred eighty separatists during a bloody confrontation. Other German patriots captured prominent supporters of Dorten and carried them out of the occupied areas to face charges of treason. Thus, the Republic of the Rhine fell as fast as it had arisen. On January 9, 1924, loyal Germans shot and killed Heinz Orbis and four of his followers, ending the short life of the Republic of the Palatinate. The final defeat of the separatists was in Pirmasens, where the people set fire to the city hall and killed seventeen separatists trying to flee the flaming building.

Although the Rentenmark and the economic policies of Stresemann brought an end to the inflation, and the effort to tear the Rhineland from Germany met with violent resistance, political stability did not follow. On November 23 the Social Democrats, who objected to the Rentenmark because they believed it favored the rich and neglected the interests of the worker, forced Stresemann to resign. Dr. Wilhelm Marx, a prominent judge and leader of the Center party, tried to form a new government with Stresemann as foreign minister. However, this too met with failure because the Social Democrats and Nationalists refused to support Marx unless he endorsed tax reform and the establishment of an eight-hour work day. Unable to form a cabinet, the government dissolved the Reichstag and called for elections on May 4, 1924.

The election of 1924 showed the discontent of the people with the republic and its political leaders and an ominous growth of radicalism. The Communists grew from four to sixty-two delegates. The Nationalists gained twenty-five members and emerged with ninety-five, to become the second-largest party in the Reichstag. The Nazis, who had formed a coalition with several other radical groups, won thirty-two seats and entered the parliament for the first time. Although the Center lost only a few delegates, the other moderate factions lost heavily; the People's party lost one-third of their former strength, while the Democratic party lost one-fourth of their seats. Although the Social Democrats lost only two seats and remained the largest party in the Reichstag, they did not recapture the Ministry. Instead, after failing to persuade the Nationalists to join the government, President Ebert reappointed Marx, with Stresemann as foreign minister.

The Germans were not alone in their opposition to the French invasion of the Ruhr. The British, ever mindful that economic chaos in Germany could harm English trade, resented the failure of Paris to discuss the plans to occupy the Ruhr before taking action. Some in

London believed that the occupation of the Ruhr would make it more difficult to collect reparation payments from the angry Germans. London appealed to the United States for assistance in an effort to force the French to change their policy. The Americans also objected to the French action, and Secretary of State Charles Evans Hughes called for a reassessment of the reparations question during an important speech in New Haven, Connecticut. Unable to resist the combined pressure of London and Washington, Paris agreed on November 20 to call a conference of the Allies to discuss the whole issue of reparations and the method of payment.

On January 15, 1924, the representatives of the Allies met in Paris. After long debates the conference recommended a series of proposals known as the Dawes Plan, named after the chairman of the sessions, Charles G. Dawes of the United States. The Allies agreed that before Germany could meet the reparations, it must have a stable currency and a balanced budget and that the Germans could pay approximately 2.5 billion marks a year. However, the Allies realized that before the Germans could pay that amount, economic recovery would have to begin. Therefore, they required the Germans to deliver only 110 million gold marks in 1926. The next year the amount would increase to 500 million gold marks, and after 1928 to 1,250 million gold marks annually. The diplomats also decided that at first only one-fourth, and later only one-half, of the payment would come directly from the German government. The rest would come from a tax on transportation and through dividends from large industrial corporations and the railroad system, which was to be placed under an international commission. Finally, the Allies decided to take control of the German National Bank from the government and to place it in the hands of the International Grand Council, although the board of directors would remain under German control.

In July and August 1924, the representatives of the Allies met to consider the recommendations of the Dawes commission. Stresemann tried to persuade them to discuss the evacuation of the Ruhr, but they refused to consider this issue. Eventually the German foreign minister won a private promise from the French representative, Edouard Herriot, that he would work for the removal of the French forces from Germany. He kept his word, and the French left the Ruhr by August 25, 1925. Prime Minister Ramsay MacDonald of England wanted to reach agreement with the French and, after several discussions, the Allies officially approved the Dawes Plan.

However, the Dawes Plan met with serious opposition within Germany. Although the government had endorsed the program as early as April 16, important provisions required the approval of the Reichstag. The law placing the German National Railroad under international control required a two-thirds majority of the German parliament because it meant a change in the constitution. Although the Center and People's parties supported the legislation, the approval of the Nationalist party, the second largest faction in the Reichstag, was required for passage. The leading party of the right was reluctant to support a program that many believed would allow the Allies to further enslave the German people. The party itself consisted of large ideological groups that violently opposed the bill. The Pan-Germans in the Nationalist party were determined to resist all efforts to reach agreement with the Allies, and the monarchists refused to cooperate with the Weimar government.

The supporters of the Dawes Plan put great pressure on the members of the Nationalist party in an effort to guarantee passage of the legislation. The Center and People's parties offered membership in the government if the right dropped its opposition. They even threatened to resign and appeal to the people in an election if the plan failed to gain approval. However, the most important effort to persuade the Nationalists came from traditionally conservative circles. The industrial and agricultural interests hoped that agreement with the Allies would restore the shattered economy. Even Hans von Seeckt announced support for the Dawes Plan, hoping that agreement with the Allies on the reparations issue would cause the French to withdraw their troops from the Ruhr. On August 28, as the Allies and the German people waited breathlessly, the Reichstag voted on the enabling legislation. About half of the members of the Nationalist party yielded to pressure and the bills passed. On September 1, 1924, under the direction of Parker Gilbert, an American named by the Allies, the Dawes Plan went into effect. It brought new life to the German economy, and a new Reichmark, backed by gold, replaced the Rentenmark. Under the Dawes Plan, which lasted until the adoption of the Young Plan in 1929, the Germans paid 7,970 million gold marks in reparations.[2]

Stresemann's success in dealing with the Allies and the economic recovery that followed caused the voters to express a renewed confidence in the republic in the election of December 7, 1924. The moderate parties won new strength. The Social Democrats gained thirty-one additional seats and the People's party, and the Center and Democratic parties each won three to six additional seats. Although the German Nationalists gained six new delegates, the other extremist parties lost much of their support. The Nazis lost over half and the Communists more than one-fourth. President Ebert turned to Hans Luther, who was able to organize a coalition government of moderate parties.

Just as it seemed that Germany was at last on the road to economic and social recovery from the setbacks of the past two years, President Ebert died on February 28, 1925. The election of a new president reopened the political strife and ended in a major victory for the right. Since Ebert had been chosen by the National Assembly, the election of his successor would be the first national election for a chief of state ever held in German history. On March 29 the people went to the polls to elect one of seven candidates from the major parties and several from the minor parties to the highest post in the government. Karl Jarres of the Nationalists, with 10,416,655 votes, and Otto Braun of the Socialists, with 7,802,496 votes, were the leading candidates. However, the other contenders had won enough support to deny Jarres the majority required by the constitution.

In the new election, the leaders of the various parties realized that as long as each faction supported one of its members, the chance of success would be slim. The Center and Social Democrats formed the People's Block behind former Chancellor Wilhelm Marx. He was a moderate who was acceptable to both the moderate left and the moderate right. Alarmed by the popularity of Marx, the conservative parties decided to put forward a popular war hero, Field Marshal Paul von Hindenburg. Hindenburg, who had retired to his home in Hanover, at first resisted, but finally, on April 9, he announced his acceptance of the candidacy of the coalition of the German People's party and the Nationalists party, which had formed the Reich Block. After a short campaign, during which Hindenburg appealed to the nationalism of the people and Marx to their desire for peace and economic order, the people gave Hindenburg 14,655,766 votes, Marx 13,751,615, and Ernst Thälmann of the Communists 1,900,000. Because the constitution required only a plurality for election on the second ballot, Hindenburg became president of Germany.

The election of Hindenburg indicated the true attitude of many Germans; they decided to support one of the chief representatives of the old order and to reject the man put forward by the parties that had created the republic. Hindenburg, a monarchist at heart, only tolerated the constitution as a temporary form of government. He was dedicated to his task and tried to follow the law. However, he was seventy-eight at the time of his election, and as he became more senile, he grew more and more dependent on his advisers. He viewed the military as his personal sphere of influence and considered Seeckt an arrogant man who tried to deprive him of his just authority. When Seeckt caused an uproar in 1926 by allowing the eldest grandson of the exiled kaiser to participate as a temporary volunteer in military maneuvers, the president supported the demand of the minister of war for his resignation. Seeckt yielded and went to China to assist Chiang Kai-shek in his struggle with the Communists between 1933 and 1935. Hindenburg then appointed General Wilhelm Heys, a member of his staff during the war, chief of the army. A year later the president's control of the army became complete when Gessler resigned in the wake of charges that he had allowed an official of the Ministry of War to lose 20 million marks through speculation. Hindenburg then named Gröner minister of war.[3]

At the same time that the right had captured the highest position in the national government, the chances for international peace were better than they had been at any time since the end of the First World War. The League of Nations began a series of negotiations designed to guarantee that Europe would never again become a battlefield. On October 2, 1924, the League endorsed the Geneva Protocol. This agreement, the work of Prime Minister Ramsay MacDonald of England and Eduard Beneš of Czechoslovakia, proposed that all nations agree to settle disputes by compulsory arbitration and branded any country that refused to submit its case to a third party an aggressor. However, the Geneva Protocol died because MacDonald fell from power and Stanley Baldwin, his conservative successor, refused to commit Great Britain to the plan.

At this moment Stresemann stepped in and salvaged the effort to insure peace in Europe. The German foreign minister, afraid that France and England would reach a solution to their disagreements, leaving Germany without the ability to play the Allies off against each other, offered on February 9, 1925, to guarantee the western borders of Germany as defined by the Treaty of Versailles. The British foreign secretary, Austen Chamberlain, responded to Stresemann's proposal by opening discussions with Paris. The French foreign minister, Aristide Briand, demanded that Germany also guarantee its eastern boundaries and join the League of Nations. Stresemann, like many Germans, refused to acknowledge the legitimacy of the Polish Corridor, and for a while it seemed that the discussions would end in failure. However, the British were not interested in the fate of Poland and persuaded Briand to drop his demand.

With initial agreement reached, the foreign ministers of Germany, Britain, France, the United States, Italy, Poland, and Belgium met at Locarno, Switzerland, on October 5, 1925, to hammer out the final terms of the agreement. The conference produced a series of treaties guaranteeing the Franco-German and German-Belgium frontiers and paved the way for Germany to become a member of the League of Nations. Stresemann proved to be a successful diplomat and won a concession from the members of the conference, who agreed that a nation would only be obligated to participate in sanctions imposed by the League as far as it was militarily capable of such action. Since Germany was required to remain weak militarily, Berlin was automatically excused from the obligation to lend troops to the League. The members of the conference signed the Treaty of Locarno on December 1, 1925, and Germany took its place as a full member of the League of Nations.[4]

The "spirit of Locarno" that resulted from the agreement meant that at last Germany became a respected member of the family of nations and that a new era of international cooperation had begun. For the next several years, international tension remained at a low level. The growth of understanding and the feeling of goodwill reached a high point when the signatories of the Treaty of Locarno signed the Kellogg-Briand Pact. This agreement, the result of a joint effort by Briand and Secretary of State Frank B. Kellogg of the United States, outlawed war as a means of solving international problems. It seemed that the era when nations resorted to violence was at an end and that no longer would the specter of death and destruction haunt Europe. However, the good intentions of the leaders of Europe could not keep the peace, and almost ten years later they would be locked in a new war that would surpass even the First World War in its horrors. Perhaps had they solved the knotty problem of reparations more effectively and taken steps to solve the conflict caused by the Polish Corridor, the Kellogg-Briand Pact would have become more than just a scrap of paper.

Upon learning of the new relations between Germany and the western powers, the leaders of the Soviet Union feared that Berlin would abandon the Treaty of Rapallo. The Russian foreign commissar, Gregory Chicherin, went to Berlin to discuss the future of German-Soviet relations and to try to win assurances that the Reich would not turn its back on Moscow. Stresemann proved to be as effective a negotiator with the Russians as he had been with the French and British, and he signed the Treaty of Berlin on April 24, 1926. This agreement reaffirmed the Treaty of Rapallo and pledged both nations to seek friendship and understanding on all economic and political questions. The pact also provided that if either nation were attacked without provocation, the other would declare its neutrality and refuse to participate in an economic boycott aimed at the warring power. Stresemann followed the signing of the treaty with assurances to the British and French that the agreement between Germany and the Soviet Union would in no way hinder Berlin's obligations to the League of Nations. Thus, under the guidance of Stresemann's able hand, Germany had reached accord with both Moscow and the western powers and had removed the stigma of the First World War.

The Dawes Plan and the Treaties of Locarno and Berlin marked the beginning of a new era of stability for the Weimar Republic. Luther continued to govern with the support of the moderates until May 1926, when once again Marx became chancellor. Only two significant squabbles broke the relative calm. The first concerned the question of the property of the former royal houses. Although the princes had lost all political power during the revolution, they still held vast quantities of wealth, including luxurious castles. The Social Democrats and Communists campaigned vigorously for the passage of a law confiscating the princes' holdings and giving them to the state. However, the nationalists, arguing that such an act would violate the property rights of the royal families, fought any attempt to deprive them of their wealth. On June 20, 1926, the German people voted on the issue, and 14,455,184 voted to take the princes' holdings while about one million favored letting them keep their possessions. However, since the constitution required that a majority of all registered voters approve the measure, it failed, and the princes retained their wealth. Yet the vote is important because it shows that a large number of Germans had turned from the monarchists.

The second controversy that shook Germany in the mid-1920s concerned the role of religion in the public schools. The constitution gave the federal government the power to control education but left the question of religious instruction unanswered. As a result, three types of schools had developed: schools where pupils of all confessions attended and received religious instruction separately according to their affiliation, schools belonging to a single religious group, and secular schools without religious instruction. In July 1927 Walter von Keudell, the minister of the interior, introduced legislation that would place all schools under state regulation and give confessional schools the same status as secular or interdenominational establishments. The Social Democrats, opposed to all religious influence over education, fought the legislation with such determination that a crisis ensued, causing Marx to resign and call for new elections on May 20, 1928.

The results of the election showed a definite turn against the radical right and toward the left, and the moderate parties lost several important seats. The German Nationalists lost thirty delegates, and the National Socialists returned only twelve of the fourteen men they had sent to the previous session. The Social Democrats emerged with renewed strength, gaining twenty-two additional seats, for a total delegation of 153. The Communists elected fifty-four deputies. The division of the Reichstag between the rival parties denied any one group the majority necessary for the formation of a government. Finally, the Social Democrats once more returned to the chancellorship when Hermann Müller formed a coalition government. Once again Stresemann became foreign minister. Thus, in 1928 the republic seemed relatively safe from the attacks of the radical right, but in a few years, as a new economic crisis developed, the right would again threaten the very existence of the Weimar Republic.

Although the reforms of Stresemann had led to a brief period of economic stability, recession gripped the German people by 1925. The inflation had left prices artificially high, and in 1925 businesses began to fail, causing a new wave of unemployment to spread across the Reich. Two million men lost their jobs, and another two million worked shorter hours for less pay. The renewed economic problems caused many industrialists to seek a solution through the formation of cartels that would eliminate competition while holding prices at a reasonable level. Meanwhile, the Frankfurt firm of I. G. Farben gained control of the German chemical and dye industry, and the United Steel Works dominated the steel industry. Other German industrialists began to study the techniques of the Americans and introduced new and more efficient machines and methods to increase productivity and to save manpower. Under the influence of the new organization of industry and automation, the recession began to end.

In 1926, as the British coal miners went out on strike, the Germans moved in to sell coal to markets that before had belonged to the English. Foreign trade improved as the "spirit of Locarno" began to be felt in economic circles, and by 1927 Germany began to experience the first real prosperity since the end of the First World War.

Despite the onset of good times, the workers continued to remain in a difficult position. The modernization of the factories decreased the need for skilled workers, and the inflation made the eight-hour day and the shop councils obsolete. Even with the short recovery, unemployment remained a chronic problem during the Weimar years. By 1929 more than three million workers had lost their jobs. The general decline in the status of the worker also affected the labor unions. In 1923 the government had recognized the right of collective bargaining and decreed that all disputes not solved through normal channels would be submitted to compulsory governmental arbitration. Nevertheless, this policy only politicized labor relations and led many workers to blame the government and the republic for unsatisfactory conditions.

The domination of industry by the cartels was echoed in agriculture. Despite demands during the revolution that the large Junker estates be broken up and divided among the peasants, the landholders had escaped unscathed and continued to wield great power. They organized into a Green Front that acted as a lobby to protect the large landholders from the demands of the peasants. Through protective tariffs, modernization, and the introduction of better management techniques through electrification, better use of fertilizer, and finally some mechanization, German agriculture began to recover from its postwar depression. By 1928 agricultural output had reached its prewar level. Yet, the next year, the coming of the depression destroyed all the gains of the 1920s and halted the growth of farming.

The effectiveness of the Dawes Plan greatly aided the general recovery of the mid-1920s. Parker Gilbert, the chief Allied representative in Germany, used his influence to persuade American bankers to loan money to German industry to enable it to expand its operations and purchase new equipment. He also exchanged German marks for stronger foreign currencies to meet the reparation payments. Even with the success of the Dawes Plan, Stresemann approached the Allies in September 1928 to request a revision of the program. Six months later the Allies met to discuss Stresemann's request. After much debate, the committee submitted its recommendations to the Germans on April 13. The Young Plan, named after Owen D. Young, the American chairman of the meetings, recommended that Berlin pay amounts ranging from 1,700 million to 2,400 million gold marks annually for a period of seventy-four years.

The Germans were horrified at the size and length of the payments and immediately requested a revision of the plan. Schacht, now president of the German National Bank, offered to pay 1,650 million gold marks annually for no longer than thirty-seven years. When the Allies rejected this, Young suggested a compromise that both sides accepted on June 7, 1929. The revised Young Plan required the Germans to continue payments for fifty-nine years, or until 1988. The first installment would be 1,700 million marks. This amount would gradually increase, until a level of 2,428.8 million would be reached in 1966, for a total of 121,000 million marks in reparation payments. The plan also provided for the establishment of the Bank of International Settlements under the control of all governments concerned, including Germany. The program allowed payments to come from taxes and railway receipts and abolished many foreign controls over the German economy. Finally, if the United States ever consented to cancel any part of the inter-Allied debt, the reparations would be decreased accordingly. On August 6 the Allies met in The Hague and accepted the Young Plan after agreeing to withdraw their troops from the Rhineland.[5]

Stresemann used his influence to persuade Chancellor Müller to accept the Young Plan and persuaded the People's party to remain in the government; unfortunately, he died on October 2. With the death of one of the greatest statesmen of the republic and a defender of the Young Plan, the opposition began to organize a national campaign to reject the decision of the government. Alfred Hugenberg of the Nationalists formed a national committee to fight the plan; he gained the support of Franz Seldte of the Stahlhelm, Heinrich Class of the Pan-German League, and Hitler. They introduced the Law Against the Enslavement of the German People renouncing the "War Guilt Clause" of the Treaty of Versailles and all obligations to pay reparations to the Allies. This law demanded the imprisonment of all officials who agreed to treaties recognizing the validity of the reparations. The national committee organized a campaign designed to whip the German people into an anti–Young Plan frenzy and circulated a petition that slightly over 10 percent of the population signed. However, while many resented the agreement, very few believed that such an extreme act as the imprisonment of Müller was justified. Twelve members of the Nationalist delegation in the Reichstag resigned from the party in protest and formed several small splinter groups. When the election on the law, necessitated by the successful petition drive, took place, only 13.8 percent of the voters favored it, and it failed.

Thus, with the enlightened leadership of Gustav Stresemann during the middle 1920s, the German people had entered a new period of political and economic stability. Through effective diplomacy the Allies had agreed to revise the reparation demands and to accept Germany as a respected member of the family of nations. The stability brought new strength to the supporters of the Weimar Republic, and the radicals declined in influence. Unfortunately, the optimism of 1928 and early 1929 was short-lived. Far across the Atlantic a new economic crisis was brewing that would again plunge the German people into poverty and give new strength to the foes of the Weimar Republic.

10

Society and Culture in Weimar Germany

The decay of the German empire, its bloody death, and the chaos of the Weimar Republic stimulated a flurry of artistic activity. The men and women of letters and art had been among the first to realize the hollow nature of the showy reign of William II and to question the values and methods of the nineteenth century. As the war brought ruin and destruction to the once-proud empire, many sought meaning by attempting to revive the styles of the past, and others created bold new art forms. Some proclaimed the end of all hope for a better world. Still others called for leadership to bring Germany out of its troubles. The authors, artists, and composers of the Weimar Republic showed the diversity of German thought and the deep search for new values to replace those that had been shattered on the battlefields of the First World War. In this quest they experimented with new forms and methods and transformed older styles into a new and vibrant art. Later, when stability came with Stresemann's reign, some artists rejected the experimentation of the first years of Weimar and returned to a more stable form. Simultaneously, the society of Germany in the 1920s reflected both the depth of discontent and the rejection of the old standards.[1]

One of the first artistic movements to leave its impact on the culture of Weimar Germany was impressionism. Beginning in France with the works of painters like Auguste Renoir and Claude Monet, impressionism tried to describe not an object or a moment but the impression it made on the artist and his subject. It began in the latter part of the nineteenth century when men and women rejected the physical pictures of realism for a deeper mental portrayal of their subjects. The new science of psychology and the writings of such men as the great Viennese physician Sigmund Freud helped men and women tear themselves from the patterns of the past to create a new and important form of literature and painting.

Arthur Schnitzler was one of the first followers of the new literature of the mind. His works describe the shallow society of prewar Vienna and attempt to picture, in terms that would later be considered Freudian, the feelings and thoughts of his characters. In *Anatol*, written in 1893, he tells of the inner emotions of a person who finds little in life except an unfulfilling search for sexual pleasure. *Liebelei* (1895) portrays the heartbreak and final suicide of a girl who learns that her lover has been killed for carrying on an affair with a married woman. Although Schnitzler was not a German, his work portrayed in vivid terms the shallow society of prewar Europe and foreshadowed the pessimistic literature of the stormy Weimar years.

The search for meaning by German authors stands out clearly in the writings of Rainer Maria Rilke. Rilke, born and educated in Prague, completed his studies at the University of Munich. He spent his unhappy life trying to find higher values amid the destruction that surrounded him and finally turned to mysticism as an answer to his burning desire to make some sense out of life. He married in 1901, but his restless soul could not accept the confines of marriage, and he left his wife shortly after she gave birth to a daughter. Rilke's quest for meaning took him to far away places like Russia, where he studied the mysticism of the Orthodox monks, and to Paris, where he sought out the great sculptor Auguste Rodin to learn that an artist's chief tool is inspiration.

This great poet began writing before the destruction of the great war swept through Europe and continued writing amid the turmoil of the postwar era. In his *Book of the Hours* (1905), he turns to his experience in Russia to portray the discussions of a simple Russian monk on God, nature, and man. He boldly proclaims the brotherhood of man and the importance of divinity, stating that even in death man finds life. The senseless fighting shook Rilke from his cautious optimism, and in 1923 he produced his famous *Duisner Elegies*. These complex poems, named for the town of Dunio on the Dalmatian coast, where he spent part of 1912, show a man unable to find comfort in a confused universe. Rilke, however, found meaning amid pain and suffering, declaring that even these come from God and must be borne with strength. In *Sonnets to Orpheus,* Rilke carried his mystical conception of art to its highest point, arguing that through poetry man and things are transformed and brought into harmony.

Rilke's cautious optimism amidst pessimism is also found in the work of Thomas Mann. Mann, the son of a wealthy grain merchant from the Hanseatic city of Lübeck, stands out as one of the giants of world literature. He attempted to describe in his works the great social and political conflicts of his era. In his first great work, *Buddenbrooks* (1901), Mann discusses the decline of a wealthy family of his native Lübeck. The younger generation is unable to manage the family business effectively, and they allow their lives to sink into meaninglessness and valuelessness. The story ends with the death of the last member of the family, Hanno, who is incapable of living the creative life of an artist within the materialism of bourgeois society. This theme also serves as the basis for one of Mann's most important works, *Death in Venice*, the story of an artist who meets his death because of his inability to tear himself away from Tadzio, a Russian boy symbolizing beauty, in time to escape an epidemic. *Death in Venice* illustrates the alienation of the true artist from the material world.

Mann's greatest work was written in 1924 as political and economic chaos engulfed his homeland. In *The Magic Mountain,* Mann rises above the confines of mere Impressionism to tell of Hans Castorp's search for the meaning of life. The hero visits a cousin suffering from tuberculosis in a sanatorium in Davos, Switzerland, and becomes entrapped by the magic of his surroundings, which weave a spell around him, causing him to stay in this artificial world. Amid the senseless quest for pleasure through frivolous games and lovemaking, symbolized by his infatuation with Clawdia Chauchat, a Russian woman, he discusses the whole scope of man's intellectual development with an Italian rationalist, Settembrini, and a Jesuit, Naphata. Once, Castorp escapes the Magic Mountain on a skiing outing, only to become blinded by the sterile white of the snow and to flee once again to the safe confines of the sanatorium. Finally, the First World War blasts him from his comfortable existence. He is last seen going to almost certain death on the fields of France. *The Magic Mountain* is one of the most important artistic works of Weimar Germany and world literature. Its author, who received the Nobel Prize for literature in 1929, would flee nazi Germany to seek freedom of expression in the United States.

Mann's effort to reconcile the world and the artist is echoed in the attempt of Hermann Hesse to find harmony between the forces of good and evil. Born in Calw in Württemberg on July 2, 1877, Hesse studied for the ministry at Maubronn but left the seminary to learn a trade as an apprentice to a clockmaker and then as a bookseller. Unable to find satisfaction in business, he finally turned to writing. Hesse, who would receive the Nobel Prize for Literature in 1946, fled his native Germany during the First World War to live until his death in Montagnola, Switzerland. In *Damien,* written during the turmoil of 1919, Hesse tells of a boy who learns that both darkness and light come from the same source. In *Siddhartha* (1922), Hesse, whose father had been a missionary in Asia, describes the quest for the meaning of life by Siddhartha, an Indian youth. The hero leaves the comfort of his Brahmin home to live in the forest as a follower of yoga. Finding that asceticism fails to quiet his troubled soul, Siddhartha becomes a disciple of a beautiful courtesan and tries a life of materialism and sensual pleasure. This, too, ends in disillusionment. Finally, after failing to find an answer in the teachings of the Buddha, Siddhartha becomes a ferryboat driver. There, at the feet of an old man, he learns that only through becoming one with nature can one find the true significance of life. The alienation of man is the theme of *Steppenwolf* (1927). In this work, Hesse tries to tell of the battle between man's animal instincts and the confines of civilization by describing the failure of Harry Haller to flee the restrictions of bourgeois society. In *Narziss und Goldmund* (1930), Hesse reaches a solution to his problem by depicting the monastic life of Goldmund, who renounces the world, and the sensual life of Narziss, who tries to live life to its fullest. He concludes that both men have found a path to God.

Although one usually thinks of impressionism as a movement among French artists like Auguste Renoir and Claude Monet, several German painters produced works of this school. Max Liebermann, born in 1847, the son of a Berlin manufacturer, began his career as a realist. However, by the turn of the century he had rejected the photographic realism of the past to try to capture the essence of his subjects. His landscapes are full of the gray of the sand of his native Brandenburg, and his portraits attempt to capture the inner personality of his subjects. His colors are austere, like his environment. Another German impressionist was Max Slevogt, born in 1868. Slevogt studied at the Academy of Fine Arts in Munich and then left the south to live in Frankfurt and later in Berlin. Unlike Liebermann, Slevogt used vivid color to create his images. He painted bright landscapes and intense psychological portraits. Along with Liebermann and Slevogt, others, like Louis Corinth and Fritz von Uhde, created works that conveyed the inner feeling of their subjects rather than just their outward appearances. Yet, like all impressionists, the German masters of this school created realistic, though not photographic, images.[2]

While some authors and painters tried to describe the emotions of their subjects, others attempted to return to the forms of the past to recapture the idea that beauty and art in themselves had great value. Ricarda Huch wrote historical tales, such as *The Defense of Rome* and *The Battle for Rome,* about the decline of the ruling class in Italy. Hugo von Hoffmannsthal returned to the mystery play of the Middle Ages to create *Everyman,* to be performed in front of Salzburg Cathedral. In *The Rose Cavalier,* he produced a gay tale of love and intrigue in eighteenth-century Vienna to be set to music by the composer Richard Strauss. He also wrote *The Woman Without a Shadow* for the celebrated musician. At the same time, a group of "divisionist" painters attempted to create mosaics on canvas. Men like Curt Hermann and Paul painted vibrant images of color that emphasized the balance between contrasts and outward appearance. Others, like Fritz Mackensen and Fritz Overbeck, tried to recapture the rhythm and mystery of nature in their works. Finally, a group of "draftsmen," like Th. Th. Heine and Karl Arnold, used satirical cartoons to criticize society.

The transformation from untraditional forms to more conservative ones is also found in the music of Richard Strauss. Born in Munich in 1864, the son of a horn player in the court orchestra, Strauss achieved fame at an early age, becoming assistant to Richard Wagner's conductor, Hans von Bülow, when twenty-one. He conducted in 1890 and became the leader of the court orchestra in Munich four years later. Strauss believed that the purpose of art was to reflect the culture of a certain time and people. He wrote many works, of which his tone poems like *Thus Spake Zarathustra* (1896) and *A Hero's Life* (1898), his *Domestic Symphony* (1903), and his many operas still have an important place in the repertoire. The tone poem *Till Eulenspiegel's Merry Pranks* (1895) and his operas *Salome* (1905) and *Elektra* (1909) reject melodious forms to create powerful and untraditional works that combine the large orchestra of romanticism with the new music of dissonance. However, his later works, such as the operas *The Rose Cavalier* (1911) and *Ariadne on Naxos* (1912) are more conservative and represent a return to the melodious forms of romanticism.

Strauss would become a symbol of the radical music of the 1920s and rise to great heights.[3]

The attempt to return to the spirit of romanticism led some authors to try to recreate the disciplined style of the Classical era. Neoclassicism rejected the emotion of neoromanticism and the feeling of impressionism, stressing instead precision of language and the victory of the heroic soul over decadence and pessimism. The most important author to attempt to regain the "noble simplicity and quiet greatness"[4] of classicism was Stefan George. He was born in Rüdesheim in the Rhineland in 1868 and educated at Bingen and Darmstadt. He achieved fame before the First World War as a poet and literary critic, arguing in the pages of *Blätter für die Kunst* ("Pages for Art") that literature must strive for artistic quality without becoming a vehicle for social criticism. However, he soon began to use his art to forward his personal political concepts. In *The Seventh Ring* (1908), George glorified Maximin, a heroic youth who rejects weakness and womanly virtues. During the chaotic years of the First World War and the Weimar Republic, he called for discipline and leadership. In *The War* (1917) he denounced weakness and called for loyalty and devotion to the heroic leader who will bring victory to the fatherland. In 1929, as the depression gripped Germany, he wrote *The New Reich,* proclaiming the need for a great leader to lead the Reich out of its troubles and into a new era of culture in which the German people would revive the splendor of the Holy Roman Empire and its rich traditions. Many of George's ideas laid a foundation for the nazi principle of leadership. Like the National Socialists, he preached the necessity of devotion to duty and unquestioned obedience to a strong leader. However, he was not a follower of Hitler and rejected the nazi movement as a collection of rowdies. Before he died in 1933, he demanded burial in Switzerland rather than in the newly born Third Reich.

George's work inspired a group of dedicated followers to build one of the most important intellectual circles of Weimar Germany. Choosing the biography as their mode of expression, they elevated the major figures of civilization to new heights. Max Kommerell praised Goethe and Herder, while Ernst Bertram rediscovered Nietzsche. Emil Ludwig rejected the dry devotion to scholarship that had characterized the works of German historians since Leopold von Ranke to produce a group of "popular" biographies. Ernst Kantorowicz, a member of the Free Corps during the early years of the republic, wrote a multivolume study of Emperor Frederick II, who emerges as a mighty leader and the creator of the Renaissance through his superhuman feats and his support for the study of the classics of antiquity. George and his disciples helped create a cult of leadership that led many to look for a strong man to lead Germany out of the abyss into which it had fallen. Many would find such a man in Adolf Hitler.

Other artists rejected the discipline of neoclassicism to stress the inner feelings of their subjects as they fought to survive in a depressing world. This art form, called expressionism, was dominated by morbid and grotesque themes that portrayed the hopelessness of human existence. The chief difference between expressionism and impressionism was that impressionism portrayed the impact of outside objects on the mind of a person, while expressionism dwelt on the inner feelings and related these feelings to the outside world. Like impressionism, expressionism began in the prewar years and continued to develop during the Weimar period. Frank Wedekind wrote of the struggle of adolescence in *The Awakening of Spring* (1891), and Heinrich Mann, Thomas Mann's older brother, described the destruction of a teacher by a nightclub performer in *Professor Unrat* (1905). This work served as the basis for one of the most important films of pre-nazi Germany, *The Blue Angel*, which helped Marlene Dietrich gain stardom in 1930. Gottfried Benn used his training as a physician to describe the fleeting nature of life in intense poems that picture the rotting flesh of a cancer victim or the decay of the body of a drowned girl as vermin and rats devour her lifeless flesh. Aldred Döblin discussed the alienation of man in his *Berlin Alexanderplatz*. This novel, written amid the economic and political breakdown of 1929, tells of the failure of a man to reenter society after his release from prison. Döblin uses the impersonal metropolis of Berlin as a symbol for the dehumanizing aspects of modern society.

One of the most important authors to bemoan the depersonalization of the modern world was Franz Kafka. Kafka, born in 1883 in Prague, then a part of the Habsburg Kingdom of Bohemia, studied law at the German University of Prague and earned a tedious living in an insurance office before his death from tuberculosis in a sanatorium near Vienna in 1924. Perhaps more than any other German author, Kafka was able to capture the alienation of man from a society he was unable to understand, much less influence. In *The Trial* he tells about K, an insignificant bank clerk who suddenly finds himself brought before a court for a crime that is never clearly specified. All his efforts to escape his fate end in failure. *The Castle* shows the inability of a newcomer to gain acceptance in a new village, where the lord lives in a forbidding castle. Finally, his short story "The Metamorphosis" tells about a traveling salesman, Gregor Samsa, who awakens one day to find himself transformed into a large insect. He tries vainly to communicate with his former loved ones, who can only react to his new form with disgust. Running through all of Kafka's work is the inability of the small person to cope with the forces that shape his life. In a real sense, Kafka symbolized the loss of optimism that had come with the carnage of the First World War and the troubled times that followed.

German art flowered in the period of expressionism and related movements. The men and women of painting and architecture boldly rejected the old forms of realism and impressionism to create a new and daring form. At the turn of the century Paula Modersohn-Becker paved the way for the new art through the lively use of color and form to illustrate the inner soul of the peasant women and children featured in her work. Even before 1914 several important movements developed to further the new art. In Dresden Ernst Ludwig Kirchner, Erich Hecker, and others formed "The Bridge" to support paintings in an abstract and primitive style. In December 1911 a group of ambitious artists staged an exhibition entitled "The Blue Rider" in Munich, giving rise to another school of German painting. Marianne von Werfkin, Franz Marc, Alexi von Jawlensky, and others emphasized color and stark outlines and rejected realism to uncover the naked soul of their subjects. After the disillusionment of the First World War and the Revolution of 1918–1919, Berlin became the center of a defiant school called DaDa. Like its nonsensical name, the followers of DaDa, Raul Hausmann, George Grosz, and others, rejected all conventions to produce a somewhat unorganized and playful art. Related to DaDa, the surrealistic movement of Max Ernst and Heinrich Hörl created a new and fantastic world of strange people and objects. Finally, Walter Gropius, an architect whose works reveal stark lines and uncluttered clarity of purpose, organized a community of artists and craftsmen in Weimar in 1919 in the Bauhaus. Artists of all types flocked to the Bauhaus, which moved to Dessau in 1925 to produce everything possible, from weaving to painting. Gropius and his followers strove to teach their students the essential unity of art and craft. Through Bauhaus and other schools, artistic endeavor reached new heights that shattered the older and more traditional patterns in a quest for artistic expression.

Max Beckmann and Paul Klee were two of the most important painters of the 1920s. Born in Leipzig in 1884, Beckmann studied at the Weimar Academy and visited Paris. He stood above the confines of any school to create some of the most striking works of any modern artist. Using painting, etching, drawing, and woodcutting, he often distorted his features to show the helplessness of man in his environment. Klee, born in Bern, Switzerland, in 1879, studied at the Munich Art Academy and traveled through Italy. He joined the "Blue Rider" circle in 1911 and went to the Bauhaus in 1920. From 1931 until his dismissal by the Nazis, Klee taught at the Düsseldorf Academy. While Beckmann's works maintain some semblance of reality, Klee's paintings are totally fantastic. Often using stick figures, he attempts to reflect his ideas through dreamlike illusions. Beckmann and Klee represent the ultimate rejection of the realistic painting of the nineteenth century and the new devotion to the abstract.

The era of expressionism also saw the development of important new forms of music through the work of Arnold Schönberg. Born in Vienna in 1874, he began to teach himself to play the violin and even to compose at eight. While working in a bank to support his family after his father's death, Schönberg studied a brief time under Alexander Zemlinsky, his only teacher. Finally, after playing in amateur orchestras and conducting a worker's chorus, he began his career as music director of the Buntes Theater in Berlin in 1901. He returned to Vienna a few months later to teach such important musicians as Alban Berg and Anton Webern. He joined the Austro-Hungarian army during the First World War and served as professor of composition at Berlin Academy of Arts from 1924 until the advent of the Third Reich. He believed that music must provide a revelation of a higher existence that man must continually strive to reach. His first works, such as the tone poems *Transfigured Night* (1899) and *Pelles and Melisande* (1902–1903), use traditional forms and reflect the influence of romanticism. However, in 1908 in *The Book of the Hanging Garden,* he rejected ths usual concept of tone to create a radical music that lays aside the difference between consonance and dissonance. Schönberg's atonal style matured in his *Three Piano Pieces* (1909) and *Pierrot Lunaire* (1912). In 1923 he unveiled a new technique utilizing twelve tones, instead of the usual octave, in his *Five Piano Pieces.* His compositions, many of which are difficult for the untrained ear, represent the height of expressionism in German music and have had a significant impact on the development of twentieth-century music.

The expressionist movement had an important influence on the newly developed art of motion pictures. In 1920 the public of Berlin saw Erich Pommer and Robert Wiene's film, *The Cabinet of Dr. Caligari*. Based on a story by Hans Janowitz and Carl Mayer, it takes place in the mind of Francis, a madman confined to an insane asylum. He fantasizes that a certain Dr. Caligari, who travels about showing his somnabulist, Cesare, is using hypnotism to force Cesare to commit terrible crimes. In his dreamworld, Francis follows Caligari to an insane asylum, only to learn that Caligari was its director and had gone mad. The film ends with the revelation that the whole story is the product of Francis's diseased mind and his cure. Robert Wiene, the director, used expressionistic sets and lighting to create a set of eerie images on the screen to symbolize the insanity of the times. This film provided the example for other motion pictures that expressed the instability of early Weimar Germany.[5]

The destruction of older forms of artistic expression paralleled the rejection of all forms of traditional morality in the society at large. Faced with continuing economic and political chaos, many Germans sought escape through an orgy of hedonism. Berlin became the center of the new cult of decadence. In dozens of bars, amusement parks, and theaters, thousands forgot their troubles and drank themselves into a stupor. Women, liberated from the confines of the past, announced their freedom by smoking in public, dressing in the new style of the flapper, and openly flaunting promiscuity and sexual perversion. The wild strains of American jazz drove the waltz from the ballrooms, and new dance crazes, like the Charleston and Black Bottom, shocked traditionalists. Nothing was sacred in the cabarets and nightclubs of the German capital; performers ridiculed everyone and everything. Men dressed as women to attend transvestite balls by the thousands. High school boys earned extra money by dressing in female clothing and selling their favors on the streets. From Berlin the cult of decadence spread to other cities, as all Germany joined in the bacchanalia.[6]

However, the experiments of expressionism did not destroy reality completely. The uneasy calm of the Stresemann era led to the flowering of still another artistic school, the New Matter of Factness, which rejected the extremes of expressionism to emphasize the real world. The terror of the war and the senseless death of thousands of young men at the beginning of their lives formed a major theme for the literature of the period. Erich Maria Remarque wrote *All Quiet on the Western Front* in 1929 to show in graphic detail the life of the frontline soldier in the stench and filth of the trenches. However, Ernst Jünger, influenced by Nietzsche, glorified the war as a means to break the chains of the past. In *The Storm of Steel* (1920) he told of his experiences in battle and praised the war as a liberator that had killed the sentimental humanism of the past and marked the birth of a new world, in which technology would lead man to great achievements. In *The Worker* (1932) he tells of a new society led by the technician and soldier, who would destroy the old Christian virtues and give birth to a new era of greatness.

Other authors criticized the society of the past but, unlike Jünger, turned leftward. The most important such writer was Bertolt Brecht, born of an upper-middle-class family in Augsburg in 1898. Brecht studied medicine at the University of Munich, where he saw firsthand the gory destruction of his fellow human beings by the war. His experiences shattered the bourgeois idealism of his youth, and Brecht dropped out of school. Instead of becoming a physician, he turned to writing to express his belief that capitalism had reduced man to the level of an animal and had been responsible for the suffering of the Weimar era. In so doing, he developed a new form of drama that rejected the unities of Aristotle and attempted to influence the audience through slides, songs, and other such techniques designed to alienate the spectator and to constantly remind him that he was only watching a play. Brecht's dramas are a picture of the disillusionment felt by many in the wake of the First World War. In his first play, *Baal*, written in 1918, as Germany struggled to survive the defeat, he tells of a man who rejects all morality to live as a beast, murdering and raping his fellow humans. In *Drums in the Night* (1922) he utilizies the turmoil of the Revolution of 1918–1919 as a background for the story of a returning prisoner of war who comes home longing to be reunited with his loved one, only to find her pregnant. Finally, in 1928, in *The Three Penny Opera*, he uses the themes of John Gay's *Beggar's Opera* for a thinly disguised satire of the economic exploitation of his age. In this play, interspersed with songs by Kurt Weill, one of Germany's leading jazz composers, Brecht tells of the beggers in eighteenth-century London and of the misdeeds of Mack the Knife. Brecht continued to produce important works from exile during the nazi era. After the Second World War he rejected the West and sought sanctuary in the newly formed Communist state of the German Democratic Republic.

The rejection of expressionism is also important in the development of music in Weimar Germany and the work of Paul Hindemith. Born in 1895 in Hanau, near Frankfurt, he began his career in a jazz band, too poor to afford formal training. Eventually, through the support of a wealthy businessman, he obtained an education in the Music Academy of Frankfurt. He became the concertmaster of the Frankfurt Opera in 1915 and achieved fame through participation in the Donäusingen Music Festival in 1921. Six years later he went to the Berlin Academy of Arts, where he taught until forced into exile by the Nazis in 1934. Greatly influenced by Johannes Brahms and Johann Bach, Hindemith rejected Schönberg's twelve tones in an attempt to salvage the concept of tonality through a more traditional harmonic system. He tried to bridge the gap between the composer and his audience by a more simplistic style and by producing works for neglected instruments, such as the trombone and double bass. He produced over two hundred fifty pieces, including his operas *Cardilac* (1926) and *Mathis the Painter* (1934), his collections of songs *The Young Maid* (1922) and *The Life of Mary* (1923), and music for youth groups, bands, and radio programs. Like Strauss and Schönberg, Hindemith represents one important aspect of the culture of Germany in the 1920s.

As well as producing a wealth of literary, artistic, and musical works, the Weimar Republic gave birth to several important academic societies. As artists and craftsmen gathered at the Bauhaus, scholars flocked to several centers to conduct their studies. In Hamburg, Aby Warburg founded the Warburg Institute to recapture the spirit of the classics. Warburg, Fritz Saxl, Ernst Cassirer, and others dedicated themselves to the study of human cultural history, producing important studies of philosophy, art, literature, mythology, and religion. Meanwhile, students of psychology gathered at the feet of Max Eitingon, Hanns Sachs, and Karl Abraham in the Psychoanalytical Institute of Berlin. Even Sigmund Freud, the father of modern psychoanalysis, lectured in Berlin on his theories of man and his subconscious. Finally, after 1924 students of political science assembled at the Institute for Social Research of the University of Frankfurt, under the direction of Carl Grünberg, a well-known socialist intellectual.

The study of the past flowered during the Weimar Republic. One group of historians dedicated themselves to proving that their fatherland had not been responsible for the outbreak of the First World War, publishing an impressive collection of documents and secondary works on the subject. Other students of history attacked larger questions. Oswald Spengler, born in Blankenburg in 1880 and educated in mathematics and science at the universities in Munich, Berlin, and Halle, produced one of the most ambitious studies of the philosophy of history in modern times. In 1918 and 1922, as his homeland struggled with the aftermath of a lost war, Spengler published his massive *Decline of the West*. He argued that every civilization possessed a unique culture that belonged to it alone. Comparing civilizations to biological forms, Spengler theorized that every culture passed through several distinct phases and that the West had passed through its period of growth and creativity and had entered its decline. Spengler denounced the materialistic society of the cities and praised the more instinctive feelings of the people of the soil.

Another influential historian of the Weimar era was Friedrich Meinecke, born in Salzwedel in 1862. Unlike Spengler, Meinecke was a professional historian. He served on the faculties of the universities of Strasbourg, Freiburg, and Berlin. He edited the *Historische Zeitschrift* ("The Journal of History") from 1893 until forced to resign by the Nazis in 1935. Meinecke wrote many significant historical works, the most important of which were his *Cosmopolitanism and the Nation State* (1908) and *Machiavellism: The Doctrine of Raison d'Etat and Its Place in Modern History* (1924). Meinecke saw the modern state as one of the dominant factors in history. It shaped the thoughts and actions of its leader to fit its needs. He believed that no ruler, no matter how powerful, was strong enough to resist the might of the state, which forced him to do things he would not normally do to serve its interests.

Although a literary critic and not a historian or political scientist, Moeller van den Bruck had a major impact on the theories of the state. Born in Solingen in 1876, he left secondary school to travel around Germany. He wrote some literary criticism and in 1923 published his most important work, *The Third Reich*. He denounced the Revolution of 1918–1919 as the work of traitors who had betrayed the victorious army. Bruck violently criticized the socialists and liberal founders of the republic as shortsighted men who failed to realize the true needs of Germany. He called for the birth of a new fatherland, or Third Reich, dedicated to the greatness of the German past and embodiment of the true "spirit" of the folk. Nothing, not even race or anti-Semitism, could be allowed to stand in the way of the quest for a new Germany. Bruck called for the destruction of the old parties and economic systems in favor of a nation organized into a hierarchy along the lines of the corporations of the Middle Ages. Bruck had a major impact on German thought. He became a Nazi, and it was no accident that Hitler chose to call his state the Third Reich.

The cult of the folk grew during the Weimar Republic. Forming the foundation of national socialism and influencing other political groups, such as the Nationalists, the religion of the folk continued to spread among the youth. The schools and universities became centers of the movement. Thousands of young people supported the Kapp Putsch and wore swastikas to display their sentiments. Influenced by racist textbooks, some boys even began to play "Aryan and Jew" as others played cowboys and Indians. Youth groups adopted the ideas of the cult of the folk, as racism spread through all elements of society. Even the centers of higher learning were not immune to the growth of racial hatred. In 1919, even before Hitler had gained a following, the fraternities meeting in Eisenach voted to expel Jews and all members who married them. In 1927 the German Students' Organization defied the wishes of the government by calling for the purging of Jewish students from the universities. Anti-Semitic students protested the hiring of Jewish professors, and in 1931 the campuses of the Reich erupted in a series of ugly anti-Semitic riots. Even the faculty failed to stem the growth of racism, and many Jewish professors lost their positions. Thus, the growth of culture during the 1920s had failed to destroy the spread of radical racism and the cult of the folk.[7]

The fall of the empire ushered in a period of daring experimentation in all aspects of German culture. Artists, musicians, and writers rejected the standards of the past to attempt to create bold new forms. At the same time, the wave of pessimism brought with the First World War and the stormy 1920s led men like Kafka and Beckmann to use art to describe the hopelessness of man and his condition. Many sought to escape the terrible reality of inflation and domestic turmoil by falling into hedonism. Others responded to the challenge to traditions by rediscovering the forms of the past and denouncing the excesses of expressionism. Weimar Germany gave birth to a multitude of artists, authors, composers, and scholars, each attempting in his own way to capture the truth. However, the excesses led to a reaction. It was no accident that the official program of national socialism pledged to rescue German art and society from the anarchy into which it had fallen. Many solid citizens responded to the new culture with horror and supported the reactionary programs of the Nazis and other rightist groups. The freedom of Weimar Germany would soon die as a new tyranny would grow to crush all who dared to champion the freedom of the 1920s.

11

The Depression

The cautious optimism of the Stresemann era and the uneasy stability that it brought ended suddenly, when a new economic crisis, which had roots in America, plunged Germany into depression once again. Millions of men and women lost what faith they still had in the republic when they were thrown out of work and forced to wander the streets in search of ways to feed their families and pay the overdue rent. The leaders of Germany, incapable of the vision of an Ebert or a Stresemann, vainly tried to restore economic order. Instead, they only made the situation worse by their failure to tear themselves from the outdated economic concepts of the nineteenth century. As Germany sank deeper into depression, many turned to extremist movements that promised to end the crisis by radical action.

One such group was Hitler's National Socialist party. During the Stresemann era, the nazi movement came to the end of the period of growth of the early twenties and showed signs of becoming a mere footnote to history. However, during this period of stagnation, Hitler was busy laying the foundation for his final confrontation with the republic. He entered Landsberg Prison on November 11, 1923. Here, he lived more as a guest of the state than as a criminal.[1] The authorities allowed him to receive gifts. Emil Maurice, and later Rudolf Hess, served as his personal servant and secretary. He passed his days writing his memoir, which he entitled *Mein Kampf* ("My Struggle"). In this poorly organized and rambling work, Hitler told his life story and outlined the basic concepts of national socialism. In fanatical tirades he denounced the republic as a government of the weak. Hitler preached extreme nationalism and hatred for the Jews. He argued that

Germany needed a strong leader who would destroy the enemies of the "superior" Aryan race. Finally, he demanded that living space for the master race be carved from the lands of inferior peoples. Millions later bought copies of this book, and it became the bible of the Third Reich. In the meantime, deprived of Hitler's active guidance, the party entered a period of dormancy. The führer discouraged any effort to carry on the work without his supervision, lest a potential rival arise.

On December 20, 1924, Hitler became a free man. He immediately set out to revive the fallen fortunes of the national socialist movement. On February 27, 1925, he returned to the Bürgerbräu Celler, the site of the Beer Hall Putsch. There, while four thousand dedicated followers cheered, he announced the rebirth of nazism. However, the Bavarian government knew of the danger of Hitler's rhetoric, and within a few days after his triumphal return to the Bürgerbräu Celler, it forbade him to make further public speeches. All the other states, except Thuringia, Brunswick, Württemberg, and Mecklenburg-Schwerin, followed the example of the southern state, depriving the Nazis of one of their chief weapons. However, the ban was of little avail, for the nazi movement proved impossible to destroy without more radical methods, and the leaders of Germany lacked the courage to blot out the growing cancer. Perhaps, had they realized the great danger of Hitler, and had they taken additional steps, Germany and the world would have been spared the disaster that followed.

However, a more serious threat to Hitler came from within the party itself, through the work of Gregor Strasser. Strasser, the son of a middle-class Bavarian family, had joined the party in 1920. He abandoned his career as a druggist to devote his complete energy to the organization. He became the local leader in Lower Bavaria and participated in the abortive Beer Hall Putsch. Strasser and his brother, Otto, emphasized the socialistic aspects of the party program and refused to acknowledge the absolute authority of Hitler. After the führer's release from prison, Strasser emerged as the leader of the northern wing of the movement, which had headquarters in Berlin. He founded the *Berliner Workers' Paper* and published a biweekly magazine, the *National Socialist Letter.*

Strasser also brought one of the most important future leaders of the Third Reich into the movement, Paul Josef Goebbels, who served as editor of the *National Socialist Letter.* Goebbels was born in the Rhineland town of Rheydt on October 29, 1897, the son of a factory clerk. He was unable to serve as a soldier in the First World War because of his clubfoot and turned his attention instead to studies of philology at the University of Heidelberg, from which he received a doctorate in 1921. While a student he flirted briefly with socialism and communism but rejected the left because of its opposition to nationalism. In his early years Goebbels, who later filled the press and airwaves with hatred for the Jews, was not an anti-Semite. He studied under Jewish professors and for a time was engaged to a girl of Jewish ancestry. After graduation from the university, he tried to become a successful author and journalist, but failed. In 1924 he became friends with several Nazis and met Strasser, who asked him to become editor of the *National Socialist Letter*.[2]

Throughout 1924 and 1925 Strasser and his followers continued to challenge Hitler's leadership. In 1926, during the debate on the fate of the holdings of the former princes, the inevitable conflict developed that destroyed this serious threat to Hitler's control of the party. Strasser, reflecting the more socialistic brand of nazism, demanded that the party endorse the effort to seize the wealth of the former rulers. However, Hitler, who was receiving large donations from the former Duchess of Saxe-Anhalt, violently opposed any effort to deprive the princes of their possessions. On February 14, 1926, Hitler summoned Strasser and his followers to a conference to determine the official stand of the organization on this important issue. He deliberately chose a working day so Strasser's followers, who were mainly workers, could not attend the meeting. After a bitter confrontation between the two men, Strasser lost his support. Even Goebbels, who had once demanded that the party expel Hitler, sided with the majority. Thus, the führer emerged once again as the undisputed leader of the party. Strasser quickly lost his power, although he remained in a position of leadership until his murder by Hitler's supporters during the Blood Purge of June 27, 1934.[3]

With complete control of the party, Hitler set out to revive and strengthen the movement. On July 3, 1926, he presided over the first national rally since 1923. He choose Weimar, the city that had given birth to the hated republic, because it was in Thuringia, one of the few states that did not forbid him to make public addresses. He made Goebbels district leader in Berlin in October 1926. Three years later he appointed this master of the art of welding public opinion his chief of propaganda. Hitler began the reorganization of the Brown Shirts, or Storm Troopers. He found an effective commander in Pfeffer von

Salmon, a former officer of the Free Corps and participant in the Kapp Putsch. Salmon had proven his worth as the leader of the movement in Westphalia and the Ruhr. Under strict instructions that the party would attempt to gain power only through legal methods, he rejected the semimilitary pattern of Röhm, who had resigned in 1924 because of disagreements with Hitler. Instead, Salmon molded the Brown Shirts into a group of effective streetfighters who could beat their opponents into silence. The private army of the party grew to a membership of 60,000, four times its size during the Beer Hall Putsch.

Despite Hitler's success in reorganizing the party, he lost the support of one of his most valuable allies, Ludendorff. The aged field marshal accused the party of failure to combat the influence of the Roman Catholic Church, and he left the party. Ludendorff never rejoined Hitler's supporters, who could not afford to endanger their strength in Bavaria by an open break with Roman Catholicism. In 1933, when his former commander, Hindenburg, appointed Hitler chancellor, Ludendorff telegraphed his opposition, accusing the aged president of handing Germany over to a madman. When Hitler offered Ludendorff a field marshal's baton in April 1935, he indignantly refused. Despite his snubbing of the Third Reich, he received a state funeral with full military honors after his death on December 20, 1937.

Ludendorff's defection signaled the beginning of a major decline in party strength. With the coming of relative stability under Stresemann, men no longer turned to extremism, and national socialism entered a period of retrogression. Despite a membership of 175,000, the Nazis were able to gain only 2.6 percent of the vote in the election of 1928. Even this poor showing allowed them to send twelve delegates to the Reichstag. Although the small nazi group was outnumbered by 479 members of other parties, the Reichstag provided a national platform for the spread of Hitler's ideas. The decision to enter the elections marked an important change in tactics. Hitler and his followers realized that illegal attempts at violent revolution were doomed to failure and that only through legal methods and the subversion of the democratic processes of the republic could the movement ever hope to achieve success.

The short-lived stability that had robbed national socialism of much of its appeal ended abruptly on October 24, 1929, when the New York Stock Exchange crashed. Unable to manage their affairs in the United States, the American banks recalled the short-term loans that had enabled Germany to achieve a measure of prosperity, causing a crippling panic to seize the weak German economy. Vast unemployment again raised its sinister head, and by 1932 six million workers had lost their jobs, bringing the danger of eviction from their homes and starvation to 43 percent of the labor force. At the same time, the national income plunged 20 percent, leaving Germany in the grip of one of the most serious depressions of its history.

The government, deprived of Stresemann's brilliant leadership by his death on October 3, 1929, was unable to halt the spreading crisis. Chancellor Müller resigned on March 27, 1930, after a futile attempt to cope with the chaos. President Hindenburg, in an effort to provide desperately needed leadership, appointed the head of the Center party, Heinrich Brüning, chancellor. Brüning was the son of an upper-middle-class family in Münster. He had studied languages, history, and economics before being swept into the First World War, where he served as a commander of a company of machine gunners on the Western Front. After the peace he rose to prominence as the leader of the Christian Trade Unions, and in 1924 he became a Center deputy in the Reichstag. He won fame for his work on the budget committee, and four years after his election he became the leader of the Center party. Upon his appointment as chancellor in 1930, he was forty-five, the youngest chancellor in German history. Despite his knowledge of politics and economics, Brüning failed to provide the leadership that the Reich so badly needed. He quarreled with Hindenburg, who refused to study his long and complex reports, and lacked the ability to inspire the people. Brüning was a dedicated nationalist who hoped to restore the fatherland to the position lost in the First World War. However, he was too conservative and lacked the vision needed to solve the crisis.[4]

Brüning believed that a balanced budget was the first step in restoring the shattered economy. In 1930 he presented an austerity program that won the approval of the Reichstag because it provided large subsidies to the agrarian interests. However, the rising unemployment doomed his effort to balance the budget. By April 1930 the deficit had risen to 400 million marks, and within a month it had increased to 1.1 billion marks. Dedicated to fiscal responsibility above all, the chancellor proposed to raise badly needed revenue by special taxes on government employees. Although he was able to gain support from the Reichstag for this program, it earned much resentment from the people because the army and police received special exemptions from the tax that other government employees had to pay.

Brüning's program failed to stem the rising crisis and won the opposition of many who demanded decisive action. On July 16, 1930, the Reichstag voted 256 to 193 to condemn his administration. Spurned by the legislature, Brüning took the drastic step of invoking Article 48 of the Weimar constitution, which allowed the government to rule by decree during a national crisis. The departure from democratic form led eventually to dictatorship and paved the way for the Nazi tyranny. Naturally, the leaders of the opposition valiantly fought the chancellor's abandonment of democratic government and introduced a resolution denouncing his attempt to rule without the consent of the Reichstag. Although the proposal lost by a narrow margin, Brüning angrily persuaded President Hindenburg to dissolve the Reichstag and call for new elections, hoping that a new parliament would be more sympathetic to his programs.

The chancellor was mistaken, however, for the spread of deprivation had brought with it a rebirth of extremism. When the German people went to the polls on September 14, 1930, many turned to the simplistic, but attractive, message of national socialism. When the Reichstag reconvened, Wilhelm Frick led 107 rowdy, brown-shirted Nazis into the company of the stunned assembly. Before the fateful election, Hitler's followers had only twelve deputies and did not represent a serious threat to the stability. Now they commanded more members than any other party except the Social Democrats, who held 143 of the 577 seats. At the same time, the Communists emerged with seventy-seven delegates, making it the third largest party in the Reichstag. Thus, a significant number of Germans, driven to desperation by the magnitude of their plight, had turned to radical groups that threatened the existence of the republic. The new strength of the extremists was a blessing for the threatened chancellorship of Brüning, for although his Center party only commanded the allegiance of sixty-eight members of the Reichstag, the terrified Social Democrats agreed to allow him to remain in office, lest the Nazis gain control of the ministry.

The depression was the decisive factor in the growth of national socialism into a large national movement. Many Germans found in Hitler's anti-Semitism a simple reason for their plight. He told them that they had not failed, but that they had been betrayed by the corrupt politicians and money-grabbing Jews. Every new wave of crisis increased the appeal of the Nazi movement. For the first time it attracted large numbers in areas such as East Prussia, where before the outbreak of the depression it had only won the support of a small minority. At the same time, revitalized under the leadership of Ernst Röhm, whom Hitler had called from his exile in Bolivia and placed in charge of his private army on January 5, 1931, the Brown Shirts grew by alarming proportions. In 1931 the Storm Troopers had 170,000 members, and by 1932 almost half a million men marched behind the hooked cross.

As the popular support of the government quickly eroded, the economic crisis continued to spread. Chancellor Brüning lacked the vision to take the bold steps necessary to restore the shattered economy. Unable to realize that a departure from the ineffective economic theory of the past was needed, he attempted to balance the budget, reduce the deficit, and stabilize the currency. He slashed the salaries and pensions of all government officials and cut the budget by two-thirds. At the same time, foreign banks, faced with a deepening panic in their own countries, recalled the short-term loans that had enabled the Germans to meet the reparation demands of the Allies. This further drained the federal budget of desperately needed funds. Brüning's program brought further disaster. At a time when workers stood idle because there was no need for the goods they could produce, the ability of many Germans to buy the surplus wares was curtailed by the austerity of Brüning's budget.

As the distress continued to grow, the Foreign Ministry, inspired by the ideas of Bernhard Wilhelm von Bülow, the nephew of the former imperial chancellor, persuaded Berlin to take the bold step of negotiating a customs union with Austria. It was hoped that this would ease the depression by providing for a free flow of goods between the two Germanic states. Naturally the German right, remembering that the first step toward national unification in the nineteenth century had been the Prussian Customs Union, favored the proposal as the beginning of the creation of a greater German Reich, consisting of Germany and Austria. When the agreement was made public on March 19, 1931, the French, ever fearful of a strong Germany, immediately objected. Supported by the Czechs, who also feared a revitalized Germany, Paris appealed to the International Court of Justice in The Hague. After short deliberation, the court ruled that the proposed customs union was a violation of the treaties of St. Germain and

Versailles, and a rather embarrassed Berlin was forced to drop the proposal.

The failure of the customs union had a disastrous impact on the already fallen German economy. On May 11, 1931, concern over the certain victory of the French led to the failure of the Credit Anstalt of Vienna. This bank controlled almost two-thirds of the industry in the former Habsburg state, and its failure led to further deterioration of the finances of central Europe. Naturally, this had an adverse impact on Germany, as alarmed foreign creditors withdrew even more funds from the hard-pressed German banks. Between June 8 and June 12, 1931, the German National Bank lost over 500 million marks through such withdrawals.

The looming danger of a massive failure of German banks in the wake of the fall of the Austrian Credit Anstalt caused Brüning to seek an end to the reparation payments, which were bleeding the Reich beyond its ability to pay. On June 5, 1931, he met with Prime Minister Ramsay MacDonald at the estate of the head of the English ministry at Chequers. The desperate chancellor pleaded with his English counterpart to support his request for a revision of the Young Plan. However, MacDonald, realizing that such a proposal would meet with strong objections from Paris, refused to agree until he had a chance to talk with the American secretary of state, Henry L. Stimson, who was to visit England the next month. Unable to convince the British to support his request until they had received American approval, Brüning returned to Berlin with little hope of relief.

At this point Germany received help from an unexpected quarter. On June 20, 1931, President Herbert Hoover of the United States issued a call for a moratorium on all payments of intergovernmental debts. The surprised Germans welcomed word of Hoover's proposal with great joy. At last it seemed that the reparations, which had hung like a great weight around the necks of the Germans for so long, would be removed to allow them the time to put their financial house in order. However, the hope felt in Berlin was premature. The French, resenting Hoover's failure to discuss the issue with them before acting and fearing the harm losing the payments would do to the tottering French economy, immediately protested. The Americans and British, not willing to allow the French fear of the Germans to lead to further economic problems, sent delegations to Paris to discuss the issue. After two weeks of stormy debates the French agreed to a compromise on July 6. This agreement would require Berlin to meet the payment quotas set by the Young Plan for 1931 and 1932, but agreed to return the money to Germany through a loan to the German National Railroad.

Despite the favorable compromise reached by the Allies, the possibility that the Hoover moratorium would fail as a result of French objections, caused a renewed financial crisis in Germany. The worried foreign banks increased their withdrawals, compounding the disaster. At the same time, the German people feared that they would lose their hard-earned savings, and they flocked to the banks to secure their money before it was too late. The German National Bank might have stepped in with loans to help the commercial banks meet their obligations and avert disaster. But, Hans Luther, the head of the National Bank, refused to take such a step, fearing that it would deplete the government's gold supply and cause a serious inflation. Luther did try to borrow money from banks in London, Paris, and New York to aid the hard-pressed German banks, but these banks, having difficulty with their own problems, refused his request. Finally, spurred by the bankruptcy of Nordwolle, one of the largest textile mills in the country, the Darmstädter Bank appealed desperately for help. However, the heads of the rival banks refused to aid their competitor, and on July 13 the Darmstädter Bank closed its doors, unable to meet its obligation. The arrogant bankers refused to appeal for aid from the National Bank, believing that the failure of their rival would have no adverse impact on their business. However, they were wrong, for news of the closing of one of the largest financial institutions in the Reich caused a general panic, as frantic people tried to withdraw their savings before a similar fate could befall their own banks. By noon on July 13, 1931, the crisis had forced all the banks in Germany to close, causing millions to lose their life savings in a single day. Attempting to bring order to the financial confusion, the government declared a two-day bank holiday, but it was August before most of the banks could reopen their doors to the clamoring public.[5]

The failure of the banks led to still more decline in the economy at large, and a frantic Brüning went to Paris on July 19 to beg for a loan. The French, mistrustful of the Germans, refused to grant his petition unless he agreed to place the German economy under direct foreign control. They also demanded that the German chancellor agree not to seek revisions of the Young Plan. Unable to accept the stiff conditions of the French, Brüning turned to London for support. However, the British refused to consider loaning the Germans money that would be sent to Paris. Instead, the English informed Brüning that only a cancellation of the reparation payments would solve the crisis. Finally, the French agreed to loan Berlin $100 million but this was not enough to save the faltering German economy.

Unable to gain assistance from abroad, Brüning decided to take several drastic steps. On December 8, 1931, he invoked Article 48 of the constitution to reduce all fixed prices by 10 percent and place all other prices under the control of a federal price commissioner. He also decreed the lowering of all interest rates and rents to prevent further foreclosures and evictions. At the same time, he raised taxes and again slashed the salaries of government officials. The chancellor further attempted to balance the budget by reducing social insurance payments. Finally, he decreed that all wages would be reduced by about 10 percent, to their level of January 1927. Brüning's policy of reducing government expenditures and of raising taxes only worsened the crisis by depriving the economy of the funds needed to increase the purchasing power of the people so they could buy goods from the overstocked businesses. At the same time, he refused to follow the lead of the British, who had devalued the pound sterling on September 21, 1931, by going off the gold standard. Had the chancellor done the same to the German mark, this would have made German goods more competitive on the international market by reducing their price. Instead, German goods became more expensive and lost valuable markets because the United States, followed by England, Italy, and Switzerland, raised tariffs to reduce foreign competition with native businesses. It is quite natural that the German chancellor would fear inflation after the disaster of the early 1920s, but the early 1930s had different problems and required different solutions.

As Germany continued to sink into economic disaster, the British, realizing that the plight of the Reich could only weaken the economy of Europe as a whole, demanded action by the Allies. Believing that the only solution to the international depression lay in ending the reparations, London forced Paris to agree to the convening of an international meeting of experts to discuss the issue. At Basel, Switzerland, on August 18, the conference issued its report, called the Layton Report after the editor of the proposal, Walter Layton of the *London Economist*. This document argued that new loans to Germany would not solve the problem as long as the German economy was weakened by continued reparation demands. Therefore, the Allies must take more radical action, lest the economic decline of Germany weaken the finances of other nations. The British responded favorably to the Layton Report and pressured the French to agree to a meeting of the Allies on January 18, 1932, to discuss the whole question of reparations. However, Paris, refusing to abandon the demand for payment of the damages of the First World War, stalled the opening of the meetings for several months.

The failure of the British to persuade the French to take swift action intensified the economic distress in Germany. The Reichstag had been robbed of most of its voice in determining national policy by Brüning's constant invocation of Article 48, and the government fell more and more into the hands of incompetent bureaucrats. The increasing severity of the depression and the inability of the government to cope with the situation played into the hands of Hitler and his National Socialists. The Nazis made major gains in local elections held in 1931, as the movement grew from a regional party to a national force. Hitler, freed by the expiration of the laws forbidding him to speak in public, tirelessly spread his message of anti-Semitism and antirepublicanism to increasingly willing ears. The party also began to attract many youths who had become disenchanted with the republic and its failure to bring economic relief. The party held colorful youth rallies, during which Hitler and others harangued their listeners with the promise of a rebirth of national glory and prosperity once the Nazis seized power. On October 17 and 18 Hitler spoke to a huge gathering of supporters in Brunswick, the only state with a Nazi, Dietrich Klagge, in the ministry.

The Nazi growth continued throughout the next several months, as thousands sought a solution to their distress and found the Nazi message an easy answer. The party press developed from one daily paper with a circulation of slightly over 10,000 in 1926 to thirty-six papers with a readership of 431,000 in 1931. Hitler also won valuable support from the industrialists. On January 27, 1932, the führer spoke to a meeting of the Industry Club in Düsseldorf. At first these captains of German industry were skeptical because they considered Hitler merely a rabble rouser. However, they too could not resist the power of his voice as he warned them of the danger of a communist revolution. Following his victory at Düsseldorf, Hitler spoke to other representatives of business at sessions in Bad Godesburg and Hamburg. Here, too, he won support. The industrialists so feared the Sovietization of the Reich that they began to contribute large sums to the nazi movement. Herein lies one of the keys to Hitler's victory. As he continued to threaten the German people with the possibility that the Marxists would take advantage of the depression and stage a revolution, many believed that Hitler was their only salvation from a communist tyranny.

At this crucial period, when the depression crippled the economy and the National Socialist party grew daily, President Hindenburg's term as president was due to expire on May 5, 1932. Brüning and his supporters tried desperately to avoid an election that could sweep Hitler into office. First he proposed the election of the ancient field marshal as regent for life, with one of the sons of the crown prince named as his successor. This would have restored the monarchy; so it met with the approval of the right. It also would have deprived Hitler of an opportunity to campaign for president. However, the Social Democrats were devoted to the republic and refused to consider such a proposal, forcing the chancellor to attempt another plan. In desperation, he contacted the exiled kaiser to ask if he would consider returning. However, William replied that he would only consent to regaining power if the government agreed to restore the other dynasties. Since Brüning knew that this would never gain the approval of the Reichstag, he dropped the plan. However, he made one last effort to avoid the election. He suggested that the Reichstag grant the aging president two additional years in office. Since this would require the support of two-thirds of parliament, Brüning tried to win the support of the right. However, Alfred Hugenberg, the leader of the Nationalist party, rejected the proposal, and Hitler demanded Brüning's resignation and new national elections as the price for nazi support. Brüning reluctantly agreed to hold the elections.

The election of 1932 could not have been held at a more difficult period of German history. The founding parties of the Weimar Republic could do little but hope to withstand the onslaught from the right and left by rallying around as unlikely a person as the chief representative of imperial Germany, the aging Hindenburg. The Communists, hoping to profit by the economic crisis, nominated Ernst Thälmann. The radical right also decided to make an effort to capture the highest office in the republic and supported Theodor Düsterberg, an official in the Stahlhelm. Naturally, the rising National Socialists saw in the campaign a golden chance to gain national exposure for their führer. However, Hitler was still legally a citizen of Austria and could not run for president unless he could gain German citizenship. Realizing that the chances of persuading Hindenburg to grant Hitler

German citizenship were unlikely, the Nazis sought another way to make their leader eligible. They found it in Article 110 of the Weimar constitution, which provided that any person with citizenship in one of the states would automatically become a citizen of the nation. They also discovered that if a state government would agree to appoint Hitler to office, no matter how unimportant, he would become a citizen of that state, and therefore a citizen of the Reich. Wilhelm Frick, who was the leader of the nazi delegation in the Reichstag and also a member of the government of Thuringia, proposed that he persuade his fellow ministers to appoint Hitler commander of the police at Hildburghausen. However, the proud führer rejected this office as beneath his dignity. At this point, Dietrich Klagge, a member of the government of Brunswick, offered to secure the appointment of Hitler as professor of education at the Pedagogical Institute in Brunswick. Fortunately for the standards of German higher education, this suggestion was also rejected. Finally, Klagge won Hitler an appointment as an official of the delegation from Brunswick to the upper house of the German parliament. Thus, Hitler became a citizen of Brunswick and of Germany and could run for president.

In the weeks before the election, all sides carried on a fierce campaign. Hitler flew all over Germany speaking to cheering crowds, while his supporters covered the streets with nazi posters. However, when the people went to the polls on March 13, 1932, only 30.1 percent supported the nazi leader. Hindenburg received slightly less than 50 percent, Thälmann won about 13 percent, and Düsterberg less than 7 percent. Since no one received a majority, a new election was called for April 10. Terrified that the fanatical leader of the Nazis might capture the presidency of the Reich, the parties of the right and middle united solidly behind Hindenburg. Although Hitler once again carried on a furious campaign, he lost to Hindenburg, and the ancient field marshal won another term as head of the Weimar Republic. It is a sad testimony to the weakness of German republicanism that the only alternative they could offer to Hitler was a man who had served the exiled kaiser and longed for a restoration of the monarchy.

The violent nazi campaign for the election of their leader frightened many Germans. Wilhelm Gröner, the minister of war, decided that something had to be done to stop the Brown Shirts from harassing their opponents. However, he realized that if the Storm Troopers were banned, the government would be legally bound to take similar action against the Reichsbanner of the Social Democrats. Brüning knew that if the ministry suppressed the Reichsbanner he would lose the needed support of the Social Democrats, and he refused to agree to Gröner's proposal. However, the continuing violence of the brown-shirted nazi army had to be halted, and on April 5, 1932, the governments of Prussia, Bavaria, Saxony, Württemberg, Baden, and Hesse demanded that the national government act or they would dissolve the Storm Troopers on their own authority. Pressured by the states, Gröner, supported by Kurt von Hammerstein, the chief of the army, and General Kurt von Schleicher, persuaded Hindenburg to sign a decree on April 11 dissolving the Brown Shirts.

Naturally, the Nazis refused to accept the attack on their private army and violently objected. They won the support of some of the younger members of the military and prepared to defy the decree. The National Socialists also stepped up their campaign for power and won control of the diets of Prussia, Hamburg, Anhalt, and Württemberg, while winning a substantial delegation to the diet of Bavaria in local elections held on April 24. On May 10 Gröner attempted to defend his action before the Reichstag, but he only met with humiliation as the Nazis, led by Göring, drowned his statement with a chorus of insults. Greatly embarrassed by his reception, Gröner sent Hindenburg his resignation. The Nazis continued to defy the government, the members of the Storm Troopers simply shedding their uniforms. Finally, after a stormy session ending in a brawl between their members and the Communists, the Nazis elected one of their followers, Hans Kerrl, president of the Prussian diet. Unable to stem the growing economic crisis and the rise of national socialism, Brüning resigned in disgrace on May 29, 1931.

Thus, the uneasy stability of the Stresemann era ended abruptly with the outbreak of the depression. The leadership of the republic stood powerless before the rising unemployment and hunger and could do nothing but attempt to restore the stability through a desperate effort to balance the budget and lessen governmental expenditures under Chancellor Brüning. The spreading crisis enabled Hitler to revitalize the almost defunct Nazi party and to pose a serious threat to the old leadership. Although Hitler was unable to secure election to the presidency of the republic, the Weimar coalition was so devoid of effective leadership that they could do little but stand behind the conservative presidency of Hindenburg in an effort to stop Hitler. Despite his failure to achieve election, Hitler was able to lead his party to victory in several local elections and to send a loud nazi delegation to the Reichstag. Although the Weimar Republic would continue a precarious existence for another year, it was only a matter of time before Hitler and his followers would seize power and put an end to the democracy.

12

The Birth of the Third Reich

Although Hitler had failed to defeat Hindenburg, the National Socialists were far from subdued. As the continuing economic crisis drove more and more to seek answers for their plight, the simple message and primitive emotional appeal of the führer and his brown-shirted followers won more and more supporters. The bankrupt political leadership could do little but make a feeble attempt to save the embattled republic from the extremists and proved totally incapable of rising to the task. Finally, all the hopes and dreams of the men who had assembled in the city of Goethe to create a new Germany turned to dust, and a new era of tyranny began that caused many to long for the days when the authoritarian kaiser was more of a joke than a serious threat to mankind. The story of the death of the Weimar Republic and of the attempt to establish a government of the people is partially the tale of the intense rivalry of two men, Kurt von Schleicher and Franz von Papen. As they fought for personal power and the destruction of each other, they not only destroyed themselves, but also the very republic they claimed to serve.

Kurt von Schleicher was a soldier who had been fortunate enough to gain the friendship of important people. He was from the heart of the Hohenzollern Empire, Brandenburg, where he was born on April 7, 1882. He began his rise to influence by joining the Third Foot Guards, where he became friends with Oskar von Hindenburg, the son of the future president. Through diligent work and attention to duty, he gained the notice of another future leader of the Republic, General Wilhelm Gröner, then on the staff of the military academy. When Gröner left his teaching duties to assume the command of the transport section of the general staff, he took Schleicher with him, and thus began Schleicher's rise to power. The young officer served for a while on the Eastern Front, where he won the Iron Cross, before his superiors assigned him to desk duty. Schleicher might have ended his career in relative obscurity in the service of the press office of the army had not Gröner remembered his former student and appointed him his personal assistant when he became quartermaster-general in October 1918. During the stormy early years of the republic, Schleicher served his military masters by developing contacts with the Free Corps, and Seeckt rewarded him by giving him increasing authority in political matters. When Gröner became minister of war in 1928, he turned to Schleicher to head the political division of the ministry. Through his ties with Gröner and access to Hindenburg through Hindenburg's son, Schleicher rose to a position of great importance in the republic and finally to the office of chancellor.

Schleicher's chief political ally and eventual opponent was Franz von Papen. Papen, the son of a wealthy Westphalian family, was born in Werl on October 29, 1879. A dapper gentleman, he married a rich heiress and spent his spare time with horses. During the First World War, Papen, called by some "a hat without a head" because of his bungling manner, joined the army and became military attaché to the German embassy in the United States. Here he conspired to violate the neutrality of the Americans by supporting sabotage and by setting up a munitions factory in Bridgeport, Connecticut. Although the plant could not openly manufacture supplies for the Germans, it could use valuable raw materials that might have aided the British. He also attempted to set up a spy network and disrupt the production of war materials by influencing workers of German and Austrian ancestry to deliberately slow down their work. When one of his associates fell asleep on an elevated train in New York City and lost a briefcase containing incriminating documents, the American officials discovered Papen's plans and demanded his recall. Undaunted by his disgrace in the New World, he continued to serve his fatherland in Palestine, where he lost another set of confidential papers dealing with German attempts to aid the Irish revolt. After the war Papen, a devout Roman Catholic and monarchist, decided to turn his talents to politics and joined the Center party because he believed that this moderate body had more chance of success than the rightist groups.

After the resignation of Brüning, the aged Hindenburg searched for a new chancellor. Schleicher, able to influence the president through his son, suggested the appointment of Papen, then a Center deputy in the Prussian Diet. Papen, jumping at the opportunity to assume the leadership of Germany, approached the chairman of his party, Dr. Ludwig Kaas. However, Kaas, unwilling to allow a local politician to rise to such heights, refused to agree. The ambitious candidate accepted the post, but by refusing to yield to pressure from Kaas he lost the support of his own party. With Schleicher as minister of war, Papen began his stormy career as chancellor. Like Brüning, Papen was a conservative who believed that fiscal responsibility and a balanced budget were the key to recovery. He slashed expenditures for social programs and unemployment insurance, but he did try to provide some relief through public works projects to provide jobs for the idle workers. However, like his predecessor, his efforts only caused the situation to worsen, and Germany sank deeper and deeper into economic chaos.[1]

At first it seemed that Papen's government would bring some relief to the troubled land. On June 16, after being delayed by the French for several months, the representatives of the Allies met in Lausanne, Switzerland, to discuss the problem of the reparations. The Germans asked the victors to accept the Layton Report, but the French, ever mindful of the destruction caused by the First World War, refused to accept the German demand. Instead, Paris suggested that the payments continue, but at a lower rate than those of the Young Plan. Finally, after several weeks of arguments, the conference agreed to cancel the reparations in return for a German payment of 3 billion gold marks to a fund for European reconstruction. Thus, on July 9, 1932, the German people were freed at last from the burden of the hated reparations.

It is difficult to determine the precise impact of the reparations on the German economy. Between 1921 and 1932 the Germans paid a total of 23,18 billion gold marks in reparations. However, at the same time the Germans obtained large international loans to cover part of the expense of the reparations. Despite the assistance provided by the loans, it is clear that the reparation payments greatly added to the growing deficit of the German government. For not only tax revenues went directly to the Allies, but also industrial wealth that could have been taxed to lessen or eliminate the deficit. Thus, the reparations drained valuable resources that might have been utilized to improve the condition of the German economy. In addition to the economic impact of the reparations, they contributed to the growing indignation of the German people, who resented the victors and the German politicians who yielded to their demands. Therefore, the reparations did have a negative impact on the history of the Weimar Republic and did play a major role in the disenchantment that allowed a man like Hitler to gain control of Germany.

Meanwhile, in an effort to win support in the Reichstag, Papen persuaded Hindenburg to call for new elections. However, he made a fatal mistake by allowing the National Socialists to reorganize the Storm Troopers. Free of governmental repression, the brown-shirted hoard set about beating their opponents into submission and committing 322 violent acts in Prussia, not including Berlin, between July 1 and July 20. They even invaded Altona, a suburb of Hamburg famous for its pro-Communist element, and brutally murdered seventeen Reds. The bloodshed so infuriated the chancellor that he decided drastic action was needed to restore order. He persuaded the president to invoke Article 48 of the Weimar constitution on July 20 and to appoint him commissar of Prussia. Naturally, the duly elected government of the northern German state protested this violation of their rights, but after being threatened with military occupation of their offices, they yielded. Papen removed the socialist officials of the Prussian government and gave their posts to his fellow conservatives. Finally, to cope with the violence, President Hindenburg declared a state of emergency and placed the police under control of the military.

Although Papen had successfully overthrown the government of Prussia, he emerged from the election for the new Reichstag on July 31 robbed of most of his support. He could count on only 44 of the 608 delegates to stand behind his program. At the same time, Hitler's forces benefited from the confusion and more than doubled their delegation from 107 to 230. The Communists emerged with 89 seats. The Social Democrats, the strongest supporters of the constitution, lost 10 seats and formed a rather small block of 133. The Center gained 7 seats for a total of 75 and the Democrats shrank to a mere 4 delegates. Thus, the Weimar coalition consisted of only 212 deputies, and the foes of the republic held a clear majority of 356 of the 608 members of the Reichstag. The inability of the political leaders to deal with the depression had led a majority of the people to cast their votes for parties that openly sympathized with the overthrow of the republic.

Since the Nazis had emerged as the largest group in the German parliament, Papen was forced to attempt to win their support. On August 13 the gentleman chancellor offered the leader of the Brown

Shirts the post of vice-chancellor. However, Hitler had no desire to accept anything less than the highest office in the government. He met with Papen and the president that same day and demanded the chancellorship as the cost for nazi support. Considering Hitler and his men little better than ruffians, Hindenburg indignantly refused to consider him for the post. The session ended without agreement, and the president issued a statement to the press describing Hitler's stubborn attitude. His failure to cooperate with the former field marshal only cost him valuable support, for the average German could not understand his refusal to join the government. On August 30 the newly elected Reichstag met and promptly elected Hermann Göring its chief officer. Göring, who had been severely wounded during the Beer Hall Putsch, had spent several years in exile with his wife in Sweden. The pain from his wound had been so great that he had become a morphine addict and had been confined to an asylum for treatment. He returned to Germany in 1927 and the next year joined the nazi delegation to the Reichstag. Realizing that he could not count on the cooperation of the legislative body, Papen had obtained an undated decree from Hindenburg dissolving the Reichstag and calling for a new election. However, when the Communists introduced a motion to censure the government, the chancellor had forgotten to bring the document with him to the session. At a crucial moment the Nazis called for a recess so they could discuss the communist proposal. This gave Papen the time he desperately needed to send a messenger to his office to bring him the decree. However, even armed with this document, Papen was unable to escape censure, because Göring simply ignored his persistent attempts to gain the floor and allowed the Reichstag to pass a vote of no confidence against the ministry by 512 to 42. The issue decided, Göring recognized Papen, who formally dissolved the parliament and called for new elections.

The election of November 6, 1933, the last held before Hitler's victory, was a defeat for the rising nazi movement. Hitler's arrogance in dealing with Hindenburg had offended many. Three days before the election the Nazis had alarmed conservatives by joining the Communists in support of a strike by the transportation workers in Berlin. If the willingness of Hitler's men to work with the hated Reds was not enough to shock the middle classes and industrialists who had supported the Nazis out of their fear of communism, the violence that accompanied the strike convinced them to turn from national socialism. The strikers tore up streetcar rails, blocked switches with cement, tore down overhead lines, and terrorized strike breakers. As a result of this mistake, the Nazis lost 61 deputies and emerged with only 196 delegates. However, the strike had an opposite effect on the Communists, who actually gained a few seats. At the same time, the Social Democrats and Centrists lost even more votes and became minor parties. Once again Papen had failed to win the support of the people.

The chancellor desperately tried to put together a ministry that would win the favor of the majority of the Reichstag. However, the Social Democrats and Center refused to endorse the government. Once again Papen turned to Hitler and offered him several posts. But Hitler, undaunted by the defeat at the polls, held out for the chancellorship and declined to enter the government. The führer wrote Hindenburg a letter demanding appointment, and the president once more declined his ultimatum, announcing to the press that government by Hitler would lead to a dictatorship. Finally, Papen decided that only drastic action could provide Germany with a stable government. He met with the president and presented a fantastic scheme, proposing the dissolution of the Reichstag and the parties, if necessary, and rule by decree. The president hesitated to violate his oath to the constitution. Schleicher, whom Hindenburg had summoned for advice, could do little but suggest that an agreement be reached with the Nazis or the moderate parties. Finally, persuaded by Papen's invocation of William I's acceptance of Bismarck's plan to violate the Prussian constitution and tired and irritable after the long discussions, the president gave his tentative approval to Papen's plan.

However, when the ministry met on December 2 to discuss the chancellor's radical proposal, Schleicher dealt it the death blow. He argued that the dissolution of the Reichstag would only lead to violence and possibly to a bloody civil war at a time when the Reich was in no condition to undergo such a tragedy. To support his argument, he summoned Colonel Eugene Ott to inform the startled ministers that the army was too weak to withstand a combined nazi and communist revolt. After a stormy discussion, during which Papen argued frantically for his plan, the cabinet voted to oppose his drastic idea. When the chancellor reported his failure to gain the support of his ministers, Hindenburg could do little but refuse to consider rejecting their advice and risking a civil war. He informed Papen that he was no longer capable of holding office and that he had decided to give Schleicher a chance to restore order to Germany.[2]

The general immediately began the search for support from the

Reichstag. Realizing that Hitler would never consent to any office lower than the chancellorship, he tried to cause a split in the national socialist ranks. He approached Gregor Strasser, the leader of the leftist wing of the party and well-known critic of Hitler, and offered him the post of vice-chancellor. Strasser's first inclination was to accept, but he failed to win the approval of his fellow Nazis. He met with Hitler, Goebbels, and Göring to persuade them that failure to accept a position in the government would only harm the party and could lead to another election, which could cause a further decline in nazi strength. However, the other leaders of the party refused to allow the chancellor to destroy the unity of the movement. Göring and Goebbels charged that Strasser had submitted to defeatism, and Hitler reacted with fury to Strasser's dealings with Schleicher. The angry führer accused him of treason to the party for being willing to even discuss the issue with the chancellor. Finally, unable to persuade the leaders of the party to allow him to accept the post, Strasser rejected the offer and left for a vacation in Italy, a defeated and discredited man. Violently angry at the attempt to break the party into rival factions, Hitler dramatically threatened to kill himself, and by so doing beat the membership into line. He created a new central party commission under his old friend Rudolf Hess and demanded that all party officials and members of the Reichstag sign an oath of unquestioned loyalty to his leadership. Thus, Schleicher's attempt to gain support by causing a split within the National Socialists met with miserable failure and only strengthened Hitler's hold on the movement.

Urgently in need of support for his government, Schleicher turned to the other parties. He tried to gain the sympathy of the Social Democrats by promising a bold program of reform to provide jobs for the unemployed and land for the peasants by breaking up the large estates of the Junkers. However, even this met with failure because the Socialists refused to cooperate with a man who had played a role in the dissolution of the Prussian government. Schleicher's vain courting of the Social Democrats only weakened his position by depriving him of the much needed support of the Nationalists. They were shocked by what they considered Schleicher's surrender to "bolshevism" and his willingness to sacrifice the landowners to gain the approval of the Social Democrats. They turned a deaf ear to his frantic pleas for support. Thus, Schleicher had failed to win the allegiance of the Socialists and had lost the loyalty of the Nationalists.

A complete failure as a politician, Schleicher met with the president on January 23, 1933, to propose the dissolution of the Reichstag and rule by decree as the only solution to the deadlock. The president was horrified by Schleicher's plan. Had he not been the chief opponent of Papen's similar effort of the month before? Had he not argued that such a drastic violation of the constitution would only lead to a civil war that the army could not win? Without hesitation, Hindenburg rejected Schleicher's effort to turn Germany into a military dictatorship. Unable to control the Reichstag and failing to persuade the president to allow him to rule by decree, Schleicher's ministry could only last a few weeks more.

Since the chancellor was unwilling to allow Papen another attempt to organize a ministry after his certain fall, he came to the conclusion that the only way to bring order would be to appoint Hitler as chancellor. He considered the nazi leader a weak man, whose sole ability was to arouse the rabble. Schleicher thought that once in power Hitler would be forced to drop the more radical aspects of his program and assume a more moderate course. He also believed that it would be easy for the military to dominate Hitler once his inability to rule became apparent. If this failed and Hitler attempted to put his ideas into effect, Schleicher and his friends thought that Hitler would be such a complete failure that the Nazi movement would dissolve after their leader's radical programs had made him into a joke. On January 27 Schleicher sent his friend, General Kurt von Hammerstein, to discover Hindenburg's attitude toward the idea. But the president refused to discuss the issue and coldly suggested that the general confine his activities to the military and leave politics to the politicians.

During the next few days political machinations reached a feverish pace as both Papen and Schleicher tried to influence the president. Papen wavered between favoring a coalition government headed by himself and Hitler and a ministry led by himself with strong military backing. Schleicher, determined to prevent the reappointment of Papen, worked behind the scenes to secure the appointment of Hitler. On January 28 Schleicher formally resigned, after charging the aged president with betraying his trust by negotiating with Papen. After the former chancellor left, Papen arrived to try to persuade the president to award the head of the ministry to Hitler. However, despite the seriousness of the situation, the president could not bring himself to allow the Bohemian corporal to take office. During the next few days, almost alone, the ancient field marshal resisted the efforts of Papen and Schleicher to convince him to yield to Hitler's demands.

Despite Hindenburg's attitude, Papen threw himself into negotiations with Hitler and Alfred Hugenberg, the leader of the Nationalist party. Hugenberg, whose support Papen badly needed if he were to succeed, was reluctant to join a government dominated by the Nazis and demanded guarantees that Hitler would not attempt to establish a dictatorship. Meanwhile, the nazi führer demanded not only the chancellorship but also the office of Reich commissar of Prussia, a position that both Papen and Schleicher had occupied while serving as chancellor. The nazi leader also refused to work with the existing Reichstag and demanded new elections as the price for agreement. Papen, knowing that Hindenburg would certainly reject both demands, neglected to transmit them to the president when he reported the results of the discussions. Instead, he tried to persuade Hindenburg that Hitler was really much more moderate than he seemed and could easily be controlled.

Unable to solve the knotty problem of who would assume the chancellorship, Hindenburg decided to take a bold step to preserve the independence of the military. He recalled General Werner von Blomberg from Geneva, where he was a member of the German delegation to the International Disarmament Conference, and planned to make him minister of war. Papen had suggested the appointment of General Werner von Fritsch, but the president did not know him well and preferred to rely on a man he thought would stand up to Hitler. Unfortunately, Blomberg would be no match for the nazi leader. Hindenburg asked Papen to become vice-chancellor in the event of Hitler's appointment, and to agree to be always present when the leader of the Brown Shirts met with the president.

With Hindenburg's resistance to Hitler weakening, Papen undertook renewed negotiations. He met with Hitler and Göring, and Hitler finally agreed to drop his demand for the office of Reich commissar of Prussia if Göring would receive the important post of minister of the interior. However, he refused to reconsider his demand for new elections, and Papen finally agreed to take up the matter with Hindenburg. The former chancellor then met with Hugenberg and Franz Seldte, the leader of the Stahlhelm. Both men were worried that Hitler would use the office of chancellor to establish a nazi dictatorship. However, Papen argued that this would be impossible since Hindenburg was inclined to appoint Hugenberg minister of economics, and Seldte could use the Stahlhelm to challenge the Storm Troopers. Finally, they agreed. Thus, Papen had won the support of the most important factions to be represented in the new government.

That same day Papen visited Hindenburg to report that he had reached an accord with Hitler and Hugenberg. This time, he informed the president of Hitler's demand for new elections, but he neglected to mention Hugenberg's violent opposition to the proposal. At first Hindenburg hesitated, but he finally agreed to formally appoint Hitler as chancellor at eleven the next morning. Thus, Papen had won. Hitler's appointment was virtually assured despite the serious opposition of the conservatives, who disliked his violent manner and considered him a mere demagogue who would lead the fatherland into further disorder. Hindenburg had been unable to cope with the situation, perhaps because of his advanced age and the loss of his will to continue to fight for what seemed a lost cause.

Meanwhile, unaware of the outcome of Papen's efforts and worried that in the end Papen would once again emerge as chancellor, Schleicher tried to play a role in the discussions. He and his supporters had been alarmed at the recall of Blomberg, which they suspected was a part of a clever plot by Papen to assume office. So Schleicher sent von Hammerstein to Hitler to seek information. However, the führer was unwilling to tell Schleicher more than necessary lest he need his help in case Papen were really only creating a diversion to conceal his real plan. Hammerstein, not knowing of the outcome of the negotiations and still believing that Papen had a chance of becoming chancellor, hinted that Hitler could count on the support of the army in a struggle with Papen and Hindenburg. After Schleicher's emissary left, Hitler ordered the Storm Troopers to prepare for action if the army resisted his appointment.

During the next few hours all kinds of fantastic rumors circulated through the German capital. Still unaware that Hitler and Papen had reached agreement, Schleicher sent Werner von Alvensleben to meet with Hitler at Goebbels's home. Alvensleben, who found the Nazis optimistic but worried about the possibility of Papen's appointment, informed Hitler that Schleicher was prepared to mobilize the garrison in Potsdam to seize control of the capital to keep Papen from office. Naturally, this announcement did not remain a secret long, and within a few hours many, including Hindenburg, believed that Schleicher was preparing for a military putsch. The irony is that the president and his followers thought that Schleicher would take such a drastic step to *prevent* the appointment of Hitler, not to *insure* it, as Alvensleben had implied to Hitler. Early the next morning Blomberg arrived at the Anhalter Railroad Station and immediately Oskar von

Hindenburg and Major von Kuntzen, Hammerstein's adjutant, tried to get to him. The president's son ordered Blomberg to report immediately to his father, and Kuntzen presented a command to report to Hammerstein. Without hesitation Blomberg announced that an order from the president took precedence over any command from Hammerstein and proceeded to the head of state to assume control of the War Ministry.

While Blomberg was obeying the command of his president, Papen was once more trying to persuade Hugenberg and Seldte to join a ministry under Hitler. Aware of the strong opposition to the Nazi leader among their fellow conservatives, Hugenberg and Seldte hesitated to accept his appointment. At this crucial point Papen told them that unless the new government took office that morning, Schleicher would call up the army and establish a military dictatorship. Beaten into submission by this threat, Hugenberg and Seldte finally agreed. However, a few hours later, when they stood waiting to see the president, they renewed their objections to Hitler's demand for elections. With the impatient Hindenburg waiting, Hitler and Hugenberg argued as Papen appealed to them to reach an agreement. Finally, the president sent word that they must cease their argument at once, for he would not be kept waiting. Pressured by the president's demand for their appearance, Hugenberg and Seldte finally yielded and joined Hitler in the presidential reception room. There, without ceremony, the aged president appointed Hitler chancellor of Germany. Thus, on January 30, 1933, Hitler became the head of the government.[3]

With the appointment of Hitler, Germany embarked on a course that shortly would destroy the last vestiges of democracy and create one of the most totalitarian states in history: the Third Reich. Although the Nazis were willing to use legal methods to gain power, once they had it they had no intention of allowing others the same chance. Soon the new brown-shirted masters of Germany destroyed all possible opposition and ended freedom of thought and expression. They disbanded all rival political organizations and beat their critics into silence. In the process the once free Germany became a prison. Where once farmers had harvested their crops, concentration camps sprang up to hold those who dared to resist the rule of the führer. Berlin, a city whose gay night life had once been world famous, became a sinister world of goose-stepping Storm Troopers and hooked crosses flying from the towers of great churches.

Hitler lost no time in his plan to turn Germany into a national socialist state. He had been able to goad Hindenburg and the Nationalists into holding new elections and had used every means possible to pressure the German people into voting in his favor. Although Hitler had decided against banning the Reds outright, lest this only enlarge the socialist vote, he ordered government agents to disrupt the meetings of the followers of Marx and Lenin. Naturally, the Nazi government harrassed the social democratic and centerist press to keep them from challenging Hitler's rule. Since the government owned the radio, Hitler and his followers gained almost exclusive use of the airwaves.

At the same time, the new masters of Germany used semilegal methods to browbeat the opposition into silence. The Storm Troopers spread a wave of terror, brutally beating and torturing anti-Nazis and disrupting meetings of rival parties. When no other method would destroy the brave foes of the new dictatorship, the Brown Shirts began kidnapping their opponents. They tore over 100,000 persons from their families, coming sometimes in the night and carrying a husband and father away while his wife and children looked on in terror, unable to do anything to help their loved one. Since the barracks of the Storm Troopers were too small to hold such large numbers of political prisoners, they began building special camps early in 1933. By the end of that fateful summer, about fifty concentration camps stood where once flowers had grown or factories had carried on their work.

While the Nazis attempted to beat their opponents into submission, a major event took place that gave Hitler the key to absolute power. On the cold evening of February 27, 1933, the flames of the burning Reichstag building lit the night sky. Hitler immediately made every effort to convince the people that this act of terrorism was the first step in a well-planned communist attempt to seize control of the Reich and establish a Soviet dictatorship. The police arrested Martinus van der Lubbe, a crazed Dutch ex-Communist. Lubbe confessed to the crime, and the authorities began rounding up those suspected of assisting him in his terrible deed. Ernst Torgler, the leader of the Red delegation to the Reichstag, surrendered to the police the next day to answer charges of involvement. On March 9 the police arrested four Bulgarian Communists, charging them with participation in the plot. The four stood trial in Leipzig on September 21, but despite the efforts of the Nazis to implicate them in the act of arson, the court found only Lubbe guilty. The Dutchman met his death by decapitation on January 10, 1934.[4]

Whether or not Lubbe acted alone is one of the great mysteries of history. The Communists charged that the Nazis set the fire to stir up public opinion. Supposedly, nazi agents entered the basement of the building through an underground passage between Göring's residence and the Reichstag and spread incendiary chemicals, while Lubbe, above, set the fire. However, there are serious reasons to doubt the authenticity of the communist charge. It is questionable that the Nazis would have risked the involvement of a foreign vagabond who might have yielded to pressure to tell the truth. The night watchman had made his rounds a half hour before the fire, and the last deputy left the building at 8:38 P.M. Lubbe set the fire at 9:00, and the Nazis would not have had enough time to spread the chemicals and escape before being trapped in the fiery inferno. Had the Brown Shirts entered the building through the tunnel, they would have made a great deal of noise as they walked on the sheet metal floor. Yet Paul Adermann, the night porter at the palace of the president of the Reichstag, where Göring resided, testified at the trial that he heard no strange sounds. Finally, Göring, who placed great value on his possessions, lost several valuable items in the fire. If he had known of the plot, he almost certainly would have removed them. All that can be proven beyond a doubt is that Martinus van der Lubbe set the fire.

Despite the strong possibility that the fire was a surprise to Hitler and his men, he took advantage of the event. He persuaded Hindenburg to issue an emergency decree on February 28, 1933, suspending civil liberties, including freedom of the press and speech and the right of habeas corpus. Armed with this, the Nazis made one last effort to crush their opponents in the final days before the election. The government prohibited political meetings by non-Nazis and suppressed the press organs of rival parties. The National Socialists built the red threat into an issue to frighten the people into voting for the swastika as the only alternative to communist dictatorship. On March 5, 1933, the Germans went to the polls for the last time in a semifree election and gave the Nazis only 43.9 percent of the vote, less than they had given the Weimar coalition in 1919. Despite the nazi reign of terror, the Communists retained 12.2 percent and the Socialists 18.2 percent, down slightly from the last election but still a third of the vote. The Center and Bavarian People's parties emerged with their strength unchanged, with a total of 14.4 percent, and the Nationalists retained 8 percent, down from 8.8 per cent in the last election. Thus, in their last chance to express their opinions, the majority of the German people refused to cast their votes for the National Socialists.

Having achieved what they proclaimed as a glorious victory at the polls, the Nazis next turned to the state governments in their effort to become the absolute masters of the Reich. They already controlled the regimes of a few small states such as Thuringia, the two Mecklenburgs, Oldenburg, Brunswick, Anhalt, and Lippe, but they had been unable to gain a foothold in the governments of Bavaria, Württemberg, Hesse, Saxony, and the three Hanseatic cities. Following the example of Papen in Prussia, they crushed the last shred of independent government in Germany. Storm Troopers caused riots all over the Reich to prove that the local officials could not keep order in their areas. In one state after another the Nazis persuaded Hindenburg to appoint commissars to take over the functions of local government. By the end of March 1933 the Nazis had wiped out the last traces of local autonomy.

At the same time, Hitler was busy trying to consolidate his position in the government by a masterful appeal to the traditional loyalties of the German people. On March 21, the date of the convening of the first German Reichstag by Otto von Bismarck, in 1871, the führer presided over the ceremonial opening of his Reichstag in the Potsdam Garrison Church. Here, Hitler and the deputies to the parliament gathered to pay homage to the glories of Germany's past. President Hindenburg, clad in his field marshal's uniform and his chest blazing with his decorations from the First World War, marched down the aisle, pausing to salute the empty chair of the exiled kaiser. Standing near the tombs of Frederick William I, the soldier king, and his son Frederick the Great, the aged president appealed for support for the new government, invoking the ancient spirit of Prussian duty represented by their meeting place. Then Hitler stood to address the crowd. As silence fell on the assembled dignitaries, the führer praised the triumphs of the past and condemned the "traitors" who had submitted to the Allies in 1918. Finally, the new master of Germany claimed that his victory had restored the lost honor of the fatherland and had opened a new era of greatness. After finishing his address, Hitler, appealing further to the traditions of the past, went to the tomb of Frederick the Great to pay tribute to this symbol of the glory that once had been Prussia. All at once, a crescendo of trumpets, drums, and rifle salutes broke the silence, as the German army, followed by the Storm Troopers and the Stahlhelm, marched before Hindenburg, Hitler, and Crown Prince William, the symbol of the exiled Hohenzollerns. That evening thousands of brown-shirted Nazis filled the streets of Berlin with singing and the flames of their torches as they marched through another symbol of Prussia's glory, the Brandenburg Gate. The festive day ended with a gala performance of Richard Wagner's tribute to German art, *The Mastersingers of Nuremberg*, conducted by William Furtwängler.

After subjugating the states, destroying the left, and appealing to the traditional loyalties of the German people, Hitler turned to the Reichstag. He presented the Enabling Act, granting his cabinet legislative authority. However, such a radical change in the constitution required the support of two-thirds of the members of the Reichstag. The Nazis and their nationalistic allies did not have delegations large enough to force passage of the bill. So Hitler was forced to appeal to the Center for support. However, the Center hesitated to grant such sweeping powers to the Nazi-dominated ministry. The führer met with Dr. Ludwig Kaas, the leader of the Center, and pleaded for his approval by promising that no law would go into effect without Hindenburg's approval, that a small committee would review all proposed acts, and that the new power would not be used against the Center party. Hitler further pledged himself to respect the independence of the judiciary and the principle of equality before the law for all except Communists. With these guarantees, Kaas reluctantly agreed to support the measure, but he failed to gain a written statement of Hitler's promises.

Amid great tension, the Reichstag opened on March 21 in the Kroll Opera House. Göring, president of the legislative body, opened with a speech appealing once again to the past and promising a new age of glory. Two days later the Reichstag met to discuss the Enabling Act. As the delegates assembled they walked through a column of uniformed Nazis, who then followed them into the hall, standing threateningly around the room. In this atmosphere Hitler addressed the deputies, denouncing the weak Weimar Republic and pledging the rebuilding of the fatherland. Hitler also called for a new birth of morality and the cleansing of the schools, theaters, movies, literature, press, and radio of all subversive elements. He pledged his government to protect the rights of the churches as long as they supported the state, and he proclaimed a war on unemployment and a restoration of the shattered economy to create a new era of prosperity. Finally, Hitler spoke of peace, praising not only fascist Italy but also France and the Soviet Union.

When the Reichstag reassembled a fiery debate followed, during which Otto Wels, the leader of the Social Democrats, heroically pleaded with the members to remember the principles of democratic government and to reject the attempt to deprive the Reichstag of its constitutional powers. However, his appeal failed, for Kaas spoke in favor of the act, reminding Hitler of his promises. The Reichstag finally approved the act by a vote of 441 to 91. Thus, Hitler's victory had been complete. He and his followers had gained total control of Germany, and the hated Weimar constitution became a document of the past.

Thus, the Weimar Republic had yielded to its chief enemy without a struggle. The political leadership of Germany had failed to provide an effective government. As the multitude of parties sank deeper and deeper into petty squabbles between themselves, the republic sank into stagnation. When the Weimar coalition could do no more than turn to a symbol of the old order in their drastic effort to defeat Hitler, the republican ideal suffered an irreparable blow. Hindenburg was loyal to the constitution, but he lacked the ability to provide decisive leadership. He really longed for the good old days of the Kaiser and was incapable of resisting the onslaught of the National Socialists. Had the leaders of the parties forgotten their rivalries and sought to unselfishly strengthen the republic by working together to combat the economic crisis and the growth of national socialism, Hitler might not have won the final victory.

The military also failed. Ebert and his fellow founders of the republic had been unable or unwilling to destroy the old military establishment. Instead, the army became a state within the state, led by men who supported the government because it was their only alternative, but who did so without any real commitment to democracy. The army under Seeckt and Gröner was more concerned with its own position than the welfare of the republic and became a bastion of rightist ideas. Had Ebert and the founders of the republic destroyed the old military establishment and created a new republican army loyal to the ideals of the constitution, German history might have been radically different.

An important failure of the republic was its unwillingness to take decisive action against its foes within Germany. Hitler attempted to overthrow the government through a violent revolution in 1923. Instead of placing him in prison for a long period and crushing the nazi movement after the Beer Hall Putsch, the government was content with half-hearted measures that only weakened the movement temporarily. The leaders of the republic failed to take decisive action after the Kapp Putsch. Even after the army refused to defend the republic, the government failed to purge the rightist elements who had refused to oppose Kapp. The Communists also escaped severe punishment for their attempt to overthrow the constitution. Although, in dealing with the left, the leaders of the republic acted decisively, they failed to take similar measures with the right. Certainly, the unwillingness of the leaders of Germany to destroy the radicals was a major factor in Hitler's victory.

The Allies also played an unwitting role in the destruction of the Weimar Republic. Wilson seemed to promise a fair and moderate peace; but, instead, the Allies delivered the Treaty of Versailles. The victors also demanded high reparation payments from the defeated nation. Although it would be an oversimplification to blame the reparations alone for the many economic problems of Weimar Germany, it is clear that they did not help preserve economic stability. Even if the reparations did virtually no harm to the German economy, many believed that they did. What people think is always more influential than what is actually the case. By forcing the founders of the republic to accept the treaty and the reparations, the Allies helped to discredit the founders in the eyes of many Germans. This provided grounds for the rightist charge that the Weimar coalition, which had accepted the treaty and designed the republic, had betrayed the fatherland. Once many Germans lost faith in the republic and its founders, as is shown by the election of 1920 that gave a majority to the critics of the constitution, it became impossible for the republicans to gain the support needed to challenge the growing radicalism of the right. Even the Stresemann era, with its relative stability and the revisions of the reparation payment schedule in the Dawes and Young plans, failed to restore completely faith in the republic. The coming of the depression and the refusal of the French to recognize the importance of radical revision or elimination of the reparations, until forced to do so by the combined action of the English and Americans, provided the right with the opportunity to seize power legally. The failure of the Allies to realize that their policies only alienated the German people helped to condemn the republic before it even had a chance by discrediting the one element in German politics that might have been able to provide a viable alternative to national socialism.

In a real sense, the major reason for the failure of the Weimar

Republic lay with the German people themselves. Schooled in the nationalism of the prewar era and the cult of the folk, and beset by economic and political chaos, they were unable to develop the commitment to democracy necessary for the salvation of the republic. They had never really participated in their government under the rule of the princes and an authoritarian kaiser, and they were unable to cope with their new political power. When the republic failed to deal effectively with the Allies and the economic distress, many Germans lost what little faith they had in their leadership and turned instead to the old traditions of duty and order. Thus, when Hitler appealed to their subconscious feelings, many responded favorably, and the Third Reich became a terrible reality. Naturally, as almost always, the nazi leader lied to the people. Had he told them that he would turn their country into a tyranny and adopt an aggressive foreign policy that would lead the Reich to war, perhaps the German people would have refused to fall victim to his effective speeches.

Yet Hitler's victory was not inevitable. Germany had other traditions, and had the climate been different these might have triumphed over the extremism of the Nazis. German culture had produced many great philosophers of humanism, whose ideas could have provided the foundation for a successful democracy. The end of the First World War provided a golden opportunity to create a liberal state in place of the empire. Unfortunately, a combination of many factors prevented this, and paved the way for the destruction of freedom in Germany. Had events taken a different turn in 1918 or 1919, had the victors adopted a more realistic policy toward the defeated nation, had the politicians been more courageous, and had the people been able to devote themselves to the success of the republic, Germany and Europe might have been spared Hitler's tyranny.

In conclusion, Hitler did not really destroy the Weimar Republic. He merely completed a process begun by others. In a real sense, the democratic republic did not fall on January 30, 1933, when Hitler assumed office, or even on March 23, 1933, with the passage of the Enabling Act. It ended on July 16, 1930, when, unable to command the allegiance of the majority of the Reichstag, Chancellor Brüning invoked Article 48 of the Weimar constitution to rule by decree. Once the head of the ministry began to reject democratic forms, the transformation of Germany into a dictatorship had begun. Brüning's successor, Papen, also unable to win the support of the Reichstag, failed to reverse the trend. Instead, he continued to rule by decree, ruthlessly crushing the freely elected government of Prussia. Hitler, who came to power not by revolution but by legal means as the leader of the largest faction of the Reichstag, did not depart from established traditions when he turned Germany into a dictatorship. He merely used the precedents set by others to complete a process already begun.

13

The Nazi Dictatorship

The passage of the Enabling Act marked the beginning of the nazi tyranny. With the power to dictate his will to the German people, Hitler and his friends had the might to transform every aspect of German society and government to fit the ideology of national socialism. During the Coordination, or *Gleichschaltung,* period, the nazi masters of Germany forced every individual, group, or organ of the state to conform to the principle of strong leadership by the führer. They turned Germany into a vast prison, stamping out every vestige of freedom of action or thought. Every real or potential opponent of Hitler felt the full wrath of the hated secret police, and those who were lucky enough to escape with their lives found themselves living little better than animals in concentration camps. It was the Jews, the symbol to the Nazis of all that was evil, who met a most horrible fate at the hands of their new lords. They watched helplessly as the Storm Troopers destroyed their businesses and burnt their places of worship.

Hitler's first use of his new power was to eliminate the state governments, already under the control of his commissars, as potential rivals to the national government. On March 31, 1933, the ministry issued a decree dissolving all state diets, county, city, and town councils and reorganizing them according to the results of the national election of March 5, 1933. However, this was only a preliminary step, for on April 7 Hitler announced the Second Law for the Coordination of the States with the Reich, which swept away the last remnants of local sovereignty and handed all power to special governors appointed by the führer. Hitler became the head of the Prussian government. On January 30, 1934, the führer asked for, and received from the Reichstag, the passage of the Law Concerning the Reconstruction of the Reich. Proclaiming it the will of the people to abolish all borders between the citizens of Germany, the new legislation completed the process begun a year earlier by destroying the powerless state governments and by placing control of local affairs in the hands of the minister of the interior, Wilhelm Frick. On February 14 Hitler signed a decree abolishing the Upper House of the Reichstag and granting its powers to the ministry. Thus, the Third Reich had ended the long struggle between the states and national government that had dominated much of modern German history.[1]

While destroying the local governments, the Nazis also worked to crush all possible political opposition. Hitler had already used the burning of the Reichstag to ban the Communists, and on June 22, 1933, the minister of the interior announced the dissolution of the Social Democrats. Accompanying the decree, the Nazis issued a statement accusing the socialist leadership of treason for organizing antinazi activity from exile in Prague. The rulers of Germany also charged that the police in Hamburg had found evidence of a socialist plot to betray the fatherland. Seeing the futility of resistance, the leaders of the Democratic party announced its end a few days later. Hugenberg of the Nationalists had joined Hitler's cabinet on condition that the Brown Shirts respect the rights of his organization. However, the Nationalists were also the target of nazi oppression. After Hugenberg's resignation from the ministry on June 29, the Nationalists followed the example of the Democrats and ceased to exist. The Center party, under the leadership of Brüning, who had become head of the organization after Kaas had gone to Rome following the passage of the Enabling Act, tried valiantly to withstand the Nazi oppression. However, after the pope showed his willingness to negotiate with Hitler, the Center lost one of its most important supporters and ceased to exist on July 5. On July 14, 1933, Hitler issued a decree recognizing the National Socialists Workers' party as the only legal political organization in the Reich and forbidding the organization of rival parties. Finally, on December 1, the ministry issued an order unifying the Nazi party with the state. Thus, the nazi seizure of the government became an accomplished fact.

After bringing the government under total control, the Nazis turned to the "coordination" of the labor movement. In 1933 the Free Trade Union of the Social Democrats had a membership of 4.5 million, the Christian Unions of 1 million, and the liberal unions of

500,000. Hitler, remembering the ability of organized labor to cripple the nation through a general strike, such as that which had toppled the Kapp Putsch, realized that the Nazis must bring the unions under control. At first the leaders of labor, aware of Hitler's power and brutality, cooperated with him, but this was not enough. On April 1, 1933, he issued a decree declaring May 1 the Day of National Labor. The first of May had long been dedicated to the solidarity of the working classes, but because of its association with Marxism, the leaders of the Weimar Republic had refused to recognize May Day as a national holiday. Now Hitler decreed that all workers must join the managers and owners to demonstrate for the new national socialist state on May 1. On that day Hitler addressed a large rally of workers assembled at Tempelhof Field in Berlin. The führer proclaimed that the birth of the Third Reich spelled the end of class differences and the advent of a new unified Germany dedicated to the principles of national socialism. In this and similar rallies throughout the Reich, many workers demonstrated their faith in their destiny under Hitler's leadership.

After the speeches and songs had subsided, Hitler set about destroying the labor unions. The next day bands of Storm Troopers seized the offices of the unions, their newspapers, and banks and sent the leaders to join the other potential opponents of the dictatorship in the concentration camps. On May 10 the new Nazi-dominated German Labor Front held its first national congress. This group grew to a membership of 20 million which was greater than that of the old unions. However, it made no real effort to represent the grievances of the workers. Instead, labor trustees, appointed by Hitler on May 19, 1933, set wages and controlled working conditions. The Labor Front, led by Robert Ley, became an arm of the Nazi party dedicated to indoctrinating the proletariat with the principles of Hitlerism. However, the Labor Front did make an effort to win the support of the workers by assuming the functions of social welfare programs from state and private organizations.

Perhaps the most successful and popular program of the German Labor Front was the Strength Through Joy organization. This movement was designed to win the enthusiastic sympathy of the workers by making them feel that they had a right to enjoy the privileges formerly reserved to the upper classes. It supported an ambitious program of theatrical performances, concerts, operas, films, sport and hiking groups, and adult education. It subsidized the development of a people's car, or Volkswagen, promising that soon every working family would own their own private automobile. Although only a few actually received Volkswagens, this aspect of the Strength Through Joy movement outlasted national socialism and even today forms one of the most important industries of the Federal Republic of Germany. The movement also sponsored special travel programs for the workers to rural vacation spots and foreign countries like Norway and Italy. Two ships took eager workers on holidays, previously available only to the rich. Although few actually had an opportunity to take advantage of the cruises and trips, and some parties actually consisted of more upper-class men and women than workers, the travel program became a symbol of the new classless society of nazi Germany.

The nazi rulers of Germany were also interested in the fate of the agricultural areas. Alfred Hugenberg, the minister of economics and agriculture, sponsored a program to raise prices to benefit rural interests and enable them to escape the crushing debts many had incurred during the agricultural depression. Since Hugenberg was a Nationalist and of doubtful loyalty to Hitler, Alfred Derres emerged as the chief nazi agrarian planner. Born in Argentina, Derres had written several books in the late 1920s advocating a new agrarian order based on the peasants who had come from the pure German soil. He became Hitler's chief adviser on agricultural affairs and organized party work in rural areas. After Hitler's assumption of power, Derre worked to bring the German farmer under nazi control. He charged the leaders of the Nationalist Reich Land League with corruption and engineered their replacement with trusted Nazis. This successful effort discredited Hugenberg, and on June 29, 1933, he handed in his forced resignation. That same day, Hitler's cabinet divided the Ministry of Economics and Agriculture into the Ministry of Economics under Kurt Schmidt and the Ministry of Food and Agriculture under Derre.

The Nazis supported an ambitious but only moderately successful program to bring relief to the hard-pressed German farmers. Influenced by the cult of the folk, the new masters of Germany tried to build an agrarian economy based on small farms toiled upon by peasant families. On May 15 and September 29, 1933, the government issued decrees forbidding the sale, mortgage, or division of holdings of 7.5 to 10 hectares. Since this would mean the inheritance of the farm by only the oldest son, the government also sponsored a program to create new farms for those unable to inherit their fathers' lands. During the period of the Third Reich, despite violent opposition from the holders of large estates, the rulers of Germany supported the formation of 20,748 new farms, with a total area of 325,611 hectares. However, the leaders of the Weimar Republic had created 38,711 new farms, with an area of 429,934 hectares. Thus, Hitler's efforts to establish new landholdings fell short of those of his predecessors.

At the same time, the government placed complete control of prices and distribution in the hands of the Reich Food Estate, *Reichsnährstand*. This body supported high prices in an effort to stimulate production. Although the farmers received more money for their products, a combination of bad weather and a labor shortage prevented the hoped for rise in supplies. Grain reserves actually fell from 22.5 million metric tons in 1931 to 21.1 million metric tons in 1935. Other agricultural products, such as livestock and dairy products, experienced a similar decline. In addition, farm income increased only slightly, far less than industrial income. Thus, the attempt to stimulate agriculture failed to live up to the expectations of Hitler and his followers.

Despite the relative failure of nazi agrarian policy, the party tried to win the enthusiastic support of the farmers as it had won the sympathy of the workers. The government, following the example of the successful demonstrations of May 1 for workers, proclaimed October 1, 1933, the Memorial Day of the German Peasants. On that day Hitler spoke to 500,000 farmers near Hamlein, exhorting them to join their fellow Germans in bringing a new day of prosperity to the fatherland. All over the country farmers attended similar rallies to pledge their loyalty to their führer.

Nazi policy toward big business was like its policy toward the farmer—torn between those who advocated measures for the little men and those who sympathized with the captains of large industry. After Hitler's victory the radical wing of the party called for an economic revolution that would destroy the hold of big business over the German economy and create a corporate state on the model of fascist Italy. Max Frauendorfer, head of the party Office of Corporate Organization, Otto Wilhelm Wagener, the party's chief economist, and the leaders of the Storm Troopers argued that the new economy must be built on the interests of the folk. However, the supporters of big business successfully withstood the demands of the radicals. On February 20, 1933, the leaders of the Reich Association of German Industry met at Göring's home to contribute three million marks to the nazi cause. Hjalmar Schacht, head of the national bank, and Walter Funk, chief of the party's Committee on Economic Policy, argued for a policy favoring the interests of big business. Hitler, unwilling to offend a group that had provided him with so much money, declared his opposition to the radicals and demanded Wagener's resignation. However, the conflict between the radicals and the conservatives continued until the bloody purge of 1934.

The leaders of industry favored cooperation with Hitler as a means to achieve a strong state and a strong economy. Although a few members of the Reich Federation of German Industry resigned, Gustaf Krupp, the head of the Krupp munitions empire, remained its president. In June the federation joined the Association of German Employers to form the Reich Estate of German Industry. On February 27, 1934, the Law for Preparing an Organic Structure of the German Economy granted the Ministry of Economics the power to organize trade associations. On November 27, 1934, the government established the National Economic Chamber as the head of an elaborate hierarchy of industrial and trade organizations under the control of the Ministry of Economics. Each businessman was required to join either one of the one hundred local chambers of industry and commerce or one of the seventy local chambers of handicrafts. These organizations were under the supervision of twenty-three regional economic chambers, which were controlled by seven national groups representing industry, trade, banking, insurance, power, tourism, and handicrafts. Each businessman had to join the local and regional organizations and the national chamber controlling his specific industry.

Despite the efforts to "coordinate" every aspect of industrial activity, Hitler and his aides granted special privileges to their supporters in big business. The government supported the monopolies and even organized cartels in areas not already under their control. The masters of nazi Germany also favored the concentration of wealth and power in the hands of a few individuals or groups of individuals. In 1934 the government issued a decree granting tax benefits to corporations willing to convert to private ownership by one person or a few persons rather than by many individual stockholders. Thus, despite the demands of the radical Socialists within the party, the actual leaders of the Third Reich favored a policy that allowed the leaders of big business to consolidate their power.

Although nazi economic policy favored the interests of the large cooperatives and cartels, the leaders of nazi Germany made an appeal for the support of small businessmen and retailers. Many shopkeepers had joined the nazi movement to crush the large department and chain stores and consumer cooperatives that had taken many of their customers. On May 3, 1933, the Nazi Fighting League of the Industrial Middle Class persuaded the masters of the new Germany to establish the Reich Estate of Trade and Handicrafts to regulate the retail trade. The government also issued the Law for the Protection of Retail Trade, which banned the expansion of department and chain stores and promised to protect the interests of the small tradesman. Meanwhile, party organizations such as the Fighting League, the Storm Troopers, and the women's organization sponsored boycotts of the large stores. Hitler and his advisers enforced these boycotts by decrees increasing taxation of the large establishments and other similar measures. However, the power and size of the large stores worked to their advantage, and after 1934 government harassment halted, allowing them to continue to capture most of the retail trade.

The nazi effort to destroy consumer cooperatives met with a similar fate. Hitler halted Papen's policy of granting subsidies to the cooperatives on April 27, 1933, and the Labor Front and other nazi groups took over their direction. In March 1934 the small retailers were able to force the cooperatives to agree to limit their membership. The next year the government ordered them disbanded and introduced new taxes designed to favor their competitors. Through the campaign against consumer organizations, the government was able to force 72 of the largest cooperatives to disband, although 1,187 smaller ones survived. Finally, the nazi directors who had taken over the remaining cooperatives were able to prevent their destruction, and by 1934 the campaign had ended. Thus, once again, nazi economic policy began by favoring the interests of the middle class and ended by supporting their chief competitors.

The nazi financial policy was much more successful than the other aspects of the economic program. Hitler's chief goal was to end unemployment through public works projects and rearmament. He announced a major program to build a series of superhighways that would provide many needed jobs and would serve important military needs. In September 1933 the construction of the first autobahn began. In the first year of the Third Reich, the government spent 3 million marks on the project. By 1938 this had increased to 916 million marks a year. The government sponsored other public works projects costing 1.5 billion marks. Meanwhile, Hitler and his advisers spent 60 million marks to rebuild the war machine. Through these programs, Hitler was able to reduce unemployment and to begin to lead Germany out of the depression. Naturally, many of the newly employed workers became strong supporters of the führer.

During the early years of the Third Reich, the chief architect of governmental finances was Horace Greeley Hjalmar Schacht, the son of a former emigrant to the United States who had returned to his fatherland in 1871. The financial wizard of nazi Germany studied economics at the University of Munich and became a director of the national bank at thirty-nine. He served as an economic adviser to the occupation forces in Belgium during the First World War and returned to become president of the German National Bank in 1923. Schacht had been an important figure in Stresemann's economic programs but became a supporter of Hitler, believing that a nazi victory would restore a strong government. Schacht used his influence in the early years of the Third Reich to defeat the attack on big business by the radicals. He became minister of economics in August 1934.

Schacht immediately began a program to increase government revenues. He devised a plan to create a new semiofficial currency, the Mefo bills, from *Metallurgische Forshungsgesellschaft* ("Metallurgical Research Corporation"). This was a firm created with government support by several large businesses. It had the power to issue bills of credit to be redeemed at 4 percent interest. Schacht persuaded many people to buy these Mefo bills, thus providing new sums of money to the hard-pressed government. At the same time, taxes increased, providing yet another source of revenue. Through Schacht's efforts, the government gathered six billion marks for the rearmament program.

The chief financial expert of the Third Reich also attempted to curtail the flow of German currency to foreign merchants. Schacht devised The New Plan to place all imports and exports under strict governmental control. He negotiated agreements with countries in Latin America and southeastern Europe to obtain needed raw materials by barter rather than cash. He also established special clearinghouses to handle those transactions requiring change of currency. A German buyer of a foreign product would deposit marks in the clearinghouse, which in turn would pay the exporter in the currency of his own country, thus curtailing the export of German marks. Meanwhile, Schacht worked to limit imports to only those items absolutely needed to support the rearmament campaign.

However, Schacht soon fell into sharp disagreement with Hitler.

The führer sought a program to make Germany independent of foreign sources of raw materials. For example, at the beginning of Hitler's reign, Germany imported 80 percent of its iron ore from Sweden, Spain, Luxemburg, Norway, and Greece. It obtained 85 percent of its oil from North and South America. Under pressure from Hitler, Schacht, who became special commissar for the war economy in 1935, attempted to utilize existing firms to produce synthetic raw materials. In 1933 he persuaded I. G. Farben to begin production of synthetic oil by agreeing that the government would buy the oil for ten years at a fixed price. He tried to negotiate similar agreements with other firms. However, his progress was not fast enough to please the impatient Hitler, who demanded increased spending on rearmament and the program to make the Reich independent of foreign raw materials. Finally, because of this disagreement and Schacht's criticism of the campaign against the Jews, he lost his position. In 1944, he would be thrown in prison for association with the plot to assassinate the führer.

Hitler turned to his old comrade in arms, Hermann Göring, to develop the German economy along lines more acceptable to his long-range goals. In March 1936 the führer appointed his friend commissioner of foreign exchange and raw materials. Although Schacht remained minister of economics for another year, Göring emerged as the master of the economy. He announced the Four Year Plan, designed to make the Reich completely self-sufficient within four years. Hitler endorsed the project and informed businessmen that they would have to meet the needs of the Reich or perish! The government issued decrees regulating all aspects of the economy, including wages, prices, and production quotas. Göring and his advisers controlled the distribution of credit, manpower, resources, and transportation facilities.

However, Göring was not totally successful in dealing with the large corporations. He demanded that they increase iron ore production by 10 million tons. They refused to comply, arguing that it would be cheaper to import iron ore from Sweden. Finally, the economic tsar of the Third Reich established the Hermann Göring Works to produce iron from domestic sources. Although he hoped that the new firm would produce 4 million tons annually, it was able to produce only a small amount of the quota, and in 1942 it manufactured only one-fourth of the projected pig iron. The failure of the Hermann Göring Works led to plans, after the annexation of Austria in 1938, to develop Austrian ore and to build a steel mill at Linz. However, this project failed. Despite this setback, Göring was able to build on Schacht's programs to sponsor agreements with other business firms. I. G. Farben was successful in its efforts to produce synthetic oil, and by 1940 the supply had tripled. Meanwhile, firms made enough artificial rubber to make Germany independent of foreign sources. Domestic production of aluminum also increased. Although operations to mine bauxite ore greatly expanded, German sources could only provide 10 percent of the needed ore, and additional supplies had to be imported from Hungary and Yugoslavia. Thus, the Four Year Plan did not make Germany completely self-sufficient and was a failure in many ways, but it did stimulate domestic production of materials formerly imported from abroad.

Another important aspect of German society that Hitler sought to dominate was the military. The führer had made an effort throughout his career to win the support of the army and constantly invoked the traditions of the Prussian officer corps as an example for all Germans to follow. Hitler realized that he could never crush the strong traditions of independence among the soldiers; so he adopted a policy designed to win their support while attempting to bring the military under his complete control. On July 20, 1933, he issued a new army law abolishing the authority of civilian courts over military matters. He also ended the practice of the election of spokesmen to represent the interests of the enlisted men. Naturally, this won the approval of the officers who resented the attempts of the founders of the Weimar Republic to curtail their power.[2]

Hitler did not rely solely on his efforts to gain support from the officers; he also tried to place loyal party members in important positions within the military. He acknowledged the appointment of Werner von Blomberg as minister of war by Hindenburg in the last hours before his own appointment. Blomberg had served as a staff officer during the First World War and as commander in East Prussia during the last years of the Weimar Republic. He was sympathetic to the goals of national socialism; so he immediately began removing supporters of Schleicher and replacing them with loyal Nazis. However, his dedication to the führer caused much resentment among the officers, who saw the nazi rule as merely an interlude in preparation for the restoration of the monarchy. When Hitler and his minister of war attempted to appoint Walter von Reichenau, a moderate Nazi and former chief of staff at Königsburg, chief of the army command, they met with stiff resistance from Hindenburg. The aging field marshal resented the efforts of the Nazis to interfere in what he considered the private affairs of the military, and he regarded Reichenau as unqualified for such an important position. When Blomberg threatened to resign unless the old soldier approved Reichenau's appointment, Hindenburg coldly informed him that he had the right to resign his political position, but he had no right to question the wisdom of his military superiors. Finally, Colonel General Werner von Fritsch, a close friend and adviser to Hitler, became chief of the army command. Although Hitler continued to enlarge his control over the military, he was never able to win the complete support of the officers.

Related to the conflict between Hitler and the army leadership was the question of the role of the Storm Troopers in the new Germany. Under Röhm's effective leadership, Hitler's private army grew to rival the army itself. By December 31, 1933, the membership of the Stahlhelm had joined the Brown Shirts, as had many former Communists who wanted to save themselves from the consequences of their earlier activities by joining the victors. However, the rapid growth of the S.A. (the abbreviation for the Storm Troopers) only alarmed Hitler, because Röhm openly sympathized with the more radical Nazis who called for an enactment of the socialistic aspects of the official party platform. Thousands read the press of the Storm Troopers, which praised their leader but seldom found space to speak of the accomplishments of Hitler. The Brown Shirts established their own private air force, medical service, engineer corps, and intelligence service. They also usurped the power of the local authorities by enforcing a swift and brutal S.A. "justice" against the critics of national socialism.

The strength of Röhm's forces grew to such an alarming proportion that finally, on December 1, 1933, Hitler appointed him minister without portfolio in the hope of winning his unquestioned loyalty. However, Röhm used his new position to enhance that of the Brown Shirts. In February 1934 he outlined a proposal to unite the command of the armed forces into a single organization headed by a minister. Naturally, he hoped that Hitler would name him to this post. However, upon hearing of this threat to the traditional independence of the army, Hindenburg flew into a rage and thwarted Röhm's plan. Undaunted by this setback, the head of the S.A. only increased his efforts. He established a special Storm Trooper foreign office that began to deal with foreign diplomats as if it had replaced the foreign office. Röhm sponsored elaborate banquets in honor of foreign emissaries and even attempted to open negotiations with the French ambassador, Andre Francois Poncet. Röhm also argued that his forces should become the new German army and replace the traditional military command.

Naturally the officer corps resented the rapid rise of the Storm Troopers. They considered military activities their exclusive right and resented the gang of streetfighters and drunkards who dared to challenge their position. Blomberg and his fellow officers decided to win Hitler's support by showing that the military could be turned into a nazi organization. In February 1934 the minister of war announced that members of the military could wear the swastika as a part of their official uniform, and he began a program to include the indoctrination of the ideas of the führer in the training of every soldier. On May 25 he issued a statement on the duties of the German soldier that clearly obligated all members of the armed forces to fight for the Third Reich and its leader.

Hitler, resenting the radicalism and independence of the S.A. and realizing that he could not afford to alienate the military, finally decided that Röhm and his followers had to be crushed. The führer learned in May that Hindenburg was in poor health, and Hitler feared that the Storm Troopers might use his death as an excuse to seize power for themselves. On June 7, 1934, Röhm vacationed in Bad Wiessee, thirty miles south of Munich. Aware of the possibility that his enemies might use his absence as an excuse to move against the S.A., he granted the Brown Shirts a month's furlough. At the same time, he announced that this should not be misinterpreted as a sign of weakness, for after their rest, the Storm Troopers would return to achieve new heights. However, Hitler decided to act swiftly and telephoned Röhm at his retreat on the evening of June 27 to order him to call a meeting of the leaders of the S.A. at Bad Wiessee at nine on the morning of June 30.

With the trap laid, Hitler flew to Munich from Bonn in the darkness of the morning of the scheduled meeting. He then drove to Bad Wiessee. There, in the early hours of June 30, 1934, Hitler and armed policemen burst into the room of the sleeping leader of the S.A. and personally arrested the startled Röhm. He also seized the leaders assembled at the resort, including Edmund Heines of Silesia, who was found sleeping with a homosexual. They took their captives back to Munich and threw them into prison, where Hitler's men brutally murdered Röhm after he refused to take his own life. The führer issued a decree removing Röhm from office and ordering the Storm Troopers to obey his commands or suffer expulsion from the organization and the party. The führer also ordered his own forces into action, and all over Germany loyal men seized local S.A. headquarters, killing all who resisted. Nazi bands hacked the body of the former commissar of Bavaria, Gustav von Kahr, to pieces and threw it into a swamp; others murdered Gregor Strasser. Even Schleicher had not won immunity for his help to Hitler the year before. An armed band broke into his home, filling his body with bullets as he sat at his desk, his helpless wife watching in horror. In all, two hundred people lost their lives during the Night of the Long Knives, and Hitler emerged the unquestioned master of the nazi movement.

Then Hitler became the absolute head of the German Reich. On August 1, 1934, tired after a long and active life, Hindenburg died, and the führer lost no time in announcing the combination of the office of president with that of chancellor. The next day he ordered all members of the military to swear to give their lives, if necessary, in the service of Hitler as the absolute führer of the Reich. Seventeen days later 45,473,635, or 95.7 percent of the qualified voters, went to the polls to express their approval of Hitler's actions in a national plebiscite. After the votes of almost a million had been declared invalid, 89.9 percent favored Hitler's rule. Thus, by the end of the summer of 1934, Hitler was the supreme dictator of both the Nazi party and the German Reich.

The chief author of Hitler's complete victory over the S.A. was Heinrich Himmler, head of the *Schutzstaffeln,* ("Security Units") or S.S. Hitler had formed the S.S. as a private bodyguard after his release from prison, and on January 6, 1929, the führer appointed Himmler head of the S.S. Himmler, the son of a teacher from Munich, was born on October 7, 1900. He served briefly in the First World War. An agriculturalist by education and profession, Himmler had participated in the Beer Hall Putsch and had joined the party in 1925. Leaving his chicken farm to serve his leader, Himmler proved to be an effective organizer and increased the membership of the S.S., or Black Shirts, from 290 to 52,000 by 1933. Reinhard Heydrich, a former lieutenant in the navy, who had been discharged for corruption, was Himmler's chief assistant. In 1932 Himmler named Heydrich chief of the security service of the S.S.[3]

Under Himmler's guidance, the S.S. consisted of several divisions. The General S.S. formed a more respectable form of the Brown Shirts and attracted university graduates, government officials, and physicians. The Active S.S. consisted of three additional groups: the Personal Guard Regiment of the führer, which by 1933 had been enlarged into a fully armed division; the Armed S.S., which served as a private army, played a major role in the Blood Purge of 1934, and later served as a combat force during the Second World War; and the Death's Head units, which administered the concentration camps. The S.S. formed a bulwark of dedicated Nazis fanatically loyal to the führer and willing to do anything at his command. During the Third Reich, the S.S. would become one of his most effective instruments of terror and would spread their ghastly influence to conquered territories during the Second World War.[4]

In addition to his role as head of the S.S., Himmler also emerged as the leader of the police. In March 1933 Göring placed the Prussian political police under the Ministry of the Interior. The next month he created the hated Secret State Police, or Gestapo, in Berlin and established Gestapo offices throughout the Reich. The secret police rooted out all possible opposition to the nazi dictatorship and acted outside the authority of the courts. Although Himmler had brought the Bavarian police under his control in March 1933, and within a few weeks had gained domination over the police of every area except Prussia, he was still subject to Göring's orders. Finally, on July 17, 1936, Hitler appointed the head of the S.S. as chief of the German police. Himmler, free of supervision, integrated the criminal police with the Gestapo and divided the constabulary into two divisions. The first, the Order Police, had jurisdiction over local matters such as fire control, streets and roads, public works, and protection against air raids. The second, the Security Police under Heydrich, controlled the Gestapo, the criminal police, and counterespionage activities. In 1938 Himmler organized the Security Police into ten groups to control every aspect of German life, including the churches, the press, homosexuality, and political oppression. On September 27, 1939, Heydrich became the chief of the Reich Security Office, which regulated all aspects of police activity. The well-organized police of the Third Reich respected the civil rights of no one. They often pounced on a suspected enemy of the state by night, tearing him from his sleeping family and carried him away to oblivion in police vans. The police were assisted in their reign of terror by the organization of the special People's Court on April 24, 1934. This five-member tribunal had the power to try cases of treason against the Reich.

Himmler controlled the concentration camps through the S.S. The first camps had been established after the mass arrests of thousands of Socialists and Communists on February 28, 1933, when the prisons and headquarters of the S.A. were too small to accommodate the captives. On March 30, 1933, Himmler opened an S.S. concentration camp in the abandoned barracks of an old power plant in Dachau, near Munich. During the next few weeks, S.S. units established fourteen additional camps, including Columbia House, a special prison in Berlin. In 1934 Himmler founded the Death's Head units, so-called for the skull on their collars, to administer the camps. On June 20 Black Shirts replaced the S.A. guards in the remaining camps.

The model camp was Dachau, under the command of Theodor Eicke, who was from Alsace-Lorraine. During the First World War he served as a paymaster in the military. When peace came he joined the police but was expelled for his extreme rightist political activities. Eicke joined the S.S. in 1928 after working in the security department of I. G. Farben. That year he fled to Italy to avoid imprisonment for his part in a terrorist bombing, and he did not return to Germany until February 1933. Before assignment to Dachau, Eicke was under the care of Dr. Werner Heyde, a psychiatrist in Würzburg, who later headed the nazi euthanasia program. In 1934 Eicke participated in the capture and murder of Röhm. That same year, he became inspector of concentration camps. At Dachau, Eicke presided over a world of terror and brutality in which the prisoners were subjected to inhuman conditions and punishments administered in an impersonal manner by members of the S.S. In Dachau and other camps, the sadistic guards forced their captives to stand for hours clad in flimsy clothing in the dead of winter for roll calls. They beat prisoners, made them stand naked in the snow, threw them into pits, and even tortured animals before releasing them to attack the weak inmates. Some guards killed prisoners for sport by shooting them or injecting poison into their bodies. They gave the inmates substandard food and medicine. Rudolf Höss, the future murderer of millions, served at Dachau under Eicke.[5]

Although the first months of the Third Reich had led to the mass arrest and imprisonment of thousands, the middle period saw a decline in the number of prisoners. In 1937, with only 10,000 inmates, the masters of Germany began to dissolve some of the camps, so that the next year only three camps, staffed with about 1,000 members of the Death's Head units and 120 S.S. men, were still in existence.

However, in 1938 a new reign of suppression began, which included "antisocial" elements such as homosexuals, criminals, political prisoners, Jehovah's Witnesses, and those who did not work well. The camps once again were filled with captives. The anti-Jewish campaign of November 9, 1938, added another 30,000 prisoners, although many were released after a few weeks if they would agree to leave Germany. By the beginning of the Second World War, about 25,000 people lived a tortured life at the hands of the S.S. Death's Head units. During the war the camps would experience a rebirth and serve as the sites of one of the greatest crimes in modern history: the mass extermination of millions of Jews, Slavs, Gypsies, and others.

One of the most sinister aspects of Himmler's program was his effort to create a "super" race. He was a dedicated believer in the official nazi ideology of the racial superiority of the Aryan peoples and established the S.S. Race and Land Settlement Office. This arm of Himmler's empire checked the background of applicants to the S.S. to insure their racial purity, and it sponsored a program to settle Aryans on land seized from so-called inferior peoples. Before the Second World War, only a small amount of land was settled under the auspices of the office, but after the conquest of Poland and parts of the Soviet Union, Himmler and his followers planned to extend this program to the occupied areas.

In December 1935 Himmler sponsored the formation of the Lebensborn movement to create a new race of supermen to rule Europe in the future. This plan, one of the most immoral of all nazi schemes, advocated large families and encouraged unwed mothers of acceptable racial background to offer their children to the führer. This organization set up special homes where these nazi children could be born and cared for until they could be adopted by Aryan families. The first of these "baby farms" was built at Steinhöring, near Munich, in 1936. Unwed pregnant women came here to have their babies, after which the officials reported the births not to the local authorities but to the Lebensborn headquarters in Munich. The children received names in a nazi parody of Christian baptism. Only healthy infants had the right to stay in the homes; sickly or deformed babies were sent to other institutions, where many died.

Himmler expected every S.S. officer to become a father, and often promotions depended on a man's ability to sire a child. Because many S.S. officers were unwed, and also to encourage the married ones to have as many children as possible, special breeding houses were established. In Munich the S.S. rented a house where the future fathers could be entertained and have sexual intercourse with willing women of the proper racial background. After the woman became pregnant, she went to Steinhöring to have her baby. Since such a program would arouse the moral indignation of many Germans and violate the moral image of the Third Reich, the S.S. made every effort to keep this activity secret. Guards surrounded the Lebensborn buildings, and participants swore to absolute secrecy. After the Second World War, many former Lebensborn workers claimed that the homes were merely charity homes for unwed mothers. With the fall of the Third Reich, many of the children born as a result of the Lebensborn movement were adopted by American, Swiss, or English parents. Many believed that their parents had died in concentration camps or were killed in the fighting. In the tragic aftermath of Hitler's tyranny, a few discovered their origins and tried, without success, to discover their true parents.

The nazi racial policy reserved a special place for the 500,000 Jews living in Germany. One of the basic principles of national socialism was violent anti-Semitism, and Hitler was determined to eradicate all Jewish influence in the Reich. On March 26, 1933, he ordered Goebbels, the minister of propaganda, to organize a boycott of all Jewish businesses to begin on April 1. However, before the action could begin, mobs of brown-shirted thugs began their own spontaneous campaign. They broke in and looted or destroyed Jewish shops, harassed Jews on the street, and took every opportunity to intimidate the Jews. Naturally, news of these outrages, transmitted in urgent letters and telegrams to relatives and friends abroad, caused a wave of anti-German feeling to sweep the world. In the United States, sympathizers began a boycott of German products. This action so startled Hitler and his friends that they began an effort to counter stories of anti-Semitic acts by organizing the Central Committee for Defense Against Jewish Atrocity and Boycott Propaganda. However, despite denials of harassment of the Jews, the party organized local boycott committees and on the appointed day placed two brown-shirted sentries at the door of every Jewish business to inform the would-be customers that shopping there would be helping the enemies of the Reich. Finally, because of foreign pressure and fears of economic sanctions, the boycott ended on April 4. Nevertheless, the damage had been done, and the first step toward Auschwitz and Dachau had been taken.[6]

After the end of the boycott, Hitler and his advisers began a campaign to deprive the Jews of all civil rights. On April 7 the ministry enacted the Law for the Restoration of the Professional Civil Service, the first of over four hundred anti-Jewish acts to be issued during the nazi tyranny. This legislation provided for the elimination from the bureaucracy of all Jews and anti-Nazis. On April 25 the government issued the Law Against the Overcrowding of German Schools and Institutions of Higher Learning to bar non-Aryans from access to universities and other schools. A few weeks later the government decreed a purge of the faculties of the schools and universities of all Jews and other critics of Hitler. Other acts forbade Jews from participation in the cultural and journalistic professions. On July 14 the Law on the Revocation of Naturalization and Annulment of German Citizenship deprived Jews naturalized during the Weimar Republic of their citizenship. Later, the Hereditary Farm Law of September 29 forbade persons with Jewish ancestry from inheriting land. Even the Jewish religion was not immune to persecution, for on April 21 the government banned shehitah, the ceremonial killing of animals by Jews. Thus, within the first few months of the Third Reich, Jews found themselves robbed of many of the civil rights they had fought so hard to obtain in the last century.

In charge of the legal persecution of the German Jews was Wilhelm Frick, who was born in 1877, the son of a teacher in the Palatinate, and who earned a law degree from the University of Heidelberg. After several years of private practice he found a position in the police of Munich, where he spent the First World War. During the Revolution of 1918 the Communists arrested him, and he became a fanatical rightist. He was attracted to national socialism and participated in the Beer Hall Putsch. In 1924 he was elected to the Reichstag as part of a pro-nazi coalition of Nazis and the German Folkish party. After several years in the parliament, where he became the leader of the brown-shirted faction, Frick became the minister of the interior in Thuringia, the first Nazi to hold a position in a German government. In 1933 Frick became the minister of the interior and assisted in the drafting of anti-Semitic legislation.

The anti-Jewish frenzy reached a crescendo in 1935. Nazis organized new boycotts of Jewish businesses and forcedly kept Jews from attending theaters, swimming pools, or other public places. Whole towns fell under the influence of the fanaticism and posted signs prohibiting Jews from entering the city limits. The campaign reached its height during the Nazi party rally at Nuremberg on September 15, 1935, where, to a crowd of cheering admirers, Hitler announced the Nuremberg Laws. These acts deprived anyone with three Jewish grandparents of all rights of citizenship and forbade marriage and sexual relations between Aryans and non-Aryans. Hitler also forbade Jews to employ any German woman under forty-five as a house servant, lest they enter into a forbidden relationship. Thus, the German Jews lost even those rights not already taken from them by earlier legislation and became mere subjects of the German Reich. Many Jews left their possessions to flee the persecution or sent their children abroad to live with relatives, and thus, by 1938, there were about 375,000 Jews still living under the Nazis.

A new wave of anti-Semitism swept the Third Reich in 1938, bringing the most violent persecution prior to the outbreak of the Second World War. In April of that fatal year, Göring ordered all Jewish businessmen to register their assets and make them available to the government for its economic program. Additional laws prohibited Jews from entering the stock exchanges or the real estate trade. By summer the government required all Jews to carry special identification and to add Israel or Sarah to their names to make them more easily identifiable. On October 4, 1938, the government required all Jews to register all assets of more than 5,000 marks so they could be controlled by their Aryan masters. Meanwhile, nazi thugs continued the campaign of harassment and intimidation.

The continued persecution naturally led to much resentment and finally to a violent reaction. The cause was the case of some 17,000 Polish Jews expelled from Germany in late October. Because the government of their homeland, in the midst of its own anti-Semitic movement, had canceled their citizenship and refused to allow them to enter, they spent several weeks at the border waiting for a solution to their problem. Finally, Warsaw relented and allowed them to enter. However, Herschell Grynspan, the son of one of the Polish Jews, decided to take his vengeance for the mistreatment of his father and assassinated Ernst von Rath, the German ambassador to France, on November 7, 1938. Hitler and his advisers claimed that the murder was part of an international Jewish conspiracy to destroy Germany and intensified the anti-Semitic propaganda. Thousands of Germans throughout the Reich attended memorial services for the slain diplomat.

The campaign reached a new level of violence on November 9, the anniversary of the Beer Hall Putsch. Goebbels delivered a stinging indictment of the Jews and launched a new offensive in the war against the Jews. That evening bands of Storm Troopers, preserving the illusion of spontaneity by not wearing their uniforms, led a series of bloody attacks against the few remaining Jewish businesses. Throughout Germany the nazi criminals beat defenseless Jews mercilessly, killing dozens. They lit the cold November night with the flames of two hundred fifty burning synagogues and covered the streets with the glass of broken windows from Jewish shops. By morning the rabble had demolished over 7,500 businesses. The government, disclaiming all responsibility, charged the Jews with inciting the riot and demanded that they pay the cost of repairing the damage. In addition, the Reich charged the Jews fines totaling a billion marks and sent 30,000 innocent Jews to concentration camps. Throughout the next few months the persecution intensified, and new laws forbade Jews from leaving their homes at night or from owning gold, silver, radios, or telephones. Finally, the Nazi rulers of Germany began moving Jews to special ghettos and introduced forced labor.

Only those Jews willing to emigrate, leaving behind all their possessions, could escape the terror of Nazi anti-Semitism. Even before the riots of November 9, 1938, the so-called Reichskrstallnacht, the masters of the Third Reich had adopted a policy designed to stimulate the Jews to leave Germany. For example, a memo sent to all diplomats of the Third Reich in June 1937 stated that the major objective of Berlin was to force the Jews to emigrate. In early 1938 Adolf Eichmann of the Central Office of the S.S. established the Central Office for Jewish Emigration with headquarters in Vienna. During the months that followed, Eichmann successfully persuaded almost 200,000 Austrian Jews to leave their homes. On January 24 of the next year, Göring, who had decided after the riots of November 9 to unify the various agencies dealing with Jewish emigration, instructed Wilhelm Frick to form the Reich Central Office for the Emigration of the Jews. This office, headed by Heinrich Müller until October 1939, when leadership passed to Eichmann, successfully convinced thousands of Jews to leave their homes and move to other nations. However, the outbreak of the Second World War made Jewish emigration impossible and led the masters of the Third Reich to seek other methods of dealing with the Jews, eventually leading to the deaths of millions of defenseless Jews in the gas chambers.

In addition to Frick, Goebbels, Göring, Himmler, and others, two other men played major roles in the Third Reich, Rudolf Hess and Martin Bormann. Hess joined the movement in its earliest days and served as Hitler's secretary in prison while the führer dictated *Mein Kampf.* After the fall of Strasser in 1932, Hitler named Hess head of the party's Central Political Committee. The next year he became Hitler's official deputy. Martin Bormann, who was Hess's chief assistant, was born in 1900 in Halberstadt, the son of a sergeant in the cavalry. After leaving secondary school without a diploma, Bormann became an official at the estate of the Treuenfels in Herzberg. He served briefly in the field artillery in the last days of the First World War. With the restoration of peace, Bormann joined several anti-Semitic organizations and became a Nazi in 1927. He worked for the party as a journalist in Thuringia and as a member of the Storm Troopers; he married Gerda Buch, a fanatical Nazi, in 1929. By hard work and dedication to detail, he rose in the ranks of the party and became Hess's chief assistant. From this position Bormann became one of the most powerful men in nazi Germany. He spent hours distilling lengthy documents into abbreviated form for his führer and prepared the thousands of documents that served as Hitler's chief source of information and as the basis for many of his actions.

Although the leaders of nazi Germany attempted to convey an impression of middle-class respectability to the public, their private lives were anything but respectable. Goebbels carried on sordid affairs with actresses seeking his favor as dictator of German culture. At one point his wife threatened to divorce him. Only the personal intervention of Hitler, informed of the intimate details by Göring, prevented a national scandal. Göring, whose first wife, Carin, died shortly before the nazi victory, married Emmy Sonnemann, a beautiful actress, in 1935 after a torrid affair. The vain head of the Four Year Plan used his power to live a life of ostentatious splendor. He filled his apartment in Berlin and his estate, Carin Hall, north of the city, with a large collection of valuable paintings and other art objects. Even Bormann shared in the debauchery by keeping a mistress with the full approval of his wife. The secondary figures of the Third Reich fought like children for the favor of the führer and sought every means to undermine the positions of others. Göring's agents placed taps on the telephones of all his potential rivals, and Himmler's men monitored the private conversations of everyone, including Göring and his wife.[7]

The efficiency of Bormann and his rivals freed the führer for other pursuits, for Hitler still fancied himself an architect. He employed

Albert Speer as his chief adviser for his ambitious building projects. Speer was born in Mannheim on March 19, 1905, the son of an architect, and he studied at Karlsruhe, Munich, and Berlin, joining the staff of the Technical Institute in Berlin. Hitler began to notice Speer's work, whose plans for the new Reichstag building greatly impressed him. They spent hours discussing Hitler's plans to rebuild Berlin into a city worthy of the Third Reich. On January 30, 1937, Hitler appointed Speer inspector general of buildings for the renovation of the federal capital. According to the model, the new city would center on a large avenue, running three miles from the Reichstag to a huge domed meeting hall with a diameter of 825 feet and enough room for 150,000 people. An arch more than 400 feet high would stand at the other end of the thoroughfare. Large and impressive governmental buildings were to stand along the boulevard, which would end in two large railway stations, serving all parts of the Reich.[8]

Hitler had other plans for Speer and called him to his office in January 1938 to assign him the task of building a new chancellory within a year. Speer and his assistants spared no expense and kept two shifts of workers busy on the construction. When completed, the new building was a mighty monument to national socialism, designed to impress and fill with awe the foreign diplomats who later made their pilgrimage to negotiate with the führer. At their arrival, they drove through two large gates into an impressive court, and they then climbed an outside staircase to a reception room. To instill a proper attitude of humility, the diplomats had to walk through several other impressive rooms, including a 480-foot-long gallery, twice as long as the Hall of Mirrors at Versailles, which had been the scene of Germany's humiliation in 1919. Finally, they entered the reception room of the master of Germany. Standing on a slippery marble floor, which increased their feeling of insecurity, they encountered the führer, surrounded by four statues representing the virtues of Wisdom, Fortitude, Prudence, and Justice.

Despite the ostentatious chancellory, Hitler's personal habits were rather austere. He dined regularly with about fifty officials who had earned the privilege of eating with their leader. Hitler arrived in the reception room about three in the afternoon and spent about twenty minutes in informal discussions. Then the servants ushered the master of Germany and his guests into the dining room, where they ate a simple meal of meat with vegetables and potato with a dessert. They had a choice of mineral water, Bavarian beer, or inexpensive wine.

Hitler, who normally drank no alcoholic beverages, was content with mineral water; he was a vegetarian, so ate no meat. During the session he entertained his friends with stories about his experiences in the First World War and discussed political issues. A few of the highest placed Nazis received invitations to return for the evening meal. Once again the fare was simple, in keeping with Hitler's tastes. However, for a short time he consumed caviar with great lust, until he realized its cost and ordered his cook to discontinue such frivolities. During the evening repast Hitler led a discussion of petty matters and avoided political issues. After dinner the führer led his guests to a lounge to watch a film, which he selected after consultation with Goebbels. Usually it was a popular movie of the day. Selecting films banned to the general public on occasion, he favored light musicals or dramas, and he avoided productions dealing with the outdoors. The almost frantic way in which he sought to surround himself with adoring groups is an indication of the insecurity of the leader of the Third Reich.[9]

Hitler spent much time at his private retreat in Berchtesgaden, away from the busy atmosphere of Berlin. There, near Salzburg, Austria, he built his summer home high on the Obersalzburg. Bormann surrounded the area with fences and buildings to house the führer's servants and bodyguards. Here, Hitler repeated the scene in Berlin, with a few chosen guests, taking them on daily hikes through the wooded mountain wonderland. He kept them up until early in the morning with films and discussions of politics or anything that came into his head. Hitler often played with Blondi, his Alsatian dog, or received delegations of admiring peasants.

At Obersalzburg and within the secret confines of the chancellory, Hitler lived a private life in which he allowed himself time to fulfill his sexual desires. Although there are many accounts of Hitler's perverted activities, such as sadomasochism, or of his impotency, reliable sources indicate that he led a normal, if not somewhat active, sex life. There is certainly no factual basis for accounts of syphilis or other venereal diseases, nor is there any conclusive evidence that his sexual organs were underdeveloped. He was fond of the female figure, especially full-bosomed figures, and he enjoyed watching films of stripteases or films that emphasized the body of the female.

Although he was often uneasy around beautiful women, he carried on several affairs and often invited actresses to visit him. He always treated women courteously, kissing their hands and bowing to them. In 1924 his sister, Angela Raubal, came to live with him as his housekeeper. Hitler developed a strong attraction to Geli, her daughter, who moved into his apartment in 1929 after his sister had gone to live at the Obersalzburg. However, on September 18, 1931, she committed suicide. Upon learning of the death of his beloved, Hitler fell into a fit of despair and only the vigilance of Hess kept him from taking his own life. He never recovered from the loss of Geli and kept her room in Munich as she had left it as a memorial. Every year, on the anniversary of her death, Hitler visited this shrine and paid an emotional tribute to his lost love.

Geli Raubal was not the last love of Hitler's life. One day in 1929 he met Eva Braun, a pretty, but simpleminded, blue-eyed blonde working in the studio of Heinrich Hoffmann, the party photographer. He took her to operas, films, and on picnics, and in 1932 she moved into his apartment. Eva was completely devoted to Hitler and allowed him to keep her hidden from the public to preserve his image of respectability. She spent much of her time confined to Berchtesgaden and only rarely appeared in public in Berlin. She enjoyed smoking and dancing, despite Hitler's disapproval of these activities, and carefully hid them from him. The master of the Third Reich was so unresponsive to her needs that on November 1, 1932, she shot herself, and on May 28, 1935, tried to end her life with sleeping pills. Eva Braun would remain with Hitler until the end, and finally, as the Third Reich came to a crashing end around them, she would become Hitler's wife, only to perish along with her husband.[10]

Throughout his career Hitler was troubled with serious health problems. After the suicide of his niece in 1931, he went into a fit of anxiety, and his health suffered greatly. Thereafter, he gave up meats, a needed source of protein. This only compounded his physical problems. He spent sleepless nights, and severe stomach pains wracked his body. In 1936 he came under the care of Dr. Theodor Morell, who was born in 1886 in Hesse. Morell studied medicine at Giessen, Heidelberg, and Paris and served as a medic during the First World War. After the war he moved to Berlin, where he became a society physician specializing in venereal diseases. In 1933 he joined the Nazi party. Morell filled Hitler's body with strong drugs, prescribing Dr. Köster's Antigas Pills, a potion containing strychnine and belladonna. Despite, or rather, as a result of, Morell's treatment, Hitler's condition continued to worsen. His gums and tongue often became inflamed, and he developed a heart murmur and an enlarged left ventricle. In 1937 Hitler decided that his frail health would lead to an early death and thereafter began to accelerate his plans to avenge the loss of the First World War.[11]

Thus, after his appointment as chancellor, Hitler set out to dominate all aspects of German society and politics. The Nazis ruthlessly crushed all opposition outside of and within the party and brought all facets of the government under their control. Heinrich Himmler and his black-shirted troops imprisoned thousands in concentration camps, where they lived a subhuman existence. The Jews found themselves deprived of all civil rights, their shops looted and destroyed, and their synagogues burned by mobs of fanatical Nazis. At the same time, Hitler and his economic advisers took bold action to reduce unemployment. They rejected traditional economic theory and its observance of strict fiscal responsibility and spent the sums necessary to revitalize the German economy on public works projects and rearmament. As we shall see in the next chapter, Goebbels's propaganda machine instilled in the people a sense of confidence in the new regime that may have played as great a role in the recovery as the economic measures. Ironically, the nazi regimentation of German society had one lasting impact that may have been the most important legacy of the Third Reich. Programs such as Strength Through Joy and the opportunity for ability to rise high in the various party organizations and the new bureaucracy broke down the old aristocratic order and replaced it with a new sense of equality. For the first time in modern German history the wellborn lost their domination of culture and society, and working men and women enjoyed privileges hitherto reserved for the aristocracy. To be sure, the well born did not lose their status, but they had to move over to make room for the people.

14

Culture in the Third Reich

While the nazi masters of Germany busily crushed all rival political groups, they brought all aspects of German culture under strict party control in an effort to unite the people behind their new leaders. The Nazis denounced as depraved much of the art, music, and literature of the Weimar era, driving most of the major writers, painters, musicians, and creative minds of the Reich into exile. Inspired by the pageantry of Wagner's operas and the barbaric ideology of national socialism, Hitler and his deputies sought to create an atmosphere that would appeal to the primitive emotions of the people and lead them to join the brown-shirted throng without pausing to realize the true nature of the nazi tyranny. Germany became an exciting land, with one ceremony after another; the radio and cinema communicated the message of hate and racism while lulling the people into a false sense of well-being. Not even the churches were spared in the effort to indoctrinate the people. Arising from the cult of the folk of the last century, Hitler's disciples called for the development of a German Christianity to replace the religion of their fathers. These prophets of the Third Reich transformed Christ into a blond-haired Aryan. Naturally, a few brave souls resisted the desecration of their religion and the subversion of German culture by the new barbarians. But this was to little avail, for few listened to their desperate call, and most simply joined the mob as they marched to the beat of the nazi drummers.[1]

Symbolic of the mood of the Third Reich were the party rallies, which provided the people with excitement while working them into a feverish pitch of fanaticism. Beginning on August 30, 1933, thousands of dedicated followers of the new German leader gathered at the Zeppelin Field in Nuremberg to pledge their loyalty to their führer. Yearly they came, and yearly the rallies served to inflame the masses with the spirit of the Third Reich. All the party leaders and Hitler gathered to receive the homage of the faithful. Radio and film carried the spirit and excitement of the meetings to thousands of Germans who were unable to leave their homes and jobs to pay their tribute to the leader of the Third Reich.

Each rally opened with a gala performance of Richard Wagner's hymn to German art, *The Mastersingers of Nuremberg,* by the Berlin Opera. Significantly, not all appreciated their leader's love of Wagner's powerful music. In 1933 Hitler found, much to his chagrin, an almost empty opera house. Hardly suppressing his fury, he ordered his police to search the hotels, beer halls, and restaurants of the city to bring the unfaithful party functionaries to the performance by force if necessary. Thereafter, regardless of their personal feelings, no official dared miss this tribute to German art.

The leaders of nazi Germany made every effort to carefully orchestrate the August 30 rallies to fill the hearts and minds of the people with the excitement of life under their beloved leader. Goebbels and others spent weeks planning every small detail of the events to create a spectacle worthy of the new Germany. In 1934 Albert Speer, Hitler's architect, planned a monstrous rally to highlight the gathering and to leave the spectators breathless. Thousands of local party leaders marched onto the Zeppelin Field, proudly bearing their chapter banners. Above, dozens of spotlights focused their rays on the flags, sending the reflections of the silver eagles on their staffs in all directions. At the same time, 130 searchlights, placed at intervals around the stadium, cast columns of light over 20,000 feet into the dark sky to create the image of a huge hall, which served as the Valhalla for the worship of the new Teutonic religion. In the rally, immortalized by Lini Reifenstahl's frightening film, *The Triumph of the Will* (1936), thousands of workers marched onto the field bearing spades as soldiers carried rifles to swear their allegiance to Hitler. During some rallies, thousands of dedicated followers marched in a circle in the form of a huge hooked cross, bearing torches that sent their swirling flames into the night, as a brilliant salute to the Third Reich.[2]

Finally, after a week of tireless demonstrations and dozens of fiery speeches, Hitler reviewed his troops, standing in the marketplace beneath the towers of a medieval church, an almost pathetic reminder of a time when men served another Lord. During the parade, the streets of Nuremberg, lined with Gothic buildings and churches, echoed with the thunder of thousands of boots as they pounded the cobblestone. The S.S., the S.A., the army, the Hitler Youth, and other groups marched past their leader, all singing lustily. Above the tumult of the voices and the marching, the imperial castle stood as a reminder of the glorious past.

The huge Nuremberg rallies served as a pattern for other celebrations of the nazi faith. Every laying of a cornerstone, every opening of a new factory, and every other event served as an excuse for the pageantry of nazi Germany. On May 1, 1933, the workers joined in a demonstration of faith in their leader. Five months later the somber judges joined in the movement by celebrating the Day of the German Jurist at Leipzig. There, outside the Supreme Court building, clad in banners bearing nazi slogans, the robed justices gathered to listen to Hans Frank, the chief legal expert of the party, proclaim the principles of nazi law. The next day Frank and Professor Wilhelm Kirsch of Munich addressed the deans of the law schools on their obligation to serve the cult of the folk. That same day Hitler spoke to 500,000 farmers near Hamelin. The führer celebrated the Day of German Art two weeks later by laying the foundation stone of the House of German Art in Munich. Every year on the anniversary of the abortive Beer Hall Putsch, Hitler and his henchmen led a solemn procession from the Bürgerbräu Celler to the Hall of the Soldiers. The German people found themselves constantly involved in festive celebrations to the glory of national socialism and being called upon to pledge faith in their new leader.

The mastermind of the seizure of German culture was Joseph Goebbels. On June 30, 1933, Hitler granted him supreme authority over all aspects of artistic life and journalism. To tighten his control, the Nazi tsar of culture formed the Reich Chamber of Culture on September 22, 1933. This body consisted of sections for literature, press, radio, theater, music, and fine arts and had complete control over who could produce work and the form that creations must take. Goebbels appointed pro-Nazi artists, such as author Hans Friedrich Blunck or world-famous composer Richard Strauss, heads of the various sections of the chamber. Goebbels and the chamber served as a means to dominate culture and prevent artists unsympathetic to the goals of National Socialism from practicing their art. More than a thousand Jewish and "Marxist" journalists found themselves thrown out of work and their positions taken by persons willing to sacrifice their creativity to serve the Third Reich. On October 4, 1933, Goebbels decreed that all editors of newspapers and political magazines must be pure-blooded Aryans. He also held all editors personally responsible for the contents of their publications and forbade the printing of anything not acceptable to the party. Naturally, he alone held the right to determine what was satisfactory.

Under Goebbels's strong hand, art became another means to indoctrinate the people in the ideology of national socialism. He severely condemned the abstract art of the Weimar era as decadent and "Jewish." He demanded that all art clearly and simply portray the official view of the pure Aryan race as contrasted to that of the dark Jew. Paintings and sculpture became hymns to the beauty of the blonde-haired, blue-eyed Nordic type. Fair peasant maidens and athletic youths dominated canvasses and statuary as symbols of the cult of the folk. Many works were studies of the nude body in which every muscle stood out to show the ideal physique of the healthy member of the "master" race. Other works portrayed nature and the soil as the mystical source of the German people.

The cult of the hero formed another important theme of nazi art. To inspire the youth and the people to devote their lives to following the führer in his campaign to restore the lost glory of the ancient Teutons, works praised the accomplishments of heroes of the past like Frederick the Great. Others created new models for the people to emulate, such as Albert Leo Schlageter, who died fighting the French in the Ruhr in 1923, or Fritz Todt, the builder of the autobahn, who burned to death when his plane crashed as he was flying to report to Hitler. Naturally, many works pictured the führer as the new savior of the German people. One painting by Hermann Otto Hoyer, entitled, *In the Beginning Was the Word,* shows the young Hitler as he addressed a gathering of early party members. Hubert Lanzinger painted Hitler dressed as a medieval knight, carrying the swastika-adorned flag as if leading the Reich on a grand crusade.

Even the stage became a part of the ideological indoctrination of the people. Theater was made accessible to Germans from all walks of life in an attempt to entertain them while teaching them the ideas of the party. Classical plays by men like Goethe and Schiller, as well as the nationalistic works of Kleist and his contemporaries, found a major place in the repertory. Naturally, the Reich Chamber for Music sponsored festive performances of Wagnerian opera to glorify German mythology. Even operettas by Strauss, Lehar, and others found a place on the Nazi stage, as a means to reach those less inclined to the heavy works of Wagner. The works of foreigners like Shakespeare and Rossini were performed, provided they did not violate the ideas of national socialism. At the same time, Goebbels banned productions by Jews and such classics as Lessing's *Nathan the Wise,* which condemned anti-Semitism, as decadent and unworthy of performance on the stages of the Reich.

Goebbels also dominated the airwaves. He realized the possibility of reaching every man, woman, and child through the radio. The Reich Broadcasting Chamber utilized this important medium in the campaign to indoctrinate the people. The airwaves carried all party rallies and all speeches by Hitler and other leaders. Goebbels also cleverly interspersed the propaganda with light entertainment. Goebbels saw that the best conductors, orchestras, and performers produced works to lull the people into a false sense of prosperity that would hide his real intent. He used his economic influence to support the manufacture of cheap radios so that every home could afford to own a receiver. To reach as many people as possible, he placed loudspeakers on the streets, in restaurants, factories, and other public places. He even encouraged managers to allow the workers time off from their duties to listen to important programs.

Goebbels also used the motion pictures as a means to spread Hitler's gospel; he created the Film Credit Bank to gain economic control of the industry. By 1937 the Reich Propaganda Ministry had bought the last independent film company, thereby gaining control of all motion pictures made and distributed in the Reich. He condemned the painted stars of Hollywood and encouraged German film personalities to reflect in their dress and manner a pure Aryan race. Films concentrated on themes such as the folk, health, the youth, the ideal German family, travel, anti-Semitism, as in *Jud Suss,* one of the most notorious pictures of the nazi period, and other subjects that served the needs of the party.

The nazi domination of culture included literature. Even before the founding of the Reich Chamber of Literature, the party purged books by authors like Heinrich Heine, Thomas Mann, Upton Sinclair, H. G. Wells, and others, from the shelves of libraries and bookstores. On May 10, 1933, the students of the University of Berlin marched to the library in procession, seized unacceptable books, and built a huge bonfire. Similar scenes took place all over Germany as thousands of books went up in smoke, carrying with them the intellectual freedom of the German people. Goebbels forced authors to produce works that fulfilled the needs of the party and taught the basic concepts of national socialism. Some authors glorified the cult of the leader and called on the people to dedicate themselves to following great men like Hitler. Others idolized the soil as the mystical force that shaped the destiny of the people. Of course, fervent nationalism and racism served as major themes of nazi literature. Because of the confines of nazi ideology and control, the literary works of the Third Reich were of little artistic value. A nation that had produced men like Goethe, Schiller, Heine, Kafka, and Mann had rejected its rich heritage to serve the demands of Hitler and his followers. The nazi era was one of the most barren periods of German literature and culture.

The cultural dictatorship that robbed German literature of creativity also called for rigidly defined family roles. In a reflection of the "leadership principle," which taught the folk to render unquestioning obedience to their leader, the ideal German father was to be the absolute master of his wife and children. Women had no status as persons outside of the family, and their chief function was to produce healthy children who would grow up to serve the fatherland. In 1938 the government began to award Honor Crosses, resembling Iron Crosses, to new mothers. As the perfect Aryan male was to be slender, healthy, blonde-haired, and blue-eyed, so the nazi woman was to exhibit similar characteristics. She was to be pure and natural, shunning such artificial symbols of decadence as lipstick, powder, and makeup. The ideal woman of the Third Reich was chaste, for despite the excesses of their private lives, Hitler and his followers supported traditional sexual morality. She would never allow herself to participate in "savage" dances like the Black Bottom and the Charleston and never listened to jazz, considered by the Nazis a savage music produced by an inferior people, stemming from the jungles of darkest Africa.[3]

Even the youths were not immune to the plot to mold all Germans in the nazi image. The party gained strict control of education, and beginning in Prussia and spreading throughout Germany, it revised the curriculum and textbooks to serve the needs of the Third Reich. The new studies centered on the racial doctrines of nazism as well as the proper nationalist interpretation of history and literature. To teach the youths the proper respect for physical fitness, Hitler's schoolmasters required all pupils to spend at least five hours each day in exercise. Naturally no one failed to overlook the possibility that the pupils would be the soldiers of the future. Teachers constantly reminded their charges of the obedience and respect due their führer and taught them to love him as the savior of the German people. In one school in Cologne, the impressionable children even said "prayers" to their leader, thanking him for restoring the glory of the fatherland and providing them with bread and safety. Hitler appointed Robert Ley to supervise the nazi revision of the educational system. Ley established several Adolf Hitler schools for the lower grades and order castles for higher education; but few sent their children to these schools, and so they had only a limited impact.

Naturally, higher education fell victim to the ideological needs of the Third Reich. Before 1933 each state administered its colleges and universities independently. However, on April 30, 1934, Hitler appointed Bernhard Rust, a leader in the Storm Troopers and former party chairman in Hanover, minister of education. All institutions of higher learning came under the centralized control of the Reich, which supervised curriculum and the selection of professors. The faculty members, who had traditionally guarded their academic freedom, became mere organs of the nazi machine, subject to dismissal if they failed to uphold the principles of the party. The state required all professors and instructors to join the National Socialist Association of University Lecturers, led between 1935 and 1943 by Dr. Walter Schultze, head of the public health service in Bavaria. The state used the civil service laws to eliminate Jewish instructors. The party controlled curriculum and introduced new courses in racial science while sharply curtailing classes in natural science and other subjects considered unnecessary by the authorities.

In addition, the students felt the full impact of the nazi dictatorship. Even before 1933 many students influenced by nationalistic professors, resentment of the Treaty of Versailles, and the cult of the folk had taken up the hooked cross. In 1931 the nazi students had enough power to elect Gerhard Krüger, the head of the National Socialist Student Union, president of the National Organization of German Students. After Hitler came to power, all students had to join the National Organization of German Students. The state required prospective students to serve at least six months in the Labor Service, performing manual work with youths of all classes to impress on them the equality of all Germans. To obtain admission to an institution of higher education, all had to provide, besides valid academic credentials, proof of Aryan blood, which they could accomplish by showing that their grandparents had not been Jewish or by membership in one of the party organizations. They also had to show that they were free of a criminal record. Thus, the schools became centers of national socialism.

The nazi program for indoctrination of the youth did not stop when they left the classroom. In June 1933 Hitler appointed Baldur von Schirach youth leader of the German Reich. Schirach was born in Berlin in 1907, the son of the director of the Court Theater. He joined the Young German's League, one of the youth organizations that mixed hiking and camping with the cult of the folk, and he joined the party in 1925, working as a recruiter at the University of Munich. Six years later Hitler named him the party's national youth leader. Schirach organized the Hitler Youth, which by 1932 had a membership of 107,956. However, other youth groups, such as the groups dedicated to the cult of the folk and the Catholic Youth, had a combined enrollment of ten million. Of course the führer of the junior branch of the party set out to bring all rival groups under his control. In 1933 Schirach sent a group of his followers to occupy the headquarters of the Reich Committee of German Youth Associations. Finally, on December 1, 1936, Hitler disbanded all non-nazi youth groups and ordered all young people to join the Hitler Youth or the Society of German Maidens, proclaiming that all youth must dedicate themselves to the service of the folk and the Reich.[4]

The Hitler Youth sought to shape all boys from six to eighteen into the nazi mold. The program stressed physical fitness through hiking, camping, and an active sports program. It also taught the members of the junior branch of the party the importance of racial purity and obedience to the führer. Schirach even organized military training for the older members of the organization so that, when the time came, they could take their place in the army, the S.A., or the S.S. They wore brown uniforms and were filled with a sense of their role in the crusade to restore Germany to its proper place in the world. At six, a boy became an apprentice and received a book in which to record his physical and ideological growth. When ten years old, each lad took a test in athletics, camping, and history. If he passed, he joined the Young Folk, after swearing complete devotion to Adolf Hitler. Finally, after eight years of training, an adolescent became a full-fledged member of the Hitler Youth.

Since the Hitler Youth was a male organization, the Nazis organized a corresponding organization for girls. They learned the proper role of a woman as a mother and loyal wife. They wore white blouses, blue skirts, and heavy marching boots. Their leaders taught them the nazi concept of the Aryan race and physical fitness while advising them to aspire toward the Aryan concept of beauty, the pure, blonde-haired, blue-eyed woman. They learned to shun cosmetics as the product of the degenerate culture of the Jewish-dominated Weimar Republic. Members of the Society of German Maidens underwent a series of trials and apprenticeships similar to that of their brothers. At six, a girl became a member of the junior wing of the movement, advancing to the Young Maidens at ten, and finally, at fourteen, to full membership in the Society of German Maidens.

At eighteen, both young men and women joined the Labor Service. The men worked on public works projects or on farms, while their sisters took care of families in rural areas or joined their brothers in the fields. The members of the Labor Service lived in camps or in the homes of farmers. Naturally, the large groups of healthy young men and women led to moral problems, despite the official party doctrine of chastity. Many girls became pregnant and had children out of wedlock. The indoctrination of the youth also shook the family structure of nazi Germany. The leaders of the Hitler Youth and the Society of German Maidens taught their charges to spy on their families and to report any anti-nazi sentiments. Many parents lived with the fear that their sons and daughters would report any critical remark or activity to the authorities. Thus, in all aspects of their youth, the Germans became targets of nazi indoctrination. They spent hours in their schools learning Hitler's ideas of race and nationalism. They passed their free time in the Hitler Youth or in the Society of German Maidens mixing play with education. Hitler and his supporters hoped to produce a new breed of German through these programs, in preparation for the time when the "super race" would rule the world.

Since Goebbels, Schirach, and the other leaders of the Third Reich were dedicated to bringing all aspects of society under party domination, it was only natural that they would attempt to do the same with the churches. Even before the advent of national socialism, the cult of the folk had produced a so-called German Christianity. The leaders of this group pictured Christ as a blue-eyed Nordic who resembled an ancient Germanic chieftain more than the Lord of Peace found in the Bible. They condemned the Old Testament and the writings of St. Paul as a Jewish attempt to subvert the true message of

Christianity. After Hitler's appointment, the "German Christians" proclaimed their belief in the nazi state and in Hitler as God's chosen instrument to lead the German people. These fanatics demanded the unification of the local Protestant churches into one national church. Although Hitler seemed to have few religious beliefs and was a Roman Catholic, at least in name, he took an active part in the efforts to unify the local groups into a national church. He appointed Ludwig Müller, a follower of German Christianity, adviser for Protestant affairs on April 26, 1933. In an effort to create a national church, the government sponsored elections to a national synod on July 23, in which all Protestants over twenty-three could participate. As a result of party propaganda, Müller's followers won a majority of two to one. The national synod met at Wittenberg, the birthplace of the Reformation, and elected Müller bishop of the German Reich on September 27. On April 19, 1934, Müller issued a decree unifying the local churches into the German Evangelical Church under his leadership. The next year Hitler recognized the new body, placing it under the control of Hans Kerrl, the minister for church affairs.[5]

Meanwhile, Müller set out to bring the church into line with the goals of national socialism. He announced that a true German Christian must regard Hitler as a gift from God and called for obedience to the wishes of the prophet of the Third Reich. Over 20,000 enthusiastic people assembled in the Berlin Palace of Sports on November 13, 1933, to listen to a speech by Reinhardt Krause, one of the chief spokesmen for "German Christianity." In an emotional speech, Krause invoked the teachings of Martin Luther and called national socialism the completion of the Reformation. He demanded the purging of all Jewish elements from the faith, shouting that, just as a true German should not buy a necktie from a Jew, he should not derive his religion from his racial and cultural enemy. He screamed that only pure-blooded Aryans had a right to occupy a German pulpit. His speech whipped the mob into such a frenzy that they unanimously shouted their approval of a motion demanding the dismissal of all clergy unwilling to support the principles of the führer.

Krause's fanaticism caused a major reaction. Even Müller realized that such radicalism would only offend the majority of German Protestants and immediately removed Krause from office. However, this step did not silence the supporters of traditional Christianity. On November 14 Hans Meiser, the Protestant Bishop of Bavaria, called for a national protest at a meeting celebrating the Reformation. The two most important leaders of the anti-nazi movement in the church were Martin Niemöller, pastor in Dahlem, a suburb of Berlin, and Dietrich Bonhöffer, a professor at the University of Berlin. Even before the election of Müller, they realized the threat to their religion and organized the Pastor's Emergency League. On September 7 they announced that anyone supporting "German Christianity" had cut themselves off from the communion of the faithful. During the national synod at Wittenberg, Bonhöffer and his friends boldly defied the Nazis. When they failed to gain a hearing, they nailed a statement to the trees lining the streets of the city condemning the attempt to subvert the basic doctrines of the church. In October Bonhöffer went to England to inform G. K. A. Bell, the Anglican Bishop of Chicester, and other leaders of the Church of England of the nazi threat to the faith. The Pastor's Emergency League continued to grow under the able leadership of Niemöller, and by the end of the first year of the Third Reich it had a membership of six thousand, about one-third of the clergy.

The conflict between the German Christians and the Pastor's League split the German Protestant Church into three major factions: the followers of Müller, the supporters of Bonhöffer and Niemöller, and the conservatives, who stressed the authority of the state and appealed to moderation. Hitler, realizing the harm that strong religious opposition could do to his position, decided to intervene personally in the conflict. On January 25, 1934, he, Goering, Frick, and Hess met with seventeen Protestant leaders, including Müller and Niemöller. Despite the führer's attempts at persuasion, the conference accomplished little, and Niemöller refused to be intimidated. Two days later, the bishop of the Reich met with the other bishops and convinced them to sign a statement of unconditional support for the government and its leadership. This caused two thousand frightened clergymen to withdraw from the Pastor's League.

Since the leadership of the Protestants and the majority of the clergy had allowed the nazi dictators to pressure them into obedience, Niemöller became more militant in his defense of the faith. On January 31 he sent the bishops a letter scolding them for abandoning the Gospel and the church to national socialism. Niemöller and his supporters met in Barmen on May 29 to discuss the issue and formed the Confessing Church. They agreed to resolutions denouncing the German Christians and calling for obedience to Christ and the Bible as the only valid expression of the faith. Finally, on October 20, 1934, the members of the Confessing Church denounced the bishop of the Reich and announced their decision to cease all dealings with the existing church government until it returned to the true faith.

Hitler and his advisers realized the serious threat to their efforts to indoctrinate the people posed by the new organization and set out to destroy it before it became a center of anti-nazi agitation. On July 16, 1935, the führer appointed Hans Kerrl, the Prussian minister of justice, Reich minister of church affairs. Biding his time for a few years, lest he cause a major revolt, Kerrl finally, on February 13, 1937, demanded that all members of the church recognize the absolute authority of the state and accept the nazi doctrine of race, blood, and soil. Since the brave defenders of the Christian faith refused to yield, they felt the full terror of the nazi tyranny. Squads of Gestapo agents and others raided the parsonages of the land and sent eight hundred members of the Confessing Church to prison. On July 1, 1937, Niemöller received the reward for his defense of the faith and the police seized him. The court sentenced him to seven months in jail on March 2, 1938, and ordered him to pay a fine of 2,000 marks. Since he had already suffered imprisonment for eight months, the officials set him free. However, his freedom was short-lived, for that night the Gestapo drove up to his house and took him to the concentration camp at Sachsenhausen. Since even Hitler did not dare murder a man with his popularity, he received special treatment as the führer's personal prisoner. The officials transferred him to Dachau in July 1941, and there, a few yards from the death chambers, he spent the remaining years of the Third Reich. Bonhöffer was not so lucky. Although he escaped imprisonment until 1943, the agents of modern barbarism tore him from his family and friends in 1943, and on April 8, 1945, he became a modern martyr to the Christian faith. Bonhöffer's letters and writings while in prison form one of the most striking testimonies of devotion to the Christian faith, and they have become one of the most important works of modern Protestant theology.

Hitler's efforts to bring the Roman Catholic Church of Germany under his control were much less successful than his campaign against the Confessing Church had been. Roman Catholicism was a strong international religion, with a powerful and prestigious leader in the pope. The nazi masters of Germany could not challenge the pope for fear that they would alienate the many Roman Catholics who had supported the Brown Shirts in their rise to power. Even Hitler was a Roman Catholic, at least in name. He could not overlook the Catholic Center party's support of the Enabling Act. As early as March 28, 1933, the German bishops met at Fulda to issue a statement permitting the faithful to become active members of the Nazi party. Unable to challenge the Papacy directly, Hitler decided to negotiate. He sent Dr. Ludwig Kaas to Rome to meet with Pope Pius XI. Aided by Franz von Papen, Kaas negotiated a concordat with the Vatican, which both sides signed on September 10, 1933. This agreement guaranteed the right of the Roman Catholic Church to maintain its schools without governmental interference. Hitler pledged to respect the right of the Church of Rome to publish papal statements and to full freedom of religion. In return, the pontiff agreed to disband all Roman Catholic political and social organizations.

However, no sooner had the leaders of the Third Reich signed the concordat than they began violating it by interfering with church schools and youth organizations. As early as September 3, a week before the agreement went into effect, the bishops met in Fulda to send a letter to their pontiff charging the Nazis with violating the rights of the German Catholics. Naturally, the semipagan "German Christian" movement caused great alarm in Catholic circles. During Advent in 1933, Cardinal Michael von Faulhaber, archbishop of Munich, preached a series of sermons denouncing the racism of national socialism and defending the Old Testament. Other clergy joined Faulhaber's bold protest against the attempt to revive paganism. The faithful sent detailed letters to Rome informing the pope of the true nature of the Third Reich, and their priests openly defied the dictator by such acts as forbidding children to give the nazi salute or celebrating Mass for those killed fighting the nazi tyranny. Finally, influenced by the brave protests from Germany, Pius XI placed Rosenberg's *Myth of the Twentieth Century* on the index of prohibited books, a direct challenge to Hitler and his henchmen.

The pope's defiant act led to increased tensions between Berlin and Rome. On March 1 Cardinal Karl Joseph Schulte, archbishop of Cologne, issued a statement condemning as contrary to orthodox doctrine the nazi concept of race and the superiority of "Aryan" peoples. He also denounced in stinging words the efforts of the German Christians to purge Christianity of so-called Jewish elements. Schulte's statements led the Nazis to attack the church much as they had attacked rival political groups. On March 25, 1934, a rowdy band of Hitler Youth savagely molested a group of Catholic Youth. A few days later, a pro-nazi mob stormed the residence of the bishop of

Würzburg to protest his refusal to remove an anti-nazi priest from his parish. Other Roman Catholics, however, were more sympathetic to Nazism. Archbishop Conrad Gröber of Freiburg urged loyal support for the government and criticized the anti-nazi clergy. Although the prelate would later denounce Hitler, he praised the führer for his efforts to create a Christian state in Germany. In May Abbot Ildefons Herwegen of Maria Laach not only called for support of Hitler but lauded fascism in glowing terms. Bishop Wilhelm Berning of Osnabrüch joined the Prussian state council.

However, the pro-nazi Catholics were only a minority. On August 28, 1935, the bishops issued a pastoral letter calling for devotion to Christ above the state and reminding the faithful of their obligations to their church. This led to renewed violence as brown-shirted thugs harassed prelates, priests, and laymen who refused to sacrifice their beliefs at the altar of national socialism. Finally, on March 14, 1937, Pope Pius XI formally denounced national socialism in his encyclical *With Deep Anxiety*. The angry Pontiff charged the Third Reich with violating the terms of the Concordat of 1933 through violence and illegal persecution. He strongly condemned the Nazis for their anti-Christian character and declared that no loyal Roman Catholic could support Hitler's racial theories. The document, written in secret and smuggled into Germany through Cardinal Faulhaber, was read on Palm Sunday, March 21, in all churches. Thus, the Roman Catholic Church had declared war on national socialism. The dictators of Germany reacted with a vengeance. The government declared the document treasonous and ordered the Gestapo to arrest all who had participated in its distribution. Many priests, nuns, prelates, and laymen were rounded up and thrown into the concentration camps, which provided the Catholics with a new group of martyrs for their faith. Relations between the Third Reich and the Roman Church would improve after the election of Eugenio Pacelli as Pope Pius XII in 1939. The new pope was more sympathetic to Hitler than other leaders of the Roman Catholic Church had been.

Hitler and his supporters had turned Germany into a totalitarian state. Virtually every aspect of society and culture came under party domination. Authors, musicians, and artists lost the right to create freely and became servants of the nazi dictatorship. The party tried to dominate the personal lives of the people by subjecting them to a constant barrage of propaganda and by trying to mold them into the nazi stereotype of the ideal male and female. The new barbarians tried to encourage children to reject the values of their parents and to dedicate their lives to the service of the führer. At every turn of their lives, in school, in the Hitler Youth, and in the Society of German Maidens, the youth of Germany became the targets of indoctrination. Even religion was not sacred to the cynical leaders of Germany. They attempted to desecrate the faith by introducing their renewed paganism and by openly violating their word to the pope. Those who dared raise their voices in protest became the targets of violence or lost their freedom to spend their days in the stinking, rat-infested prisons and concentration camps. Germany became a land without personal freedom that would not tolerate independent thought and action.

15

Nazi Foreign Policy 1933-1936

While Hitler and his aides were busy crushing all possible domestic opposition and dealing with unemployment, the führer was engaged in conducting an aggressive and opportunistic foreign policy. He dreamed of the day when, freed from the restrictions of the Treaty of Versailles, Germany could once again take its place as a major European power. Although he never forgot his long-range goals as defined in *Mein Kampf* and his speeches, Hitler was realistic and flexible enough to refuse to risk losing everything by leading Germany into a war before it was capable of fighting. He supported the agitation of his followers in Austria, but he quickly retreated when faced with the possibility of war with Italy. He negotiated favorable agreements with the English to allow him to rebuild the German navy and with the Polish to guarantee his eastern frontier while he concerned himself with other matters. Meanwhile, he sponsored the rearmament of Germany so that he could negotiate from a position of strength. Finally, he took advantage of the preoccupation of Europe with the Italian aggression in Ethiopia to remilitarize the Rhineland.

While it would be a gross oversimplification to regard Hitler's statements as a detailed outline of his foreign policy, he did set forth several long-range goals that his actions reveal played a role in determining his foreign policy. Hitler openly proclaimed his chief goal of reuniting the Reich with the territory lost at Paris and creating a greater German empire that would include all German-speaking peoples. He advocated the unification of Austria with the Reich, a direct challenge to the treaties that had ended the First World War. Hitler directly spoke and wrote of force as the only possible way to achieve the reunification of Germany.[1]

One of the most important concepts of the foreign program defined by the führer was the need for living space for the Aryan peoples. He was greatly influenced by the school of geopolitics developed by Rudolf Kjellen, a Swedish political scientist who published *State as an Organism* in 1916 and was taught by Karl Haushofer of the University of Munich. Haushofer, editor of the *Magazine of Geopolitics* (Zeitschrift für Geopolitik), taught his students that a state must have a large enough agricultural base to support its population. Hitler, introduced to Haushofer by Hess in the early days of national socialism, took the ideas of geopolitics and united them with the basic concepts of the cult of the folk to create a basis for much of nazi foreign policy. Hitler argued that the Aryan people must have control of a living space that would provide enough food and raw materials for the super race. He looked not to overseas colonies, but to the vast steppe occupied by the Slavs. Hitler, who considered the Slavs an inferior people, demanded that the Germans renew the push to the east and conquer the fertile breadbasket of Poland and the Ukraine. He was also interested in the oil fields of the Caucasus.

To achieve Aryan domination of eastern Europe, Hitler advocated a policy of struggle and alliances. He saw the French as the chief enemy to German expansion, arguing that the traditional effort of Paris to achieve hegemony over Europe while keeping the Germans weak and divided could be defeated only by force. To destroy the natural enemy of the German people, Hitler looked to the British, traditional opponents of French domination of the continent. Hitler hoped to form an alliance with the English that would commit London to his quest for living space while guaranteeing the solidarity of the British colonial empire. The führer looked to the Italians as another ally in his pursuit to destroy French domination, because he believed that Rome, like Berlin and London, shared a desire to oppose the French effort to dictate to the peoples of Europe. Of course, Hitler spoke against any long-range agreement with the Soviet Union because Moscow would resist German control of Poland and the Ukraine, an important part of the Soviet empire. Hitler considered international communism a Jewish plot to enslave mankind.

The first concern of Hitler's foreign policy was an effort to free the German people from the confines of the Treaty of Versailles. His first opportunity to demonstrate the new aggressive independence of Germany came immediately after his assumption of power. On February 2, 1932, the League of Nations summoned the major nations of the world to a disarmament conference in Geneva. The Germans opened the session with a demand for equality with the other powers and the right to build up its forces to the level of France or at least to that of Poland and Czechoslovakia. Naturally Paris objected to this demand, and the meetings reached a deadlock before they had a chance to consider the basic issue of disarmament. Finally, the delegates decided to adjourn until they had a chance to consult with their governments about the knotty issue.[2]

On February 2, 1933, the conference reopened. Hitler, who had no intention of allowing any agreement to thwart his plans to rearm Germany, decided to send a delegation, fearing that refusal to participate while he was still trying to secure his power in Germany would lead to protests from France and England and might even cause a war. Once again the German delegation demanded equality with France, and again Paris objected to the German ultimatum. Instead, the French demanded the creation of an international police force to supervise any agreement and guarantee that all signatories abided by its terms. Of course Hitler did not agree to this plan, and a new deadlock developed. On March 16 Ramsay MacDonald, prime minister of England, suggested a compromise that allowed the Germans equality with France but called for a reduction of all armaments by half. However, Paris then demanded the inclusion of Storm Troopers in the number of soldiers allowed Germany, and Hitler resoundingly rejected this demand. He persuaded the aged president and the ministry to announce German withdrawal from the conference and the League of Nations on October 14, 1933. The next month the führer appealed to the German people to express their approval of his actions in a plebiscite; confidence was expressed by 95 percent of the voters. With Germany in the hands of the aggressive Nazis and all hope of universal disarmament destroyed by Berlin's withdrawal from the League of Nations and the conference, the Geneva Disarmament Conference ended in failure, and the foundation for the tensions that later erupted into the Second World War was laid.

Significantly, neither France nor England was the first to challenge the new aggressive foreign policy. Instead, Poland, realizing the potential threat to its national existence, rose to the challenge and attempted to stand up to Hitler and his supporters. The cause of the conflict was the city of Danzig, placed under Polish administration by the Treaty of Versailles. Many members of the German-speaking majority of the Baltic port had flocked to the nazi movement as a means to protest their status as a protectorate of Warsaw. The rapid growth of the Brown Shirts alarmed the Poles, and in March 1933 Polish marines landed on the Westerplatte Peninsula, near Danzig. Hitler realized that he could not afford a war with Poland that might plunge Germany into armed conflict with France, Poland's ally in the West since 1921. He ordered the Nazis in Danzig to restrain themselves and began negotiations with Joseph Pilsudski, the Polish dictator. On January 26, 1934, both nations signed a nonaggression pact that provided for a solution to all disputes by negotiation. It was agreed that the treaty would run for ten years and after that time could be ended on six months notice by either party. Hitler had achieved a major victory, for he had driven a wedge between Warsaw and Paris and had managed to secure his eastern frontier while he turned his attention to other matters.

The new friendship between Berlin and Warsaw greatly alarmed the Soviet Union. Stalin and his fellow Bolsheviks had feared a Nazi victory and had sent aid to the German Communists. Hitler and his followers had denounced Marxism and Moscow in stinging terms, and the Soviets feared a possible breakdown of the good relations they had enjoyed with Germany since the Treaty of Rapallo of 1922 and the Treaty of Berlin of 1926. Although Hitler renewed the latter agreement in May 1933 and silenced much of Goebbels's anti-Soviet propaganda, the agreement between Germany and Poland caused great concern in the Russian capital. Stalin abandoned the communist campaign against the governments in the West and began to speak of a popular front of Communists and other leftists against the threat of fascism. In February 1934 he signed a nonaggression pact with France, and in September the Soviet Union joined the League of Nations.

With Germany's eastern border secured through the agreement with Poland and the renewal of the Treaty of Berlin with the Soviet Union, Hitler was able to turn his attention to one of his major goals, the unification of Austria with Germany. Austria, formed from the German-speaking portions of the defunct Habsburg Empire, had long been a center of German nationalism. Even before 1918 various groups had demanded the destruction of the multinational state and unification with the German Reich. In 1904 Walter Riehl and several others had organized the German Workers' party of Austria on a platform of radical nationalism. After the abdication of the last Habsburg ruler, Charles, on November 12, 1918, the Austrian National Assembly had voted to become a part of Germany. However, the victors in Paris, fearing the development of a strong Germany, specifically forbade the annexation of Austria by Berlin. Therefore, Vienna had formed a republic dominated by the Christian Democrats, led after 1932 by Engelbert Dolfuss.

The Allied prohibition of unification of the two major German states caused resentment and fed the growing nationalist movement. National socialism found many supporters in the former Habsburg lands, where Riehl's group continued to agitate. In August 1920 Riehl met Hitler and persuaded him to come to Austria in early October to speak at meetings at Innsbruck, Salzburg, St. Pölten, and Vienna. Riehl became a staunch Nazi and was one of the few allowed to address Hitler in the familiar *Du* form. In 1926 his followers organized the National Socialist German Workers' party of Austria as a branch of the larger German organization. Two years later Hitler began to send badly needed funds to finance Riehl's activities, and in November 1930 the Nazis won 110,000 votes in the national elections. Although they failed to gain enough support to send a delegation to the Austrian parliament, Hitler realized the importance of continued activity. In 1931 he sent Theodor Habicht, a businessman and local nazi leader in Wiesbaden, to Linz to coordinate the Nazi effort in Austria. Habicht organized the movement on a national basis and established units of Storm Troopers to intimidate opposition groups.[3]

Throughout 1931 and 1932 the Austrian followers of Hitler continued to gain support. The party bought a house in Vienna to serve as national headquarters and organized local party cells in every city and town of the small country. The Brown Shirts began a campaign of terror against opposing groups on June 30, 1932, with an attack on a club near the Vienna Zoo and began street fighting with groups of Social Democrats. The Nazis organized over three hundred meetings and orchestrated an anti-Semitic campaign characterized by violence against Jews and their businesses. Soon bloody fighting swept the peaceful alpine country as the Austrian Nazis copied the actions of their German counterparts.

Hitler's victory in Germany inflamed the situation and led Chancellor Dolfuss to take action before the Brown Shirts could destroy order and forcedly turn Austria into a conquered province of Germany. An alarmed Dolfuss decided that the violence of the Nazis could only be met by radical solutions; on March 4, 1933, he disbanded the

Austrian parliament and announced his intention to rule by decree. Four days later the new dictator banned political meetings and the wearing of party uniforms. However, the determined Nazis refused to be intimidated and openly defied the chancellor by marching through the streets of Vienna in full nazi regalia on March 29 while the police stood by unable, or unwilling, to enforce the law. Hitler, who openly demanded German annexation of Austria and who supported his followers in their struggle, decided to use economic coercion to force Dolfuss to yield. On May 27 the masters of the Third Reich announced that all tourists traveling to Austria would have to pay a fee of 1,000 marks. Hitler hoped that this would destroy the tourist market, one of the chief sources of income in the depression-gripped land, and he believed that this would force Dolfuss to resign and call for new elections, which the Nazis could use to seize power.

However, the Austrian leader refused to allow Hitler to pressure him into surrender. On June 14 he ordered Habicht to leave the country and five days later officially banned the Austrian Nazi party. But the followers of the hooked cross in the former Habsburg state merely went underground and destroyed all evidence that could be used against them by the authorities. They continued to distribute literature, and the Brown Shirts met secretly in homes or on the streets. Meanwhile, the German frontier guards smuggled nazi newspapers and publications across the border, providing yet another source of propaganda. Goebbels used his power over the radio to blanket the airwaves with criticism of Dolfuss aimed at the peoples of the central European state. Habicht gave over twenty radio speeches between July 1933 and February 1934 calling upon the Austrians to revolt against the dictatorial measures of their chancellor and demand unification with the Third Reich. While the German radio aimed Hitler's message across the border, German planes flew overhead dropping thousands of leaflets. Hitler's agents sabotaged bridges and buildings and attempted to undermine the faith of the people in the ability of their leadership to withstand the nazi challenge.

Dolfuss, who realized that he could not defeat his enemies, sought to avoid a German invasion or nazi revolt through negotiations. He approached the führer hoping to find a way out of his dilemma through compromise. However, Hitler's price was high—an immediate lifting of the ban on the Nazi party. The leader of the Third Reich also demanded that Dolfuss appoint Habicht as vice chancellor and give at least half the positions in his cabinet to the Nazis. Even if Dolfuss were willing to yield to Hitler's ultimatum, his army, the heir to centuries of anti-German feeling, refused to allow him to compromise Austrian independence. The chancellor rejected Hitler's proposal. Meanwhile, at the insistence of his military, Dolfuss had begun to look for an ally in Benito Mussolini.

The fascist dictator of Italy sympathized with the Nazis, but he had no desire to endanger his country by sharing a common border with the aggressive Third Reich. Instead, he preferred to support an independent Austria to act as a buffer state between himself and Hitler's Reich. He therefore came to Dolfuss's support, but like his German counterpart, his help had its price. He demanded that the Austrian chancellor, who had already suspended democratic institutions, turn his country into a fascist state. Dolfuss, willing to do almost anything to gain support in his struggle against the Germans, accepted the Duce's advice and issued a decree banning all political organizations except his own fatherland front. However, the Social Democrats, who opposed all forms of fascism, decided to fight the new challenge to democracy. They called upon all workers to join a general strike that would cripple Austria and force Dolfuss to restore the constitution. The chancellor, who had stood up to the Nazis, refused to tolerate a leftist revolt. He summoned the army and ordered them to seize the socialist headquarters. This only led to renewed opposition as the leftists fortified themselves in a workers' apartment complex, Karl Marx Court. The military surrounded them, and, after several days of bloody fighting, broke through the barricades and arrested the leaders of the Social Democrats. With victory achieved, Dolfuss set about organizing Austria along fascist lines.

Hitler was greatly alarmed by Mussolini's opposition to his plans. On June 14 he went to Venice, and there, amid the decaying splendor of the mistress of the Adriatic, he attempted to negotiate with the Italian dictator. Mussolini proved adamant. He angrily told his northern counterpart that he would never tolerate German annexation of his neighbor and implied that he would go to war if necessary to protect Vienna from aggression. Unable to convince the duce to reconsider his position, a crestfallen Hitler returned to Germany. He ordered Goebbels to suspend the propaganda campaign and instructed Habicht to adopt more moderate methods.

However, the Austrian Nazis refused to allow the Italian dictator's threats to cool their determination to seize control of the government. They disobeyed Hitler's orders and acted without informing him of their plans. On July 25, 1934, a band of 154 dedicated Nazis, disguised in Austrian army uniforms, burst into the chancellory and shot the terrified Dolfuss at a range of two feet, leaving him to die an agonizing death four hours later. Meanwhile, other conspirators had captured the radio station and announced the chancellor's resignation and the beginning of a national socialist revolution. Hitler, who apparently had no prior knowledge of the plot, was at Bayreuth watching a performance of Wagner's *Das Rheingold*. He received word of the murder with great excitement, and he ordered the preparation of a press release praising the deed and promising the unification of the two German states. To appear completely uninvolved in the plot, he went to dinner as usual while awaiting further news from Vienna.

Despite the death of Dolfuss, the Austrian republic failed to fall. Kurt von Schuschnigg, a lawyer from Innsbruck and member of Dolfuss's cabinet, organized the loyalist forces and quickly suppressed the rebellion. Upon hearing of the abortive nazi revolt, Mussolini immediately mobilized four divisions and sent them to the Brenner Pass ready to face the German army if necessary. Hitler, in no position to risk war with Italy, repudiated the plot and ordered his aides to halt the publication of the press release supporting the conspiracy. He also forced Habicht to resign and closed the Austrian headquarters in Munich. The führer sent Franz von Papen to Vienna as the new German ambassador to develop friendly relations with Schuschnigg's government. Austria had gained a few precious years of freedom, but Hitler had not abandoned this important portion of his program, for he simply realized that he must develop better relations with Rome before he could take action. In a few years nazi troops would march through the former Habsburg capital, and Hitler would return to the scene of his youthful humiliation in triumph.

The failure of the first attempt to annex Austria led to an intensification of another of Hitler's major goals, the rearmament of Germany. The Treaty of Versailles had limited the German army to a total force of 100,000, had forbidden the introduction of conscription, and had severely limited the size of the artillery and munitions. The hated peace further reduced the German navy to six warships and prohibited the Germans from possessing either submarines or an air force. Hitler, who had come to power partially on the promise to rid Germany of the chains of the treaty, almost immediately on assuming power began to plan the rebirth of Germany as a major military power.

On February 1, 1934, he appointed Werner von Fritsch commander in chief of the army under Blomberg, the minister of War. Hitler instructed Fritsch to begin immediate preparations to construct a strong military. To build an army larger than that demanded by the Treaty of Versailles, Hitler's military advisers appealed to the precedent set by Generals Gerhard von Scharnhorst and August von Gneisenau. These Prussian leaders had defied similar restrictions imposed by Napoleon by simply shortening the period of active service in order to build up a large reserve that could be mobilized in the event of renewed fighting. In January 1934 a secret decree ordered the reduction of the length of active service from twelve years to one. After a year of training, a soldier would join a unit of the reserves. Thereby Hitler's generals could build up a large force of men ready to take up arms at a moment's notice. At the same time, the military began active recruitment, and by October 1934 the army had 240,000 men, more than twice the number allowed by the Treaty of Versailles. The leaders of the military also trained and equipped 200,000 policemen to act as an auxiliary force. Finally, on March 16, 1935, Hitler openly defied the victors of the First World War by announcing the resumption of universal military conscription, another direct violation of the Treaty of Versailles. Of course the rapid enlargement of the army meant a corresponding growth in the officer corps.

When Hitler appointed Fritsch commander in chief of the army, he made Erich Räder head of the navy. Räder threw himself into the rebuilding of the sea forces of the Reich. Hitler provided him with 830 million marks, which he spent building new ships, including two battle cruisers, the *Scharnhorst* and the *Gneisenau*. Räder also ordered construction of two cruisers and several destroyers. Because the führer was not prepared to openly risk the wrath of the Allies by building a fleet of submarines, Räder, building on the clandestine activities of the Krupp firm in Finland, gathered in Kiel the materials needed to build submarines. He also ignored the restrictions of the hated treaty and increased the size of the navy from the authorized 15,000 to 25,000 in 1934, and to 34,000 in 1935. Thus, Germany was well on the way toward challenging the British domination of the seas.

Since Hermann Göring, Hitler's old comrade in arms, had been commander of the famed Richtoffen squadron during the First World War, it was only natural that the führer would ask him to organize a German air force, or Luftwaffe. Realizing that the Allies would never tolerate such an open breach of the Treaty of Versailles and that the Reich was not yet strong enough to withstand Allied pressure, Göring decided to proceed with caution and build a secret air force. With the assistance of Karl Bodenschats, his former adjutant during the First World War, and Erhard Milch, chief of Lufthansa, the national airlines, Göring began to plan for the creation of a large Luftwaffe. He used the facilities of Lufthansa and those of the League for Aeronautical Sports to train future pilots. He goaded Hjalmar Schacht, the nazi economic tsar, into giving him funds to build the first prototypes of the new planes, and he commissioned Ernst Udet, another member of the Flying Circus, to design and test a bomber that would dive at an object and then drop its bombs directly on target. Slowly the air force began to take shape, and after 1936, when Hitler officially overthrew the Treaty of Versailles, production went into full force.

The Krupp works was the major armament firm in Germany. It had been founded by Friedrich Krupp in 1811 and was headed by Gustaf Krupp. These industrialists from Essen had built a vast industrial empire by providing several generations of Prussian soldiers armaments of all sizes. Krupp had been an early supporter of Hitler and had rallied his fellow industrialists in support of the nazi drive for power. During the Weimar years, when the government feared the wrath of the French and British and refused to openly break the Treaty of Versailles, Krupp had kept his designers busy preparing weapons for the day when Germany could once again openly build an army. Through subsidiaries in the Netherlands, Finland, and Spain, Krupp had built and tested prototypes for a new fleet of submarines. After the nazi victory, Krupp stepped up this aspect of his work and built parts to be stored secretly in Kiel, which were to be assembled when Hitler gave the order. Meanwhile, this famous company was busy preparing other weapons for Hitler's new army.[6]

I. G. Farben, the chemical cartel formed in 1926 by Carl Duisberg and Carl Bosch, performed services for the rearmament effort similar to those of the Krupp works. During the First World War the German chemical industry had developed processes to create synthetic substitutes for materials normally imported from abroad. Shortly after the nazis assumed power, Carl Krauch, a director of the vast Farben enterprise, informed Erhard Milch, Göring's chief assistant in the Air Ministry, of the willingness of his firm to produce artificial gasoline. Milch contracted Vollard Bockelberg of the Army Ordnance Office and worked out an agreement that would guarantee Farben the funds needed to expand its facilities at Leuna for the production of synthetic gasoline from coal. The army approached Farben in September 1935 to request the development of a substitute for rubber that could be used to make badly needed tires for military vehicles. The scientists working for Farben perfected a system to produce the needed material, and with government assistance the firm established a plant at Schkopau to produce synthetic rubber the next year. Throughout the next few years I. G. Farben would provide many valuable products to feed the growing German war machine.

Despite Hitler's efforts to keep his program of rearmament secret from the Allies, the British and French, who had superior intelligence operations, learned of the Nazi program. On March 25, 1935, a few days after the führer reintroduced military conscription, the British sent Sir John Simon and Anthony Eden to meet with Hitler and his aides in Berlin. They found the nazi dictator in an uncompromising mood when they suggested the negotiation of a collective security agreement that would guarantee peace and international boundaries. The adamant führer not only refused but also demanded that the British allow Germany to create an army of 550,000 men consisting of thirty-six regular divisions and one weapons S.S. division. Unable to persuade Hitler to reconsider his ultimatum, the English diplomats returned home, having failed in their mission. However, London, realizing the danger of German rearmament, approached the equally alarmed French. On April 11, 1935, the two countries issued a statement pledging both nations to collective security, to the independence of Austria, and to disarmament. The two Allies also appealed to the League of Nations, which voted one week later to protest German rearmament and threatened action if Berlin failed to abide by the terms of the Treaty of Versailles.

The declarations of London and Paris and of the League of Nations threw Hitler into a rage. He issued an angry note challenging the authority of the League of Nations to judge Germany. The führer also tried to challenge the Allies by appearing ready to reach agreement with them. On May 21, 1935, he spoke to an adoring crowd to answer the charges against the Reich. Whipping his listeners into a patriotic frenzy, he denounced the League and the Soviet Union in fiery terms, but he also held out an olive branch to the world. Hitler strongly denied any plan to conquer neighboring nations, including Austria, and offered to sign nonaggression pacts with countries bordering the Reich as a pledge of his word. Finally, the führer promised to abide by the terms of all international agreements that Germany had freely signed.

Hitler accompanied his peace campaign by an effort to drive a wedge between the French and the British, who were alarmed by the Franco-Soviet nonagression pact, and he sent Joachim von Ribbentrop to London. Ribbentrop was born in Wesel on April 3, 1893, the son of a former officer in the army who had resigned his commission in protest of the dismissal of Bismarck and had accepted a position in a bank. The future nazi diplomat traveled with his family to Switzerland and France, where he learned to speak fluent French. When eighteen he went to Canada to work at various jobs, from banking to road construction, and he learned to speak English. In 1914 he returned to Germany to fight for his fatherland in the First World War, where he was a successful soldier, earning the coveted Iron Cross and becoming a lieutenant in the service of Hans von Seeckt. After the war he went to Berlin to work for a firm specializing in cotton imports. In 1920 he married Annalies Henkel, of the champagne family, and became a liquor and wine wholesaler. Five years later the clever Ribbentrop persuaded a noble aunt to adopt him, thereby winning the right to put "von" in his name. He joined the Nazi party in 1932 after deciding that they would achieve their goals. He used his knowledge of foreign languages and foreign countries to rise in the nazi hierarchy and become the führer's chief adviser on foreign affairs. On June 18, 1935, he successfully negotiated a naval agreement with the British. This masterful piece of diplomacy allowed Germany to build a navy 34 percent as large as the British navy, but with as many submarines as the British navy. Naturally, the announcement of this agreement alarmed the French because Hitler had achieved his goal.

A few months later events in Africa played into Hitler's hands, enabling him to begin building good relations with Mussolini. The Italian dictator was determined to enlarge his overseas empire and sent his troops into Ethiopia on October 7, 1935. He hoped that the British and French concern over nazi Germany would lead them to ignore his aggression. He was wrong. London and Paris refused to stand by idly while the Italians conquered the monarchy of Haile Selassie. On November 18, persuaded by the pleas of the Ethiopian emperor, the League of Nations condemned the Italian action and called for economic sanctions against Rome. However, the superior army of the duce was more than a match for the poorly armed Ethiopians, who threw spears and arrows at their foe equipped with modern weapons. On May 5, 1936, the Italians marched into Addis Ababa, formally annexing the empire four days later. The violent protests from London and Paris drove Mussolini to seek closer relations with Hitler, thereby preparing the way for the formation of an alliance.

The conflict over Ethiopia provided Hitler with a golden opportunity to rid himself of the Treaty of Versailles. With London and Paris preoccupied with events in Africa, the führer decided that the time had come for the remilitarization of the Rhineland. Ever since the end of the First World War, the Allies had forbidden German troops to occupy the strategic Rhine area. One of Hitler's major goals was to rid Germany of this humiliating state of affairs. Originally, he planned to take this bold step in 1937, but the Ethiopian crisis diverted attention from Germany and prompted him to take immediate action. After receiving assurance from the duce that he would oppose retaliation against Germany, Hitler ordered Blomberg to begin immediate preparations to march into the Rhineland. On "Z-Day," March 7, 1936, which was a Saturday, chosen to catch the weekending English off guard, the army marched across the forbidden line, occupying Trier, Aachen, and Saarbrücken. The reappearance of German troops for the first time since the end of the First World War led to great rejoicing among the people. Cheering crowds lined the streets as they marched by, and pretty girls handed flowers to the enthusiastic soldiers.

Meanwhile in Berlin, Constantin von Neurath, Hitler's foreign minister, tried to win the friendship of the alarmed Allies. Neurath was born on February 2, 1873, of petty south German nobility. After studying at the universities of Berlin and Tübingen, he entered the diplomatic service in 1901. Before the First World War he served in London. He was a captain in the army during the conflict and won the Iron Cross for bravery. After the war he reentered the foreign service and served as ambassador to Denmark, Italy, and Great Britain before Franz von Papen appointed him minister of foreign affairs in 1932. Although Neurath despised the Treaty of Versailles, he was not a Nazi, and would finally leave Hitler's service in 1938. As a part of the führer's peace offensive, timed to avoid conflict over the remilitarization of the Rhineland, Neurath met with the French, Italian, and British ambassadors to inform them that the Franco-Soviet treaty had violated the Treaty of Locarno, thereby justifying the German action. However, on the führer's instructions, he proposed the signing of a twenty-five year nonaggression pact by Germany, France, and Belgium. To soothe the English, he offered them a treaty limiting the size of the Luftwaffe, and he further suggested the creation of a demilitarized zone along the Franco-Belgian-German border.

However, the British and French refused to allow the German peace offensive to turn their attention away from the violation of the Treaty of Versailles. Paris indignantly rejected Neurath's offer because it would require the destruction of the Maginot Line, France's chief defense against a German attack. The French vehemently protested the remilitarization of the Rhineland and persuaded the League of Nations to pass a resolution formally denouncing the German action. However, the British prevented Paris from more substantial action. Many Englishmen accepted Hitler's guarantees of peace and felt that the provisions of the peace of 1919, forbidding the Germans to have troops in the Rhineland, had been an unfair violation of the rights of sovereignty. Even those in Britain who failed to sympathize with Hitler's actions had no desire to risk war and considered the French protests too extreme. Had the French and British acted decisively to prevent the breach of the Treaty of Versailles, Hitler would have been forced to back down and might have lost sufficient support from the military, which feared war, to cause his fall from office and to prevent another war.

Meanwhile, Vienna, realizing the failure of the French and English to meet Hitler's challenge and aware of the rapid growth of the German military, decided to seek closer relations with Berlin. Kurt Schuschnigg, Dolfuss's successor, forced the anti-German vice-chancellor, Prince Starhemberg, to resign and opened discussions with the Germans. After securing the approval of Mussolini, the two nations signed a treaty on July 11, 1936, whereby Berlin recognized the independence of the former Habsburg territory. The Austrian chancellor also promised close cooperation with the Third Reich. As a sign of his good faith, Schuschnigg released over one thousand Nazis from prison and lifted the ban on the importation of newspapers from the Reich. Meanwhile, Hitler met with the leaders of the Austrian Nazis at Berchtesgaden. After ordering them to avoid any action that could threaten the new friendly relations between the two Germanic states, the führer told them in no uncertain terms that unification could not come through violence and revolution but only as the result of evolution and legal activity.

By 1936 Hitler had achieved the first major goal of his foreign policy, the destruction of the Treaty of Versailles. He had reorganized the military and begun a program of rearmament designed to create a machine that would challenge his enemies and back his demands on other countries with the threat of death and destruction. He had begun to win the friendship of Mussolini and had taken the first step toward the annexation of Austria. Hitler and his advisers had boldly challenged the British and French by sending German troops into the Rhineland, and they had confronted no significant resistance. In 1936 the führer had achieved victory on all fronts and was well on the way toward achieving his goal of making Germany a major European power.

16

The Road to War

The remilitarization of the Rhineland was only the first of several defiant acts by the German dictator. During the next few years Hitler took advantage of every opportunity to bring more and more people under the shadow of the Third Reich. Like a greedy beast, the more Hitler achieved, the more he wanted. He won the friendship of Mussolini by joining him in interfering in the Spanish Civil War to help a fellow fascist ruthlessly crush the freedom of his people. He took advantage of the strength of the Austrian Nazis to force Schuschnigg virtually to surrender the independence of the former Habsburg state in preparation for its annexation by the German Reich. He then championed the cause of the Sudeten Germans against the Czech government. In the crisis that followed he used a mixture of threats and promises of eventual peace to persuade the English and French to allow him to carve out a large chunk of the Slavic state for the German Reich. Yet many Germans feared that the führer's risky diplomacy would lead Europe into a terrible war and organized an effort to overthrow the tyrant before he destroyed Germany and the rest of Europe with it. But the heroes who dared to oppose him found themselves unable to stem the rising tide of Hitler's power and could do little but feebly appeal to the French and English for help. Unfortunately, the leaders of the strongest nations in Europe lacked the courage to rebuke the German dictator, and by failing to do so, they allowed him to emerge a victor. Finally, Hitler's greed led him to make a pact with Stalin, the dictator of Soviet Russia, to shatter Poland. Eventually the British and French realized that their agreements with Berlin had been in vain and that only armed force could halt the nazi menace.[1]

After defying the French and British by sending his troops into the Rhineland, Hitler found another opportunity to extend his power by interfering in the Spanish Civil War. The once-great empire had sunk to a level of turmoil and revolution. From 1923 to 1930 General Miguel Primo de Rivera ruled the troubled land as an absolute dictator. After his fall the weak king, Alfonso XIII, failed to restore order and finally fled on April 14, 1931, after the Republicans had won a series of local elections. For the next few years anarchy reigned in the kingdom, as the rightist Falangists, led by Jose Antonio Primo de Rivera, the son of the fallen dictator, fought the Socialists and Communists. The Communists, Democrats, and Socialists formed the Popular Front and acquired control of the Spanish parliament, the Cortes, electing Manuel Azana, a Republican, president on May 10, 1936. However, the moderate head of state failed to control his leftist supporters, and they set out to deprive the large landowners of their domination of the countryside and to confiscate the vast wealth of the Spanish Roman Catholic Church. Finally, the rightist military in Morocco, led by General Francisco Franco, revolted on July 18, 1936, beginning a bloody civil war that raged for the next three years.[2]

The conflict in Spain provided Hitler with an opportunity to cast Germany in the role of a great power. At the beginning of the conflict, Johannes Bernhardt, a German agent in Spain, realized that the Third Reich could not only make a great deal of money by selling supplies to the rightists, but also could place a government in Madrid friendly to the basic ideology of fascism. Bearing letters from Franco pleading for help, Bernhardt flew to Berlin. Unable to gain a hearing at the foreign office, he appealed to Rudolf Hess for assistance. The deputy party leader sympathized with Bernhardt's arguments and arranged for him to meet with Hitler in Bayreuth, where he was attending the Wagner Festival. There, on July 22, caught up in the heroic mood of Wagner's powerful music, the führer committed Germany to come to Franco's aid without even consulting his chief advisers.

Hitler saw the conflict as a chance to distract the British and French while he continued to rebuild his military. He also hoped to cement his relationship with Mussolini, who had already agreed to help Franco. Naturally, Hitler was concerned that a leftist victory in Spain would strengthen the French Communists and directly threaten the security of Germany. Eventually Hitler sent supplies and over 100,000 men to aid the Falangists in their fight with the left. Hitler, however, had no desire to help Franco achieve a quick victory, because as long as the war raged he could concentrate on other matters while the world focused its attention on the struggle for Spain. He sent several Junker 52s, which the future Spanish dictator used to fly his men from Morocco to the mainland. During the war Germany sent 1.6 million tons of iron ore and 956,000 tons of pyrites. Giving Göring a chance to test his air force under combat conditions, Hitler sent the Condor Air Legion. This force of 6,750 men terrified the world with the brutal bombing of Guernica, a Republican stronghold, in 1937.

Hitler and Mussolini were not the only dictators to interfere in the Spanish Civil War. Joseph Stalin, who saw the struggle as a conflict against fascism, sent four hundred trucks, fifty planes, one hundred tanks, and four hundred pilots and tank drivers to aid the Popular Front. He also sent a large group of advisers from the Comintern to help the leftists plan their strategy. Meanwhile, liberals and leftists throughout the world championed the struggle against Franco, and hundreds flocked to join the International Brigade to fight in support of the Popular Front. All the British and French could do was to plead vainly for nonintervention by both sides. London and Paris tried without success to organize a blockade of Spain that would halt the shipping of men and supplies to both sides. The war devastated Spain, leaving a path of death and destruction as both sides fought. Finally, on January 26, 1939, Franco drove the Republicans from Barcelona, their last stronghold, and established a dictatorship that lasted until his death in 1975.

Out of cooperation in the Spanish Civil War, Italy and Germany developed a relationship that culminated in the formation of the Rome-Berlin Axis. Hitler realized that as long as the Italian dictator supported Schuschnigg's government in Vienna, his hope of German annexation of Austria was in vain. Therefore he sought to develop ties with Mussolini that would allow him to carry out his policy without fear of Italian intervention. On June 29, 1936, even before the beginning of the Spanish Civil War, Hitler instructed the ambassador to Rome to inform Count Galeazzo Ciano, the duce's son-in-law and foreign minister, of his willingness to recognize the new Italian empire. On September 23 Hans Frank, Hitler's minister of justice who spoke fluent Italian, arrived in Rome to invite the duce to visit the Third Reich. Frank told the delighted Italian dictator that the führer was willing to recognize his domination in the Mediterranean since Hitler was interested in the Baltic and Eastern Europe.

Negotiations continued for the next few months and led to the signing of a formal treaty of alliance. On October 24 Ciano visited Hitler at his mountain retreat at Berchtesgaden. The führer received his guest with all the flair normally reserved for visiting royalty and impressed him so much that he signed a secret agreement providing for close cooperation between the two fascist states. Although the pact was supposed to be kept secret, an excited Mussolini announced to a crowd of his cheering supporters in Milan on November 1 the formation of a new relationship with Hitler. The duce characterized the new friendship as an axis running between Berlin and Rome, around which all those desiring peace could revolve. After further discussions Mussolini visited Hitler in Munich on September 23, 1937. Hitler's aides carefully organized a show of nazi pageantry designed to impress their visitor with the power of the Third Reich. Hitler arrived at the train station in his special train to meet the duce as he alighted from his railroad car. Mussolini spent the next few days in a whirlwind of activity. Thousands of thundering S.S. troops marched through the streets of the Bavarian capital to pay tribute to the duce, who attended numerous banquets at which nazi dignitaries toasted the achievements of their sister fascist state. Mussolini was the honored guest at army maneuvers in Mecklenburg and inspected the Krupp munition works in Essen. Finally, the triumphant tour climaxed when he and Hitler addressed 800,000 enthusiastic persons in the Field of May in Berlin. Although a violent thunderstorm suddenly appeared, sending the crowd running for cover, the soaked Italian dictator left Germany greatly impressed by the might of nazi Germany. Back in Rome, he announced his decision to join the Anti-Comintern Pact on November 6, 1937. Thus, Hitler had at last won Mussolini's friendship, a friendship that would cause him great trouble in the dark years of the Second World War.

The Anti-Comintern Pact was the product of successful negotiations concluded the preceding year between Germany and Japan. The Asian empire had fallen under the control of ultra-nationalistic military men who desired to create a new Asia under Japanese domination. After the Mukden incident in 1931, Tokyo resigned from the League of Nations in response to condemnation of Japanese aggression against China. Condemned by the international community and fearing the growth of Asian communism, the Japanese began to seek new allies. Hiroshi Oshima, the military attaché in Berlin, began discussions with Ribbentrop. The Nazis, willing to recognize the Japanese as an Aryan race because of the fair Ainu peoples of the northern islands, were sympathetic to Oshima's proposal for the formation of an anticommunist alliance. Since Hitler believed that Japan might keep Russia and the United States occupied in the event of war, he signed the Anti-Comintern Pact on November 23, 1936, providing for joint action to combat the threat of communism. After Mussolini agreed to join in 1937, an agreement had been reached that provided the basis for a full-scale alliance in the Tripartite Pact of September 27, 1940. In this treaty, Germany and Italy recognized Japanese predominance in Asia in return for recognition by Tokyo of German and Italian predominance in Europe. The agreement also provided for close cooperation among the three nations. Significantly, it clearly stated that the pact was not meant to threaten the position of the Soviet Union, with which Hitler had signed a nonaggression pact.

At the time that Hitler was busy negotiating with Rome and Tokyo, he was seeking the friendship of the English. He believed that Germany had no real conflict with the British and that he could persuade London to agree to recognize his aspirations in Eastern Europe in return for recognition of the British Empire. In August 1936 he appointed Ribbentrop ambassador to the Court of St. James with instructions to persuade the English to sign an alliance with the Third Reich. Although the nazi foreign policy expert had negotiated effectively with London the year before on the naval agreement, he was not a good diplomat. He was arrogant and lacked the charm and skill necessary for effective diplomacy. He failed in repeated attempts to win the support of the English and finally decided that the British would be Hitler's chief opponent in any future struggle.

However, in May 1937 Neville Chamberlain became prime minister of England. This dapper gentleman was dedicated to peace at any price and sympathized with the nationalism of the German-speaking peoples of Eastern Europe. On November 19, 1937, Edward Frederick Wood, the earl of Halifax, arrived in Berchtesgaden to meet with the nazi leader. Halifax assured the führer of the commitment of the British to anticommunism and that London would be open to suggestions for a revision of the Treaty of Versailles. He also told Hitler that the English would consider adjustments in the status of Austria, Danzig, and the German-speaking areas of Czechoslovakia, provided that any changes took place through negotiations and not through force. Although Hitler had failed in his effort to gain an alliance with the English, he was encouraged by the willingness of the British to discuss a revision of the eastern boundary of the Reich.

However, even as he was informing the world of his desire for peace, Hitler had not forgotten the long-range goals of his foreign policy. On November 5, 1937, a few weeks before Lord Halifax's mission, he summoned the commanders of the military and the foreign minister to meet with him in the chancellory. Since Colonel Friedrich Hossbach has provided history with an account of this secret conference, it is usually referred to as the Hossbach Memorandum.[3] The führer told the startled officials that the German people could only fulfill their destiny through the "acquisition" of enough "living space" to provide the food and raw materials necessary for a great power. Unlike the colonial powers of the nineteenth century, the Reich had to look to the east for fertile lands to fulfill this need. Hitler realized that he could not hope to achieve his goals through simple negotiations; so he knew he must be prepared to use force. Aware that the army could only be sustained for a relatively short period of time, the führer proposed that Germany prepare for action by 1943 or 1945 at the latest. He also suggested that every possible means be found to keep the Spanish Civil War going as long as possible to weaken the French and to occupy the British. If necessary a means had to be found to persuade Mussolini to strengthen his position in the Balearic Islands possibly to cause a war between France and Italy. Then Hitler proposed that while the rest of Europe was involved in the conflict in the Mediterranean, Germany would move to annex Austria and Czechoslovakia. The führer also told his terrified visitors that if the opportunity came, possibly through the outbreak of a domestic crisis in France, they must be prepared to move before the target date of 1943. While the contents of the Hossbach Memorandum do not reveal that Hitler intended to start a major war, for he stated that he believed that England and possibly France would agree to German annexation of Czechoslovakia, they do show that Hitler was willing to resort to force to achieve his long-range goals. Neither can the Hossbach Memorandum be considered a timetable for Hitler's planned diplomacy. He did not hesitate to take advantage of the opportunities to annex Austria and to crush Czechoslovakia years ahead of 1943. Significantly, Hitler failed to discuss either Danzig or his frequently expressed wish to conquer the Ukraine. The Hossbach Memorandum, however, does reveal that Hitler was more interested in achieving the goals of his foreign policy as outlined in his speeches and *Mein Kampf* than in preserving the peace in Europe.

Hitler's startling announcements led to a heated discussion, lasting several hours. One by one, Foreign Minister Neurath, Minister of War Blomberg, and Commander of the Army Fritsch voiced their strong reservations to Hitler's risky plans. The leaders of the military informed their determined leader that he had failed to consider the strength of the French army and the weakness of the German forces. They maintained that rearmament could not possibly proceed fast enough to build a military capable of intimidating the combined forces of the French and the British. Even Neurath warned the führer that his plans could lead only to disaster. Only Göring seemed willing to support Hitler's ambitious proposals. Yet the meeting ended with the dictator of the Third Reich as determined as ever to carry out his dangerous plans.

Hitler's shocking program crystallized the opinion of many leaders of the German army that he must be stopped before he brought the Reich to the brink of a war it was not prepared to fight. Even before 1937 many generals had turned against the führer and had begun to conspire to sabotage his risky plans. Many members of the elitist army had always regarded Hitler as an upstart, neither qualified to meddle in military matters nor capable of mastering them. They had reacted with horror to the bloody purge of June 30, 1934, and several had defied Blomberg's direct orders to attend the funerals of Schleicher and others who had lost their lives in the nazi campaign of revenge. Werner von Fritsch resented Hitler's failure to consult the army before announcing the resumption of conscription. Most of the officers disapproved of the rapid rearmament program, believing that Hitler and his aides had no understanding of complicated military matters and had sacrificed good planning and quality for speed. Several had protested the decision to defy the Treaty of Versailles by sending troops into the Rhineland and had unsuccessfully attempted to persuade the führer to withdraw the forces before the English and French took action. Others resented the growth and power of the Weapon S.S., Hitler's private army commanded by Himmler. Fritsch, a devout Christian, and several of his fellow officers opposed the pagan character of national socialism and the efforts of the "German Christians" to subvert the church. Now they realized that if they allowed Hitler to carry out his mad scheme, he would destroy the army and Germany.[4]

One of the most important leaders of the antinazi movement among the military was Rear Admiral Wilhelm Franz Canaris, the head of the Office of Military Intelligence. Canaris, born on January 1, 1887, was the son of a wealthy manufacturer in Aplerbeck, near Dortmund. After secondary education he joined the navy and studied at the Naval Academy at Kiel, spending the First World War in German intelligence. When the British sank his ship, the *Dresden,* off the coast of South America, the Chilean authorities arrested and interned him and his fellow sailors on an island. He escaped, and after a daring flight through South America in disguise, he returned to Berlin ready for further assignment. From there he went to Spain to continue his work in German intelligence. He caught malaria and tried to return to Germany disguised as a Franciscan friar. However, the Allies captured him, and he only escaped death through the intervention of his Spanish friends, one of whom was Francisco Franco, the future dictator. He finally returned to Germany by submarine, narrowly eluding capture by the British. After recovering from his illness, he spent the rest of the war commanding a submarine.[5]

Following World War One, Canaris helped reorganize German military intelligence, and on January 1, 1934, he became its leader. The crafty officer soon became disenchanted with Hitler and organized a group of like-minded officers into a group called the Black Band (Die Schwarze Kapelle). He went to Spain in 1936 to assist Franco, but he took advantage of the situation to instruct Don Juan March, the son of a fisherman who had risen high in the ranks of the Falangists, to contact Stewart Graham Menzies, the chief of MI-6, British intelligence, to inform him of his doubts about Hitler's leadership. He sent Captain Robert Treeck to England to penetrate Menzies's social circle to establish ties with the British, and he also contacted Major Francis Foley, Menzies's representative in Berlin.[6]

One of Canaris's chief allies in his campaign to prevent Hitler from carrying out his risky plans was General Ludwig Beck. Beck, born in 1880, was a member of the personal staff of Crown Prince Rupprecht of Bavaria during the First World War. After Versailles, Beck remained in the army and became chief of the general staff in 1934. Like many of his fellow officers, Beck considered Hitler and his Nazis a band of ruffians who could not be trusted with the fate of the German people. After receiving warning from Canaris, he tried to tell Schleicher of Hitler's plans for a purge. He defied Blomberg by attending his friend's funeral and proclaimed him a fallen hero. Despite Hitler's command of absolute secrecy, both Neurath and Fritsch had told Beck of the meeting of November 5, 1937. Thereafter, Beck became a determined antinazi, dedicated to the overthrow of Hitler and his regime.

Hitler, through the work of the security service of the S.S., which was commanded by Reinhard Heydrich, and the statements of Blomberg and Fritsch, realized the strength of antinazi sentiment among the military. He was determined to bring the army under his complete control and sought an excuse for Blomberg's dismissal without causing a major crisis. He found it when the general married Eva Gruhn on January 12, 1938. Shortly after the wedding, which Hitler and Göring attended, Count Wolf Heinrich von Helldorf, chief of the Berlin police, gave the delighted commander of the air force a report charging that Blomberg's bride and mother-in-law had been arrested for prostitution while operating a massage parlor. Armed with the incriminating evidence, Göring took advantage of the situation, allowing the charges to be leaked to the proud officers through a series of anonymous telephone calls while his allies circulated rumors about Blomberg's new wife. Finally, after Hitler had returned from a holiday in the south, Göring informed the führer that Blomberg had disgraced the traditions of the officer Corps by marrying a "common whore." Armed with Hitler's rage, Göring confronted the shocked minister of war to demand his resignation. On January 26 Hitler met with the field marshal to formally dismiss him.

However, Blomberg's fall created more problems for Hitler and his nazi cohorts than it solved, for it placed the even more hated Werner von Fritsch, commander in chief of the army, in the post of minister of war. At this crucial moment, Himmler stepped forward and gave Hitler a file charging the bachelor officer with homosexuality. This gave the führer his chance to rid himself of one of his most persistent critics. On the same day that he dismissed Blomberg, Hitler summoned Fritsch to answer the accusations in the presence of Göring and Himmler. The officer denied the charges, but suddenly Himmler produced a man named Schmidt who testified that he had seen Fritsch engaged in homosexual activity with a youth in Potsdam in 1934; Schmidt had been blackmailing Fritsch ever since. Hitler suspended the shocked commander, who was too surprised to protest. Thus, Hitler had destroyed the two strongest spokesmen for the traditional independence of the military.

Fritsch refused to allow his name to be besmirched by the false charges. With the support of his fellow officers, he demanded the right to defend himself in a formal court-martial. He obtained the services of Count Rüdiger von der Golz and prepared his defense for the trial, which opened in Berlin on March 10, 1938. Meanwhile, further investigation by the Gestapo revealed that Schmidt had actually been blackmailing a retired officer named Frisch, not General von Fritsch. Despite this revelation, Schmidt repeated his charges at the trial, claiming that he had received money from both men for a guarantee not to reveal their homosexuality. Finally, Golz's expert cross-examination revealed serious inconsistencies between the Gestapo report and Schmidt's charges and forced him to admit that he had lied. The court voted to acquit Fritsch, but he did not return to his old office.

Hitler used the scandals to bring the military under his absolute control. After the dismissal of Blomberg and Fritsch, Hitler wrestled with the problem of their successors. Göring and Reichenau both wanted the post, but the führer realized that the other officers would oppose their appointment. On January 27 Blomberg met with Hitler to express his feelings on the subject. The disgraced former minister of war, hoping that his cooperation would insure his appointment to some office once the crisis had passed, recommended Göring as the logical choice. However, Hitler rejected this suggestion, arguing that his old comrade in arms lacked the qualities necessary for such an important position. Then Blomberg suggested that Hitler become his own minister of war, an idea that the führer liked. On February 4, 1938, he announced the formation of the Supreme Command of the Armed Forces, or O.K.W., under his personal direction. He also appointed Wilhelm Keitel chief of the Supreme Command of the Armed Forces. The new chief of staff was born on his father's farm near Gandersheim in Hanover on September 22, 1882. Despite his non-Prussian origins, Keitel joined the army in 1900 and served on the general staff during the First World War. Keitel was sympathetic to the goals of national socialism, but he resented the pretentions of the S.A. To soothe the wounded pride of Göring, Hitler awarded him a field marshal's baton.

Although Hitler had brought the military under his control, he sought a means to draw attention away from his troubles with the army. He found it when Chancellor Schuschnigg of Austria showed an interest in meeting with him to discuss relations between the two countries. Since the failure of the Nazi Putsch in 1934, Schuschnigg had ruled the former Habsburg land with an iron hand. Despite the treaty of 1936, the Austrian leader had not lifted the ban on the Austrian Nazi party. Deprived of support from the Reich, which had no desire to offend Mussolini, Hitler's Austrian followers had gone underground to produce illegal newspapers and pamphlets to spread their message. They painted swastikas on buildings and other monuments and prepared for the day when once again the Storm Troopers could march through the streets of Vienna. During this period the Nazis had capitalized on the disastrous effects of the depression to win much support among the rural classes. On February 4, 1938, Hitler instructed Franz von Papen, the minister in Vienna, to suggest that Schuschnigg meet with the führer at his mountain retreat near the Austrian border. The chancellor, wishing to develop friendly relations with his powerful neighbor, readily agreed.

Eight days later, in the heights of the Alps, the dramatic confrontation between the two determined men took place. Schuschnigg attempted to place the talks on a friendly basis by commenting on the spectacular view of the mountains and the countryside with the towers of Salzburg in the distance. However, Hitler was in no mood for pleasantries and demanded that they discuss the important differences between the two countries. The fanatical führer shouted at the startled Austrian that Vienna had betrayed his goodwill and had begun to fortify the border. He screamed that since Schuschnigg obviously had no desire to deal with him in an upright manner, he must accept his demands or suffer the consequences. Then, without giving the chancellor an opportunity to reply, he led him to lunch. While they ate, Hitler, who just a few moments before had yelled threateningly at his guest, became a gracious host. However, this was merely a facade, for the führer had not forgotten his anger.

After they finished the meal, the harried Austrian found himself in front of Papen and Ribbentrop, who then gave the unnerved Schuschnigg the German demands. He must allow the Nazis to openly carry on their activities and appoint several members to high office. The Germans also demanded that Schuschnigg agree to allow Berlin to dominate the Austrian military and economy. Significantly, before leaving Vienna, Schuschnigg and his advisers had decided to appoint Arthur Seyss-Inquart, the leader of the Austrian Nazis, to a governmental post and to lift some of the restrictions against nazi activity. Hitler's agents had learned of these decisions, and the führer had formulated his ultimatum accordingly. Aware that Hitler demanded much more than he had decided to accept, and that agreement to Hitler's proposals would mean the end of Austrian independence, Schuschnigg vainly tried to reason with the führer. However, Hitler was in a stubborn mood and briskly refused even to discuss the issue. Suddenly, he summoned General Keitel and banished Schuschnigg from his presence. When the general arrived, Hitler told him that he had no orders. It had been a clever ruse to convince the Austrian Chancellor that if he refused to sign the ultimatum, Hitler would order his troops to march into Austria. Unaware that he had been tricked, Schuschnigg signed the agreement and left to inform his colleagues of Hitler's severe terms.[7]

In Vienna Schuschnigg fulfilled the agreement and appointed Arthur Seyss-Inquart to the crucial post of minister of the interior. Seyss-Inquart, the chief German agent in Austria, was born in 1892 in Iglan, which is in present-day Czechoslovakia, and moved to Vienna in 1907. He fought the Russians during the First World War, but had enough time to receive a law degree while home on leave in 1917. After the war, he became a member of the German Brotherhood, an ultranationalistic and anti-Semitic organization that had among its members such important people as Englebert Dolfuss, the future Austrian chancellor. He became a nominal Nazi in 1932 and entered the government as a state counselor in 1937. The next year he became the minister of the interior, as Hitler had demanded at Berchtesgaden. This important post allowed him to control the police and other important aspects of the government. Shortly after receiving this important office, he flew to Berlin to receive instructions. Throughout the next few weeks he maintained close contact with Hitler's aides.

Because Hitler had justified his demands on the contention that the majority of the Austrian people supported unification with the Third Reich, Schuschnigg decided to take the bold step of calling for a national plebiscite on March 13 to settle the question definitely. However, the Austrian chancellor had no intention of risking the possibility of a pro-nazi vote. The crucial vote would take place only four days after the announcement, before the Nazis could organize an effective campaign. The ballot would not be secret and all the election machinery would be securely in the hands of Schuschnigg's supporters. Only those born before 1914 would be allowed to vote, thereby preventing the many youthful Nazis from participating. Hitler had not planned for an election, but he decided to act at once, lest Schuschnigg have grounds to tell the world that the Austrian people had no desire to lose their national independence to become a province in Hitler's empire. Furious over Schuschnigg's plans to prevent pro-unification forces from influencing the vote, Hitler ordered Keitel to begin plans for Operation Otto, an invasion of Austria developed the year before and named for Otto von Habsburg, the claimant to the imperial throne. He also sent Prince Philip of Hesse to Rome to seek Mussolini's support. Hitler instructed his messenger to inform the Italian dictator that Schuschnigg had violated the agreement reached at Berchtesgaden and had begun to suppress the German nationalists while plotting to join Czechoslovakia in an attack on the Reich. The führer also ordered the prince to tell the duce that Schuschnigg's oppressive regime had led to a popular revolt and only German intervention could restore order. Finally, on March 11 Hitler issued an ultimatum demanding the postponement of the plebiscite.

Faced with the threat of armed invasion and unable to gain support from Rome, Schuschnigg backed down and agreed to postpone the crucial vote. However, this was not enough; Seyss-Inquart and other nazi sympathizers in the government met with Wilhelm Miklas, president of the Austrian republic, to demand the chancellor's immediate resignation. At first the president, aware that the fate of the nation was in his hands, refused to yield to the nazi demands. However, at that moment bands of uniformed Storm Troopers began marching through the streets. A group surrounded the chancellory, while other members of the brown-shirted band seized city halls and governmental offices throughout the country. Aware that he could no longer resist, Schuschnigg resigned, leaving Miklas with the decision of his successor. Significantly, before leaving office the chancellor ordered the Austrian army to avoid any conflict with the Germans and to withdraw from the border, thereby giving Hitler an invitation to send his armies into the former Habsburg state. At first president Miklas refused to hand Austria over to the agents of Berlin, but the threat of violence and Seyss-Inquart's persistent demands caused him to yield, and on March 11, 1938, a Nazi became chancellor of Austria.

After Seyss-Inquart assumed office, it was only a matter of time until the swastika-bearing conspirators crushed the last vestige of independence in the land that once had ruled a vast empire. Hitler's agents instructed their puppet that he should announce that he could not keep order and request assistance from the Reich. Then the German army would march across the border. At this crucial moment in the history of the Austrian people, Seyss-Inquart regained his courage and refused to be a part of Hitler's plan. Instead, he asked Berlin to postpone action. However, Hitler refused to allow the doubts of a subordinate to stall his plans, and he ordered his forces to prepare to invade Austria at dawn on March 12. To provide proof that the new chancellor had invited German intervention, Göring prepared a fake telegram requesting that Hitler send troops to restore order, which Goebbels read to the world over German radio. At this point all the preparations had been made, and Hitler waited anxiously for word from Rome. Finally, at 10:25 in the evening, Prince Philip of Hesse called from Rome to tell an overjoyed Hitler of Mussolini's personal assurances of support. Thus, the führer had overcome the last obstacle to his lifelong dream of the unification of the two German-speaking lands into one Reich.

At dawn on March 12, thousands of German troops crossed the border to march to Vienna, while overhead Göring's Luftwaffe buzzed through the air. Deserted by their leaders and unable to withstand the might of nazi Germany, the stunned Austrian people could do little but cheer the invader, and pretty girls gave the soldiers flowers as a sign of goodwill. The Austrian army stood by powerless and watched the destruction of their state as German forces occupied all strategic points. However, the invasion was not a total success, for the hulks of broken-down trucks and tanks littered the roads, a signal that Hitler's generals must concentrate more intently on the perfection of their equipment.

His forces in possession of his homeland, the excited master of the Third Reich traveled to Linz that afternoon. There, thousands of adoring citizens of this city on the Danube cheered as the victorious dictator rode through the streets. He spent two days in the city of his youth, pausing to lay a wreath on the grave of his parents and to telegraph Mussolini his appreciation for his support. On March 14, amid the enthusiastic cries of the people of Vienna, Hitler returned in glory to the city of his youthful humiliation. At last he had revenged the disgrace and poverty of the past. He stood on the balcony of the former imperial palace, where such greats as Maria Theresia, Joseph II, and Francis Joseph had lived and worked, to address the cheering throng. Church bells pealed throughout the city and the nazi flag flew from the Gothic towers of St. Stephen's Cathedral. Hitler announced a new era in history that would unite the German people under the banner of "One People, One Reich, One Leader." He left the city of baroque and rococco monuments to a more glorious past after only a day because of the bad memories it evoked. Hitler spent the next few days touring the countryside to receive the tribute of the

Austrian people, who on April 10 went to the polls to cast 99.08 percent of the vote in favor of union with Germany. Himmler's S.S. combed the streets for all who might oppose Hitler's nefarious schemes, arresting 76,000. Finally, the victors erased all signs of the past by abolishing the Austrian parliament and renaming Austria, "East Mark." Thus, one of the most important struggles of German history had been ended. Ever since its rise from the ashes of the Thirty Years War, Prussia had fought with Austria for control of Germany. Hitler's triumphant march was a symbolic end of the conflict. The heirs to Prussia's general staff had conquered without bloodshed the capital of their former enemy while England and France looked on, unable to take action to prevent this violation of the now worthless Treaty of Versailles.

Hitler and his greedy followers were not content with the annexation of Austria, and they found another opportunity to enlarge their empire through the destruction of Czechoslovakia. Formed from the union of the former Habsburg territories of Bohemia and Slovakia after the First World War, Czechoslovakia had a highly vocal minority of 3.5 million Germans, about 24 percent of the population, living in the Sudetenland, the area bordering the German Reich. Although the Sudeten Germans had long been radical nationalists, the majority cooperated with the government in Prague during the first years of the republic. However, a sizable number had organized gymnastic societies, which, like similar groups across the frontier, had become centers of German nationalism. When the depression spread economic chaos throughout Czechoslovakia, many Sudeten Germans began to look for deliverance from their plight and found it in the example of the National Socialists. In 1934 Konrad Henlein, a leader of the gymnastic societies and a bank clerk, organized the Sudeten German Homeland Front. The next year he transformed this organization into the Sudeten German party. Aided with generous subsidies from Berlin, this new political party successfully captured two-thirds of the German vote, emerging as the second-largest party in the Czech parliament.[8]

In the spring of 1938, Hitler was prepared to use the Sudeten Germans to provoke a crisis that would enable him to destroy Czechoslovakia. He instructed Ribbentrop to direct personally the Sudeten Germans. On March 16 Ernst Eisenlohr, the German minister in Prague, persuaded Henlein to agree to place his organization under the control of Berlin. Twelve days later the Sudeten German leader arrived in the capital of the Third Reich and met with Hitler. After meetings with the führer, Ribbentrop, and other important officials, he learned that Berlin expected him to demand so many concessions from Prague that the government would refuse, thereby provoking a major crisis. In Czechoslovakia Henlein quickly organized a series of riots to coincide with municipal elections. Naturally, the Czech officials attempted to restore order, giving Hitler grounds to claim that the Slavic majority was persecuting the German people of the Sudetenland. On April 24, during a meeting of his party, Henlein announced his program. The Karlsbad Demands, named for the city where the meeting was held, called for local autonomy for the Sudeten Germans, a German civil service in the Sudetenland, protection of the rights of the Sudeten Germans and the Homeland party, and compensation for the alleged persecution of the Sudeten Germans by the Czechs.

Meanwhile, Hitler had instructed his generals during the fateful meeting of November 5, 1937, to begin planning Case Green, the invasion of Czechoslovakia. As designed by Keitel and Alfred Jodl, the commander of the national defense section, Plan Green provided for a massive ground attack from the west, with a simultaneous air offensive designed to destroy the Czech air force and important fortifications. Then the German army would attempt to defeat the Czech army before it had a chance to retreat to Slovakia and occupy Bohemia and Moravia. On May 30 Hitler signed the formal order approving an invasion of Czechoslovakia according to Plan Green by October 1, 1938. However, learning of the German troop movements and motivated by the unrest in the Sudetenland, President Eduard Beneš mobilized 400,000 men and sent additional forces into the troubled borderlands. At the same time, the British and French diplomats in Berlin informed Hitler that any threat to the independence of Czechoslovakia would lead to war.

The Czech mobilization and threats from the British and French led many German officers to conclude that Hitler's risky plans would lead to a war that the Reich could not win. The leader of the opposition was General Ludwig Beck, chief of the general staff. On May 30 he told General Walter von Brauchitsch, commander in chief of the army, that if the military allowed Hitler to carry out his plans, a major disaster would result. For the next few months Beck's fears continued to grow. In July he bravely suggested that if Hitler insisted on his daring scheme, the generals should resign in protest and seek civilian support to remove him. Early the next month the führer ordered the generals to meet with him at Jüterbog, during planned exercises, and Beck decided to take action. He persuaded Brauchitsch to call the commanding generals to a secret meeting on August 4. At first Beck planned to have von Brauchitsch read a specially prepared speech calling for resistance, but he finally decided to speak to the officers himself. Although he was able to convince all present of the danger of Hitler's plans, he could not persuade them to agree on a plan to prevent the führer from leading Germany to destruction, and the meeting ended in failure.

However, Hitler learned of Beck's efforts to undermine his authority and decided to seek the support of the younger generals, whom he believed would have more courage than the older officers. He invited a group of them to his mountain retreat and lectured them for several hours about his plans to create a greater German Reich. Even Hitler's effective rhetoric failed to convince all present of the wisdom of his plans, and General Gustav von Wietersheim bravely questioned his contention that the British and French would not go to war over Czechoslovakia. At Jöterbog, Hitler once again pleaded for support and announced that if he failed to achieve his goals through negotiations, he would use force to crush the Czech state. Aware that his opposition to the führer's plans had compromised his position, Beck resigned on August 27 after speaking to his men on the historic independence of the German military.

Meanwhile, Brauchitsch and his aides were making final preparations for the execution of Case Green. In August the German air attaché in Prague traveled to the Sudetenland to find suitable areas for Luftwaffe landings. Brauchitsch decided that the army would stage fake maneuvers as a cover for the movement of forces to their positions surrounding Czechoslovakia while others would station themselves in the west to repel any invasion from France. At the same time, thousands of Germans crossed the Czech border in a clandestine fashion to reinforce Henlein's forces, and the S.S. prepared for mobilization.

Despite the preparations for Case Green and Beck's resignation, the opposition to Hitler's plans had not vanished. General Franz Halder, Beck's successor, decided that radical action was necessary to prevent Hitler from leading Germany to a disastrous defeat. Building on Beck's work, Halder found other generals willing to join in a conspiracy to depose the führer and to build a new civilian government that would immediately seek friendly relations with the French and

British. He contacted Colonel Hans von Oster of military intelligence, who organized the members of the Black Band in support of the plot. According to the plan, the military, commanded by General Erwin von Witzleben, leader of the forces in Berlin, would revolt on September 29, two days before Case Green was to go into effect. With the additional support of the division in Potsdam commanded by General Walter von Brockdorff-Ahlenfeldt, the army would seize all governmental offices. Meanwhile, General Erich Höpner and his armored forces from Wuppertal would capture the S.S. troops in Munich to prevent their march to Berlin in support of their führer. Other forces would arrest Hitler, Himmler, and Göring and take them to Bavaria to await trial. Hans von Dohnayi, an attorney in Oster's service, prepared the case against Hitler, using his medical file from the First World War to prove that an Allied gas attack had left him insane and unfit for leadership.[9]

Aware that success would depend on the willingness of the British and French to stand firm in their threat of war should Germany violate the sovereignty of Czechoslovakia, the conspirators attempted to contact the British government. They sent Ewald von Kleist-Schmenzin, a supporter of the Black Band, to London to inform the English that if they would stand firm, the German army would move to overthrow the hated national socialist dictatorship. Canaris used his contacts with British intelligence to prepare for Kleist's secret mission, and he flew to a small airport near the British capital, where Menzies's representatives met him. They took him to the Hyde Park Hotel, and he dined with Lord Lloyd of Dolbran, a representative of MI-6. While the two men ate in secrecy, the German informed his host of the details of the plot and asked for support. However, despite their interest in the conspiracy, the British were unwilling to commit themselves to war over Czechoslovakia. The next day Kleist discussed the plan to overthrow Hitler with Robert Vasittart of the British foreign office, and again he asked the British to agree to threaten war in support of the plot. Kleist also unsuccessfully asked the English to agree to consider favorably requests from a non-nazi government for a peaceful revision of Germany's eastern frontier. On August 17 he met with Winston Churchill, who explained that the English system of government would prevent any prior commitment to resist Hitler by force. Finally, Kleist secretly returned to Germany to inform Canaris of the unwillingness of the British to make an agreement. However, despite the failure of his mission, the conspirators continued to plan the overthrow of the nazi regime.

Tensions over the Sudetenland continued to grow. Although the Karlsbad Demands threatened the unity of the nation, the Czech officials opened negotiations with Henlein and his followers. They even expressed a willingness to submit the issue to arbitration by a neutral party, should negotiations fail. Finally, in early September, Prague indicated its willingness to accept most, if not all, of the Karlsbad Demands. Naturally, such a solution to the conflict would fail to fulfill Hitler's aggressive intentions. Therefore, during a speech at the Nuremberg rally on September 12, he provoked a new crisis by vehemently denouncing the Czechs as an inferior people unfit to rule the Germans of the Sudetenland. The day after the führer's fiery address, Henlein, on instructions from his German masters, announced that the concessions made by Prague were out of date. He further demanded the expulsion of all Czech police from the Sudetenland and the transfer of all local authority to representatives of his party. To meet the new threat, Prague mobilized its reserves and occupied the Sudetenland. Henlein fled to Bavaria and announced the organization of a force to free his people from Czech oppression.

At this point the British government stepped in to prevent a war, granting Hitler his demands without forcing him to fight, and dooming the plot to overthrow the nazi tyranny to failure. The British prime minister, Neville Chamberlain, who favored peace at any price and sympathized with the cause of the Sudeten Germans, had sent Lord Walter Runciman to Prague as early as August 3 to advise Beneš to yield to the German demands. On September 15 the British prime minister came to Berchtesgaden to negotiate face to face with the leader of the Third Reich. Encouraged by the willingness of the British to come to terms, Hitler decided to ask for even more than Henlein had demanded. He told the shocked Chamberlain that he would not be satisfied with anything less than regional autonomy for the Sudetenland, with special guarantees of German rights. He also informed his guest that France must renounce its alliance with Czechoslovakia. After discussion, the intimidated British prime minister agreed to Hitler's ultimatum and planned another meeting for September in Bad Godesberg, a suburb of Bonn.

Believing that he had guaranteed the peace of Europe, Chamberlain returned to England to report to his fellow ministers. Supported by Lord Runciman, who now argued that Britain should persuade Prague to allow Germany to annex the Sudetenland, Chamberlain had no trouble gaining the support of the ministry. On September 18 French Premier Edouard Daladier arrived in London to discuss the issue. The French leader listened to Chamberlain's report and agreed that the two nations should attempt to convince the Czechs to accept Hitler's demands. A few days later the British and French ambassadors in Prague informed Beneš of their recommendations. Deserted by London and Paris, the Czech leader could do little but yield on September 21.

Meanwhile, influenced by the ease with which he had won his demands, Hitler decided to press Chamberlain further. On September 22 the British prime minister arrived at Bad Godesberg. There, in a hotel overlooking the scenic Rhine, Hitler told the shocked Englishman that the agreement reached at Berchtesgaden was outdated and that new concessions would be necessary. The führer then informed Chamberlain that Germany would not be satisfied with anything less than the outright annexation of the Sudetenland. The startled English leader tried in vain to persuade Hitler to moderate his demands and the meeting adjourned after a stormy discussion. The next day the führer produced a map with the areas to be annexed by Germany clearly marked. After Chamberlain asked for time to consider Hitler's new ultimatum, the leader of the Third Reich announced that if agreement were not reached by October 1, the German army would march. Chamberlain angrily tried to persuade Hitler to reconsider this plan, but he only received assurances that the Sudetenland would be Hitler's last territorial demand. Just as it seemed that negotiations would end in a deadlock, a messenger rushed into the room to announce that Beneš had ordered a general mobilization of the Czech military. Taking advantage of Chamberlain's surprise at this new development, Hitler responded that despite the Czech provocation he was willing to continue negotiations. Chamberlain agreed to submit Hitler's proposals to Prague for consideration, and the meeting ended.

For the next few days Europe was on the verge of war. Prague ordered general mobilization, and France called up 500,000 reserve forces. The British ordered the navy to prepare for action and began to dig antitank ditches in London. On September 26 Hitler gave a fiery speech to a crowd in Berlin, stating that his patience was at an end and demanding acceptance of his ultimatum. Neither London nor Paris proved willing to go to war to save Czechoslovakia. On September 27 Chamberlain announced that England would not fight to protect the interests of a country so far away from Britain. The next day Daladier, influenced by the reports of Paul Stehlin, the French air attaché in Berlin whom Göring had pointedly allowed to inspect the might of the Luftwaffe, decided to propose further negotiations. He called for a meeting of Chamberlain, Hitler, Mussolini, and himself in Munich to prevent a major war.

On September 29, at the Brown House in Munich, the headquarters of the Nazi party, the leaders of Germany, Italy, France, and England met to hammer out a solution to the crisis. Significantly, the Czechs, whose fate was being decided, were prevented from participation in the discussions. Beginning at noon and lasting until two the next morning, the four heads of government argued the issue and finally agreed to accept Hitler's demands. Then, as the führer and his aides celebrated, Chamberlain and Daladier signed the treaty that spelled the end of Czechoslovakian security. The Treaty of Munich allowed the German troops to march unopposed within forty miles of Prague, an area containing the major Czech defenses. Before departing the next morning, Chamberlain met Hitler again to sign a nonaggression pact between Germany and England. The prime minister then returned to announce to a relieved people that he had successfully achieved a lasting peace. Unfortunately, he later found that Hitler's word was just as fragile as the piece of paper he waved before the cheering crowd at the airport.[10]

The Munich Agreement was one of the most important steps toward the Second World War. Chamberlain's faith in Hitler's goodwill was misplaced, and in less than a year the nazi armies smashed the peace that the prime minister and his people so wanted. The willingness of France and England to give Hitler the Sudetenland without forcing him to shed any German blood made him a hero and destroyed the conspiracy to rid the world of his rule. Hitler's success convinced him that the British and French would rather yield to his every demand than risk war with the Third Reich. This led him to demand more and more, until he finally forced the unwilling British to resist, lest all of Europe become a satellite of the Third Reich. Hitler's aggressive foreign policy convinced the British that war between England and Germany was inevitable. Had Chamberlain refused to allow Hitler's threats to intimidate him, Halder and his supporters might have been able to oust the führer and thus prevent an even greater disaster. Naturally, there is a chance that the revolt would have been a failure, but nevertheless, Hitler's position would have been so weakened that he would not have been able to challenge the British and French for several more years, if ever. It should not be overlooked that the Munich Agreement did give the British and

French a year to prepare for the final confrontation, but if they had not lacked the courage to stand up to Hitler in 1938, perhaps they might have been spared the horror of the Second World War.

After Munich, Czechoslovakia ceased to exist as an independent nation. In addition to losing the Sudetenland to the Nazis, Prague lost the Trans-Olzan area of Silesia to Poland, and Hungary gained sections of Slovakia. Even Hitler was not happy with the Sudetenland, but he took advantage of an opportunity to destroy the remainder of the Czech state. Hitler championed the cause of the Slovaks, who had resented Czech domination for years. Encouraged by the example of the Sudeten Germans, the Slovaks formed a government on October 6, 1938, with Joseph Tiso, a Roman Catholic priest, as prime minister. A few weeks later Tiso informed Hitler that he had placed the fate of his people in the führer's hands. While negotiations continued between Prague and Tiso's government, the Hungarians under Admiral Nikolaus Horthy, the "regent" for the exiled Habsburgs, attempted to take advantage of the conflict to annex large areas of Slovakia. Soon after the Munich Agreement, Horthy demanded possession of much of Slovakia. Naturally, Prague refused to accept this demand, and Hitler intervened on November 2, 1938. In the Vienna Award, negotiated between Ribbentrop and representatives of the two nations, Budapest received possession of a large area of Slovakia. However, this concession did not satisfy the land-hungry Hungarians. On November 20 Budapest demanded the right to occupy the Carpatho-Ukraine within twenty-four hours. Hitler vehemently opposed this extension of Hungarian power on his southern flank and successfully pressured Budapest to drop this ultimatum.

However, the threat of Hungarian annexation of Slovakia led Hitler to support Tiso's government as a means to erect a buffer between the Third Reich and Hungary while destroying the hated Czech state at the same time. Pressured on one side by the Czechs, who refused to allow the dismemberment of Czechoslovakia that would be represented by Slovak autonomy, and on the other by the Hungarians, the Slovaks increasingly turned to Germany for support. On February 12, 1939, Vojtech Tuka, the leader of the Slovak nationalists, went to Berlin, where Hitler agreed to support his demand for complete autonomy for his people. After Tiso refused to agree to a Czech demand that he pledge never to seek separation from the rest of Czechoslovakia, Prague dismissed him and his government and proclaimed martial law, thereby causing a new crisis. Tiso fled to Berlin and sought additional support from Hitler, who was only too glad to grant it. On March 14, 1939, with German support, Tiso announced the creation of an independent Slovak state. Unwilling to seek French or British aid after their surrender at Munich, Emil Hacha, the Czech president, realized that he had no choice but to attempt to reach an agreement with Hitler; therefore, he went to Berlin, hoping to receive some guarantee of independence for the remainder of Czechoslovakia. He found the Nazis in a belligerent mood. Hitler, Ribbentrop, and Göring took turns threatening Hacha until the exhausted Czech leader finally collapsed and capitulated, asking the dictator of Germany to protect personally the Czech people. Hitler was overjoyed and took immediate action. On March 15, one day after Tiso had announced the independence of Slovakia, German forces occupied the remainder of Czechoslovakia. The next day Hitler's men marched into Slovakia in response to a request from Tiso. By occupying all of Czechoslovakia, Hitler gained territory and won the valuable prize of the Skoda armaments works at Pilsen, the largest in Europe, and its stock of weapons. Thus, Hitler turned Czechoslovakia into a German satellite through persistent diplomacy. His next conquest would not be so easy, for London and Paris had realized at last that nazi Germany was a menace that could only be dealt with through force.

The next target of Hitler's lust for power was Danzig and the Polish Corridor. Ever since the Treaty of Versailles, the Germans had resented the separation of the Baltic city and the surrounding areas from the Reich. The German-speaking population of the Polish-administered area had been fertile ground for nazi propaganda and had flocked to the banner of the hooked cross. By 1933 the Nazis of Danzig had grown strong enough to capture control of the senate of the city. In 1938 the successful German annexation of Austria and the campaign of the Sudeten Germans against Prague led Hitler's followers in this city on the Baltic to adopt a more aggressive program. Their leader, Albert Forster, even demanded the right to place a swastika on the flag of the free city. The führer of the Third Reich began a diplomatic offensive designed to persuade the Poles to yield peacefully. On September 20, 1938, even before his victory at Munich, Hitler suggested to Josef Lipski, the Polish ambassador to Germany, that Berlin and Warsaw begin discussions concerning a possible agreement on the corridor and Danzig. The dictator proposed that Poland agree to a revision of the status of Danzig and to a German railroad and highway through the Corridor. In October Ribbentrop, now Hitler's foreign minister, demanded a return of the free city to Germany and a German corridor through the Corridor to connect the city with Prussia and the rest of the Reich. Although Lipsky agreed to discuss Ribbentrop's proposals with Colonel Josef Beck, the Polish foreign minister, he informed Ribbentrop that Poland considered Danzig crucial to the national interests of the Slavic state. On November 19 Lipsky met with Ribbentrop and informed him that any German effort to annex Danzig would lead to a serious crisis between the two nations.

Lipsky's reply to Hitler's proposals did not end discussions of the fate of Danzig. On January 5, 1939, Colonel Beck met with Hitler at Berchtesgaden. The führer, believing that he could persuade the Polish official to yield to his demands, sought to win agreement by promising that in return for Danzig Germany would support a Polish conquest of the fertile Ukraine. However, after further discussions with Ribbentrop, Beck refused to commit himself on the issue and returned to Warsaw. At the end of the month Ribbentrop once again offered German aid in the conquest of the Ukraine in return for Danzig. Finally, on March 26, 1939, Beck defiantly rejected the German offer. A few days later the Poles began military preparations to defend their homeland against a possible German attack. Meanwhile, the British, who had come to the conclusion after the German destruction of Czechoslovakia that Hitler's greed for territory would only grow with each victory and eventually would even threaten England itself, decided to take action to show their support of the Poles. On March 31 Chamberlain informed the British House of Commons that England would fight if necessary to preserve Polish independence. This British guarantee only infuriated Hitler, who informed Warsaw on April 27 that its acceptance of Chamberlain's offer for support rendered the nonaggression pact of 1934 null and void.

Meanwhile, lest he fail to achieve his goals through diplomacy, as he had done with the Czechs, Hitler ordered the army to begin preparations for Plan White, the invasion of Poland. Significantly, the führer gave this order the day before the final Polish rejection of his proposals. Colonel Günther Blumentritt, chief of the training section of the general staff in Berlin, received responsibility for working out the details of the possible aggression against the Poles. After studying the Polish military, he decided to make a quick thrust from Silesia and East Prussia with the Luftwaffe acting as an advanced guard. Blumentritt hoped that decisive action would surprise the Poles and enable Germany to crush the Polish army before it could be fully mobilized. As in Case Green, the military decided to mask the movements necessary as a preliminary to the attack by a fake fall maneuver. During the time that Blumentritt was busy perfecting his plans, Goebbels used his propaganda machine to charge that Polish mobs were attacking Germans living in the Polish Corridor, and nazi agents began whipping the people of Danzig into a frenzy.

However, before resorting to force, Hitler realized that he must seek agreement with the Soviet Union. He knew that his army was not yet strong enough to face the powerful Red Army. He found a willing partner in Joseph Stalin, the Russian dictator. Stalin had offered support for the embattled Czechs before Munich and had been snubbed by the British and French. He therefore decided to attempt to protect the Soviet Union by reaching an accord with the Third Reich and at the same time approaching the British and French. On May 3 he appointed Viachaslav Molotov foreign commissar and instructed him to approach both sides with an offer for a nonaggression pact. However, London and Paris were in no haste to sign a treaty with a communist power that they had opposed since its inception. Instead of replying immediately to Molotov's offer, they sent a military mission to Moscow by ship rather than plane.

Meanwhile, Stalin decided to seek immediate agreement with the Germans. On August 14 the Russian chargé d'affaires in Berlin informed Julius Schnurre of the German Foreign Ministry that his government would respond favorably to an effort to reach agreement with the Third Reich on such issues as economic affairs, cultural exchanges, and Poland. Naturally, Hitler was anxious to neutralize the Russians before the possible attack on Poland. That same day, Ribbentrop instructed the German minister in Moscow to request Molotov to receive him as soon as possible. Stalin, in no mood for long negotiations, sought to play on Hitler's anxieties by responding that Molotov would be unable to meet with his German counterpart until the end of the month. Ribbentrop again requested an immediate meeting, but the Soviet dictator refused to waste time on discussion. Instead, he informed the Germans that they must accept the basic principles of a nonaggression pact before he would allow the nazi foreign minister to travel to the Soviet capital. On August 20 Molotov handed the text of the proposed agreement to the German ambassador in Moscow. This document provided that neither nation would take aggressive action against the other and that should one party become involved in a war with another nation, the other party would remain neutral. Hitler responded by telegraphing Stalin his personal acceptance of the Soviet proposal and once again requesting that Ribbentrop be allowed to come to Moscow as soon as possible. With German agreement assured, Stalin responded favorably to Hitler's request. On August 23, 1939, Ribbentrop met with the rulers of the Soviet Union. That night they signed the nonaggression pact that would free Hitler to carry out his conquest of Poland. Significantly, the two dictatorships also signed a secret agreement that provided for the division of Poland into spheres of influence divided by the Narev, Vistula, and San rivers. Russia received a free hand to deal with Finland, Estonia, and Latvia on the Baltic Sea and Bessarabia in the southeast in return for allowing Germany to carry out its aggressive intentions in the rest of Europe. Thus, Hitler had won one of the most brilliant diplomatic victories of his career by effectively neutralizing the might of the Soviet Union.

With the threat of Soviet intervention removed by the nonaggression pact, Hitler was ready to attack Poland. Significantly, on August 11, even before the successful conclusion of the treaty with Stalin, the führer told Count Galeazzo Ciano, the Italian foreign minister, of his decision to destroy Poland. Eleven days later the master of the Third Reich told his generals of his plan to smash the Slavic state, adding that he had first thought he could attack the West before moving east, but that recent events had led to a revision of his program of aggression. News of Hitler's plans, which the British received through their rather effective intelligence network a few hours after the führer's statement, only led London to strengthen its support of Warsaw. Thus, despite the diplomacy of the last few weeks of August, 1939, both sides had accepted the inevitability of war.

With all preparations made, Hitler ordered the German forces to invade Poland on August 26. However, a few hours after giving the fateful order he learned that Warsaw and London had signed a mutual assistance pact. That same day Mussolini informed the führer that Italy would be unable to come to the aid of the Reich in the event of war unless Germany provided the necessary military supplies. Unwilling to risk war while diplomacy might gain his ends as it had done in the case of Czechoslovakia, and aware of the importance of Italian support, Hitler decided to postpone Case White while he attempted to negotiate with London and frantically sought a list of the needed supplies from Rome. On August 28 the führer responded to a British proposal that Berlin and Warsaw enter into direct discussions, informing Chamberlain that he would expect a Polish representative to arrive in Berlin no later than August 30 with full power to settle the issue. However, the Poles, remembering the experience of Hacha, refused to negotiate under duress. Instead, Warsaw authorized the British to inform Berlin that the Poles would be willing to open direct negotiations, provided agreement could be reached beforehand on the procedures to be used for the discussions.

Meanwhile, Hermann Göring attempted a rather curious solution to the problem. For several weeks Birger Dahlerus, a Swedish businessman and friend of Göring, had attempted to act as an unofficial arbitrator between Germany and England. On August 24 Dahlerus telephoned London to inform them that he was flying to the British capital immediately with important new proposals. The British agreed to receive him, and he arrived in London to inform them that Göring had told him that if the English would recognize Germany as a European power, a peaceful solution to the conflict could be reached. The head of the Luftwaffe also suggested that the British send someone who spoke fluent German and who could clearly express the British viewpoint to negotiate with Hitler. After the meeting Dahlerus returned to Germany and reported that Hitler was willing to meet with a British representative to discuss peace between the two nations. A few days later the Swedish unofficial diplomat again flew to London, where he repeated the German proposal, adding that Hitler favored a plebiscite in the Corridor to determine which areas should return to the Reich. The British asked Dahlerus if Hitler still expected a Polish representative to arrive in Berlin by August 30. After a telephone call to Göring, Dahlerus informed his hosts that Hitler's demand was unalterable.

However, when the Polish diplomat failed to arrive in Berlin before the expiration of the deadline, negotiations reached a stalemate. At midnight on August 30, Henderson, the British ambassador to Germany, arrived at Ribbentrop's office to inform him that the Poles had agreed to begin direct negotiations. The British ambassador also requested a copy of the German demands to transmit to Warsaw. Ribbentrop then told Henderson that the führer demanded not only Danzig, but also a plebiscite in the Corridor to decide which areas would remain Polish. Significantly, when the British diplomat requested a written copy of Hitler's latest proposals, Ribbentrop refused to provide it, and threw his papers on the table while announcing that since no Polish representative had arrived within the time limit further discussions were no longer relevant. Henderson, unwilling to allow Ribbentrop's hostility to lead to a complete breakdown of negotiations, frantically pleaded with Lipsky to seek an interview with the German foreign minister. Under strict instructions from his superiors to avoid any discussions that might display a willingness to accept the German ultimatum, Lipsky agreed to meet with Ribbentrop. During his audience with the German foreign minister, the Polish diplomat received a text of Hitler's demands and stated that Ribbentrop could expect a reply from Warsaw. The German official then angrily asked if Lipsky were the Polish representative demanded by the führer. Lipsky replied that he was not, and the session ended, as did all possibility of a negotiated settlement that might prevent the Second World War.

Unable to achieve his goals through diplomacy, Hitler, still believing that the British and French would desert Poland as they had Czechoslovakia, signed the directive for Case White on August 31, 1939. That night S.S. men disguised in Polish uniforms attacked a German radio station in Giliewitz in Silesia to give Berlin an excuse for its planned aggression. Hitler rushed to the Reichstag to denounce the Polish attack on Germany. As a horrified world listened by radio, the fanatical dictator called on all Germans to dedicate themselves to the coming conflict. Meanwhile, Hitler's troops began their march into Poland. Faithful to their commitment, England immediately demanded the evacuation of all German troops and the restoration of Polish sovereignty. When Hitler refused to answer, London joined France in declaring war on Germany on September 3, 1939, thus beginning the Second World War. Unlike 1914, the German people did not greet the news of the war with cheers; instead, they sat or stood in silence, too stunned to speak.

For the next six years Europe was a vast battleground; millions lost their lives while savage aerial warfare reduced cities to rubble. The Second World War did not come about suddenly; it was the product of twenty years of mistrust and resentment. In reality, the foundation for the conflict was laid by the victors of the First World War. The Allies forced the Germans to accept a peace of vengeance and continued to weaken the German economy through excessive reparation demands. Finally, the German people turned to the Nazis to avenge the disgrace of Versailles and to restore the lost glory of their nation. The British and French refused to recognize the threat of Adolf Hitler and failed to take action to halt him before he made Germany strong enough to challenge the peace and security of Europe. Instead, they chose to seek an elusive peace and yielded to one demand after another, until they finally realized that the nazi dictator had an insatiable appetite for conquest. After receiving the Sudetenland, Hitler loudly proclaimed that he had made his last territorial demand, but a few months later, he presented an ultimatum to the Poles. In 1939 Hitler's threats failed to intimidate his opponents into surrender. The Poles refused to risk sharing the fate of the Czechs, and war came. Shaken from his illusions by Hitler's broken promises and his willingness to resort to force once diplomacy had failed, Chamberlain finally gathered the courage to realize that only force could halt the growth of nazi power. Hitler did not create the problems of Austria, the Sudetenland, and Danzig; history had done this by placing large numbers of Germans outside of the Reich. However, the führer took advantage of these conflicts to enlarge his dictatorship through encouragement of the nationalistic aspirations of these peoples and a combination of threats and diplomacy. The German dictator failed to realize that the British and French would not continue to shudder before the threat of war as they had done before Munich. When diplomacy failed to force the Poles to yield, Hitler did not hesitate to order his army to march.

17

Blitzkrieg

The opening of the Second World War marked the beginning of a savage new era of warfare. Instead of sending his troops into pitched battles, Hitler and his generals devised the Blitzkrieg, or lightning war. From the air, Göring's Luftwaffe pounded the enemy into submission, and on the ground tanks and armored vehicles raced to wipe the enemy out before they had time to react. During the first months of the Second World War, country after country fell victim to a sudden attack that left them defeated before they had time to know what had happened. In the spring of 1940, Hitler revenged the disgrace of 1918 by sending his victorious troops marching through Napoleon's Arch of Triumph while the startled French stood powerless to resist. The German army failed to crush only one country, Great Britain. Despite merciless bombardment from the air, the brave English people refused to submit to Hitler, and their persistence in the end saved Europe from a new dark age dominated by the Nazis.

The first country to feel the full force of Hitler's strategy was Poland. On the morning of September 1, 1939, the Luftwaffe fell on the unsuspecting Poles like fire from hell. The dive bombers, equipped with whistles to make their attack more terrifying, screamed down to scatter the Polish army and destroy its fortifications and equipment. Then Hitler's specially designed tanks and armored cars sped to complete the destruction of the enemy. Although the Poles fought bravely, they were no match for the superior German army. The desperate Poles prayed for rain to turn the plains into seas of mud and halt the German advance, but their prayers were unanswered, and the enemy swept across the Polish countryside destroying all last-minute defenses. Within a few days the Germans had occupied most of the Slavic republic. Only Warsaw, defended by the remnants of the army and brave civilians who dug trenches to halt the oncoming tide, refused to surrender. Throughout September the Luftwaffe bombarded the Polish capital while the radio begged for help from the British and French. Thousands lost their lives in the futile defense of their city. Centuries old palaces, churches, and homes tumbled down, victim to the German bombardment. Yet the Poles fought with their last bit of strength until they were unable to fight more, and finally, on September 27, the German forces marched through the battle-strewn streets.[1]

In Moscow, Stalin watched with horror the speed of the German advance. But he realized that Hitler's success not only threatened the security of Russia, but also gave the Soviet Union a chance to reconquer the areas lost to Poland in the First World War, which had marked the birth of the communist dictatorship. Quickly gathering his forces, Stalin sent the Red Army across the border without warning to claim a portion of the booty on September 17. Two days after the fall of Warsaw, the victors divided the devastated Polish state in half, and Stalin began the conquest that fulfilled the dreams of the Tsars, bringing Russian domination to Eastern Europe. Meanwhile, the British and French stood idly by, unable to move with the speed required to aid their besieged ally. All Paris could do was reinforce the Maginot Line, the massive fortification running from Switzerland to the Belgian border. The British could do little more than send a force to France under Lord John Gort to join in the wait for the German onslaught.

While the British and French waited breathlessly for the coming attack, Hitler decided to seek peace, for despite his willingness to use force against Poland, he had no desire to fight a long war with the Western powers. Although the führer assured Mussolini of the ability of his forces to defeat the British if necessary, the terrified duce sent Count Ciano to Berlin to urge Hitler to seek negotiations immediately. On October 6 the führer spoke to the Reichstag and the world. Amid the cheers of those present, the nazi dictator praised his army for its decisive victory against the Poles and then offered peace to London and Paris. He even promised to begin general disarmament talks. However, the British and French, weary of a man who had violated the agreements reached at Munich, refused to consider his offer. Therefore, on October 9 he ordered the army to begin plans for Case

Yellow, an attack on Holland, Belgium, Luxemburg, and France, to begin as soon as possible. The military again opposed Hitler's risky plans. Brauchitsch and others begged the führer to postpone the attack until spring. Hitler refused to yield to his plea and shouted that he would move regardless of the fears of the generals. He issued further orders in preparation for Case Yellow on October 18 and November 20, and on November 29 he ordered the navy and Luftwaffe to prepare for the destruction of British shipping and industry. However, nature intervened with a severe winter to prevent Hitler's planned attack, and 1940 passed without the expected confrontation. Both sides settled down to a period of "phony war," called Sitzkrieg by the Germans, during which both sides did little more than fire an occasional shell or make propaganda broadcasts.[2]

Meanwhile, Canaris and his supporters in the Black Band worked feverishly to sabotage Hitler's plans. Even before the attack on Poland, the brave head of German military intelligence sent Lieutenant Colonel Gerhard von Schwerin to London to warn the British of Hitler's plans to attack Poland. After the fall of Warsaw, the dedicated foes of the nazi tyranny organized a conspiracy with Halder's support to march on Berlin with the aid of two divisions of tanks from Poland to overthrow the hated dictatorship. They planned to arrest Hitler and try him for atrocities, declare him insane, and confine him to a mental hospital. At the same time, Canaris's assistant, Colonel Hans Oster, sent Dr. Josef Müller, an attorney from Munich, to Rome to open contacts through the pope with the British. Despite the persistent efforts of Hermann Keller, prior of Beuron Abbey and Heydrich's agent in the Eternal City, to sabotage his efforts and discover the members of the conspiracy, Müller approached the British through Father Robert Leiber and informed them of the plot to overthrow Hitler. Although London was interested in the plan and indicated that they would favor a non-nazi German government, Canaris was unable to win enough support from the army and finally postponed action until a more opportune time.[3]

Throughout the war Canaris and his agents provided the British with much valuable information, but London had a more reliable method of determining Hitler's plans—Project Ultra. In 1919 Hugo Kock, a Dutchman, had developed a code machine that Arthur Scherbius, a German, perfected and attempted with little success to sell to firms interested in protecting their secrets from competitors. After Hitler became chancellor, Colonel Erich Fellgiebel of the

German signal corps realized the potential of the device and developed it for use by the German army. The Enigma Machine, as the instrument was called, consisted of two electric typewriters connected to a series of revolving wheels. By pressing the correct key and typing the message on one typewriter, the wheels would reproduce it in code on the second typewriter. Then the message could be sent by radio to a receiver equipped with an Enigma Machine. All one had to do was press the correct key and type the coded message, which would come out on the second typewriter. In June 1938 Menzies learned that a Polish Jew, who had worked in a secret factory that built the device, was willing to help the British and French. English agents smuggled him from Warsaw to Paris and provided him with the necessary tools. He constructed a model of the Enigma Machine, which the British transported to England. Working from the Pole's model, Alan Turning, an engineer, built a computer called "the bomb" to calculate exactly which key on the Engima Machine to press to read coded messages intercepted from nazi broadcasts. Under the command of Frederick W. Winterbotham, the British built a secret base at Bletchley Park, north of London. There, utilizing the Enigma Machine and "the bomb," the British developed detailed reports of the size and strength of the German forces and their locations and orders. Project Ultra turned out to be one of the major factors in the defeat of nazi Germany.[4]

Having postponed the planned attack against the West because of the severe winter, Hitler rescheduled it for January 17. Yet on January 10, as he was making the last arrangements for the offensive, he learned that a Luftwaffe officer, carrying a copy of the battle plan, had crash-landed in Belgium while flying from Münster to Cologne. The news sent the führer into a panic. He and Göring frantically consulted Dr. Augustus Heerman, a clairvoyant brought to them by Göring's wife. Although Heerman swore that he had a vision showing the unlucky officer burning the document and assured the anxious dictator that the Belgians could not possibly have salvaged it, Hitler decided to postpone the attack while he made appropriate changes to compensate for the information Brussels might have received. Unknown to Hitler, the Belgian officials had indeed arrested the officer and had learned of his plans by thwarting his frantic effort to burn the incriminating document.

Despite the uneasy calm that had descended on the Western Front, the months after September were not uneventful, for a savage battle raged on the seas. The German submarines patrolled the Atlantic, sinking thousands of tons of Allied shipping to cut England's supply lines. Incapable of successfully fighting these monsters, the British could do little but sink a few submarines and try to keep the locations of their ships secret. During the war the submarine warfare of Germany would almost drive Allied shipping from the Atlantic. At the same time, the *Graf Spee,* a German pocket battleship, fought a relentless battle with three pursuing British cruisers. Unable to withstand the might of the Royal Navy, the captain finally sought refuge in Montevideo, Uruguay. However, the English refused to allow the Germans to escape and steamed into the harbor of the neutral nation. Cornered, the Germans sank their ship on December 13, 1939, rather than allow the British to capture it.

While Britain and France were occupied with Germany, Stalin used the war as a pretext for Soviet aggression in the Baltic, forcing Estonia, Latvia, and Lithuania to allow him to station troops on their soil, a prelude to Soviet annexation of these small countries. He demanded the same right from Finland, and also that Helsinki yield territory in the southeast and several islands in the Baltic to Russia. The fiercely independent Finns rejected Stalin's demands on November 26, and four days later the Soviet dictator declared war on the small Baltic republic. The Finns valiantly fought the Soviet invasion, but they failed to defeat the superior Red Army and signed a treaty on March 12, 1940, yielding a vast stretch of territory to the Russians.

The Soviet aggression in the Baltic led to another delay in Hitler's plans to conquer the West. The führer feared that the English would send aid to the enbattled Finns through Norway and Sweden. At the beginning of the war, through the efforts of Göring's close friends in the Swedish aristocracy, Hitler had agreed to respect the neutrality of that Nordic kingdom in return for access to desperately needed Swedish iron ore. Because of the severe Baltic winter, the iron traveled to Germany through Narvik, a Norwegian ice-free port. However, if the British intervened in the war in Finland, this essential supply would be threatened. Therefore, Hitler ordered his forces to prepare Operation Weser, the conquest of Norway, and postponed Case Yellow until the strategic port was secure in German hands. He also sent aid to Vidkun Quisling, the leader of the Norwegian fascists.

Hitler was not the only one interested in Narvik. Although Norway had declared its neutrality, the English were attacking German shipping off the Norwegian coast. On February 16, they sent a force into the territorial waters of the Scandanivian kingdom to attack the *Altmark,* a German ship, and rescue several hundred prisoners of war. Realizing the importance of Narvik, London decided to prevent its falling into German hands, and on April 8 the British and French announced that they had mined the approaches to the neutral harbor. This action gave Hitler the excuse he needed to cloak his aggression in respectability. He proclaimed that the might of Germany would protect Scandanivia from Allied imperialism and gave the order for Operation Weser. To secure Norway, Hitler also decided to attack Denmark; thus, on the morning of April 9, 1940, his agent in Copenhagen demanded that the peaceful kingdom accept German protection. The Danes, knowing the futility of opposition, yielded to Hitler's ultimatum and allowed the Germans to occupy their country. The only resistance came from a few scattered troops in Jutland and the guard at the royal palace, who fired their weapons to salvage the national honor. Thus, the shadow of the Third Reich had fallen on the first of many neutral peoples.

The Norwegians refused to yield and bravely tried to resist the German advance. Once again, Hitler's armies moved so quickly that their victim had no time to prepare an adequate defense. The small Norwegian navy fought valiantly but was no match for the superior German forces, which swept it aside to clear the way for the onslaught. The German army landed at predetermined sights while the Luftwaffe filled the skies overhead. The stunned Norwegians could do little, and Oslo fell without a major battle; other detachments captured Bergen, Trondheim, and Narvik. Nevertheless, the Norwegian people, led by their courageous king, Haakon VII, refused to surrender. The brave monarch fled his palace with nazi units in pursuit and set up his headquarters at Nybergsund. There, he urged his people to fight and pleaded with the British and French for support in the desperate struggle with the new barbarians. The Germans demanded his immediate surrender. When he defiantly refused, they tried to kill him by a savage air attack on the small undefended village. However, he had escaped to a nearby forest, vowing as he watched the destruction to resist the nazi invasion with all his might. Haakon rallied his forces and waited for deliverance by the British and French.

This time London and Paris were ready to fight. The Royal Navy sped to the Norwegian coast and sank several German ships. On April 12 the *Warspite,* which had fought the Germans at Jutland boldly sailed up Narvik Fjord and bombarded the German ships in the harbor. The next day a British force under Major General P. J. Mackesy arrived at Harstad, on an island on the approach to Narvik. Meanwhile, the Allies decided to liberate Trondheim, in the middle of the kingdom, and thereby divide the enemy into two groups. On April 16 a force of British infantry and French Alpine troops under Major General Carton de Wiart landed at Namsos, about one hundred miles north of the crucial port. Elsewhere, another British force under Brigadier Morgan landed at Andalsnes one hundred fifty miles south of Trondheim.

While Mackesy waited for the snow to thaw, De Wiart's forces began their march toward Trondheim. They planned to surround the important city and then attack in a pincer movement. However, the savage Norwegian winter blocked their advance with mounds of impassable ice and snow. They got only as far as Verdal, fifty miles from their target. They could move no further, for lacking adequate antiaircraft weapons they stood helpless before the overpowering might of the Luftwaffe. The Germans blasted the defenseless troops, forcing them to retreat and to leave their dead in the frozen wasteland. Finally, they reached Mansos. On May 2, as the Germans bombarded them from the sky, De Wiart's men boarded British ships for their escape.

The British at Andalsnes met a similar fate. They withstood the fierce winter to march through Dombas to relieve the exhausted Norwegians, who were trying desperately to halt the German advance at Lillehammer. Together they stood against the nazi blitzkrieg, and the British army fought its first battle of the war. The swiftly moving Germans unleashed unending heavy artillery fire on the Allies, blowing large gaps in their lines and sending parts of bodies flying in every direction. Although French reinforcements arrived, the Allies could not withstand the German attack and finally fled. They retreated through the mountain valleys while the Germans hit them from the air with bombardment and machine gun fire. At one point they took refuge in a railway tunnel, huddling in the cold darkness for protection from the aerial attack. Finally, leaving a road strewn with the frozen bodies of their comrades, the remnant of the Allied force reached Andalsnes, where they began their voyage to safety on May 1.

The British were more successful at Narvik. Realizing that a forward attack through the harbor would meet with failure, they decided to move from the north and cross Rombaks Fjord to attack Narvik. Reinforced by French, Polish, and Norwegian units, the British began the siege on May 27. Meeting little resistance, they captured Narvik the next day. However, by this time Hitler had turned his attention elsewhere, and the Allies needed every available man to defend France from the nazi invasion. The victorious forces therefore boarded British ships and evacuated the Nordic city by June 8, leaving Norway to its German conquerors.

In the south the main German thrust against the West had finally begun. Originally, Hitler and his advisers had decided to concentrate on Paris in a revision of the Schlieffen Plan of the First World War. However, General Erich von Manstein suggested that, instead, the Germans strike through the Ardennes and then move to the sea to prevent a British evacuation. Hitler accepted Manstein's suggestions and ordered his generals to make appropriate revisions in Plan Yellow, the invasion of France.

The day of May 10, 1940, began as any other spring day in Holland, Belgium, and Luxemburg. The sun was fiery red, spreading beams of sunlight over the colorful tulip fields and glistening playfully on the windows of the medieval buildings. The birds sang to greet the dawn. Suddenly, without warning, the ominous drone of the Luftwaffe shattered the calm, sending terror into the hearts of the peace-loving peoples of this quiet corner of Europe. While the German planes circled above the Gothic towers, shaking the stained glass of the ancient churches, well-dressed diplomats delivered a fateful message from the master of the Third Reich. Hitler demanded the right to send his troops through Belgium and the Netherlands and threatened devastation if they met any resistance. The brave Belgians and Dutch defiantly rejected the führer's ultimatum, and the invasion began.

Again the German forces moved with such speed that their victims could do little to organize their defenses. Thousands of soldiers poured across the frontier, the sound of their march echoing through the streets of the quiet border towns. From above, more Germans rained down from the heavens, which became white with German parachutes. The desperate Dutch opened the dikes, destroying their carefully planted fields. But this failed to halt the German advance, for they simply inflated their rubber boats and continued their movement. Some nazi troops fanned out to seize important bridges before their defenders could destroy them; others concentrated on strategic airfields. From the sky the bombers pounded the Dutch air defenses, annihilating them before they could act. Still, the brave Dutch refused to surrender. Their small army held out against the onslaught as every able-bodied man and woman fought the invaders. The dedicated Dutch repulsed the enemy attempt to capture the bridges leading to the strategic port of Rotterdam. On May 14 the arrogant Nazis demanded the immediate surrender of the city or its destruction. Unable to withstand continued fighting, the defenders of the town asked for terms and began negotiations. But while they talked with their captors, the Luftwaffe appeared over the city and unleashed a violent bombardment, smashing the center of Rotterdam and killing thousands of innocent civilians in a foreshadowing of the nazi reign of terror that would engulf Europe for the next several years. Finally, the wounded city surrendered, and the victorious Germans occupied the smoking ruins. With the fall of Rotterdam, the defense of Holland reached an end. Queen Wilhelmina and her government narrowly escaped capture and fled to England, and by May 14, 1940, the Netherlands was a part of the nazi empire.

Like the Dutch, the Belgians resisted the invasion of their country. Moving through Luxemburg, the Germans unleashed the full force of their new brand of warfare on the people of Belgium. They sent in specially trained forces by glider to capture the bridges over the Albert Canal before the defenders had enough time to detonate explosives to destroy them. Thousands of tanks poured across the border while overhead the Luftwaffe bombarded the Belgian forces. Their border defenses breached, the dedicated army of the small kingdom formed a line following the Meuse River to the Albert Canal. The key to the Belgian defenses was the fortress of Eben Emael. This armor-plated structure of steel and concrete controlled the junction of the Meuse River and the Albert Canal and, with it, the road to the heartland of Belgium. On the first day of the invasion eighty specially trained German commando units landed on the roof of the fortress with their silent gliders. While Hitler's tanks moved through stiff resistance to surround the strategic bulwark, the commandos used carefully placed explosives and flame throwers to turn the massive structure into a raging inferno. Still the brave defenders stood their ground. Again and again the German artillery hit the fortress as the soldiers fought bloody hand-to-hand combat with their enemies. Above, the Luftwaffe released a merciless hail of bombs, and dive bombers beat at the enemy with their machine guns. Finally, after thirty terrible hours of carnage, a white flag appeared and the battle ended. The Germans had captured the "impregnable" fortress of Eben Emael and, with it, the key to Belgium.

The remnant of the Belgian army, reinforced with French and

British forces, fell back to a line running from Antwerp to Namur and prepared to meet the oncoming Nazi army. All eyes in London and Paris were turned on the small force, for if they could hold the Germans and attack them from the north, France might be saved. But in a crucial moment, as Hitler's men marched through northern France toward the English Channel, King Leopold III lost his courage and asked the führer for the terms of surrender. The ecstatic Hitler demanded unconditional surrender, and on the evening of May 27 the beaten monarch accepted the German ultimatum. At four the next morning the guns in Belgium became silent as another nation fell before the might of nazi Germany.

An even more important battle raged in France. On May 17, after the surrender of the Netherlands and the fall of Eben Emael, the German army crossed the French frontier. Instead of heading for Paris, as in 1914, Hitler's men raced toward the English Channel to split the Allied forces in Belgium from those in France. The powerful German tanks swept through the flat countryside aided by the clear, dry weather. In vain the French artillery tried to halt the advance, but the light weapons only bounced off the thick armor of Hitler's tanks, which moved closer to the English Channel every hour. They sped along the Somme, the scene of violent fighting during the First World War, toward Amiens, and then to Abbeville, which fell, opening the way to Bologne and to the sea. Still they continued to move, brushing aside the desperate effort of the Allies to halt their advance to Bologne and then to Calais. By May 24 Hitler had achieved his goal. The Allies were split into two forces, and the swastika floated in the breeze over the English Channel.

However, the British, through knowledge of German communications, derived through Ultra, knew of Hitler's intentions to surround and capture their forces; so they planned to save their men for the defense of Britain itself. Churchill, who had become prime minister after the forced resignation of the discredited Chamberlain, ordered the English to assemble every boat that could cross the English Channel to rescue the army. The situation grew darker with every passing hour. General Maxime Weygand, leader of the French army, cancelled the plans to attack the Germans from the south to relieve the embattled British and ordered his men to dig trenches to defend Paris. King Leopold's surrender freed still more Germans to concentrate on the obliteration of the English. On May 27 the greatest body of small vessels ever assembled in the history of modern warfare began

Operation Dynamo, the evacuation of the Allied forces from Dunkirk. For the next week, small pleasure craft, fishing vessels, every vessel that could float sailed back and forth from Britain to the French coast to rescue the desperate troops. Fortunately, to allow the Luftwaffe to win the honor of victory, Hitler ordered his ground forces to refrain from attacking the fleeing English. However, bad weather grounded Göring's Messerschmitts, saving the English from what could have been one of the greatest disasters of their history. When the weather cleared, all the Germans could do was destroy the docks, forcing the men to leave from the beaches while the outnumbered Royal Air Force Spitfires valiantly held the Germans in check. Thousands of men waded into the cold waters of the English Channel holding their arms above the surf to grasp a friendly hand to pull them to safety. Day and night the mission continued, until, by June 5, 1940, 350,000 French and British soldiers had reached England. The German plan to destroy the Allied forces had been thwarted by the selfless dedication of thousands of British civilians who rallied to Churchill's call for aid.

With the British driven from the north, the Germans began the final occupation of France on June 5. The outdated French army folded before the powerful German advance. General Weygand mistakenly made no effort to halt the advance. Instead, he allowed the Germans to break through his lines, hoping, thereby, to surround and destroy them. But the modern motorized German army was more than a match for the French, who still used horse-drawn weapons. With his best men trapped on the Maginot Line, the massive complex of fortifications running from Switzerland to Belgium, Weygand could do little but harass the advancing Nazis. On June 10 Mussolini, seeing an opportunity to profit by the might of nazi Germany, declared war on France and sent his army into the south. Finally, outnumbered by two to one and unable to stem the enemy advance, the French evacuated Paris, and on June 14 thousands of Germans marched through the streets of Paris as the population stood watching.

Churchill and Franklin D. Roosevelt pleaded with the French to continue the fight, but they had no will to resist. On June 17 President Henri-Philippe Petain, the hero of the First World War, informed an overjoyed Hitler of his decision to surrender. At last the Germans had avenged the humiliation of 1918. France lay helpless before the might of Hitler's forces. Wishing to mortify the defeated French as much as possible, Hitler announced that he would receive their surrender at Compiègne, the scene of the German surrender twenty-two years before. Seated in Foch's chair in the railway car brought from its museum to symbolize the revenge, the dictator received the French delegation headed by General Charles Huntzinger. After discussing Hitler's terms with the French government in exile in Bordeaux by telephone, the pale delegation signed the death warrant of their country. The Germans would occupy the northern part of France, leaving a powerless government under Petain in the south, at Vichy. Hitler after the signing, went outside and saluted his honor guard while the band played "Deutschland über Alles," and he left in his Mercedes to celebrate the final revenge of the previous defeat of Imperial Germany.

The French yielded because they lacked the ability to fight the modernized German army, and their elderly generals refused to consider new ideas. The generals placed all their faith in the Maginot line, which the Germans simply went around, for the French refused to use their tanks to meet the advancing enemy. The tired leaders of the French army considered them mobile fortresses, suitable to do little more than guard bridges. Another reason for the French defeat was the presence of German "fifth columnists," who had entered the unsuspecting nation disguised as tourists, salesmen, or even refugees from Hitler's tyranny. When the attack began, some dressed in French uniforms and gave false orders to the confused troops. Others spread rumors among the French people to cause terror and confusion. Finally, the French lacked the stamina needed to resist the Germans. They had lost almost a whole generation during the First World War and preferred to capitulate to the Nazis rather than risk a renewal of the death and destruction they had known from 1914 to 1918.

As the führer inspected the magnificent buildings of the French capital shortly after the surrender, his military advisers gathered to discuss the future of the war. Göring advocated an immediate attack and found support from others. But Hitler believed that since his goal in Western Europe had been achieved, an invasion of Britain was unnecessary, for he believed that London would accept his offer of peace. A few days after his triumph at Compiègne, he met with his military advisers to tell them that his fondest desire was peace with Britain because he considered the continued strength of the British Empire the most important guarantee of stability in the rest of the world. Hitler had always expressed his desire to reach agreement with London. In *Mein Kampf* he wrote that because of its opposition to French domination of Europe, England was the natural ally of Germany. The führer brushed aside Göring's frantic plea for immediate action, confident that once he offered peace the British would rush to accept it. The British had no desire to form an alliance with the Third Reich. Instead, they used the time granted them by Hitler's hesitation to build their defenses for the coming invasion. Day after day went by as Hitler expected the British to request negotiations. On June 18 Winston Churchill spoke to the House of Commons to defiantly proclaim the will of his people to fight Hitler's aggression to the last man, woman, and child. The eloquent prime minister announced a new crusade against a new infidel that would determine the fate of the world for many years to come, saying that, should the war be lost, it would plunge mankind into an era of barbarism more terrible than that brought by the fall of ancient Rome. Nevertheless, Hitler believed that the British would seek peace. On July 19 he spoke to the Reichstag. In a message flashed to the world by radio, the führer praised his army for its heroic campaign in the West. After pausing to award the field marshal's baton to nine of his most trusted generals and to promote the glory-hungry Göring to reich marshal, he spoke to the British people. Standing beneath the wings of a huge eagle, Hitler once again offered peace, pleading with the English to reject Churchill's call for resistance and bring the war to an end through negotiations. But the British refused to heed Hitler's call and rallied around their government. On July 22 Lord Halifax officially rejected Hitler's offer.

Even before his speech of July 19, Hitler realized that he must begin planning the invasion of England. After meeting with his top military advisers in the quiet of Berchtesgaden, he ordered the high command to develop Operation Sea Lion, the invasion of England. The army proposed a massive operation of 100,000 men led by Field Marshal Gerd von Rundstedt. According to the army proposal, General Ernst Busch would lead his men from Calais to the area around Dover while General Adolf Strauss would sail from Le Havre to the southeastern coast of England. At the same time, Field Marshal Walter von Reichenau would assemble his men at Cherbourg and land near Weymouth in the southwest. From their beachheads, the army would fan out to occupy the south, surrounding London and forcing its surrender. Then German forces would march under the shadow of Big Ben, and other troops would occupy the rest of the island.

However, the army's ambitious project was impossible for the ill-prepared German navy. Admiral Erich Räder met Field Marshal Brauchitsch, commander in chief of the army, General Hans Jerschonnek of Göring's staff, and Hitler on July 21 in Berlin. The head of the fleet denounced the plan as foolishly impossible and announced that the navy lacked the ships necessary to support such an ambitious invasion. A few days later Räder's officers presented a report stating that they simply could not provide enough ships to transport so many men across such a wide front. At the end of July Hitler met with his top officers, and once again Räder argued against the plan, announcing that he could not hope to assemble the force necessary for Operation Sea Lion until September 15. The führer yielded to the admiral's convincing assessment of the situation and ordered Göring to beat the British into submission in preparation for the time when the Germans could move.

While the navy frantically assembled the ships and barges needed for the operation from all parts of Germany and the conquered countries, Göring prepared the Luftwaffe for the destruction of the British defenses. Operating from his luxurious train in France, the reich marshal, enjoying his role as the possible savior of the invasion of England, followed Hitler's order of August 1, 1940, to concentrate on the destruction of the Royal Air Force and the important coastal radar installations. According to the plan, once air superiority had been achieved the Germans would destroy the English ports and food supplies. However, forewarned by Ultra, the British were ready for the coming attack.

On August 8 Göring ordered his men to begin Operation Eagle, the destruction of the Royal Air Force. His attack had two goals, to disrupt the British airports through massive bombing and to force the outnumbered R.A.F. to engage in combat with his fighter planes. However, hostile weather confined the opening volleys of his attack to a few minor bombings as the English leaders waited in anticipation of the coming onslaught. On August 13 the sky cleared, and over one thousand German aircraft began to hit the R.A.F. bases. Throughout August and early September the Battle of Britain raged as valiant R.A.F. pilots fought desperately to drive the superior Luftwaffe from the sky above their homeland. Aware of Göring's strategy, Sir Hugh Dowding, commander of the British air force, refused to allow the arrogant Germans to trick him into sending his planes to certain destruction. Instead, armed with priceless information gleaned from

Ultra warning him exactly when and where the attacks would come, Dowding concentrated his limited forces where they would do the most good. Since the German fighter planes carried only enough fuel to stay above England a few minutes before leaving the bombers to their own defenses, the British tactic was a success.

Still, the persistent pounding of R.A.F. bases was taking its toll and, if continued, might have deprived Dowding of the advantage of foreknowledge of the sites of the coming bombing runs. However, on September 7 Göring made a fatal error that saved the R.A.F. from destruction. Furious over a token raid the British had made over Berlin, the humiliated reich marshal ordered his men to attack the London docks. Warned by Ultra, the British secretly assembled their firefighting equipment and waited for the German planes to break the calm that summer afternoon. While Churchill watched from the roof of the Air Ministry, the Luftwaffe unleashed its force against the defenseless docks, turning them into a raging inferno that covered the city with smoke. Again and again for the next few days, the Luftwaffe appeared over the London sky to bomb the British into submission. Göring failed; the continued offensive only made the English more determined than ever to resist the nazi aggression.[5]

On September 15 Göring ordered his men to prepare for the decisive battle, which, if successful, would prepare the way for Operation Sea Lion. However, the British were ready and met his planes with all the might the R.A.F. could muster. The shocked Germans, who believed that they had destroyed the defiant British air force, were unprepared for resistance and returned to France soon after reaching their target. Göring was determined to prove the worth of his forces and ordered them to return that same day. Once again Ultra warned the British, and they were ready to meet the coming attack. Armed with fresh supplies of fuel and bullets, the courageous R.A.F. pilots pounded the Luftwaffe from the moment it appeared over England. Unable to repel the British, Göring's shattered force dropped their bombs wherever they could and fled to the safety of their bases. The R.A.F. had won the Battle of Britain. Two days later Hitler ordered his men to dismantle the armada being assembled for Operation Sea Lion to wait for a more opportune time.

Throughout the winter of 1940 and 1941, the Luftwaffe bombed the English cities into rubble, but it never again threatened the existence of the R.A.F. With each new bombing the British stiffened their will to resist Hitler's plan to conquer Europe. Thousands died while the survivors, avoiding death by crouching for hours in shelters or in the tunnels of the London subway, emerged to find their homes and belongings destroyed by the German bombs. Yet, despite Göring's vengeance, they refused to surrender. In November he ordered the Luftwaffe to vent its wrath on other cities, spreading the destruction throughout England. On the moonlight night of November 14 the Germans hit the industrial city of Coventry, reducing its cathedral to rubble. Through Ultra, Churchill had learned of the plan, but fearing disclosure of this vital source of information, he had decided against warning the people of this unlucky city. Thousands died and over 50,000 homes were destroyed, but Ultra, the source of intelligence that was one of the major factors in the defeat of the Third Reich, was saved. The raids continued throughout the spring of 1941, until finally, as Hitler prepared for his next campaign, the invasion of Russia, the attack subsided. Once again the British people were able to sleep in relative peace.

The first years of the Second World War were a period of major German victories. Hitler's forces conquered an empire larger than any other German ruler had. The nazi blitzkrieg overcame the resistance of Poland, Denmark, Norway, Luxembourg, Belgium, the Netherlands, and France. The führer stood at the height of his power. He avenged the disgrace of 1918 and sent his victorious troops through the streets of Paris. Yet he also met a major defeat. He neglected to prepare for the attack on England in the false belief that the British would yield to his superior force and make peace with the Third Reich. He rejected the demands of some of his advisers for immediate action, and he gave the British an opportunity to organize their forces. When Hitler finally decided to launch the invasion of England, his navy was unable to provide transportation for his troops, forcing him to rely on Göring's Luftwaffe to beat the British into submission. However, armed with knowledge of Göring's plans through Ultra, the valiant British R.A.F. withstood the German attack. The blitzkrieg was at last thwarted. The swastika-bearing planes failed to destroy the English air force, and, by shifting the attack to London and the English cities, they gave the British desperately needed time to rebuild their air defenses. Despite Göring's fervent hopes, the British people refused to allow him to force them into submission. They lived to fight with a new determination to rid mankind of national socialism. The failure to conquer Britain may have been Hitler's first fatal mistake. For the next few years the British alone, in the West, withstood the nazi onslaught and concentrated their energies on the day when they would liberate France and the rest of Europe. Had London fallen as did Paris, the German dictator could have concentrated all his forces on the coming attack on Russia. Instead, the determined British forced him to fight a war on two fronts, which in the end proved to be his undoing.

18

The Fall of Fortress Europe

The first months of the Second World War marked the growth of German power to heights undreamed of by men like Frederick The Great and Bismarck. Hitler presided over an empire that dominated almost all of central and western Europe and imprisoned millions. Yet complete victory had eluded the greedy dictator. Despite the destruction of its cities by the Luftwaffe, England defied the German armies. Even while his forces were crushing his enemies in the West, Hitler began to plan his next step, the invasion of the Soviet Union. Hitler, who was alarmed about the Soviet aggression on his eastern frontier, believed that once Russia had fallen England would have no choice but to accept its fate at his hands. The führer also hoped that the defeat of the Soviets would prevent the Americans, who were already sending supplies to his enemies, from daring to intervene in the conflict. Naturally, Hitler had not forgotten his old dream of the conquest of the fertile Ukraine to provide "living space" for the "master" race. Yet, before he could concentrate on the next goal of his aggression, the need to obtain supplies from the rich Balkans and to help his ineffective ally, Mussolini, forced him to divert his attention to southeastern Europe and North Africa. Finally, he ordered his vast army to march across the steppes of Russia and, in so doing, opened the way for his defeat. Russia did not fall, and England did not surrender. The Americans entered the war after a treacherous attack by Hitler's Asian ally, Japan; Hitler's worst fears came true, and the Third Reich found itself engaged in a two-front war, which, in the end, would free the world from the curse of national socialism.

Even as Göring's Luftwaffe soared above the skies of Britain, Hitler began scheming for the invasion of the Soviet Union. On July 21, 1940, the dictator instructed Brauchitsch to begin preparations for Operation Barbarossa, the invasion of Russia. He hoped that after a battle lasting four to six weeks, Germany would tear White Russia and the Ukraine from the Soviet Union and form an association of Baltic states under German domination. On that same day he summoned his generals to meet with him at his mountain retreat to discuss the project. He told them of his vision of a vast Blitzkrieg far greater than the successful attack on the West that would not only destroy the economic capability of the Russians, but would also place the inferior Slavs under German domination. The führer told the somewhat startled generals that the fall of Russia would bring victory against England by weakening the will of the defiant British to resist. The next day Halder set hard at work on the plan for the invasion. During the next few weeks the Germans secretly moved men and supplies to the east in preparation for the coming offensive.[1]

But once again events in other parts of Europe diverted Hitler's attention from his main goal. On July 26, 1940, in accord with the secret agreement with Berlin of 1939, Moscow demanded that Rumania yield Bessarabia. Although Ribbentrop advised Bucharest to yield to Stalin's demand, Hitler began taking steps to prevent a repetition in the Balkans of the Russian aggression that had destroyed the Baltic states. Hitler and his advisers realized that Soviet domination of Rumania would deprive Germany of desperately needed oil. The situation became more complex when Hungary, influenced by the ease with which Moscow had gained a large chunk of Rumanian territory, demanded Transylvania. Hitler moved at once to use the conflict between Budapest and Bucharest as an excuse for intervention. On August 26 he sent several units to the southeast to prepare for the occupation of Rumania. Four days later he dispatched Ribbentrop to Vienna to meet with the representatives of the two nations. Although the Rumanian diplomat fainted when he learned that Hitler intended to support Hungary's demands, he could do little but agree to allow the Hungarians to occupy a large portion of Transylvania. The failure of his government to resist the dismemberment of his country led King Carol to panic and abdicate a week later, giving Hitler still another opportunity to take advantage of the situation. The new monarch, Michael, appointed General Ion Antonescu, leader of the fascist Iron Guard, head of the government. The new dictator immediately announced his decision to join the Axis and asked Berlin for assistance. Only too happy to answer Antonescu's call for aid, Hitler sent a force into the troubled kingdom a few weeks later to protect the oil supply. Thus, yet another people fell under German domination.[2]

Not forgetting his determination to conquer Russia, Hitler decided to take an additional step to crush the British. On June 30, 1940, General Alfred Jodl, his chief military adviser, had suggested that Germany win domination of the Mediterranean and cut the British communications with their empire by the conquest of Gibraltar. Other concerns prevented an immediate decision on the issue. On September 6 Admiral Räder again suggested the conquest of the strategic sea, and this time the führer accepted the idea and decided to persuade the Spanish to enter the war. A few weeks later Franco sent Serrano Suñer to Berlin to meet with Hitler and Ribbentrop. Although the leaders of the Third Reich spared no effort to impress their important guest with the might of Germany and offered assistance in driving the British from Gibraltar, long a major goal of Spanish foreign policy, the crafty Spanish diplomat refused to give the persistent Germans a definite answer.

Still determined to bring Spain into the war, Hitler decided to attempt to influence personally the Spanish dictator. On October 23 the führer arrived by train in Hendaye in southern France to meet with Franco. Hitler used all his ability to sway the stubborn Spanish leader, but at last he had met his match. Franco refused to give an answer, and Hitler flew into a rage; nevertheless, the Spanish fascist stood his ground, and Hitler tried charm. This too failed, and the two men left without reaching an agreement. Despite the reluctance of Franco to commit himself to join the Axis, Hitler ordered his generals on November 12 to begin preparations for Undertaking Felix, the conquest of Gibraltar. Hitler continued to press Franco for a definite answer. Finally, on February 6, 1941, the obstinate Spanish leader formally rejected Hitler's pleas. The enraged führer, defied by a man he had helped put in power, tried once again. A few days after Franco's refusal to join the Axis, Mussolini made a frantic appeal for Spanish support when the two met at Bordinghere, but despite the threat that Hitler might invade Spain, the determined dictator stood his ground. Although 40,000 Spanish volunteers later fought on the Russian front, Spain remained officially neutral throughout the war. In the end Franco's decision proved correct, for he alone of the fascist dictators of Europe would last through the war, and he would dominate his country until his death in 1975.

Why had he gathered the courage to withstand Hitler's persistent appeal? The answer lies partially in the work of Admiral Wilhelm Canaris, the anti-nazi commander of German military intelligence. In July 1940 the master spy and several of his aides had traveled secretly to Madrid to report on the defense of Gibraltar. He deliberately wrote a pessimistic report, stressing the ability of the British to defend their impregnable fortress. He also emphasized the major difficulties in transporting men and supplies across Spain because of the difference in the width of the Spanish railroads from those of the rest of Europe, thus requiring the reloading of German materials at the border. Canaris, who had known Franco since the First World War, also reassured his friend that Hitler would not invade Spain. He sent Josef Müller, his agent at the Vatican, to meet with Suñer in Rome to guarantee that despite the führer's demands Germany would not violate Spanish neutrality. Buttressed by Canaris's assurances, Franco became more determined than ever to keep his country, which had not recovered from the bloody civil war, out of the war, causing Hitler to meet with one of the most decisive diplomatic defeats of his career.[3]

Hitler's failure to persuade Franco to join the Axis was a serious setback, but Mussolini's ambitions led to even greater problems. The duce dreamed of turning the eastern Mediterranean into an Italian lake and of re-creating the grandeur of the ancient Roman Empire. As German forces marched into Prague in April 1939, Italian troops had overthrown the regime of King Zog of Albania and made the small Adriatic nation an Italian province. On September 13, 1940, the Italian army opened an attack on the English in Egypt, threatening the Suez Canal, the lifeline of the British Empire. A few weeks later Rome launched an invasion of Greece. Although the two dictators had pledged their loyalty to the alliance at the Brenner Pass on October 4, Mussolini had failed to inform Hitler of his plans. The führer, returning from his ill-fated meeting with Franco in a sullen mood, flew into a rage when he learned of the Italian operation. He ordered his train halted and demanded an immediate meeting with the duce. Mussolini agreed, and on October 28 he confronted Hitler in Florence. Hitler was furious and wanted to know why the Italian dictator had taken such drastic action without his knowledge. Did he not know that it could seriously threaten the stability in the Balkans and force Hitler to divert troops badly needed for Barbarossa? Barely able to contain his rage, Hitler discussed the war and left the Renaissance city after grudgingly pledging his support, a promise he would later regret.

The Italian army was incapable of facing the British. To defend Egypt and the access to the Suez Canal, the English fought mightily. They launched a surprise attack on the ill-prepared Italians on December 8 and within a few days had swept across the burning desert to capture 30,000 enemy troops at Sidi Barrani, thus beginning the invasion of Libya. After a month-long siege, the English forced the battered Italian army to surrender the fortress at Bardia. Without pausing for a rest, the British continued the offensive, capturing Tobruk on January 22 and forcing 100,000 battle-weary Italian troops to surrender. Two days later Derna fell, and the British were on the verge of driving the vanquished Italians from Africa. Meanwhile, the courageous Greeks, their strength underestimated by Rome, repelled the troops of the duce and entered Albania. On both fronts Mussolini had been dealt a humiliating defeat.

With every British and Greek victory, Hitler grew more and more concerned that Allied domination of the Balkans would threaten Operation Barbarossa and place the English in position to bomb the precious Rumanian oil fields. He reinforced his garrison in Rumania and decided that if Mussolini failed in Greece, he would have to send German forces to complete the conquest. Meanwhile, the Russians became alarmed by the German movements in the Balkans, and they charged that the Hungarian annexation of Transylvania with German support violated their agreement. On November 12, 1940, Molotov arrived in Berlin to discuss the issue. Ribbentrop assured the Soviet diplomat that England had been defeated and suggested that Moscow take advantage of the situation to move into the Arabian Sea. However, Molotov was in no mood to be fooled by the Germans and angrily demanded to know why the Third Reich had supported the Finns and intervened in Rumania. Hitler brushed aside the Russian's questions and suggested that Moscow join the Axis, promising Russian domination of the Indian Ocean after the defeat of England. However, the Russian official had no interest in the Indian Ocean. Instead he indicated that the future of the Balkans would have to be decided before Russia would consider joining the Axis. After the usual banquets and receptions, Molotov returned to Moscow without solving the issue. On November 25 Stalin informed Hitler that he would consider joining the Axis if he were allowed to place his forces in a position to control the Bosporus from Bulgaria. The führer, having no intention of yielding to Stalin's demands, approved the first draft of Operation Barbarossa on December 18. Once again diplomacy had failed, and Hitler resolved to use force to achieve his goals.

Before Hitler could turn to the invasion of Russia, he had to rescue the Italians and secure the Balkans. On December 7 the humiliated duce finally admitted his failure and begged for German aid. Hitler agreed and ordered his army to plan Operation Marita, the invasion of Greece. However, an attack on Greece led to additional complications. Before the führer could send his troops to aid the desperate Italians, he had to win the cooperation of Bulgaria and Yugoslavia. He massed his forces on the Danube in Rumania and demanded the right to send his men into Bulgaria. Tsar Boris III had no choice but to yield. He was more afraid of Moscow than Berlin and saw German troops as his salvation from a Russian occupation. He also believed that Hitler would win the war and wanted to be on the side of the victors. Therefore, on January 3, 1941, he allowed the Germans to cross the Danube into Bulgaria. On March 1 he formally joined the Axis.[4]

Despite the capitulation of Bulgaria, Hitler encountered serious difficulty with Yugoslavia. At a meeting with Prince Paul, regent for King Peter II, at Berchtesgaden on March 4, he demanded that Yugoslavia join the Axis. He also hinted that as a reward for agreement Belgrade could expect to receive Salonika after the defeat of Greece. Since the Germans had surrounded the southern Slavic kingdom on three sides, Prince Paul decided to yield. On March 25 his premier, Dragisha Tsvetkovich, and his foreign minister, Tsintsar-Markovich, journeyed secretly to Vienna to join the Axis. Hitler agreed to respect the sovereignty of the Balkan state and said that he would not transport his troops through Yugoslav territory. However, influenced by the British, the members of the army and air force of the southern Slavic kingdom had no desire to become a part of Hitler's empire. On hearing of the agreement with Berlin, they organized a plot to overthrow the government of Prince Paul and to place King Peter II in control of the government. During the night of March 26 they surrounded the palace and seized control of the capital. The new Yugoslav regime under General Dushan Simovich repudiated the pact with Hitler and announced Yugoslav neutrality.

Hitler was furious. He postponed the planned invasion of Russia while he punished the defiant Yugoslavs and beat the Greeks into submission. Immediately on hearing of the revolt, he summoned his military advisers to the chancellory and ordered Jodl to plan Operation Punishment, the destruction of Yugoslavia. The offensive opened on April 6 with a merciless Luftwaffe bombardment of Belgrade, destroying the city and killing thousands of defenseless people. At the same time, his army, with the support of the Italians, swept down from the north, entering the devastated city on April 13. The Yugoslav army frantically gathered its forces and tried to resist, but they were no match for the superior German forces. On April 17 at Sarajevo, the site of the assassination of Francis Ferdinand in 1914, they surrendered, powerless to save their country.

Meanwhile, Hitler's army moved into Greece from Bulgaria. Unable to repulse the invaders, General George Tsolakgou, commander of the northern Greek forces, disregarded his orders and offered to surrender. The failure of Tsolakgou to resist the Germans caused a panic in Athens. Premier Alexander Koryzes committed suicide on April 18. His successor, Emmanuel Tsoderos, tried to rally his forces, but the battle had been lost. The remainder of the Greek army, supported by 57,000 British troops, tried to halt the German onslaught near Mt. Olympus. Hitler's forces savagely pounded them and forced them to retreat to the south. Finally, they knew that they had been defeated and quickly repeated the feat of Dunkirk, evacuating over 50,000 men between April 24 and 31. The Germans entered Athens on April 27, and by May 1 they had completed the invasion.

From Greece the Germans swept across the sea to attack the British at Crete. The Luftwaffe bombarded the British bases while thousands of Germans parachuted onto the island. In a daring attack, Hitler's forces first cut the British communications and then began to drive them from their bases. After three weeks of fighting, the Germans were once more victorious, and the British evacuated the island as German aircraft swept down on them from the sky, killing thousands of fleeing soldiers. By June 2 Crete had fallen to the forces of the Third Reich, depriving the British of a valuable base for air operations against the Germans in the Balkans.

With the Balkans secured, Hitler was finally able to turn his full attention to Operation Barbarossa. Once again he planned a quick blitzkrieg that would destroy the enemy before it had a chance to organize its forces. The invasion was to consist of three massive thrusts. In the north, Field Marshal Wilhelm von Leeb would lead twenty-six divisions through the Baltic states to Leningrad in hope of destroying the bulk of the Soviet munitions industry and joining the Finns. In the south, Field Marshal Karl von Rundstedt, commanding forty-one divisions and a group of Rumanian soldiers, would send one section of his army from Poland to capture Kiev, and another would occupy the Black Sea coast. Then they would join for a quick thrust into the Caucasus. Between the two armies, Field Marshal Fedor von Bock would lead fifty divisions to Moscow and the Urals. Hitler hoped that by the end of the summer his troops would occupy a line running from Archangel east of Kazan and Stalingrad to the Caspian Sea east of Astrakhan.

Because of faulty intelligence, Hitler believed that once his men had crushed Russian resistance in Europe and had captured the oil fields in the Caucasus that Stalin would be on his knees asking to surrender. Hitler's agents, hampered by the necessity of working in a tightly controlled state, had underestimated the size and strength of the Red Army and the organization of Soviet industry. His intelligence so misled the führer that he believed he could accomplish his goal before the onset of winter, and Hitler made the fatal mistake of failing to supply his men with winter provisions and clothing. In the end, the failure of Colonel E. Kinsel, head of the section of military intelligence dealing with the Soviet Union, to provide Hitler with a true picture of the organization of Russian defenses and manufacturing was one of the major reasons for the defeat of the Third Reich.[5]

On June 22, 1941, significantly enough the anniversary of Napoleon's ill-fated invasion of Russia in 1812, thousands of German troops poured across the Soviet border while the Luftwaffe blasted the Russians from the air. Despite persistent warnings from Churchill, who knew of Hitler's plans through Ultra, Stalin was totally unprepared for the attack. In the field his commanders lost contact with their troops, and chaos reigned as Hitler's forces began to sweep across Russia. Finally, the Soviet leader realized the true nature of the situation and took swift action to organize his army. Slowly the Russians began to resist the oncoming Germans, as every available man threw himself into the fighting. After the loss of thousands, the Red Army began to hamper the German movement, depriving Hitler of the quick victory he had planned. Then, as in 1812, the Russian weather intervened to save the Soviet Union from destruction. The Germans choked on the dust of the dry steppe, and the harsh sun beat down upon them. Then rains turned the battlefield into a sea of mud, clogging the wheels and treads of the German vehicles and tanks. Still Hitler's forces moved toward their goal as the days turned into weeks.

Finally, on July 19, as Bock's forces moved toward Moscow, Hitler made a mistake that cost him the Russian capital. At a crucial moment the führer chose to ignore the protests of his generals and ordered Colonel Heinz Guderian to move his tank divisions from Bock's army to reinforce Rundstedt in the Ukraine. He also sent another group of Bock's men to join Leeb in the north. Had Hitler concentrated instead on capturing Moscow, instead of diverting his forces to the north and south, the Russian capital might have fallen. But deprived of badly needed men, Bock's troops were unable to break through the hastily organized defenses of Moscow. On October 14 the Germans reached Mozhaisk, sixty miles from the Kremlin. Fighting the determined resistance of Stalin's forces, Bock's advance units reached the suburbs of the Russian capital, and his main force was within twenty miles of its goal. However, as in 1812, the Russian winter intervened to deprive the invaders of victory. Hitler's ill-prepared forces floundered in a frozen hell of ice and snow. They were reduced to slaughtering scrawny horses for meat and to harvesting local grain to make bread. Although the capture of Moscow would not have insured a German victory in the war with Russia, it would have been a major psychological blow to Stalin's forces. Meanwhile, Leeb's men failed to capture Leningrad, but in the south Rundstedt was more successful. He occupied Kiev, and after bitter fighting he forced 600,000 Soviet troops to surrender on September 14. Yet, the early winter, a repetition of the winter of 1812, forced the Germans to halt on all fronts, unable to move through the ice and snow that covered the land and even prevented movements by rail.

Hitler's generals, realizing that their men were unprepared to withstand a savage winter, tried to persuade their leader to order a retreat to a more defensible position where they could regroup and prepare for renewed fighting once spring had come. But, the determined dictator refused to consider even a strategic retreat, and he ordered his men to hold their ground whatever the cost, condemning thousands of Germans to live in a frozen prison along the Russian front in fortified centers called hedgehogs. Hitler's generals, who had long doubted the wisdom of his dangerous plans, refused to accept his decision. Rundstedt, Block, Leeb, and Brauchitsch resigned in protest. Instead of finding qualified replacements to command his armies, the egotistical führer took over personal direction of the campaign.

When spring finally came, after the terrible winter, Hitler decided to hold the line in the north and to concentrate on the drive into the Caucasus. Believing the poor intelligence reports, he thought that once he had deprived the Soviets of their major source of oil, their defenses would fold and victory would be achieved. On April 5, 1942, the führer ordered his men to resume the offensive in the Ukraine. Within a few weeks the Germans had swept across southern Russia into the Crimea and had begun the siege of Sevastopol, which fell on July 1. Taking advantage of the long winter to reorganize his forces, Marshal Georgi K. Zhukov, Stalin's commander in chief, ordered the Red Army to attack the invaders. On June 28 the Russians fell on the Germans near Kursk, and, after several weeks of bloody fighting, during which thousands died, the German advance on the Volga stopped at Voranezh. However, in the south, Hitler's men continued to march, capturing Rostov on July 27 and reaching the outskirts of Stalingrad on September 19.

The battle for Stalingrad, opening on September 15, was one of the decisive engagements of the war. Zhukov rushed additional troops to the besieged city and ordered his commanders to resist the Germans no matter what the cost. Day and night the Nazis pounded the city from the air, killing thousands and turning it into a smoking graveyard. On the ground, Hitler's forces penetrated the outer defenses, but Zhukov hurled every available man at the enemy. In the hand-to-hand fighting that followed, the determined Russians repulsed the German advance and saved the city. On November 19 the Red Army began a massive counterattack, piercing the German flanks defended by Italian and Rumanian forces, and began to close in on the defeated Germans. Once again Hitler stubbornly refused to surrender or to order a retreat. His commander at Stalingrad, General Friedrich von Paulus, appealed to him to halt the senseless carnage, but Hitler stood his ground. Throughout the next months fighting raged at Stalingrad, with both sides fighting in the face of the Russian winter. Finally, on January 31, 1943, the Russians captured Paulus, and two days later the last German soldier fell. Hitler had met with one of the most decisive defeats of the war. He had lost thousands of soldiers and tons of supplies to carry out an ill-conceived offensive.

With the Germans broken at Stalingrad, the Russians began to regain the Ukraine in a massive movement. Despite Hitler's orders, the tired and weakened Germans were unable to resist the Soviet offensive. Kursk fell on February 7, followed a week later by Rostov and Kharkov. The fighting continued through the summer, but Hitler could not resist the determined Soviets. Day by day they inched toward Kiev, and on November 6, 1943, they liberated the capital of the Ukraine. Hitler lost hundreds of thousands of men, and the Third Reich began to crumble.[6]

While Hitler's forces met with a major defeat in Russia, events elsewhere were helping to prepare the way for his downfall. Although many Americans considered the war a squabble between the Europeans and had no desire to become involved in another foreign conflict, it was impossible for the United States to remain neutral. As the Third Reich continued to expand, President Franklin D. Roosevelt became more and more alarmed. On June 3, 1940, while Hitler's armies marched across France, he ordered the War Department to ship surplus and unneeded supplies to assist the British. On March 11, 1941, the American Congress passed an act providing to lend or lease materials to any nation fighting nazi aggression. When Hitler began his attack on the Soviet Union, Roosevelt immediately offered assistance. During the war the Americans spent billions to provide valuable supplies to repulse the Germans. On August 14, 1941, Churchill and the American president met off the coast of Newfoundland to discuss the war. They drew up an agreement called the Atlantic Charter, which defended the right of the peoples of the world to determine their own governments and provided for the maintenance of peace once the war ended. The two leaders also formally agreed not to use the war to gain additional territory for their own nations.

However, the United States did not enter the war because of direct action by the Third Reich. It was Hitler's Japanese ally who brought the Americans into the conflict. Washington had long been alarmed by the Japanese aggression in Asia and had constantly protested Tokyo's attempt to carve an empire from China and other Asian countries. When the Japanese invaded French Indochina on July 24, 1941, Roosevelt took immediate steps to seize Japanese assets in the United States. In October Tokyo sent two representatives to Washington to negotiate with the Americans. Roosevelt demanded an immediate evacuation of China and Indochina and promised favorable trade relations if Japan would agree. But the Japanese refused to accept the American ultimatum, arguing instead that the United States had no right to interfere in Asian problems.

As the talks continued, the Japanese planned a bold stroke to eliminate America as a power in the Pacific. The target of their attack was Pearl Harbor, the home of much of the American fleet in the Pacific. Significantly enough, the Americans had several chances to learn of the Japanese plot. Since 1934 Washington had been able to read the

Japanese code. Tokyo had a special version of the Enigma Machine, which the Americans had been able to purchase from Alexander von Kryha, the commercial agent of Arthur Scherbius, its inventor. Using this device, William F. Friedman, head of the Signals Intelligence Service, penetrated the Japanese code. Project Magic, as the Americans called their decoding operation, would provide the Allies with much valuable intelligence information. The Japanese ambassador in Berlin, General Hiroshi Oshima, sent regular reports to his superiors concerning Hitler's battle plans and the size of the German forces. The Americans intercepted these reports and promptly informed their British friends.

In addition to Project Magic, the Americans had another opportunity to learn of the Japanese plans to attack their naval base at Pearl Harbor. In June 1941 the Germans, responding to a request from Tokyo, sent one of their most trusted agents, Dusko Popov, a Yugoslav businessman, to America to study and to report on the defenses at Pearl Harbor. Unknown to Berlin, Popov, who operated under the name Tricycle, was also working for the British. He informed them of his orders, and London passed the information to Washington. Although J. Edgar Hoover, the head of the Federal Bureau of Investigation, refused to cooperate with Tricycle and once even threatened to have him arrested for violating the Mann Act because of a holiday with a girlfriend in Florida, the mission should have warned the Americans to take measures to protect their base in Hawaii. Unfortunately, neither information gained from Magic nor Tricycle's mission led Washington to take the appropriate actions, and the U.S. fleet lay vulnerable to a Japanese attack.[7]

Sunday, December 7, 1941, began like any other Sabbath. Millions of Americans went to church, slept late, or lulled away the hours with their newspapers. Suddenly, a startling announcement broke the calm. The Japanese had launched a surprise attack on Pearl Harbor. The next day the furious American president told the nation that America must enter the war, and an obliging Congress voted overwhelmingly to join the Allies in their life-and-death struggle against the Axis. Three days later Hitler, who considered America already in the war because of the aid sent his enemies, declared war on the United States, and the war became a worldwide conflict. The Americans provided badly needed supplies and fresh troops that played a major role in breaking the back of the Third Reich.

Cooperation between Washington and London became more and

more important as the war progressed. On December 22, 1941, Churchill came to Washington to persuade the American president to concentrate on defeating Hitler before turning his full attention to Japan. A few weeks later the representatives of twenty-six nations met in Washington to endorse the Atlantic Charter and to sign the declaration of the United Nations calling for a unified effort to rid the world of German and Japanese aggression. However, the new allies soon fell into serious disagreement. From Moscow, Stalin pressed America to open a second front in the West as soon as possible to relieve pressure on the besieged Red Army. The Americans agreed and tried to persuade the British to support an early invasion of Europe. However, the English military, led by General Alan Brooke, favored victory in North Africa, coupled with intense bombardment of Germany, and, when the forces of the Third Reich had shown signs of weakness, an invasion of France. The Americans, led by General George Marshall, favored Operation Sledgehammer, an invasion of Europe in 1942. When the leaders of the two forces met in London on April 8, 1942, the British persuaded their allies that the time was not right for an invasion and that they should concentrate on North Africa instead.

However, Stalin continued to pressure his allies to open a second front. On August 12, 1942, Churchill and Averell Harriman, Roosevelt's representative, met with Stalin in Moscow. The British prime minister responded, when the Russian dictator asked for relief, that his forces were not prepared and that a premature invasion would lead to disaster. Discussion of the issue continued throughout the next year; time after time the Americans tried to convince the British to open an invasion of France, and time after time the English refused to move until all preparations had been made.

The Americans saw their first action in North Africa, where the German Afrika Korps, led by Field Marshal Erwin Rommel, was locked in a bitter struggle with the British, led by Bernard Montgomery. Rommel was one of the most important and colorful generals of the Second World War. Unlike the traditional German officer, Rommel was from southern Germany, having been born in Heidenheim in Württemberg on November 15, 1891. During the First World War he won fame for a smashing defeat of the Italians in 1917, and after the armistice, Rommel remained in the army. In 1935, while at the War Academy in Potsdam, he helped train a group of Hitler Youth. Although he resigned in protest of the effort to indoctrinate the youth, he became commander of a unit of Hitler's bodyguard in 1938.

Although Rommel was at first an enthusiastic follower of the führer, he later supported the plot to rid the German people of this menace. During the campaign in France he fought bravely, and in 1941 he went to North Africa to command the German forces that took the place of the defeated Italians.

Rommel's brilliant leadership and daring escapades won him the title the "desert fox." Pounding the British, who had sent some of their troops to Greece, Rommel's forces devastated their foes and swept across the desert, reaching El Alamein, on the border of Egypt, on July 1, 1941; there they awaited Hitler's order to march on Cairo and the Suez Canal. The British were frantic. Unless they drove the Germans back, they might lose one of their most important links with their Asian empire. Taking advantage of Hitler's preoccupation with Russia, the desperate English launched a major offensive against Rommel on December 11, 1941. This time, the German commander, with some of his most valuable men having been transferred to the Russian Front, was no match for the determined British. Throwing every available man and weapon into the fray, the British surprised the Germans and their commander, who was in Germany with his family when the campaign opened. After fierce fighting they drove the nazi forces back through the desert, capturing the fortress of Tobruk on December 20.

However, the determined German commander refused to allow the setback of 1941 to destroy his army. He spent the winter reorganizing his men and preparing for a major attack to open on May 27. Once again he cut through the British forces. At El Adem, Rommel tricked the British commanded by Claude Auchinleck into attacking a group of his tanks, trapping them in a position ringed with his cannon. Although Auchinleck had learned of Rommel's plans through Ultra, he was not aware of the source of his information and decided to disregard it, which caused him to suffer a major defeat. After El Adem the British could do little but retreat, desperately trying to prevent a German breakthrough to Cairo.

Rommel swept across the undefended desert and again stood at El Alamein, only seventy miles from Alexandria. Meeting stiff resistance, he moved his forces to Alam Halfa, leaving fake tanks and trucks to fool the British. He planned to cut through the English defenses at Alam Halfa and then move north to the Mediterranean. However, the British intercepted his messages and quickly placed reinforcements across his path. They also utilized radio equipment and

The Fall of Fortress Europe 311

a code captured from John Eppler and Peter Monkaster, Rommel's spies in Cairo, to send false reports that led the "desert fox" to believe that British defenses at Alam Halfa would present no serious challenge. The crafty English managed to allow the Germans to capture a fake map of the terrain of the area to be attacked to complete their deception. On the night of August 30 the nazi commander ordered his men to begin the offensive, but no sooner had they begun than the R.A.F. swept down from the air to blast the Germans, knocking a badly needed tank unit out of the campaign. Still, the nazi army pressed on, meeting stiff resistance instead of the small group of English soldiers the fake messages had led Rommel to expect. Despite heavy losses, Rommel refused to halt the offensive. He ordered his men to move to the north of Montgomery's forces, but instead of the rocky terrain the captured fake map indicated, the Germans found deep sand that quickly halted their advance and ended the attack. Rommel had lost five thousand men and fifty tanks, and the Germans had met a major defeat at the hands of the clever British.

Throughout the summer, Montgomery prepared for Operation Lightfoot, the campaign to drive the Germans from North Africa. In a masterpiece of deception, the British concealed their increased forces along the German lines by covering their tanks with mock wooden trucks. At the same time, they built a fake supply depot and assembled a force of dummy tanks poised for a thrust in the south. Meanwhile, Rommel, aware that his supplies could not withstand a British offensive, flew to Hitler's headquarters in Russia to beg for additional fuel and equipment.

The British launched their offensive on October 23, 1942. Suddenly, their artillery shattered the calm of the desert night, and the burst of their shells on the unsuspecting Germans cast a red glow above the sandy wasteland. To further weaken the German defenses in the north, the English staged a fake attack on the Mediterranean. General George Stumme, unable to meet the British thrust because his best forces had moved to the south to await an attack that never materialized, rushed badly needed forces to the sea while the Luftwaffe bombarded the beaches. When the smoke cleared, the astonished Germans found no English troops, but only a few rubber rafts carrying smoke bombs and record players producing the sounds of battle. The deception had worked. The Germans had been defeated, and the English began the march across the North African desert.[8]

Rommel, who had been vacationing in the clean air and majestic scenery of the Austrian Alps, frantically returned to the scene of battle after stopping in Rome to beg for needed fuel and ammunition. However, warned by Ultra of the shipment, R.A.F. forces, operating from Malta, shattered the supply convoy, sending the supplies to the bottom of the Mediterranean. Deprived of the gasoline necessary to power his tanks and the shells to resist the British onslaught, Rommel organized his men and fought with all his might. But he could not halt the oncoming British, who constantly pounded his forces. Finally, on November 12, 1942, the "desert fox" ordered his men to begin the retreat. Leaving behind a trail of broken tanks and sand stained with German blood, Rommel fled to Tripoli. But the British captured this strategic port on January 24, 1943, forcing the Germans to fortify themselves in Tunisia. Rommel realized that the destruction of his supply ships had been one of the major reasons for his defeat and demanded an investigation to learn how the British had been able to find them. London, aware of the threat to Ultra, caused false radio messages to be sent, in a code the Germans could decipher, thanking nonexistent agents in Italy for their help.

While the Germans were taking a beating from Montgomery, the Americans, led by General Dwight D. Eisenhower, landed in French Morocco on December 7, 1942, in one of the largest amphibious operations in the history of modern warfare. However, Petain's forces resisted the advancing Americans, who captured Casablanca, Oran, and Algiers only after bloody fighting. At a decisive moment, when the fate of the invasion hung in the balance, Admiral Jean-Francois Darlan, commander of the French in Algiers, ordered his men to lay down their arms and allow the Americans to pass. Hitler was furious at the French surrender and ordered his troops to occupy southern France and put an end to Petain's puppet regime. Although Eisenhower, grateful for Darlan's assistance, recognized the French admiral as head of the civilian government, the feuding French refused to recognize the authority of a man who had cooperated with the Germans. On December 24, 1942, they assassinated Darlan and organized a new government of North Africa under General Henri Giraud, who had escaped from a German prison. However, the removal of Darlan did not end the fighting among the French, for a force led by General Charles De Gaulle, the self-proclaimed head of the Free French, refused to recognize his government. The constant struggles between the various groups for domination of the French forces caused the Allies many problems in the coming months and greatly hampered their efforts to defeat the enemy.[9]

From Algiers the Americans marched to Tunis to assist Montgomery. Although the Allies clearly had the initiative in North Africa, Hitler refused to accept defeat. He immediately sent reinforcements and supplies and ordered his men to hold Tunis no matter what the cost. Hoping to break the Allied attack, the Germans gathered their depleted forces and began a massive operation against the Americans at Faid Pass on February 11. After an explosive confrontation that left the site of the battle at Kasserine Pass covered with the bodies of soldiers from both sides, the powerful Germans drove the shattered Americans from the field. The humiliation made Eisenhower's men more determined than ever to defeat their enemy. Four days later they returned and overpowered the Germans, forcing them to retreat. Meanwhile, the British had advanced on the Mareth Line, the German defense in southern Tunisia. Montgomery unmercifully pulverized the Germans, pouring every available man and weapon across the desolated battlefield and driving the enemy from their positions on March 30, 1943.

With the English moving on the Germans from the east and the Americans coming from the west, the nazi forces again attempted to halt the Allies. They fortified themselves on three strategically located hills at Mateur on the road to Bizerte. As they hurled their artillery at the Allies, Eisenhower ordered his valiant forces into the battle. The Americans stormed the most important hill in the face of overwhelming odds and heavy machinegun fire. As the Germans cut them down, the Americans kept coming, and after fierce hand-to-hand fighting the hill fell, and with it, the approach to Bizerte. Although a remnant of the nazi troops continued to fight, most of Hitler's men, realizing that further resistance would prove futile, surrendered. Finally, after a battle that had raged from Algiers to Egypt, the last tired German surrendered on May 15, 1943, and North Africa lay in the hands of the victorious Allies. Hitler had suffered another major defeat, losing men and supplies that might have prevented the disaster of Stalingrad.

While their forces achieved victory in North Africa, Churchill and Roosevelt met at Casablanca on January 12, 1943, to discuss their next move. Once again Marshall tried to convince Brooke to open the invasion of France that year, and once again the British refused to agree. The Allies consented to concentrate on Operation Husky, the invasion of Sicily. As the discussions came to a close, the two leaders met with reporters to publicly reaffirm their friendship. Suddenly, without prior consultation with Churchill, Roosevelt announced that they would accept nothing less than unconditional surrender from the Axis powers. The British prime minister was shocked but powerless to challenge his ally in front of the world. The American president's unilateral statement may have been one of the most unfortunate incidents of the war, for it dashed the hopes of British intelligence that the anti-nazis would overthrow Hitler in the belief that the Allies would open negotiations to end the war. Had Roosevelt not made his startling declaration, the conspiracy to get rid of Adolf Hitler might have gained desperately needed support and ended the bloodshed months earlier, saving thousands of lives. Instead, the president's ultimatum strengthened the führer's hold on the German people, who feared another Versailles.

After the last German had surrendered in Tunis, Montgomery and Eisenhower began planning the liberation of Sicily. Hitler fully expected an Anglo-American offensive in southern Europe and ordered his spies to try to discover the target. The British again deceived the master of the Third Reich. On April 30 they dropped a corpse in the sea off Huelva, Spain, carrying a briefcase carefully packed with letters and battle plans that indicated that the attack would come in Greece. The Spanish officials found the body and alerted German agents, who inspected the briefcase and reported to Berlin. A few days later the English allowed another body, dressed in a commando uniform, to wash up on the shore near Cagliari, Sardinia. The Germans who found the body fell for the trick and reported to their superiors that the Allies were planning to attack the island. Overjoyed that his agents had discovered the Allied plan, Hitler sent Rommel to Athens to face the expected invasion; a force of crack S.S. troops prepared to defend Sardinia.

While the Germans waited for an attack that would never come, the Americans and British prepared for the occupation of Sicily, the first step toward the invasion of Italy. On July 3, 1943, Allied aircraft swept from their bases to bomb enemy positions in Sardinia and Sicily, destroying airfields and forcing the enemy to move their heavy bombers to a safer location on the Italian mainland. Six days later, despite hostile weather that blew the Allied gliders off course, drowning many soldiers and scattering others, the British under Montgomery landed near Pachina. The Americans led by General George S. Patton, one of the most colorful and unpredictable commanders of the war, began an amphibious operation between Cape Scaramia and Licata. Faced with frantic fighting by the Germans defending the island, Patton led his men through the rough terrain of western Sicily to capture Palermo on July 22. Meanwhile, Montgomery moved up the eastern side of the island, encountering heavy resistance at Mount Etna. After the arrival of reinforcements, the British overwhelmed the enemy and rushed to Messina, which the Americans had taken on August 16. Sicily fell, and thus the liberation of Europe from the Nazis had begun.

The successful Allied invasion of Sicily ended the fascist dictatorship in Italy. Defeated in the Balkans, North Africa, and now a part of his own country, Mussolini was powerless to take decisive action. On July 19 he met with the furious German führer at Feltre. His health and spirits broken by his failure, the duce could do little but sit quietly while Hitler shouted at him for five hours about the necessity of resisting the Allies with every available man. However, Hitler's lecture had little effect, for on July 24, after a stormy session lasting ten hours, the fascist Grand Council voted to remove their leader and turn power over to King Victor Emmanuel III. The Italian monarch appointed General Pietro Badoglio head of the new government. Realizing the futility of further fighting, the new Italian leader immediately opened negotiations with the Allies. In accordance with Roosevelt's decree at Casablanca, they demanded unconditional surrender, and on September 3, powerless to resist, Badoglio agreed and asked only that the Allies delay the announcement to prevent a German invasion.

Hitler was caught by surprise by Mussolini's removal and demanded to know if he could count on the new Italian government to continue the fight. Keitel sent Canaris to Italy to study the situation. He met with General Cesare Ame, who begged him to deceive Hitler to prevent a German occupation of Italy. The anti-nazi commander of military intelligence agreed, and upon his return to Germany sent Keitel a report, signed by a subordinate to protect Canaris's position, that there was virtually no danger of an Italian surrender. However, Hitler knew that once Mussolini had fallen, it would be only a matter of time before Italy left the war. He ordered his forces to occupy Rome in Operation Student and the rest of Italy in Operation Black.

The German dictator also ordered his agents to rescue the fallen Italian leader and restore him to power by whatever means necessary in Operation Oak. For the next few weeks Hitler's men in Italy flooded Berlin with reports on Mussolini as Badoglio's government moved him from island to island in the Mediterranean. Finally, they put him in a hotel on top of the highest range of the Abruzzi Apennines, at Gran Sasso d'Italia. On September 13 Otto Skorzeny led a small group of specially selected S.S. men in one of the most daring actions of the war. Braving treacherous air currents that could have dashed their tiny gliders on the sides of the mountains, they landed near the inn. Overcoming the startled guards without firing a shot, they rescued the duce. With inches to spare, Skorzeny took off in a small plane and flew Mussolini to freedom. The next day, Mussolini, scarcely able to catch his breath after his dangerous escape, met with Hitler in his bunker at Rastenburg. There, at the führer's insistence, he announced the creation of a new fascist party and the birth of the Italian Social Republic. However, his new government restored only a shadow of his former greatness, for Mussolini never returned to Rome and took no active part in the remainder of the war. Guarded by S.S. troops, he set up his headquarters in Rocca della Caminate in the north and waited in vain for the day he could once again rule Italy.

While Hitler busied himself with the rescue of Mussolini and the occupation of Italy, the Allies prepared for the invasion of the Italian mainland. On September 3, the day that Badoglio's representative signed the armistice in an olive grove near Syracuse, the British crossed the Straits of Messina without serious incident. The Allies waited for word from Bletchley on the German response. Relieved, they learned that Field Marshal Albert Kesselring, Hitler's commander in Italy, expected the main invasion to come north of Naples and had withdrawn his forces from the south. Reassured by the lack of German wireless communications and believing that the enemy had not guessed that they would land at Salerno, the Allies sailed to the peaceful beach on September 9. However, the calm was deceptive, for General Heinrich von Veitinghoff's men had sighted the coming armada and had fortified the hills over the shore. Suddenly, after the Allies had barely reached their goal, hidden German artillery burst forth in a shower of fire and lead, scattering the defenseless troops. Frantically, the British ships blasted the German position. Overhead, Allied aircraft, able to remain above the fray a mere fifteen minutes before returning to their bases for fuel, bombarded the Germans. After several days of fighting, the German line broke, and the victorious Allies occupied Salerno. It had been a costly battle, but at last the Americans and British had breached Fortress Europe.

Without pausing, the Allies raced one hundred fifty miles to liberate Naples. Aware that they could not hold the historic city, the barbaric Germans looted Naples of all they could carry and destroyed the rest. In an orgy of destruction reminiscent of the descent of the Germanic hoard on the Roman Empire, the Nazis vented their revenge on the Italians. They burned libraries, destroying priceless books and manuscripts, plundered art collections, and blew up the water, gas, and electric systems. In a final act of barbarism, the retreating Germans placed time bombs in public places that exploded long after the battle had ceased, killing thousands of innocent civilians. On October 1 the British occupied the city, gaining their first taste of the terrible destruction that they would later encounter as they liberated Europe from the nazi tyranny.

Barely pausing to rest their tired troops, the Allies began the drive to Rome. However, Kesselring fortified his position on the Gustav Line, centering on Monte Cassino, the birthplace of Western monasticism under St. Benedict. There, below a place where hooded monks had once sung their praises to the Lord of Peace, the Allied advance ground to a halt. Throughout the winter, from their perch high above the once-quiet countryside, the Germans stopped each of their enemy's moves with a shower from of artillery shells. Although the Allies drove the Germans from other positions along the Gustav Line, they could not break through this position until Monte Cassino had fallen. Supported by heavy aerial bombardment that crashed through the frescoed ceilings of the great monastery, shattering art treasures and turning the shrine into a smouldering ruin, the Allies desperately strove to drive the Germans from their fortress. They tried on February 15, and again a month later, but, although some of their forces managed to scale part of the steep mountain, they failed. It seemed that the great armies that had driven Rommel from the North African desert, occupied Sicily, and liberated Naples had met defeat. Finally, on May 15, 1944, the Allies gathered their forces for the final assault. While overhead their air force blasted the Germans, the Allies surrounded the impregnable fortress. Then, in the face of German machine-gun fire, a force of valiant Poles, fighting to revenge the rape of their homeland, penetrated the enemy defenses. On May 18 Monte Cassino fell, freeing the Allies for the march to Rome.

Meanwhile, to outflank the German line, a force of 50,000 Allied troops, commanded by General John Porter Lucas, landed at Anzio, thirty miles south of Rome. He met with little resistance because

Kesselring, acting on information from Canaris, expected the invasion at Civitavecchia. Nevertheless, Lucas failed to take the initiative and capture Rome. Instead, he halted to organize his forces and fortify the beachhead. Lucas's pause gave Kesselring the opportunity he needed to rush his men to Anzio to surround the unsuspecting Americans. Throughout the next month the once-placid resort became a living hell as the two commanders hurled wave after wave of their best forces at each other. Finally, after one of the most violent battles in the war, the Allies broke through the German lines and cleared the way for the advance on Rome. Although Lucas's fortifications had saved his troops from annihilation, his superiors relieved him of his command, and he left in disgrace. With the impasse at Anzio broken and the Germans driven from Monte Cassino, the Allies were free to resume the march on Rome, which they entered on June 4 amid the cheers of the population and the peals of bells from the great churches. From Rome they pressed on to Florence, which they liberated on August 12. However, once again the Germans fell back on a fortified position, this time along the Po River, that the Allies failed to break until the final collapse of Germany, the next year. Despite the failure of the foes of the Third Reich to advance beyond the Po, they had captured Italy and freed the homeland of fascism from Hitler's grasp.

While the English and Americans fought the Germans in Italy, the Russians began an offensive to drive the last enemy troops from their homeland and relieve Leningrad. For two and a half years the Germans had besieged the city, trying to break the will of the people. Although hundreds of thousands died of starvation and much of their city lay in ruins, the brave people of Peter the Great's "window to the West" refused to yield.[10] On January 14, 1943, Colonel General I. I. Fedyunisky's forces broke out of Orienbaum, and the following day a force of the Red Army under General I. I. Maslennikov fell on the Germans from the Neva. Facing hostile weather and fierce opposition, the persistent Russians hit Hitler's army with determination. Eventually, the enemy line broke, and the siege of Leningrad ended. Meanwhile, on January 19, braving a violent blizzard to cross the frozen Ilmen, a group of Stalin's army surrounded the Germans in Novgorod. Despite the führer's order to never retreat, the Germans could not withstand the onslaught, and, leaving their wounded to the mercy of their captors, the Germans evacuated the city while the Russian air force blasted them from above. On January 28, aware that he had been defeated, General Georg von Küchler ordered his men to move back to the Luga. Although the furious führer immediately replaced him with Field Marshal Walter Model, the Germans could not hold the line, and on February 15 Hitler ordered his forces to evacuate northern Russia.

Meanwhile, in the south, the Russians were winning the battle for the Ukraine. On December 24, 1943, the Russians began a series of attacks on the German line on the Dnieper. Aided by rain and snow that turned the steppe into a sea of mush, preventing German movements, the Russians blasted their enemy with artillery and aerial bombardment. Using oxen and horses to drag their tanks and trucks through the mud and peasants to move their supplies, the Red Army fell on the Germans, who fought behind the remains of shattered villages or in icy trenches. After some of the bloodiest fighting of the war, the German line broke and Hitler's troops fled in disorder, abandoning their heavy weapons and tanks. The Red Army encircled the last major group of German soldiers at Korsun and demanded their surrender on February 10, 1944. Hitler, who had personally assumed direction of his troops, ordered them to fight to the last man. The Luftwaffe dropped supplies to the desperate men while a relief force fought through the Russian winter to save the besieged army. Although the Germans broke through the Russian lines and rescued the bulk of their men at Korsun, the battle had been lost. All Hitler's army could do was retreat to a more defensible position. Throughout the next month the Russians blasted the enemy, crossing the Bug River on March 15. On April 10 they liberated Odessa, the last German foothold in the Ukraine. Stalin's victorious troops then turned on the Germans in Crimea, freeing Sevastopol on May 9. Thus, the Russians drove the enemy from their homeland and began the march to Berlin.

While the battle raged without ceasing on the Continent, another equally important confrontation took place in the icy waters of the North Atlantic. Since the beginning of the war, the relentless warfare of Admiral Karl Dönitz's wolfpack of submarines had sent thousands of tons of vital supplies destined for England to the bottom of the ocean. Although the Allies knew the location of Dönitz's forces through Ultra and ordered their convoys to take evasive action, the Germans continued to sink Allied shipping and threatened to cut Britain's lifeline. The Germans had broken the Allied shipping code, and they, too, knew the position of their enemy. In addition, each submarine had a device that warned it of approaching aircraft by detecting the aircraft's radar signals. In May 1943 the Allies changed their shipping code, robbing Dönitz of one of his chief weapons. The Allies also equipped their planes with a new type of radar that the Germans could not detect. Armed with the location of the German submarines through Ultra, American aircraft from Iceland and Greenland swept down undetected on the enemy submarines, forcing Dönitz to withdraw the bulk of his forces to the safety of their home ports. The German stranglehold on the Atlantic had been broken.

Meanwhile, German battleships threatened to drive Allied shipping carrying supplies to the Russians at Murmansk from the seas. The British had successfully used Ultra to hunt and destroy the *Bismarck* on May 27, 1941, after one of the most thrilling chases in the history of warfare, but the *Scharnhorst, Lützow,* and the *Tirpitz* continued to threaten Allied shipping. The British attacked these three battleships when they lay in port at Alta Fjord on September 21 with specially designed minisubmarines, crippling the *Tirpitz.* When the *Lützow* returned to Germany in December 1943, the British launched a determined effort to find and destroy the *Scharnhorst.* Led by the *Duke of York,* the British navy set out on one of the most important operations of the war at sea. Utilizing radar to find their foe and a fog cover to sneak into position, the British sank the German ship on December 26, 1943. The threat to Allied shipping had been removed, and the Battle of the Atlantic had ended in victory for Hitler's enemies.

With success in southern Italy, in the Atlantic, and in Russia, the Allies finally were ready to concentrate on the long-awaited invasion of France, called Operation Overlord. Under Eisenhower's able command, Hitler's foes gathered the largest armada ever assembled. The Americans, free at last to pour supplies across the Atlantic, shipped several million tons of materials. They organized a force of 10,000 planes and 80 ships, carrying 800 guns, to bombard the enemy positions in preparation for the liberation of the French people from the Nazis. They built a force of 130,000 men and provided them with 4,000 vessels to carry them and their supplies.

While Eisenhower, the commander of Supreme Headquarters of the Allied Expeditionary Force (SHAEF), concentrated on the preparations for Operation Neptune, the invasion of Normandy, Allied intelligence was busy with one of the most fantastic deceptions in the history of warfare, Operation Bodyguard, to convince Hitler that the invasion would come in Norway and Calais. A phantom force in Scotland, complete with a commander and false wireless traffic, posed for the offensive in Scandinavia. In southern England, under the command of General George Patton, the officer Hitler believed would lead the invasion, the Allies created another false army in position to invade Calais. Utilizing all available means, including false radio messages from double agents like Tricycle, Allied intelligence provided the Germans with a complete battle plan for the offensive in Calais. A method was devised to amplify radar echos to convince the Germans that a mighty air force was preparing for an attack, while the real force went elsewhere. Bodyguard was a complete success, for Hitler concentrated his strongest defenses at Calais to wait for the invasion that never came.[11]

The Allies also tricked Hitler into believing that the attack could not possibly come in June 1944. They captured German weather stations in the North Atlantic and provided false weather reports to convince the führer that conditions prevented an offensive in June. This guise was also a complete success. On May 30 Field Marshal Gerd von Rundstedt informed the führer that the offensive was weeks away. On June 4, two days before the day of Operation Overlord, D-Day, the Luftwaffe meteorologist in Paris predicted that weather would force the Allies to postpone any planned invasion for at least two weeks. The next day Rommel, the commander of Hitler's fortifications on the coast of France, assured Rundstedt that the Allies could not possibly take action for at least a week and left for a vacation with his family in Germany.

While Hitler and his generals rested, the Allies began their invasion on June 6, 1944. Despite hostile weather, which nearly caused the postponement of the attack, Eisenhower's forces boarded their transports and began the voyage to Normandy. The attack opened with heavy bombardment from ships and aircraft as the nervous troops slowly crept toward the beaches. Although the Germans had sunk six-pronged iron spikes into the shallow water, catching many landing craft, the determined soldiers disembarked on a front stretching from Cabourg to La Madeleine. Once again the Allies managed to surprise the masters of the Third Reich, for not only did Hitler expect the invasion to come at Calais, but also he expected it to come at a port. Instead, the English, Canadian, and American troops landed on open beaches. The bulk of the invading force met with token resistance and quickly established the beachheads. However, the Americans landing at Omaha Beach near Vierville scrambled on land in the face of fierce German fire from the cliffs commanding the area. All day they fought, facing overwhelming odds. Inch by inch the valiant Americans crept up the beach, until, by late afternoon, they had climbed the steep cliffs and destroyed the enemy pillboxes. When D-Day ended, the Allies had gained a foothold in France and had begun the liberation of the West.[12]

Despite the Allied landing at Normandy, the Germans continued to believe that the major invasion would come at Calais. Rundstedt frantically telephoned Hitler's headquarters to inform him of the attack. However, Admiral Karl von Puttkammer, Hitler's aide, told Rundstedt that he could not disturb the sleeping leader to tell him that the Allies had launched a diversionary action. The shocked commander, realizing the gravity of the situation, ordered reinforcements to rush from Calais to meet the threat, but Jodl intervened in the name of the sleeping führer to prevent the movement. With the bulk of the German forces sitting at Calais, waiting for an invasion that would never come, the Allies secured their beachheads and prepared for the march to Paris. Finally, the Germans realized that they had been deceived, but by that time it was too late to drive the Allies back into the sea.

After overcoming stiff German resistance, the Americans regrouped their forces and struck westward across the Norman peninsula to Cherbourg. The Germans, ordered by Hitler to hold the port at all costs, fought the Americans under General Omar Bradley with every available man and weapon. Striving to hold every square foot of the city, they fortified themselves in houses, cellars, and behind stone fences to resist the attack. Finally, on June 26, after four days of bloody fighting, Bradley's forces captured the city. For the next few weeks the Allies poured men and supplies through Cherbourg and gathered their strength for the destruction of the German army in France.

On June 6, 1944, the tide turned in the West as it had on January 31, 1943, at Stalingrad, in the East. Hitler's stranglehold on Europe was broken. The Russians had devastated the Germans near Leningrad and in the Ukraine and had begun the march to Warsaw. The Allies had driven the German submarines from the Atlantic and now had gained a foothold in France. Hitler had fallen prey to the Allies because he had been secure in the belief that he knew their plans and had bottled up his forces in Calais while the Allies landed in Normandy. The Germans had lost the war. Within a few weeks a group of generals would try to eliminate Hitler and free the German people of the nazi tyranny. Although a year of hard fighting lay ahead of the Allies, they had broken the back of the Axis and could find comfort in the knowledge that it was only a matter of time until their victorious troops would march through the streets of Berlin.

19

The New Order in Europe

The war that raged from North Africa to the North Cape and from Stalingrad to Normandy left millions dead and great cities devastated. Yet the destruction of the war was but one aspect of the terror that Hitler and his followers unleashed on the world. Every man, woman, and child of Germany and the occupied countries felt the full brunt of the nazi terror. When most people think about Adolf Hitler and nazi Germany, their thoughts turn toward the photographs taken by American and English troops of piles of dead bodies after the liberation of the concentration camps. Yet the gruesome image of thousands of emaciated and mutilated corpses tells only a small part of the story of the nazi holocaust. After German troops marched into Poland in 1939, the führer and his associates planned one of the greatest crimes in history—the enslavement of Europe and the destruction of whole races of people. The nazi plan was to bring a "New Order in Europe" in which the "superior" Aryan race would rule over the "inferior" non-Aryan peoples, and the Slavic peoples of the East would be driven from their land to provide living space for the super race. The story of this effort forms one of the darkest chapters in modern history, a time when men reached new depths of degeneracy through acts no civilized person would have thought possible before the Third Reich. However, not all were swayed by the fanatical speeches of Hitler and the propaganda of Goebbels. A few valiant men and women realized the true nature of national socialism and vowed to stop the war and drive the führer and his mad associates from power. Unfortunately, they did not succeed, and the Nazis rewarded their courage with more atrocities.

In the wake of the victorious German army, the S.S. of Himmler entered and established a reign of terror. The leader of the S.S. enlarged his forces from 73,000 in May 1941 to 147,000 the next year. At first the men in black shirts fought alongside the regular army, but after the destruction of Poland, special, separate S.S. units were developed to act as an arm of the Nazi tyranny.

The people of Poland were the first to feel the full weight of the "New Order." The German Reich tore Posen, Silesia, and the former Polish Corridor from the Slavic state and annexed them. In these unfortunate areas, 1.2 million Poles and 300,000 Jews lost their homes and belongings to make room for the resettlement of the land by Germans. The transport of these peoples in the severe winter of 1939–1940, without regard for their comfort or safety, left a trail of death that was not even exceeded by the effectiveness of firing squads and gallows.

The nazi rulers, not content with annexing large areas from the once-proud Polish state, placed what was left under the arch-criminal Hans Frank. Frank enforced a rule of terror that left the Polish cities smouldering in heaps of rubble and farmlands wasted, with a Polish population only a fraction of what it had been before the war. On October 26, 1939, barely after the cannon and machine-gun fire had died, the nazi masters of Poland ordered all Polish men and women from eighteen to sixty to work in factories producing the materials necessary to bring still more people under the power of the Nazis. By 1942 the Germans had forced over a million Poles to leave their homeland and families to work in the plants of the Reich.

Other peoples under nazi domination shared the fate of the Poles. France lost Alsace-Lorraine, and Slovenia lost Lower Styria and part of Carniola. Each of the occupied lands was under nazi rule, although the German yoke was less severe in the West than in the East. Collaborators like the Norwegian turncoat Vidkun Quisling governed under German supervision in Holland and Norway. Military governors ruled Belgium and occupied France, and a Reich plenipotentiary controlled the government of Denmark.[1]

In each of these areas the people made a gallant effort to defy their German rulers. At first the communist parties in the conquered lands refused to enter the conflict, condemning the war as imperialistic and following the Moscow line of noninvolvement. However, after the German attack on the Soviet Union on June 22, 1941, this policy ended, and the communist organizations became centers of resistance.

They revived the Popular Front activities of the 1930s and joined other anti-nazi forces to carry on a campaign of sabotage designed to harass their German captors. Even in weak Denmark, the brave and proud Danish people did their best to pester their nazi rulers. The Germans once ordered the Danes to provide butter and steel for the Teutonic war effort. Deciding to fulfill the command in the most economical fashion, the clever Danes mixed slivers of metal in the butter. When the S.S. ordered the Danish Jews to wear the yellow Star of David, King Frederick IX, a Lutheran, appeared in public wearing the sign. His faithful subjects followed his example, causing great confusion for their overlords.

Hitler's Germany did not let such acts of defiance pass unnoticed. One of the great atrocities of the war took place in occupied Bohemia. On the warm spring day of May 29, 1942, Reinhard Heydrich, the Reich vice-protector of Bohemia and Moravia and head of the Security Service of the S.S., rode in the open air in his Mercedes convertible on his way from his country residence to his office in Prague. Hiding behind the bushes beside the road, Jan Kubis and Josef Gabeik, members of the Free Czechoslovak Army in England who had parachuted into their homeland from an R.A.F. plane, waited for the nazi official to arrive. When he passed, they threw a bomb into the open car that exploded and shattered his spine. Heydrich died six hours later. The Germans responded savagely, rounding up and immediately shooting 1,331 Czechs and taking 3,000 Czech Jews to the concentration camps. Kubis and Gabeik fled to Prague after the explosion, and together with 120 members of the resistance sought refuge in Karl Borromeus Eastern Orthodox Church. Showing no respect for the sacred structure in their search for vengeance, the S.S. stormed the church and slaughtered all those found inside.

The most brutal retaliation for the assassination of Heydrich took place in the small village of Lidice. Early on the morning of June 9, 1942, Captain Max Rostock arrived with ten truckloads of S.S. men and surrounded the peaceful hamlet. He announced that no one would be allowed to leave and brutally killed a young boy who panicked and tried to run through the fields. Then he locked the men in the mayor's barn, stables, and cellar. Throughout the rest of the day, the men were led in groups of ten before firing squads. By the time the smoke had cleared, the blood of 172 men had been splattered on the roses in the mayor's garden. After the women were forced to stand by while their husbands and fathers were killed, the nazis packed them into boxcars for the long ride to concentration camps, where most of them died. Four pregnant women, ready to give birth, went under force to Prague to have their babies. When the babies were born, the S.S. tore the infants from their mother's arms and shot them. They then sent the terrified women to join their mothers and sisters. S.S. physicians examined the remaining children and sent those with "Aryan" characteristics to Germany to be Germanized. Infants without the correct hair and eye color and shape of the head met the same fate as their fathers and brothers under the fire of German rifles. In a ghastly conclusion to the slaughter, the Nazis burned Lidice to the ground and dynamited the ruins. They completed their terrible deed by leveling the site, reducing the once-happy village to a cleared mound of dirt.

The atrocity of Lidice was but one of many such incidents. On June 10, 1942, a detachment of S.S. men surrounded the French village of Oradour-sur-Glane. They ordered the horrified inhabitants to gather in the central plaza, where they learned that their homes were being searched for explosives said to be stored there by the underground. The Germans herded the men into barns and forced their wives and children to go into the small church. Shortly thereafter, the Nazi assassins turned the hamlet into a flaming inferno. The men who survived the fire met their death from the bullets of machine guns. Then the Teutonic invaders turned their wrath on the screaming women and children in the church. After firing on them with their weapons, they applied the torch to the building, creating a blazing tomb. In all, 642 men, women, and children died at Oradour-sur-Glane. Only ten badly burned villagers survived by pretending to be dead. Today, only the smoke-scarred remain of the church reminds the visitor that a town once stood on the spot.

The liquidation of whole villages by the Nazis was minor compared to other German acts of terror. In one of the most heartless schemes, the masters of the New Order in Europe tore countless children from their parents and sent them to the fatherland to be brought up as members of the master race. In many areas S.S. officials took children from their crying mothers and sent them to special examination stations. Here, physicians checked the slope of the nose, the color of the eyes, hair, and skin, and the size of the head. Like the children of Lidice, those who passed the test were separated from their families and sent to the Reich for forced Germanization. The brave children who refused to turn their backs on their families and nationality by adopting the language and customs of their captors met the fate of all who opposed the Nazis—death. No one knows how many children the S.S. forced to leave their homes, but in Poland alone about 200,000 parents lost their children. Even today, long after most people have forgotten the full meaning of the nazi hell, heartbroken parents still search for their lost children, and many children still try to find their parents.

As if destroying whole villages and stealing children from their parents were not enough, the nazi masters of captive Europe imprisoned millions of conquered citizens—Jews, Slavs, Gypsies, and even Germans—in inhumane conditions in the concentration camps. As the nazi tyranny expanded into other countries, it brought with it the dreaded Death Head units and their camps. By 1940 these practitioners of systematic enslavement ruled twenty concentration camps with 165 affiliated labor camps. In addition to the larger establishments, many local S.S. and Gestapo officials set up detention centers that were smaller imitations of the larger camps.[2]

The largest and most heinous part of the new S.S. empire was Auschwitz in Poland. Here, Rudolf Höss, a graduate of Dachau, reigned with the support of a detachment of fanatical members of the Death's Head unit. Höss's kingdom consisted of the main compound, with thousands of prisoners living in unsanitary and poorly heated buildings with little food, and thirty-nine subcamps scattered around the Polish countryside. In many of these satellites, prisoners slaved in factories, such as the I. G. Farben works at Bund which produced synthetic rubber. Although those lucky enough to receive assignment to the slave-labor camps escaped the most terrible aspects of life in the concentration camps, conditions were so poor that 60 percent of them died before the liberation of the camps by Allied troops at the end of the war. The millions of foreign workers who labored in regular German factories under Speer's Ministry of Arms and Munitions fared much better than the inmates of the labor camps controlled by the S.S.

So great was the Nazis' contempt for the life of the inmates of the concentration camps that they established special medical experimental stations in several camps, where a small group of about two hundred villainous S.S. physicians used prisoners as human guinea pigs. The accounts of this "scientific" research were rife with reports of the doctors' complete lack of regard for the feelings and health of the victims. In one study of the effect of high and low pressure on the human body, living prisoners were placed in pressure chambers. The prisoners were then subjected to high-altitude tests to see how much the human body could endure before being rendered lifeless. The helpless men and women were also injected with doses of typhus and jaundice so that the effects of these diseases could be studied. To understand the impact of cold and frostbite on the human physique, prisoners were forced to stand naked in the snow or to swim in ice water.

The chronicle of nazi atrocities against prisoners also included experiments to develop new weapons and methods of surgery. The researchers shot their victims with poison bullets or forced them to breathe mustard gas in order to develop new arms for the nazi attack on civilized man. In Ravensbrück, S.S. experimenters gave gas gangrene wounds to hundreds of Polish girls, who were called "rabbit girls" because of the effect of the infection on their appearance. Other physicians grafted bones onto the bodies of prisoners to study the effects of bone transplants on the human body. In Dachau and Buchenwald, Gypsies were forced to live on salt water to study the effects of dehydration. Other experiments were concerned with the development of quick and cheap methods of sterilization to destroy inferior races. The men conducting these butcherings never considered the comfort and pain of their subjects and rarely used anesthesia or sterilized instruments.

Never has science sunk to a lower level as in the nazi experiments on human subjects. Here one sees in all its terrible ramifications, the results of a political system that disregarded all traditional morality in an attempt to conquer Europe for a "superior" race and one that regarded all other peoples as subhuman and worthy only of service to the "master" race. The moral sickness even infected such men as Professor August Hirt, head of the Anatomical Institute of the University of Strasbourg. This academician wished to collect a set of human skulls for his work. However, since diseased or marred specimens were not satisfactory, and the heads of the war dead were not acceptable, Hirt persuaded the S.S. to support his work, and hundreds of prisoners of Auschwitz met their death in the name of science. After killing the subjects, the S.S. men placed the still warm heads in airtight containers and sent them to Hirt's laboratory in Strasbourg. During the Second World War the Germans committed countless atrocities against the inmates of the concentration camps. Ilse Koch, the wife of the commandant of Buchenwald, had defenseless prisoners killed so she could turn their skins into lampshades. Some

S.S. guards even made shrunken heads after murdering their charges. While the above crimes were conducted against the peoples of all races, the Nazis saved a special fate for the Jews. From its beginning, national socialism preached hateful anti-Semitism, and after 1933 it created a prisonlike environment for the German Jews. After 1939 this persecution included the Jews of other nations. The violent anti-Jewish campaign grew until it reached its horrible climax in the death camps. On September 1, 1939, Hitler laid the foundation for what was to come by ordering that all hospitals be cleared of all "incurable" cases to make room for the wounded from the front. Through an organized program of "mercy" killing, Hitler's henchmen slaughtered more than 100,000 of their own people. Christian Wirt, the chief of the criminal police of Stuttgart, developed an especially effective technique for carrying out this program; he sent his victims to their deaths in gas chambers. Once the Nazis had laid down the principle that the state had the right to determine which of its people had the right to live, it was not a great step to the murder of "inferior" races.

Hitler was obsessed with his hatred for the Jews and vowed to drive them from Europe. He even toyed with the idea of sending them to Madagascar, but the outbreak of the war prevented him from taking serious steps in this direction. Unable to force the Jews to leave Europe because of the naval blockade of the Reich, the Nazis decided to force them from their homes to areas where they could be more easily controlled. On September 21, 1939, Reinhard Heydrich, the head of the Security Police, ordered the establishment of a Council of Jewish Elders in all Jewish communities. These bodies of twenty-four male Jews were required to make lists of all Jews living in their area and to enforce the decrees of their nazi overlords. Heydrich also decreed that all Jewish communities of less than fifty be eliminated and their citizens be moved to special ghettos. Eventually, the Nazis founded ghettos in the Polish cities of Lodz, Warsaw, Cracow, Lublin, Radom, and Lvov. Here the captives lived like prisoners in areas fenced off from the rest of the city and posted with signs forbidding non-Jews to enter. Even those Jews not immediately sent to the ghettos felt the weight of nazi persecution. On August 13, 1941, the nazi conquerors of the Baltic States required all Jews living there to wear a yellow Star of David with the word Jew printed in the center in black letters. The officials also prevented Jews from using public transportation, walking on sidewalks or even attending theaters and museums. By the end of 1941 the Nazis had enforced similar restrictions on the

Jews of all the conquered territories. Naturally, many tried to flee the persecution. However, the Nazis were so dedicated to their campaign of intimidation that they refused to allow the Jews to escape by merely leaving behind their homes and possessions. On May 20, 1941, Berlin ordered the Security Police in Belgium and France to take any steps necessary to halt Jewish emigration. Yet most of the Jews made little effort to resist their captors and went quietly to their fate.

By itself, the mass deportation of millions from their homes would have been one of the most terrible crimes in history, but it was only a foreshadowing of the fate awaiting the Jews. Hitler and his followers depicted the war as the result of a Jewish conspiracy to destroy Germany. He blamed them for its outbreak, the refusal of the Soviet Union to join the Axis, and finally for the decision of the Americans to aid his enemies. Therefore, the führer vowed to seek a terrible revenge against what his diseased mind considered his chief foes. Already, on January 30, 1939, before the beginning of the war, Hitler had told the Reichstag that if the Jews forced Germany to fight a world war, they would pay with their lives.

The invasion of the Soviet Union, with its large Jewish population, provided the Nazis with a new opportunity to carry out their campaign against the Jews. Even before the invasion, Heydrich organized special groups of *Einsatzgruppen,* or occupation units, to search out and destroy all potential opposition to German rule. Divided into four units of three thousand men each, the Einsatzgruppen followed the army to enforce Hitler's rule in occupied areas. At first these murderers gathered all Jews, Communists, or other potential enemies, stripped them of their clothes, stood them at the edges of ditches, and slaughtered them with machine-gun fire. They then threw the corpses into mass graves of five hundred or one thousand and covered them with dirt and lime. However, this method of extermination failed to kill the Jews quickly enough, and the Nazis decided to seek a more efficient method. Utilizing the methods developed by Wirt for the euthanasia program, the S.S. pioneered a new system of mass murder at Chelmo, near Lodz, Poland, in December 1941. They told unsuspecting victims to get into vans for a ride to baths. However, these wagons of destruction did not take the people to wash off the dirt and grime of their imprisonment, but instead to death; the driver recycled the exhaust of the motor into the van, killing the entrapped Jews with carbon monoxide. In these death vehicles, about 150,000 men, women, and children lost their lives. In all, the Einsatzgruppen killed almost a million people; 229,052 in the Baltic alone and at least 150,000 in the Ukraine.

It soon became apparent to the Nazis that such an extensive campaign against the Jews required an effective organization. Therefore, on July 31, 1941, Göring ordered Heydrich to coordinate the "Final Solution of the Jewish Problem." After several delays, the head of the Security Police met with his aides at the former headquarters of the international police at Wannsee, a suburb of Berlin. Here, surrounded by the lakes and forests of one of the most popular resorts near the capital city, they hatched the plot to destroy the Jewish people. The first act of this heinous crime was to speed up the campaign to force all Jews in Germany and occupied areas to gather in the ghettos. Here, those able to work were separated according to sex and formed into labor gangs for drudgery in factories producing materials for use by the German war machine. The few who were strong enough to survive the work details would be eventually eliminated lest they live and form the new nucleus of the Jewish race. At Wannsee, Heydrich and his advisers planned the construction of a new ghetto in the northern Bohemian city of Theresienstadt as a detention camp for all Jews over sixty-five. Eventually, 141,000 German, Czech, and Dutch Jews traded their homes and families for the prison of Theresienstadt. Of these, only 16 percent lived to see the fall of Hitler. The chief architect of the success of this old folk's ghetto was Adolf Eichmann, the leader of the section of the Gestapo responsible for Jewish affairs. Working under Ernst Kaltenbrunner, the former head of the Austrian branch of the S.S. and Heydrich's successor, Eichmann promised elderly Jews food, living quarters, and medical care if they would sign over assets to the Reich and move willingly to Theresienstadt. Many unsuspecting Jews fell victim to this swindle and left their homes for the dismal abyss awaiting them in the camp.

After the Wannsee Conference the Nazis struck, swiftly rounding up Jews at a moment's notice for the trip east. This journey in unsanitary and unheated boxcars full of terrified people was almost as bad as the fate awaiting the victims at their final destination. They often traveled weeks without food or water, in the middle of winter, amid the stench of the bodies of those who died en route. Teams of S.S. Einsatzgruppen combed Nazi held countries, gathering Jews for transport. Adolf Eichmann personally supervised the mass deportation of hundreds of thousands from Slovakia, Hungary, Croatia, and Rumania. In 1945, after the dust and smoke of the war had settled, between 68 and 72 percent of the 8,309,000 Jews in Eastern and Western Europe before the holocaust had lost their lives.

During the roundup or after the trip, the Nazis killed those unfortunate enough to be judged unworthy of the work camps. At first they shot their victims or killed them in the vans. However, in March 1942, at Belzec, the enterprising S.S. introduced an even more horrible and impersonal method of murder; the gas chamber developed as a part of the euthanasia program. Soon, other camps followed the example, and gas chambers sprang up at Kulmhof, Sobobir, Lublin, and Treblinka, where as many as 800,000 persons died in only six months in chambers that killed 200 people at one time. The Nazis even decided to improve on this system and constructed large chambers at Auschwitz-Birkenau that could kill as many as two thousand persons at one time. As the victims arrived at the largest camp, S.S. detachments and camp officials separated prisoners able to work from their weaker comrades before they left the platform of the station. The unsuspecting Jews judged unworthy of the work camps were then told that they were being taken to bathhouses before assignment to their final place of confinement. Rudolf Höss, the commandant of the camp, introduced this clever ruse to avoid panic and riots by terrified Jews fighting for their lives, as had occurred at other camps. The commandant of Auschwitz disguised the death chambers as large shower rooms and surrounded them with well-kept lawns and flower beds. A special orchestra of young girls, clad in white blouses and navy blue skirts, lulled the Jews into a false sense of security by playing tunes from operettas and waltzes by Strauss. After the Jews arrived at the bathhouses, the emotionless S.S. guards ordered the bathers to undress and gave some of them towels to continue the masquerade. The demented Höss even equipped the death chambers with fake shower heads to conceal their true purpose. Only after the hermetically sealed door had been closed and hydrogen cyanide or Zyklon B, originally used as a strong disinfectant or insecticide, seeped through the air vents did the Jews realize their true fate.

Outside, the S.S. officials watched the terrified mass of human beings tear at the doors and at each other with their bare hands in a futile effort to escape. Even the strong doors and thick walls could not soften the pandemonium of the dying Jews screaming for help and with fear while the hissing gas snuffed out the life in their emaciated bodies. Finally, after the last cry had died, the ventilating system blew the gas from the room. Then, in a final act of inhumanity, squads of Jewish males who had been promised their lives in return for cooperation in the destruction of their brothers and sisters entered the death chamber. Clad in gas masks and heavy boots, they washed the blood from the lifeless bodies and tore the corpses apart with sharp hooks. Then they removed the gold from the teeth of the bodies to fill the nazi treasury and shaved the heads and bodies of the victims for future use in cloth and mattresses.

After salvaging all of possible use to the Nazi war machine, the Death's Head units loaded the remaining corpses on special wagons and took them to furnaces to be burned. After the ovens cooled, they made one more search for gold from their victims and then ground the ashes, completing their deed by dumping the dust that had once been the bodies of human beings into the waters of the Sola. Sometimes they saved the ashes to be made into fertilizer. One enterprising firm in Danzig even perfected a process for making soap from human fat. According to Höss's testimony at the Nuremberg Trials, at least 2.5 million persons died in the gas chambers at Auschwitz alone. Another half a million died of starvation and illness. In all of the camps, the "final solution" led to the death of between four and six million Jews, as well as countless Poles, Russians, and Gypsies.

Not all Jews were willing to succumb to their captors without a fight. In Warsaw and other ghettos, the Jews gathered weapons and prepared for their defense. On January 18, 1943, a group of the Jewish underground drove the Germans from the Warsaw ghetto after they tried to remove Jews for the concentration camps. Naturally, the Nazis vowed to avenge their defeat. Early on the morning of April 19, the S.S. surrounded the ghetto with tanks and heavy artillery. When they tried to move into the ghetto, the underground responded with a shower of homemade bombs and gunfire. The angry Germans then cut off all water, gas, and electricity and attempted to force the Jews to surrender by setting fire to the area. Thousands died in the inferno. Some tried to escape through underground sewers, only to meet a terrible death when the Germans flooded their only path to freedom. Still, the determined Jews fought; while around them the fire grew so intense that it melted the streets and consumed every building. Block by block the Germans gathered the survivors, using flame throwers and snarling dogs to drive them from their underground shelters. Finally, on May 8 the S.S. surrounded the headquarters of the underground, blocked the windows, and used poison gas to kill those who had dared fight for their lives. The Warsaw ghetto ceased to exist. The Nazis had committed yet another atrocity.[3]

Although Goebbels's large propaganda machine made every effort to fool the German people into support for Hitler and hid the true nature of the concentration camps from the world, a few gallant men and women sensed the terror of the nazi atrocities and made a brave effort to end the barbarism that had engulfed Europe. Many nameless heroes hid Jews and other targets of the nazi holocaust or provided them with false identification papers and ration cards. Some brave businessmen devised schemes to protect Jews by employing them in their factories and trying to convince the authorities that their skills were necessary for continuing production. One such humanitarian, Oskar Schindler, saved over a thousand Jews from certain death through his enamel works near Cracow, Poland.

In an effort to restore peace and democracy to Europe, others sought a more active means of resisting the tyranny of Hitler. As we have seen, one such hero was Admiral Wilhelm Canaris, who used his position as chief of the office of military intelligence to recruit men like Hans von Dohnayi and Dietrich Bonhöffer in a campaign to mislead the German leaders through false reports and to provide the resistance and the Allies with needed information. The German Communists, driven underground in 1933, also organized an effective opposition. They formed the Red Band spy ring in Berlin, which provided valuable intelligence to the Soviet Union. Others, such as the members of Canaris's Black Band, worked as agents for the West in one of the most effective espionage operations in history.[4]

One group of adversaries attempted to win support for the resistance from the West during the first months of the war. Adam von Trott zu Stolz traveled to the United States on a lecture tour, which he used to inform the American leaders of the activities of the opposition within Germany. The former mayor of Leipzig, Carl Friedrich Gördeler, contacted British, French, and American leaders for support of a revolt to overthrow Hitler and end the war. From the sanctuary of Switzerland, former German chancellor Joseph Wirt tried without success to gain assurances from British and French officials of friendly relations with a future non-nazi German government. Josef Müller, an agent of Canaris, echoed these efforts in the halls of the Vatican. However, Roosevelt's demand for unconditional surrender, destroyed hope that the Allies would negotiate with a non-nazi German government.

Even Rudolf Hess, Hitler's most trusted adviser, deserted the führer. On May 10, 1941, Hess flew to Scotland in an effort to negotiate a peace with the British through the duke of Hamilton, whom he had met at the Olympics. The nazi leader parachuted from his plane and upon landing asked a startled Scottish farmer to take him to the home of the nobleman. Hess hoped to persuade the British to allow the Reich to conquer living space in return for a guarantee of the British Empire. Although the British officials allowed Hess to meet with the duke, they rejected his proposal and placed the German in prison to await the end of the war and his trial. Hitler was furious. He denounced Hess for treason and removed him from all party offices. The fall of Hess paved the way for Martin Bormann to better his position in Hitler's entourage.[5]

One of the most important anti-nazi groups in wartime Germany gathered at Kreisau, the estate of Count Helmut James von Moltke, the great grandnephew of Field Marshal von Moltke of the First World War. Here, they organized the Kreisau Circle to discuss ways to resist Hitler and the philosophical problems created by the Third Reich. Men of all shades of political and religious opinion joined Moltke in this heroic effort. Count Yorck von Wartenburg, a descendent of the German general of the Napoleonic wars, represented the old aristocratic class. Adolf Reichwein, former professor of history at the University of Halle, contacted the socialistic resistance, and Father Alfred Delp, a Jesuit priest, joined Harald Pölchau, the Protestant chaplain at the main prison in Berlin, in forming relations with Christian groups. Together, the members of this brave band planned for the future of Germany once Hitler had been overthrown and peace restored. Proclaiming Christian principles and the brotherhood of man as the foundation for the future, they dreamed of a Europe free of strife, in which men would live dominated neither by the French hegemony of Versailles nor by the Germany of the Third Reich. They hoped that a new society would arise, in which men would live together in harmony and tyranny would become a thing of the past. Moltke even favored the destruction of the old nation-states, which had fought for centuries, and the division of Europe into small, self-administered bodies. In the end, most of the members of the Kreisau Circle, including Moltke, felt the weight of the nazi atrocities and paid for their opposition with their lives.[6]

The older generation did not stand alone in its opposition to the nazi yoke. Many young Germans joined the defiance and worked to end the nazi oppression. The most famous of these young heroes were Hans Scholl, a student of medicine at the University of Munich, and his sister Sophie, a botany student. The Scholls, several of their fellow students, and a few professors organized the Society of the White Rose, a symbol for purity. This group attempted to awaken their fellow youth to the evil nature of the nazi dictatorship. In their tireless quest for justice, they contacted other student bands at Hamburg, Berlin, and Vienna and spent much of their time copying leaflets called the "White Rose Papers." These courageous fighters sent their clandestine publications through the mails and plastered them on the walls of the Bavarian capital. They called on the German people to unite in a crusade to end the injustice of the nazi rule and the bloodbath of the war while there was still time to salvage the national honor. Some members of the White Rose painted anti-nazi slogans on buildings under the cover of the cool Bavarian night. During one nocturnal protest, Hans Scholl painted the words "Down with Hitler" seventy times on the Ludwigstrasse. Once, they stood on the balcony of the main hall of the university and showered their fellow students with anti-nazi literature. However, the rulers of Germany refused to allow their plans to be threatened by a group of scholars, and on the night of February 18, 1943, they arrested Hans and his sister. During the next few days the full wrath of the nazi dictatorship descended on Munich like a net and gathered in the leaders of the movement, including Kurt Huber, a philosophy professor, and two other students, Willi Graf and Alexander Schmorell. In an emotional trial, they defended their position and denounced Hitler and his supporters, but they, too, fell before the nazi menace and died for their beliefs.

Not all members of the resistance chose to rely on discussions and clandestine publications; some sought a more concrete way to end the nazi tyranny. Led by Colonel Count Claus von Stauffenberg, these courageous men plotted to rid the world of Hitler and the holocaust that had engulfed Europe. Stauffenberg, a member of the Swabian nobility with the exalted names of Yorck and Gneisenau on his family tree, had long been a foe of Hitler and had supported the Halder plot of 1938. Since 1943 he had served the general staff in Berlin. With the power and influence of this high office, he contacted other officers who had become disgusted with Hitler and his arrogant associates. Disguising their plot as a plan to cope with a possible revolt of the eight million foreign workers in the Reich, they planned the assassination of the führer and the overthrow of the nazi regime in Operation Valkyrie. One of the most important members of this courageous band was Friedrich Olbricht, chief of the army office in Berlin. Olbricht realized that Hitler was leading the fatherland to a disastrous defeat and sought the support of other officers who knew that the war could not be won. He also used his position to place his friends in important positions in the army commands of Berlin, Vienna, and Munich.[7]

Although the German capital was the center of Operation Valkyrie, several important men on the Russian front joined Stauffenberg in his effort to stamp out the nazi terror. Here, the leader was General Henning von Tresckow, chief of staff for Field Marshal Gunther von Kluge. This brave man had learned something of the atrocities and realized that continuing the war could only destroy the fatherland. On March 13, 1943, the führer flew to inspect the troops under Kluge, giving Tresckow his chance to eliminate the tyrant. The moment before Hitler left, one of Tresckow's associates gave a member of the führer's party a gift that was a bomb disguised as two bottles of cognac. However, the device failed to explode, and Hitler returned to his headquarters unharmed. Immediately upon learning of this, Tresckow sent Fabian von Schlabrendorff on the dangerous mission to recover the bomb before it was discovered. Schlabrendorff was successful, and Hitler's bodyguard did not suspect that their leader had almost been killed.

The failure of the first attempt on Hitler's life did not discourage Tresckow and his friends. They made another attempt to rid the German people of the curse of national socialism. Tresckow learned that Hitler, accompanied by Göring, Himmler, and Keitel, would preside over Memorial Day ceremonies at the old Prussian Armory in Berlin on March 21, 1943. Realizing that this would give them the opportunity to dispose of not only Hitler but also his major assistants, Tresckow decided that it would be necessary to persuade one of his allies to sacrifice his own life by attempting to detonate a bomb close enough to kill the führer. He convinced Colonel Rudolf von Gersdorff, chief of intelligence on Kluge's staff, to give his life for the cause of peace and freedom. On the evening of March 20, the gallant Gersdorff met with Schlabendorff in a room in the Eden Hotel in Berlin to make the last-minute plans. They decided that the colonel would hide two bombs under his overcoat and detonate them while the führer inspected a group of captured Russian weapons in the courtyard of the armory. Because of the cold of the Berlin winter, the fuses needed at least fifteen minutes. The next day Hitler arrived at the exhibit and one of his aides informed the nervous Gersdorff that the führer would only spend from eight to ten minutes viewing the captured trophies of the war instead of the thirty minutes originally announced. Since this would not give the fuses enough time to explode the bombs, Gersdorff decided to drop the attempt, and Hitler continued his terrible rule.

However, the organizers of Operation Valkyrie had a much more serious foe than bad luck, the dreaded Gestapo. The sinister secret police learned of the opposition to their leader and conducted a ruthless search for all those disloyal to the regime. These fanatics began their campaign with a strike against Canaris and the Black Band, arresting Dietrich Bonhöffer, Dohnayi, and Josef Müller. Although Admiral Canaris used his influence to postpone their trial for a year, his ability to aid the resistance had been destroyed. The trial that led the secret police to Bonhöffer and his associates soon led to Canaris, and his superiors dismissed this valuable ally of the opposition in February 1944. The next year, as the Third Reich approached its final hours, Canaris met his death at the hands of the S.S. The Gestapo did not halt their quest for the foes of the tyranny after the arrest of Canaris, but moved against the Kreisau Circle and arrested Moltke, who also felt the full power of the nazi death machine.

These setbacks failed to cool the determined Stauffenberg and his supporters, and they continued to plan the end of the Third Reich. They even attempted to win the support of Himmler by arranging a discussion between Johannes Popitz and the head of the S.S. through Himmler's personal attorney, Carl Langbehn, on August 26, 1943. This, too, ended in failure, and all Popitz discovered was Himmler's doubt that Germany could win the war. A few days later the Gestapo arrested Langbehn, ending this futile search for a break in Hitler's organization. Unknown to Stauffenberg and his associates, Himmler realized that the war had been lost and attempted to open negotiations with the Americans through Walter Schellenberg on the basis of a negotiated peace after the removal of Hitler. However, the American agents in Stockholm, where the contacts took place, held fast to Roosevelt's demand for unconditional surrender.

Undaunted by the failure to win the support of Himmler, the conspirators continued their planning and even made a list of potential cabinet members for the new non-nazi government. Ludwig Beck, a long-time foe of Hitler would be the new head of state, and Carl Friedrich Görderer would be chancellor. From his position in Russia, Tresckow continued his quest for support and even persuaded his superior, Kluge, to meet with Beck in Berlin in September 1943. The field marshal fell under the spell of the proposed head of state and tentatively agreed to back the plot. However, Kluge was injured in an automobile accident and was unable to participate in the final plans. The conspirators selected Edwin von Witzleben, a retired field marshal, to coordinate the military aspects of the plot. After the elderly officer agreed, Stauffenberg and his friends intensified their efforts and created a network of civilian and military officials ready to spring into action with the announcement of the death of the führer. They printed proclamations, leaflets, and texts for broadcast to justify the coup to the German people by denouncing Hitler for destroying freedom and leading the fatherland into an unwinnable war.

In their search for support, the planners of Operation Valkyrie approached the leaders of the communist underground. Two conspirators, Julius Leber and Adolf Reichwein, met with Anton Säkow, Frank Jacop, and Ferdinand Thomas of the Moscow-coordinated Free German Nation Committee. Realizing the danger of an alliance with the left and of Gestapo infiltration of the communist movement, Leber and Reichwein did not reveal the details of the plot but vaguely spoke of anti-Hitler measures and agreed to meet again on July 4. However, before the second meeting the Gestapo arrested Leber and Reichwein, causing the conspirators to decide to act quickly lest they, too, fall into the grasp of the secret police.

The month of July 1944 bustled with great activity as Stauffenberg and his friends made final arrangements for the liberation of Germany. On July 15 the courageous men approached Field Marshal Erwin Rommel with their plans. The "desert fox" finally agreed that if the führer refused to end the war, he should be arrested and put to trial, but he refused to take an active part in the assassination attempt. The conspirators decided that once Hitler had been removed they would offer a truce to the Allies and evacuate all occupied territories as a sign of good faith. Finally, through a stroke of luck, Stauffenberg became chief of staff for General Friedrich Fromm, commander of the home army, a position that allowed him to attend the führer's strategy meetings. On July 11 Stauffenberg journeyed to Hitler's mountain retreat at Berchtesgaden carrying the bomb that he hoped would end the nazi dictatorship. He failed to carry through the plan because Himmler and Göring were not present. Kluge and Rommel had demanded the death of these two criminals as the price for their support. Thus, the conspirators lost another chance to kill the führer. On July 15 Stauffenberg came once again within reach of his goal but decided not to detonate the bomb because neither the chief of the air force nor the head of the S.S. was present. Thus, he missed his second opportunity.

Then, on July 20, 1944, a day that will long be remembered in history, Stauffenberg's chance arrived. This time he decided not to wait. A bit nervous, he approached the führer's headquarters at Rastenburg, deep in the forests of East Prussia. In his briefcase he carried a bomb. With shaking hands, he stopped in a side building to release the timing device with a pair of pliers. He had just ten minutes to place the bomb and leave if he was to escape with his own life. It took three precious minutes to clear the final check point surrounding the building containing Hitler's headquarters. At this crucial point the guards turned back Stauffenberg's adjutant, Werner von Häften, who was also carrying a concealed bomb, which was to give added power to the explosion. Now, all depended on Stauffenberg. Once inside the building, the jittery general tried to get as close to his target as possible so the hidden bomb would have full impact. Finally, with only a few moments left to flee, Stauffenberg placed the briefcase under the heavy wooden map table and excused himself, saying that he had forgotten to make a very important telephone call. Outside, Stauffenberg joined Häften in counting the seconds in breathless anticipation. Finally, between 12:40 and 12:50, as the author of the nazi terror bent over a map spread on the table, a loud explosion shook the air. The building collapsed in a pile of rubble, killing four men. But once the smoke and dust cleared, Hitler was still alive, snatched from death by the large table that had acted as a shield and the flimsy building and open windows that had allowed the force of the blast to escape into the outside air. The führer suffered only sprains, burns, and a shattered eardrum. The plot had failed. The tyrant still lived. Men who had spent years training in the art of killing could not even kill one man.

Outside the headquarters, Stauffenberg and Häften did not wait to see if the bomb had killed their foe. They watched as the building fell into ruins and assumed that no one had survived the thunderous blast. They sped out of the compound, taking advantage of the confusion following the explosion to get past the guard and reach a waiting plane for the journey back to Berlin, where they intended to carry out the second phase of the planned coup. Upon arrival in the German capital two and a half hours later, a shocked Stauffenberg learned that no one had given the order to begin action. From the airport, he telephoned General Friedrich Olbricht at the War Ministry, demanding

The New Order in Europe

to know the reason for the delay. He learned that Olbricht had hesitated until he received confirmation that Hitler had actually died in the blast. Stauffenberg urged him to give the order at once and left for the War Ministry.

At the headquarters of the German military, Olbricht called Beck at his apartment and told him that Hitler had been killed and that Operation Valkyrie had begun. At this crucial moment, General Friedrich Fromm burst into the room to demand proof that the führer had actually perished. Olbricht then made the fatal error of calling Keitel at Rastenburg, believing that the commander of the army would report the death of the tyrant and cause Fromm to join the plot. However, Keitel told them that the attempt had failed and that Hitler had only been slightly injured. At this point, Stauffenberg arrived breathless from a speedy drive through the city and challenged the validity of Keitel's statement, arguing that he had seen the explosion and that the führer could not possibly have survived. However, Fromm believed Keitel's report and became furious upon learning that the revolt had begun. He turned angrily to Stauffenberg and demanded that he shoot himself at once. Naturally, the leader of the conspiracy refused, and a stormy scene followed that included an exchange of blows between Obricht and Fromm. At this moment, Häften and several men bearing drawn pistols broke into the room, ending the fight and forcing Fromm to go into a nearby office. After they had locked the door and cut the telephone lines to keep him from communicating with the outside, they turned their attention to coordination of the coup.

By 5:30 the operation was in full swing and supporting troops had surrounded all governmental buildings, except for the offices of Radio Germany, an omission that would lead to the downfall of the plot. Inside the war office, Stauffenberg and his aides ordered their supporters throughout Germany to arrest immediately all nazi officials and to seize control of all communications. Then, at 6:00 P.M. came the startling announcement from Radio Germany that the plot had failed and that Hitler had survived with only minor injuries. This broadcast brought on the swift collapse of the revolt. Officers from all over the Reich besieged the War Ministry with telephone calls asking if the report were true, and many supporters gave up their efforts to overthrow the nazi dictatorship, despite pleas from Stauffenberg to continue the fight to victory.

To prevent any further harmful broadcasts, Stauffenberg and his friends immediately sent Major Otto Remer and a group of men to the Propaganda Ministry. However, upon arrival, Remer fell under the spell of Goebbels, who tried to persuade him that he had been deceived and that Hitler was still alive. Finally, in an effort to convince the doubting major, the chief of propaganda took the bold step of calling Rastenburg so that Remer could speak with the führer himself. Hitler ordered the major to take immediate action to drive the traitors from the War Ministry. Thus, the stunned pro-nazi forces regained their composure and began to crush the attempt to restore democracy and peace to the German people.

At the War Ministry, Stauffenberg pleaded for support, but months of planning fell quickly apart as supporters deserted the operation. Groping for a plan to save the attempt, they made one mistake after another. They allowed Fromm to leave confinement to move to his private quarters with only a verbal guarantee that he would not escape or attempt to contact anyone outside. When three members of Fromm's staff arrived and refused to join the coup, Stauffenberg allowed them to meet with Fromm. This treacherous pro-nazi showed them a secret escape route from the building, and they fled, seeking contact with loyal forces outside. Once free, these men helped organize the resistance to the revolt. At the same time, several junior officers on Olbricht's staff, led by Lieutenant Colonel Franz Herber, joined the loyal forces and left for the fortress at Spandau to gather weapons for the counterattack. At 10:30 P.M. they broke into Olbricht's office and demanded an explanation for his behavior. Without receiving it, they left, only to return twenty minutes later bearing weapons. At this point, Stauffenberg entered the room to investigate the source of the noise. A struggle followed, during which the father of Operation Valkyrie received a wound in the arm, and the pro-Hitler forces emerged victorious and released Fromm.

Fromm stormed into the room and demanded that Stauffenberg and his men immediately surrender and face the consequences of their actions. Beck then pulled out a pistol and tried to kill himself. The bullet only scratched the surface of his skull, and he fell back into a chair as blood spurted from the wound. Fromm, realizing that he must act at once to avoid association with the plot, ordered the execution of the conspirators. After giving them a few minutes to write letters to their families, Fromm led Beck, Stauffenberg, Olbricht, and Häften into the courtyard. There, in the cool night air, under a headlight, a firing squad killed the leaders of the heroic and futile effort to end the long night of the nazi dictatorship, as Stauffenberg shouted, "Long live our sacred Germany."[8]

Outside the War Ministry, the supporters of the plot met similar fates. However, for a time there was a slim chance that the officers in Paris would be able to keep hope for a victory alive for a few hours. General Heinrich von Stülpnagel, the military governor of France, received word from Berlin that Hitler had perished and ordered his men to arrest all members of the hated S.S. The S.S. headquarters in the French capital fell without a shot. However, at this crucial point, Kluge, who had been transferred to France after his recovery from the automobile accident, demanded proof that Hitler had actually died. Like Fromm, Kluge telephoned Rastenburg and learned that the führer had survived. Stülpnagel begged Kluge to end the disastrous war by offering a truce to Eisenhower. However, the old officer was not a man to take such radical action, and he refused. The S.S. recovered its position, recaptured control of its headquarters, and moved on the conspirators. Keitel ordered Stülpnagel to return to Berlin to face trial, and the plot fell as swiftly as it had begun. After telegraphing a note of submission to the führer, Kluge took his own life rather than meet death at the hands of Hitler's henchmen.[9]

Back at Rastenburg, confusion reigned after the blast. Hitler, shaken by the assassination attempt by the highest circle of the German army, attempted to keep it secret lest it give the world the false impression that the military was not solidly behind his leadership. However, when he realized the full extent of the plot, he ordered Himmler to move at once to crush the conspiracy. At about eight o'clock that evening, Keitel instructed the army to refuse to obey any orders not countersigned by himself or Himmler. At midnight the führer, who believed that his escape was a sign of divine favor, took to the air to assure the German people that he was in good health and that the attempt had been the product of only a few demented men.

After the attempt collapsed, Hitler favored open trials, similar to those conducted by Stalin during the purges of the 1930s. Himmler successfully opposed this, arguing that public hearings would give his opponents a platform to argue against national socialism and thus weaken public morale. During the reign of terror that accompanied the trials and search for the conspirators, about five thousand persons met brutal deaths, some hanging from meat hooks. Even Rommel was not immune to Hitler's wrath and was given a choice of death by his own hand or trial for treason. After his suicide, rather than admit that the "desert fox" had lost faith in the führer's cause, the nazi leaders announced that he had died of heart failure and praised him at a formal state funeral.

Thus ends the most important attempt to free mankind from the curse of Hitler. The plan failed partially because the bomb did not kill its target and partially because of the built-in loyalty of the German officers, who refused to violate their oaths of allegiance by joining an effort to overthrow the nazi dictatorship. Had the führer died in the explosion and had the conspirators been able to move more swiftly and with more support, perhaps the war would have ended almost a year earlier, and with it, the destruction of the Jews, Gypsies, Slavs, and others and the enslavement of the peoples of occupied lands. Yet Hitler lived on, as did the machine of death that he had created.

20

The Twilight of the Gods

By 1944 the mighty empire that had once ruled all but a few small areas of Europe had been destroyed. In the West, the Allies fought the Germans on the Po and in Normandy while, in the East, their Russian comrades moved into Poland. Less than a year after D-Day, quiet once again descended on the people of Europe. They emerged from the bomb shelters and concentration camps into a world again at peace and turned to the task of rebuilding their shattered lives. Many searched in vain for lost relatives, while others learned for the first time of the horror of the death camps. Europe would never again be the same as it was on that spring day in 1914 when an obscure Bosnian radical assassinated the Austrian archduke, setting off a chain of events that would lead to two world wars. Europe was only a shadow of its former greatness, poor and dependent on help from the outside to recover from the orgy of destruction that had gripped her. Germany emerged a broken nation, under the domination of the four Allies, her people starving and her cities devastated. Heinrich Heine's prediction of the last century had come true, the force of German nationalism had run rampant and had indeed unleashed Thor's mighty hammer to smash the Gothic cathedrals.[1]

The author of much of the cataclysm was Adolf Hitler. He personally commanded his troops during much of the fighting, although he was hundreds of miles away from the battlefields. He preached the ideology that led to Auschwitz and Treblinka and overcame the opposition of the military to begin the war. Yet, despite his power, Hitler was a sick man. Under the care of Dr. Morell, the führer's health deteriorated further. The unethical doctor filled Hitler's body with as many as twenty-eight different mixtures of drugs, fake medicines, narcotics, stimulants, and aphrodisiacs. He gave him sulphonamide, which was, according to a study of the pharmacological faculty of the University of Leipzig, a mixture that did great harm to the nervous system. Dr. Morell fed the ailing dictator Dr. Köster's Antigas Pills, a mixture containing strychnine and belladona, two deadly poisons, to bring relief to his troubled stomach. Once, he even injected a concoction made from the crushed testicles of young bulls to stimulate Hitler's sex drive. The narrow escape from death in the bombing of his bunker and the failure of his armies to resist the enemy led to further deterioration. In the last months of his life, Hitler was but a shadow of the man he once had been. His mighty voice became halting and even broke on occasion. He shuffled when he walked, dragging his quivering legs to move his stooped body forward slowly. In September 1944 he could maintain his frail carriage no more and spent several days in bed, a tired, whimpering old man.[2]

Hitler's health alone could have been a major reason for the many mistakes he made during the war, but another more important reason led to his downfall. He was not a rational man. While trained psychologists may differ as to the exact nature of his condition and its causes, few deny that no normally adjusted man could have behaved in the manner of Adolf Hitler. He would fly into a rage at the slightest provocation, and he refused to listen to the suggestions of those trained in the art of warfare. He spoke of himself as God's agent, destined to lead mankind to a new era, a feeling that was only intensified by what he considered his miraculous escape from the blast of July 20, 1944. Even if his other actions had not revealed serious mental illness, the destruction of millions of innocent Jews, Slavs, Gypsies, and others in the concentration camps could not have been the work of a well man. Certainly, the brutality of his father and the tendency of his mother to give in to his childhood temper tantrums contributed to his mental and spiritual breakdown. His frustration over his failure as an artist and his life in Vienna also played a major role in creating the madman who would dominate the lives of millions. Finally, his strange relationship with the opposite sex and his inability to deal with others on a personal basis show the insecurity that led him to regard even the most well-meant criticism with hostility and illustrate the depth of his illness. Regardless of what conclusions one draws about the exact nature of his neurosis or psychosis, one must bear in mind that a raving maniac led the Germans and oppressed the peoples of Europe.

The Twilight of the Gods

From 1941 until November 1944, Hitler lived in seclusion in his headquarters in Rastenburg. There, far from the reality of the war, he attempted to direct the movements of his troops while he lived with almost monklike simplicity. He stayed in bed late because of his chronic insomnia and ate breakfast alone. Not until noon did he meet with his military advisers. After eating lunch with a few acquaintances, he tried to rest for a few hours before further conferences, which sometimes lasted until midnight. After discussions with his advisers and tea with his secretaries and Dr. Morell, the insomnia-ridden führer once again tried to gain a few hours of sleep. Despite his poor health, Hitler refused to take a vacation, believing that he must remain at his post at all times.

Finally, after a few months at the Eagles Nest, his field headquarters in the West, the dictator moved into a specially constructed bunker on the grounds of his bombed-out chancellery on January 16, 1945. There, beneath six feet of earth and sixteen feet of solid concrete, Hitler spent the last few weeks of the Third Reich. The bunker contained all he needed to live. Vents hidden amid the bushes of the garden provided fresh air, and a generator driven by a diesel engine made electricity. The first floor contained quarters for Hitler's S.S. guards and servants, as well as a kitchen and dining room. On the second floor, in twenty small rooms, Hitler directed the futile defense of Germany. The führer occupied a bedroom, living room, waiting room, and bathroom, which he shared with Eva Braun, who slept in a room next to his. Hitler even provided a kennel for Blondi, his wolfhound. The shelter housed a clinic from which Dr. Morell continued to fill Hitler's body with drugs and fought his high blood pressure with leeches, literally sucking the life from his frail body.[3]

In Berlin Hitler continued the daily regimen established at Rastenburg. He climbed from his bed at about 11:30, bathed, and then consumed his breakfast in solitude. At noon he met with his advisers to study the charts of the battles and plan the next action. In the late afternoon, surrounded by his secretaries and occasionally by his generals, he ate a lunch of vegetable soup, corn on the cob, and jellied omelets. After a nap and further discussions with his aides, Hitler stayed awake, forcing those present to listen to unending monologues of his plans for the future. From this unreal world, the führer directed the last few efforts of his once-powerful armies.

While Hitler and his aides hid deep beneath the ground, the most savage air war in history raged above them. Responding to the Luftwaffe campaign against England, the R.A.F. began a massive effort to beat the Germans into submission. At first they concentrated on destroying the Reich's valuable oil reserves, attacking civilian targets only when they could not reach their primary goal. However, as Göring's forces shifted their campaign from the R.A.F. bases to London, the British began to concentrate on undermining civilian morale by wiping German cities off the map, opening the campaign with an attack on Berlin on August 24, 1940. Suffering heavy losses to the determined resistance of the enemy, the British abandoned actions during the day by 1941 and confined their attacks to dark nights. Flying on a path designed to conceal their destination, the Allied bombers swept down on their targets in several successive waves. The first bombers dropped fire bombs, followed by attacks on the water supply and the streets to scatter the men and women desperately trying to fight the flames. Through these methods, the British hoped to turn the cities into infernos that would wipe out whole blocks at a time.[4]

On February 4, 1943, Air Chief Marshal Sir Arthur Harris ordered his forces to open an offensive to destroy the will to fight of the German people by turning their homes and factories into piles of dust. Throughout the next months, thousands of American and British bombers filled the skies above the Reich. On March 5 the Allies opened the Battle of the Ruhr, an attempt to turn a stretch from Stuttgart to Aachen into a vast wasteland. On March 5, 1943, planes blasted Essen, followed by attacks on Duisburg, Dortmund, Düsseldorf, Bochum, and Aachen. On May 29 the Americans and English destroyed almost 90 percent of the important industrial region of Barmen Wuppertal. With a path of death and destruction blasted through central Germany, the Allies shifted the attack to Hamburg, devastating the Hansa city with waves of bombers. The explosives reduced the city to rubble, unleashing fire storms that killed thousands of terrified civilians who dove into the waters of the Elbe only to find the river covered with burning napalm. Meanwhile, other missions blasted Berlin, Frankfurt, Stuttgart, and Leipzig. Every night the people of Germany scrambled to shelter amid the wail of the air-raid sirens and the thunder of the artillery defenses, emerging to search for their scattered belongings and the bodies of their friends and relations. The air war was one of the most terrible aspects of the conflict and spread more destruction than any war since the Thirty Years War of the seventeenth century. No longer could civilians remain outside the fighting. Every man, woman, and child felt the full impact of the battle.

The Twilight of the Gods

In 1944, as the fighting on land intensified, so also did the aerial bombardment of the German people. During the week of February 20 to 26, the Allied forces, utilizing their bombsights and high explosives, blasted the German defenses in yet another campaign of terror from the skies. The American and British bombers, many of which failed to return, continued the destruction of the German cities throughout the remainder of the war. The bombing reached a crescendo in the attack on Dresden of February 13–14, 1945, where 500,000 refugees fleeing the oncoming Red Army filled the baroque capital of the kings of Saxony. Suddenly the air raid sirens unleashed their shrill cry, and the people ran for every available cover. Above, the Allies dropped fire bombs and explosives, setting off one of the most deadly fire storms in the history of warfare. The flames spread through the city, sucking the oxygen from the bomb shelters and turning the once beautiful center of the city into a vast wasteland. When the fires finally subsided, 135,000 civilians lay burned to death or smothered. The Germans had been repaid for the destruction of Rotterdam, Coventry, Belgrade, and other cities. During the war the Allies, seeking vengeance for the bombardment of England, dropped 315 tons of explosives for every ton dropped by the Luftwaffe. The aerial war destroyed much of the industrial capability of the Third Reich to provide supplies for its troops, a major factor in the final victory over Hitler's forces. The warfare also lay waste the once beautiful palaces, churches, public buildings, shops, and homes of the German people. To this day, over thirty years after the end of the war, the signs of the destruction can be seen. It was due only to the accuracy of their bombsights and the sensibility of the Allies that all signs of the formerly vital German civilization were not lost. For example, the Allies destroyed the railroad station in Cologne but spared the great cathedral only a few yards away.

Significantly, neither the fighting nor the bombing had an immediate impact on the German home front. Hitler had not prepared for a long war and neglected to put the Reich on a war footing in 1939. Although the authorities introduced rationing of food and clothing as early as August 27, 1939, the German people continued to eat fairly well until the final months of the war. Finally, the reverses in Russia and the intensity of the Allied bombardment forced the leaders of the Reich to mobilize the German economy. On April 15, 1942, Hitler issued a decree establishing the Central Planning Board to coordinate the production of armaments. This body, under the leadership of

Albert Speer, whom Hitler had appointed minister of arms and munitions, had the power to control the distribution of raw materials, set production quotas, and manage transportation. Speer also had charge of over three million prisoners of war and foreign workers employed in German plants during the war. Under Speer's effective leadership, production of war materials continued to increase, reaching a peak in 1944.[5]

Although the increased pace of the conflict and the Allied bombing did not weaken civilian morale as much as the Allies hoped, they did have an impact on the attitude of the German people. From the beginning the Germans had not enthusiastically supported the war. There were no cheering crowds in 1939, only stunned silence as the people learned of the beginning of the war. The once-hysterical mobs that had greeted the führer vanished, to be replaced by a few voiceless people, motivated more by curiosity than admiration. Goebbels's propaganda began to fall on deaf ears, and the people responded with cynical jokes ridiculing their leaders. Although there seemed little danger of mass starvation until the final months of the war, fresh fruit, meat, sugar, and coffee became scarce as the fighting continued. The ceaseless bombing robbed the people of their sleep as they spent their nights huddled in the stuffy bomb shelters. The Germans grew tired of the war and greeted every rumor of peace with wild enthusiasm. Yet they continued to fight, probably out of fear of reprisals for the atrocities of the S.S. and Gestapo in the occupied countries and of a peace even more severe than the Treaty of Versailles.[6]

Hitler responded to the Allied bombing furiously. The führer, believing almost to the last that his scientists would discover new and more terrible weapon that would win the war, launched a thousand V-1 rocket bombs on London on June 14, 1944. The swift new menace from the sky, developed by a team headed by Werner von Braun, threatened even more damage than the Luftwaffe. Throughout June and July 1944 the Nazis sent two hundred rockets a day to the British. Warned only by the buzz of their engines, the English panicked. The R.A.F. was powerless to shoot down the swift V1s, and only radar and antiaircraft guns saved London from complete destruction. The Allies tried sending false reports through double agents assigned to inform the Germans where to aim their weapons, but this only caused the rockets to fall on the working-class quarter of the city, killing thousands. In the fall of 1944 the Germans launched the V-2, an even faster rocket, from Holland. Fortunately, the Allies had learned of the location of the rocket research facility at Peenemünde through one of Canaris's agents in Lisbon and destroyed it by air on August 14, 1943. Had they been able to conduct further research and construction, Hitler's scientists might have been able to develop still more powerful rockets. Finally, Allied soldiers captured the V-2 launching site in Holland and ended the attack.

Hitler's scientists, led by Werner Heisenberg, were busy working on a weapon even more decisive than the rocket, the atomic bomb. Fortunately, the British learned that the German program depended on heavy water manufactured at Rjukan, Norway. The English knew that they must destroy the plant lest the Germans develop an atomic bomb. On March 29, 1942, Einar Skinnerland dropped by parachute near Rjukan to study the plant and lead a commando raid. After an unsuccessful attack, a group of agents parachuted near Rjukan and secretly entered the plant on February 26, 1943. Although their explosives halted operations for several months, the Allies finally had to bomb the plant, killing many innocent Norwegians. On February 20, 1944, a group of Allied agents, led by Skinnerland and Knut Haukelid, planted a bomb on a ferry that carried a shipment of heavy water across Lake Tinnsjö, destroying more than fourteen tons of the valuable cargo. Had the brave men failed in their mission, Hitler's scientists might have been able to build a weapon that the mad dictator could have used to wipe his enemies off the map, leading to a nazi victory and the end of civilization as we know it.[7]

Meanwhile, before the Allies could capture the V-2 bases in Holland, they had to break out of Normandy. They continued to send false messages of a coming attack at Calais and even gathered a fleet of fake ships to fool the Germans into believing that the real invasion was yet to come. The guise worked, for on June 9 Hitler made one of the most crucial decisions of the war. He met with his generals and told them that his forces at Calais must be reinforced and under no circumstances would they be used to fight in Normandy. Meanwhile, inspired by the landing, the French people cut rail lines and enemy communications to hamper German troop movements.

Despite Hitler's persistent refusal to send reinforcements from Calais to Normandy, the Germans stood fast and refused to allow the Allies to advance into the rest of France. They fought violently, hiding behind hedges and farmhouses, forcing the Americans and the British to pay with blood for every inch. For a while it seemed that the mighty battle would turn into another nightmare of trench warfare, similar to that which had cost millions of lives in the First World War. Montgomery tried time and time again to break through the German resistance and to liberate Caen, but each time the enemy, ordered by their führer to hold the line at any cost, beat back his attack. Luckily, Kluge, the commander of the Germans in France, concentrated on repulsing the British, which gave Bradley a chance to capture St. Lo, an important rail center. On July 25, supported by a massive air strike, the American offensive began. For two days the battle raged, until the German line broke and the Allied forces poured through into St. Lo. Kluge tried to halt the Allies but could not reconstruct his shattered lines. On July 31 the Americans captured the bridge at Pontaubaut and began to send their forces into Brittany. The British and Canadians captured Caen on August 7, and the race to liberate Paris began.

Hitler was furious and ordered Kluge to regroup his forces and drive the enemy back into the sea in Operation Lüttich. However, once again the Allies knew of the German plans through Ultra. General Leland S. Hobbs gathered his troops at Mortain, the site of the coming attack, and fortified a hill outside the city. On August 7 Kluge assembled his men to drive Hobbs from his commanding position. The Allies beat back the Germans, and finally Kluge realized that he had been defeated and ordered his men to begin the retreat. The German lines in France fell apart. General George Patton, commanding the American Third Army, captured Orleans and turned toward Paris. Elsewhere, the Canadians liberated Rouen, the capital of Normandy, and the British crossed the Seine. On August 15 a group of Americans landed on the Riviera and completed the encirclement of the Germans in France.

With Allied forces advancing on Paris from all sides, the Germans could do little but evacuate the city. However, Hitler was determined to take revenge on the French for his defeat. He ordered his agents to place explosives on the bridges over the Seine and in all important buildings and ordered his commander in the French capital, Hans Speidel, to leave the city in rubble. Fortunately, Speidel refused to participate in the senseless destruction of one of the most beautiful cities in the world. Hitler ordered General Dietrich von Choltitz to carry out the destruction. He, too, refused, and Paris escaped. On August 19, 1944, cheered by the news of the coming liberation, the people of Paris revolted against the few remaining Germans. Meanwhile, Patton's tank units raced to the city to prevent a bloodbath. On August 25 Choltitz surrendered, ending four years of German occupation. As the great bells of Notre Dame pealed for joy, the people of the city filled the streets to welcome their liberators.[8]

The Allies did not pause to give their tired men a rest after the occupation of Paris, but pushed on to drive the Germans from the rest of France, crushing the last remnants of Hitler's once-mighty army as they went. The Americans moved through Reims and Metz toward Strasbourg while Patton's tanks raced sometimes as many as fifty miles a day to Nancy. In the north the Canadians moved up the coast, capturing Dieppe on September 1 and entering Belgium by the end of the month. Between the Americans and Canadians, Montgomery led his forces to Amiens, the British headquarters during the First World War, and to Brussels on September 5, moving into Holland by the end of the month to join American paratroopers in an unsuccessful effort to cross the Rhine at Arnhem. Meanwhile, a group of Americans entered Germany north of Trier, where the Allied advance was stopped as Hitler's armies hurriedly fortified themselves along the Westwall to defend their homeland. Despite this setback, the Allies freed most of western Europe from the Germans within a few weeks of the breakthrough at St. Lo.

Once again Hitler refused to accept defeat, and he gathered his forces to drive the Allies from the bases. Operating under the strictist secrecy, Rundstedt launched an attack against the Americans in the Ardennes on December 16. This time the Germans surprised the Allies. Believing that Hitler would never try an offensive through the hilly wooded Ardennes and failing to receive any sign of an impending attack from Ultra, the Allies were unprepared. Rundstedt's forces broke through the American lines and were well on the way to Antwerp to capture desperately needed fuel and supplies before the Americans and British could gather their forces to meet the new German challenge. Still, a few Americans fought the Germans with all their might and halted the advance, as Patton raced from the south through ice and snow to relieve the battered Allies. From Holland, Montgomery sped to the battlefield. Meanwhile, the Americans refused to surrender to the advancing Germans. Hitler's forces surrounded a group of Americans under Brigadier General Anthony C. McAuliffe at Bastogne and demanded his surrender. The defiant officer responded to the German ultimatum with one word, "Nuts." When the confused German asked for an explanation, one of his men told him that the reply meant, "Go to hell." Finally, the German tanks, starved for fuel, halted in the mud a few yards from an Allied fuel dump at Stavelot that contained several million gallons of gasoline. The heroic Allied forces had defeated the Germans in the Battle of the Bulge, Hitler's last gasp in the West.[9]

While the Germans met with decisive defeat in the Battle of the Bulge, the Russians pressed the Third Reich from the East. By August 29, relieved by Hitler's preoccupation with the fighting in France, the Red Army had crossed the Danube. They then moved into the Balkans. In Bucharest, King Michael led a revolution to drive the pro-German premier, Ion Antonescu, from power and join the Allies. The Russians reached Yugoslavia, where a force of anti-Germans led by Josip Broz, Tito, had been fighting the enemy. Two days later the Red Army entered Bulgaria. Thus, the Soviets crushed the Germans in southeastern Europe from all sides.

Elsewhere, another force of Russian troops moved through Poland, capturing Lvov on July 25. By the end of the month the Red Army stood on the outskirts of Warsaw. Believing that the Russians would come to their aid, the brave people of the Polish capital revolted against their German masters on July 31. However, the Red Army, motivated by Stalin's desire to see the anticommunist underground crushed by the Nazis, halted in Praga* and refused to rescue the people of Warsaw from the vengence of Hitler's troops. Throughout the next month the Germans brutally crushed the uprising and destroyed block after block of the city while Stalin's forces watched from their base in Praga. Thousands died in one of the bloodiest episodes of the entire war. On January 17, 1945, after the last Polish freedom fighter had been killed, Stalin's army occupied Warsaw. They found only a tenth of the people who had lived there before the outbreak of the war. From the Polish capital, the Red Army continued to advance, liberating Tarnow, Cracow, and Lodz a few days later. The Germans fought frantically, fearing revenge for the many atrocities committed against the Russian people and hoping that somehow the Americans and British would be the first to reach Berlin. However, their effort was to no avail. On February 20 the Russians broke through the German lines and reached a site thirty miles from Berlin.

After the defeat of the Germans during the Battle of the Bulge, the Allies resumed the offensive. For a while the Germans held their enemies at the Rohr River, running parallel to the Rhine and controlling

---

*A suburb of Warsaw.

dams that would send waves of water over the Allied troops if they were destroyed. The Americans and their British supporters fought valiantly and by February 22 had captured the dams. On March 6 Cologne fell. However, once again the Allied advance halted, for the retreating Germans had destroyed the bridges crossing the Rhine. Patton's forces moved through the Eifel Mountains and reached Koblenz, only to find the bridges across the Rhine destroyed. But Hitler's army had made one fatal mistake. They had failed to blow up the bridge at Remagen near Bonn. On March 7 the Americans captured the bridge, and the Allied forces poured into the heart of Germany. By April 11 the Americans had penetrated to the Elbe. Had Eisenhower sent his forces to Berlin, the map of postwar Europe might have been radically different. But the American commander followed his orders and allowed the Red Army to capture the capital of the Third Reich. One reason for Eisenhower's willingness to allow the Russians to capture the greatest prize of the war may have been the confusion following the death of Roosevelt on April 12.[10]

As his enemies pressed from all sides, Hitler lost all command of the situation. One minute he spoke of a victory to be won by some secret weapon; at another he told his supporters that the German people had failed and deserved destruction. He told Goebbels to order the defenders of Berlin to fight to the last man and even threatened to destroy any block of the besieged city that dared to hoist a white flag. The führer believed that if the German people failed to win the war, the Third Reich should meet a violent end, patterned after the conclusion of Wagner's *Twilight of the Gods*, in which flames consumed the bodies of Siegfried and Brunhild. Some of Hitler's advisers begged him to leave Berlin to make a last stand in the Bavarian Alps. Indeed, he had already approved Operation National Redoubt, last defense of nazi Germany from the south. He had authorized the formation of special commando groups in the Alps and had even transferred several ministries to the mountains. Allied fears of prolonged fighting in the Alps had been one reason for the decision of the Americans and British to allow the Russians to capture Berlin. Despite the arguments of Göring, Himmler, Goebbels, Ribbentrop, Bormann, and Speer when they met with him for the last time on his birthday on April 20, Hitler refused to evacuate Berlin to lead the defense of his empire. Instead, he ordered S.S. General Felix Steiner to attack the Russians. However, the offensive never materialized. As the furious führer denounced his men for their failure, charging them with cowardice and treachery, many of his chief advisers fled for their lives.[11]

By April 23 the armies of the Third Reich existed only in the imagination of its leader. That day, Speer flew from Hamburg to bid farewell to the spiritless Hitler. Suddenly an aide burst in with a telegram from Göring, safe in the south. The once-powerful leader of the Luftwaffe proposed that he personally assume the leadership of the final defense of Germany. Hitler regained his lost spirit and flew into a violent rage at Göring's treason. He removed him from all offices and ordered his immediate arrest. Hitler then commanded Colonel General Robert von Greim to fly to Berlin. Thinking that the führer had some special task for him, the officer and his test pilot, Hanna Reitsch, flew to the besieged capital, barely missing the tops of the few remaining trees to avoid Russian fire. He braved enemy artillery to reach the bunker, only to learn that he was to be the new commander of the Luftwaffe. Even during the last gasp of the Third Reich, Hitler believed in the power of his military.

The appointment of Greim and the dismissal of Göring had little effect on the outcome of the war. By April 29 the Red Army had penetrated the defenses of Berlin and was within a mile of the chancellery. Meanwhile, Himmler had fled to Lübeck to beg Count Folke Bernadotte of the Swedish consulate to persuade the Americans and British to accept a German surrender. The count flew to Stockholm and contacted the Americans and British; but, loyal to their agreement with Stalin, they refused to consider anything less than unconditional surrender and rejected Himmler's offer to allow the West to occupy Germany instead of the dreaded Red Army. Deserted by one of his most loyal followers, Hitler once again flew into a rage, but after a long tirade he sank into a chair in silence, a trace of the man who had swayed millions with his powerful voice.

That same day he summoned Walter Wagner, an official of the city of Berlin. There, with Russian shells falling on all sides, the dictator, in the presence of Goebbels and his wife, married Eva Braun. That afternoon he signed his last testament, denouncing the Jews for his defeat and naming Karl von Dönitz his successor. The next day, after hearing the last reports on the battle for Berlin, he ate lunch; after bidding farewell to Goebbels, Bormann, and the few remaining at his side, he went into his room with his bride. A few minutes later, at 3:30 P.M., the sound of a shot echoed through Hitler's underground fortress. A group of his dedicated followers entered the room to find him dead on the sofa with a bullet through his mouth and the corpse of the poisoned Eva at his side. Two solemn S.S. men formed the honor guard that carried his body, with a blanket for a shroud, into the garden. There, as the Russian artillery shells burst around them, Hitler's last supporters set fire to the body of their fallen leader, twelve years and three months from the day that he had reviewed his marching followers after his appointment as chancellor. Hitler had met his twilight of the gods.[12]

The next day the world learned of the death of Adolf Hitler, the founder of the Third Reich and murderer of millions, as the German radio played music by Wagner and Bruckner's Seventh Symphony. That evening Goebbels and his wife, loyal to their leader to the end, poisoned their frightened children and shot themselves. Then, as Walhalla had burned in Wagner's opera, the last stronghold of national socialism went up in flames. A week later General Alfred Jodl and Hans von Friedburg surrendered to the victorious Allies, and the curse of the Third Reich had passed into history.

Thus, the long night of terror that had engulfed the world ended in the smoking rubble of Berlin. Himmler took his own life rather than face trial. The Allies sentenced Göring, Rosenberg, Ribbentrop, Frick, Streicher, Kaltenbrunner, Seyss-Inquart, and Fritzsche to death for their crimes against humanity. The last minute before being taken to the gallows, Göring committed suicide to cheat the victors of their just revenge. No one knows what happened to Bormann, presumably he perished in the fighting; although at least one author has argued that he was really a Soviet agent and spent the remainder of his life in Russia.[13] The German people emerged from the destruction of their homeland to face a new world in which the spector of national socialism would never again threaten the peace and security of mankind. The victorious Allies divided Germany among themselves. Rather than the united nation-state dreamed of and fought for by generations of Germans, two separate states emerged, one allied with the West and one with the Soviet Union. The Third Reich had fallen and, with it, Germany.

Never before had any German ruler controlled as large an area as Hitler did at the height of his power; yet it all crumbled. There is no single reason why Hitler lost the Second World War. Certainly the führer had spread his forces too thin. In 1942 the armies of the Third Reich occupied an empire that stretched from North Africa to the North Cape and from the Atlantic to the Volga. No one nation could have held onto such a vast territory in the face of the combined efforts of the Allies and their supporters in the underground. The bravery of the American, British, Soviet, and other Allied troops played a major role in the liberation of Europe from national socialism. Even in the darkest days of the conflict, the dedicated soldiers and people of the Allied nations fought with all their strength; finally, they gained victory. They forced the führer to fight a war on several fronts, greatly sapping his strength, while from the skies their bombers blasted the industries and cities of Germany into oblivion. The Allied intelligence successfully penetrated Hitler's communication network through Project Ultra, and double agents constantly misled the warlords of the Third Reich.

Another reason for the Allied victory was the opposition to Hitler within his own country and his failure as a military commander. From the beginning, a significant portion of Hitler's army worked to overthrow him. When he brought war, these brave men intensified their efforts. Some, like Canaris, even provided the Allies with valuable information. Others dedicated themselves to a vain attempt to rid the world of Hitler. Although they failed, their efforts could not help but hamper the führer's campaign to rule Europe. Finally, Hitler, himself, laid the foundations for the Allied victory. He constantly refused to listen to his military advisers and made many serious mistakes. Despite the frantic pleas of his generals, he insisted on allowing his army to spend the winter in the frozen wastes of Russia. Even after the Allies had landed at Normandy, Hitler rejected the desperate request of Kluge that he send men from Calais to meet the new challenge.

The Weimar Republic and the Third Reich, together, lasted less than thirty years, a small fraction of German history. The Holy Roman Empire, the first Reich, had endured, at least in name, for more than a thousand years. Bismarck's Reich, the second, had a life of almost a half century. Yet the Weimar Republic and the Third Reich that followed it stand out to such an extent that this short era seems to overshadow all other periods of German history. Never before had Germany reached such heights in power and influence, but never before had the German people been reduced to such a level of deprivation. The Third Reich represents the greatest rule of barbarism and brutality in modern European history. Only the Soviet Union under Stalin can match nazi Germany for the wholesale murder of millions.

Every student of history must consider the proper place of the

Third Reich in German history. As we have seen, the foundation for national socialism was laid as an offshoot of romanticism. Even before Hitler began to sway the crowds in the beer halls, many Germans had adopted the extreme nationalism and racism of the cult of the folk. Yet this was but one aspect of German culture. Germany had produced such figures as Lessing, Goethe, Kant, Bach, Mozart, and Beethoven. The success of national socialism was not inevitable; it was the result of factors that, had they occurred in other countries, could have produced similar results. The Weimar Republic was founded in the wake of a lost war and a humiliating peace. The republic was never stable. Throughout its brief existence, the Weimar Republic was constantly plagued with economic and political distress as a result, partially, of the excessive reparation demands of the victors of the First World War. Even the stability of the Stresemann era was only a fleeting moment that evaporated with the coming of the great depression. As the German people searched for a solution to their problems, Hitler provided simple answers and the promise of deliverance. Finally, when the political leaders of the republic could do little but fight among themselves while severe economic problems gripped the nation, Hitler came to power. Once in office the führer transformed the Reich into an absolute dictatorship and led Germany into one of the most disastrous wars in history. When the people realized the true nature of Hitler's rule, it was too late to restore democracy and save the peace. Had they known that he would imprison and murder millions and plunge the nation into war, perhaps the German people and the world would not have allowed the tragedy of the Weimar Republic and the Third Reich to happen. Instead, lulled into a false sense of security by the lies of Goebbels and his propaganda machine, and unaware of the horror of the concentration camps, one of the most closely guarded secrets of the nazi dictatorship, they followed their führer to their destruction.

Notes

CHAPTER 1

1. For an account of the growth and influence of the Prussian military, see Gordon A. Craig, *The Politics of the Prussian Army 1640–1945* (New York, 1968). For a general history of Germany before 1800, see Hajo Holborn, *A History of Modern Germany, Vol. 1: The Reformation*, and *Vol. 2: 1648–1840*. (New York, 1959), or John E. Rodes, *Germany: A History* (New York, 1964).

2. For a discussion of the Revolution of 1848 in Germany, see Priscilla Robertson, *The Revolutions of 1848: A Social History* (Princeton, 1967); or Veit Valentine, *Geschichte der deutschen Revolution von 1848–1849*, 2 vols. (Aalen, 1968).

3. For a discussion of the Prussian Plan of Union, see Warren B. Morris, Jr., *The Road to Olmütz: The Career of Joseph Maria von Radowitz* (New York, 1976); or Heinrich von Sybel, *The Founding of the German Empire by William I*, 6 vols., trans. by Marschall Livingston Perrin and Gamalied Bradford (New York, 1890).

4. For additional information on the life and work of Bismarck see Otto von Bismarck, *Reflections and Reminiscences,* ed. by Theodore S. Hamerow (New York, 1968), A. J. P. Taylor, *Bismarck: The Man and the Statesman* (New York, 1955), and Erich Eyck, *Bismarck and the German Empire* (New York, 1968).

5. For a discussion of the development of the cult of the folk, see George L. Mosse, *The Crisis of German Ideology, Intellectual Origins of the Third Reich* (New York, 1964); or Fritz Stern, *The Politics of Cultural Despair: A Study in the Rise of the Germanic Ideology* (Berkeley, 1974).

6. For additional information on the development of nationalism in nineteenth-century Germany, see Hans Kohn, *The Mind of Germany: The Education of a Nation* (New York, 1965).

7. Friedrich Nietzsche, *The Portable Nietzsche,* ed. and trans. by Walter Kaufmann (New York, 1968).

8. Karl Marx and Frederick Engels, *Selected Works* (New York, 1974).

Chapter 2

1. For a discussion of William II, see Michael Belfour, *The Kaiser and His Times* (New York, 1972); and Virginia Cowles, *The Kaiser* (New York, 1963). For studies of the causes of the First World War, see Luigi Albertini, *The Origins of the War of 1914*, 3 vols. (London, 1953); Vladimir Dedijer, *The Road to Sarajevo* (New York, 1966); Sidney B. Fay, *The Origins of the World War*, 2 vols. (London, 1930), and Bernadotte E. Schmitt, *The Coming of the War, 1914* (New York, 1930).
2. For discussions of German politics during the First World War see Craig, *The Politics of the Prussian Army 1640–1945;* S. William Halperin, *Germany Tried Democracy: A Political History of The Reich from 1918 to 1933* (New York, 1965); Hajo Holborn, *A History of Modern Germany, Vol. 3: 1840–1945;* and Koppel S. Pinson, *Modern Germany: Its History and Civilization* (New York, 1966).
3. The most important work on German war aims is Fritz Fischer, *Germany's Aims in the First World War* (New York, 1968).
4. For a discussion of the Zimmerwald Conference and the attitude of the Socialists toward the war, see Merle Fainson, *International Socialism and the World War* (Garden City, N.Y., 1961).
5. For a complete set of documents dealing with the split within the Social Democrats, see Herbert Michaelis et al., eds., *Ursachen und Folgen von deutschen Zusammenbruch 1918 und 1945 bis zur staatlichen Neuordnung Deutschlands in der Gagenwart* (Berlin, 1962), 1: 289–306, hereafter referred to as *Ursachen und Folgen*. For the life and work of Rosa Luxemburg, see J. P. Nettle, *Rosa Luxemburg* (New York, 1969).
6. Philip Scheidemann, *Memoirs of a Social Democrat* (London, 1929), 2: 359–69.

Chapter 3

1. For a study of Wilson, see Thomas A. Bailey, *Woodrow Wilson and the Lost Peace* (Chicago, 1963).
2. For documents relating to the Treaty of Brest Litovsk, see Michaelis, *Ursachen und Folgen,* 2: 103–234. See also Louis Fischer, *The Life of Lenin* (New York, 1964), pp. 156–57, 161–75, 186–90, 195–211.
3. Ruhl F. Bartlett, ed. *The Record of American Diplomacy: Documents and Readings in the History of American Foreign Relations* (New York, 1964), p. 459.
4. For documents relating to the end of World War One, see Auswärtigen Amtes und Reichministerum des Innern, *Amtliche Urkunde zur Vorgeschichte des Waffenstillstandes 1919* (Berlin, 1924); Alma Luckau, ed. *The German Delegation at The Paris Peace Conference* (New York, 1941); and Michaelis, *Ursachen und Folgen,* 2: 374–470.

Chapter 4

1. For studies of the German Revolution of 1918, see Richard M. Watt, *The Kings Depart: The Tragedy of Germany, Versailles and the German Revolution* (New York, 1968), Arthur John Ryder, *The German Revolution of*

1918: A Study of German Socialism in War and Revolt (Cambridge, 1967); Halperin, *Germany Tried Democracy;* and Erich Eych, *A History of The Weimar Republic,* 2 vols. (Cambridge, Mass., 1962). For documents dealing with the revolution, see Michaelis, *Ursachen und Folgen,* 3: 1–221.

2. Scheidemann, *Memoirs,* 2: 580–82.

3. For the minutes of the meetings of the Council of People's Representatives, see Eberhard Kolb, ed. *Der Zentralrat der deutschen sozialistischen Republic* (Leiden: 1968).

4. For a study of the Free Corps, see Robert G.L. Waite, *Vanguard of Nazism: The Free Corps Movement in Postwar Germany 1918–1923* (New York, 1969).

5. For a discussion of the Spartacist revolt of 1919, see Erich Waldman, *The Spartacist Uprising of 1919* (Milwaukee, 1956).

6. For a discussion of the Bavarian Revolution, see Allan Mitchell, *Revolution in Bavaria 1918–1919; The Eisner Regime and the Soviet Republic* (Princeton, 1965).

Chapter 5

1. For the Preuss Report and related documents, see Michaelis, *Ursachen und Folgen,* 3: 421–23.

2. For documents relating to the development of the political parties of Weimar Germany, ibid., 465–93.

3. For a discussion of the Paris Peace Conference see Harold Nicolson, *Peace Making, 1919* (New York, 1965); and Watt, *The Kings Depart.*

4. For documents relating to the Treaty of Versailles and the German reaction, see Luckau, *The German Delegation;* and Michaelis, *Ursachen und Folgen,* 3: 331–418.

5. Nicolson, *Peace Making, 1919,* pp. 365–71.

6. For documents relating to the national assembly and the Weimar constitution see Michaelis, *Ursachen und Folgen,* 3: 464–93.

Chapter 6

1. For survey histories of the Weimar Republic see Eyck, *A History of the Weimar Republic;* Halperin, *Germany Tried Democracy;* Holborn, *A History of Modern Germany, Vol. 3: 1840–1945,* W. M. Knight-Patterson, *Germany from Defeat to Conquest* (London, 1945); Pinson, *Modern Germany;* and Hanna Vogt, *The Burden of Guilt,* trans. by Herbert Strauss (New York, 1964).

2. Scheidemann, *Memoirs,* 2: 645–78.

3. For a discussion of the leftist revolt of 1921, see Werner T. Angress, *Stillborn Revolution: The Communist Bid for Power in Germany 1921–1923* (Princeton, 1963).

4. For information on the life and work of Seeckt, see Hans Meir Welcker, *Seeckt* (Frankfurt, 1967); and Hans von Seeckt, *Aus seinem Leben* (Berlin, 1940).

5. For studies of the army during the Weimar era, see F. L. Carsten, *The Reichswehr and Politics 1918–1933* (Berkeley, 1973); Craig, *The Politics of the Prussian Army 1640–1945;* Gaines Post, Jr., *The Civil Military Fabric of Weimar Foreign Policy* (Princeton, 1973); and John W. Wheeler-Bennett, *The Nemesis of Power: The German Army in Politics 1918–1945* (London, 1964).

Chapter 7

1. For biographies of Hitler, see Alan Bullock, *Hitler: A Study in Tyranny* (New York, 1962); Joachim C. Fest, *Hitler,* trans. by Richard and Clara Winston (New York, 1967); Konrad Heiden, *Der Fuehrer* (Boston, 1944); Robert Payne, *The Life and Death of Adolf Hitler* (New York, 1973); and William L. Shirer, *The Rise and Fall of the Third Reich* (New York, 1960).
2. For discussions of Hitler's ancestry and youth, see Franz Jetzinger, *Hitlers Jugend: Phantasien, Lügen und die Wahrheit* (Vienna, 1956); Werner Maser, *Hitler, Legend, Myth and Reality,* trans. by Peter and Betty Ross (New York, 1971); and Bradley F. Smith, *Adolf Hitler, His Family, Childhood, and Youth* (Stanford, 1967).
3. For a discussion of Hitler's physical and mental health see Walter Langer, *The Mind of Adolf Hitler* (New York, 1972); Maser, *Hitler,* pp. 209–32; and Hans-Dietrich Röhrs, *Hitlers Krankheit* (Neckargemünd, 1966).
4. August Kubizek, *Young Hitler: The Story of Our Friendship,* trans. by E. V. Anderson (London, 1954).
5. For a discussion of Hitler in Vienna, see William S. Jenks, *Vienna and the Young Hitler* (New York, 1960).
6. For information on Hitler's political development, see Adolf Hitler, *Hitler's Letters and Notes,* ed. by Werner Maser, trans. by Arnold Pommenans (London, 1972), *Hitler's Secret Book* trans. by Salvator Attansio (New York, 1961); *Hitler's Secret Conversations 1941–1944,* trans. by Norman Cameron and R. H. Stevens (New York, 1953); *Mein Kampf,* trans. by Ralph Nanheim (Boston, 1943), and *Hitlers Tischgespräche im Führerhauptquartier 1941–1942,* ed. by Henry Picker (Stuttgart, 1965).

Chapter 8

1. For discussions and documents dealing with the origins of the Nazi party, see the works listed in Note 1, Chapter VII; Karl Dietrich Bracher, *The German Dictatorship,* trans. by Jean Steinberg (New York, 1970); International Military Tribunal, *Trial of the Major War Criminals Before the International Military Tribunal, Nuremberg, 14 November 1945–1 October 1946* (Nuremberg, 1949) (hereafter referred to as *The Nuremberg Documents);* Walter Hofer, ed., *Der Nationalsozialismus: Dokuments 1933–1945* (Frankfurt, 1965); Office of the United States Chief Counsel for Prosecution of Axis Criminality, *Nazi Conspiracy and Aggression,* 8 vols. 2 supplements (Washington, D. C., 1946–1948); Werner Maser, *Der Frühgeschichte der NSDAP: Hitlers Weg bis 1924* (Frankfurt, 1966); Franz Neumann, *Behemoth: The Structure and Practice of National Socialism 1933–1944* (New York, 1944); Jeremy Noakes and Geoffrey Pridham, eds. *Documents on Nazism 1919–1945* (London, 1974); Nuremberg Military Tribunal, *Trials of the War Criminals*

Before the Nuremberg Tribunal Under Control Council Law no. 10 Nuremberg, October 1946–April 1949, 15 vols. (Washington, D.C.: 1950).

2. Hitler, *Mein Kampf,* pp. 217–24.

3. For documents and discussions on the development of the party ideology and propaganda, see the works listed in Note 6, Chapter VII, and Note 1, Chapter VIII; see also A. A. B. Zeman, *Nazi Propaganda* (New York, 1973); and Adolf Hitler *The Speeches of Adolf Hitler, April 1922–August 1939,* 2 vols., ed. by Norman H. Baynes. (London, 1942).

4. For short biographies of the major figures of Nazism see Eugene Davidson, *The Trial of the Germans* (New York, 1972); and Joachim C. Fest, *The Face of the Third Reich: Portraits of the Nazi Leadership,* trans. by Michael Bullock (New York, 1970).

5. For the life and work of Hesse, see Roger Manvell and Heinrich Fraenkel, *Hess: A Biography* (London, 1971).

6. For biographies of Göring, see Charles Bewley, *Hermann Göring and the Third Reich* (New York, 1962); Leonard Mosley *The Reich Marshal: A Biography of Hermann Göring* (New York, 1974); see also Hermann Göring, *Germany Reborn* (London, 1934).

7. For documents and studies of the Beer Hall Putsch, see the works listed in Note 1, Chapter VIII, and Kurt Ludecke, *I Knew Hitler* (London, 1938), pp. 157–70; Hans Hubert Hoffmann, *Der Hitler Putsch* (Munich, 1961); and Michaelis, *Ursachen und Folgen,* 5: 417–61.

Chapter 9

1. For information concerning the life and work of Stresemann, see Heinrich Bauer, *Stresemann, Ein deutscher Staatsmann* (Berlin, 1930); Henry Ashby Turner, *Stresemann and the Politics of the Weimar Republic* (Princeton, 1963); and Gustav Stresemann, *His Diaries, Letters and Papers,* 3 vols., ed. and trans. by Erich Sutton (New York, 1935); see also the works listed in Note 1, Chapter VI.

2. For documents relating to the Dawes Plan, see The Reparations Commission, *The Expert's Plan for Reparation Payments* (Paris, n.p., 1926); Office of Reparation Payments, *The Execution of The Expert's Plan,* (Berlin, editions issued 1924–28 and 1930); and Michaelis, *Ursachen und Folgen,* 6: 59–128. For studies of the reparations issue, see Frank D. Graham, *Exchange Prices and Production in Hyper-Inflation Germany, 1920–1923* (Princeton, 1930); John Maynard Keynes, *The Economic Consequences of the Peace* (New York, 1920); and Constantino Bresciani-Turroni, *The Economics of Inflation: A Study of Currency Depreciation in Post-War Germany* trans. by Millicent E. Sayers (London, 1937).

3. For information on the life and work of Hindenburg, see Andreas Dorpalen, *Hindenburg and the Weimar Republic* (Princeton, 1964); and Emil Ludwig, *Hindenburg, Legende und Wirklichkeit* (Hamburg, n.p., 1962).

4. For documents relating to the Locarno Conference, see Michaelis, *Ursachen und Folgen,* 6: 308–454; and Stresemann, *Diaries,* 2: 171–90.

5. For documents relating to the Young Plan, see the works listed in Note 2, Chapter IX; and Michaelis, *Ursachen und Folgen,* 7: 577–634.

Chapter 10

1. Since the works of the major authors and scholars of the Weimar era are readily available at most libraries, they will not be cited in the notes. For general histories of German literature, see J. G. Robertson et al., *A History of German Literature* (London, 1966); Werner P. Friedrich, *History of German Literature* (New York, 1948); and Ernst Rose, *A History of German Literature* (New York, 1960). For a discussion of culture in general during the Weimar Republic, see Otto Friedrich, *Before The Deluge: A Portrait of Berlin in The 1920s* (New York, 1973); and Peter Gay, *Weimar Culture, The Outsider as Insider* (New York, 1968).

2. For a discussion of art in Weimar Germany, see Franz Roh, *German Art in the 20th Century* (Greenwich, Conn: 1968); and H. W. Janson and Dora Jane Janson, *The Story of Painting for Young People* (New York, 1962), pp. 146–48, 158.

3. For a discussion of music in Weimar Germany, see Joseph Machlis, *The Enjoyment of Music* (New York, 1963), pp. 345–50, 401–10; William W. Austin, *Music in the 20th Century* (New York, 1966), pp. 134–44, 294–318, 396–416; and Otto Deri, *Exploring Twentieth Century Music* (New York, 1968), pp. 263–318, 389–418.

4. "Noble simplicity and quiet greatness" were the basic concepts of German Classicism as defined by Johann Joachim Winckelmann in *History of the Art of Antiquity*, n.p., (1764).

5. For a discussion of film in Weimar Germany, see Siegfried Kracauer, *From Caligari to Hitler: A Psychological History of the German Film* (Princeton, 1966).

6. Gay, *Weimar Culture*, pp. 127–32; Friedrich, *Before The Deluge*.

7. For a discussion of the cult of the folk during the Weimar era, see Kohn, *The Mind of Germany*, pp. 306–43; Mosse, *The Crisis of German Ideology*, pp. 237–311; and Stern, *The Politics of Cultural Despair*, pp. 183–300.

Chapter 11

1. For information on Hitler's imprisonment and activities before 1933, see the works listed in Note 1, Chapter VII, and Note 1, Chapter VIII; see also Ernst (Putzi) Hanfstaengl, *Hitler, The Missing Years* (London, n.p., 1957); and Ludecke, *I Knew Hitler*.

2. For discussions of the life and work of Goebbels, see Helmut Heiber, *Joseph Goebbels* (Berlin, 1962); and Viktor Reinmann, *Dr. Joseph Goebbels* (Vienna, 1971).

3. For information on the rebirth of the Nazi movement, see the works listed in Note 1, Chapter VIII; and Geoffrey Pridham, *Hitler's Rise to Power: The Nazi Movement in Bavaria, 1923–1933* (New York, 1973).

4. For documents relating to the ministry of Brüning, see Michaelis, *Ursachen und Folgen*, 8: 2–72, 310.

5. For documents relating to the Hoover moratorium and the bank crisis, ibid., 7: 181–218.

Chapter 12

1. For discussions of the last years of the Weimar Republic, see the works listed in Note 1, Chapter VI. For documents concerning Papen's rule, see Franz von Papen, *Memoirs*, trans. by Brian Corell (New York, 1953); and Michaelis, *Ursachen und Folgen*, 8: 539–56.

2. For documents dealing with Schleicher's ministry, see Michaelis, *Ursachen und Folgen*, 8: 539–56.

3. For a discussion of the appointment of Hitler, see the works listed in Note 1, Chapter VII; Elliot Baruclo Wheaton, *The Nazi Revolution 1933–1935: Prelude to Calamity* (Garden City, N.Y., 1969); Neumann, *Behemoth;* and Bracher, *The German Dictatorship*. For a discussion of the role of the military, see the books listed in Note 4, Chapter VI; and Telford Taylor, *Sword and Swastika: Generals and Nazis in the Third Reich* (Chicago, 1969). For source materials, see Ludecke, *I Knew Hitler;* Hofer, *Der Nationalsozialismus:* Noakes and Pridham, *Documents on Nazism;* International Military Tribunal, *The Nuremberg Documents;* Papen, *Memoirs,* pp. 225–64, and Michaelis, *Ursachen und Folgen,* 8: 740–66.

4. Wheaton, *The Nazi Revolution,* pp. 251–64; and Fritz Tobias, *The Reichstag Fire* (New York, 1964).

Chapter 13

1. For studies of the history of Germany from 1933 to 1939, see the works listed in Note 1, Chapter VIII; David Schoenbaum, *Hitler's Social Revolution: Class and Status in Nazi Germany 1933–1939* (Garden City, N.Y., 1966); and Wheaton, *The Nazi Revolution.* For primary sources, see also Bella Fromm, *Blood and Banquets: A Berlin Social Diary* (New York, 1942); Adolf Hitler, *Rede und Proclamationen 1932–1945* ed. by Max Domarus (Würzburg, 1962); William L. Shirer, *Berlin Diary: The Journal of a Foreign Correspondent 1934–1941* (New York, 1961); and Albert Speer, *Inside the Third Reich* (New York, 1973).

2. For studies of the military under Hitler, see Wheeler-Bennett, *The Nemesis of Power;* Craig, *The Politics of the Prussian Army;* and Taylor, *Sword and Swastika.* For documents, see Rudolf F. Absolon, ed., *Die Wehrmacht im Dritten Reich,* 3 vols. (Poppard am Rhein. 1969); International Military Tribunal, *The Nuremberg Documents;* and Office of U.S. Prosecution, *Nazi Conspiracy and Aggression.*

3. For documents and a study of Himmler see Roger Manvell and Heinrich Fraenkel, *Himmler* (New York, 1964); and Helmut Heiber, ed., *Reichsführer! . . . Briefe an und von Himmler* (Stuttgart, n.p., 1968).

4. For a study of the S.S., see Heinz Höhne, *The Order of The Death's Head: The Story of Hitler's S.S.,* trans. by Richard Barry (New York, 1967).

5. For personal accounts of life in the concentration camps see Eugen Kogan, *The Theory and Practice of Hell* (New York, 1975); and Germaine Tillion, *Ravensbrück* (Garden City, N.Y., 1975).

6. For discussions of the fate of the Jews under Hitler, see Lucy Dawidowicz, *The War Against the Jews, 1933–1945* (New York, 1975); Raul Hilberg, *The Destruction of the European Jews* (Chicago, 1961); Nora Levin, *The*

Holocaust: The Destruction of European Jewry 1933-1945 (New York, 1968). For documents, see Raul Hilberg, *Documents of Destruction: Germany and Jewry 1933-1945* (Chicago, 1971); International Military Tribunal, *The Nuremberg Documents;* and Office of U.S. Prosecution, *Nazi Conspiracy and Aggression.*

7. For short biographies of the leaders of the Third Reich, see Davidson, *The Trial of the Germans;* and Fest, *The Face of the Third Reich.*

8. Speer, *Inside the Third Reich,* pp. 187-91.

9. Ibid., pp. 133-34.

10. For a discussion of Hitler's attitude towards women, see ibid., pp. 138-39, 596-97; Langer, *The Mind of Adolf Hitler;* Maser, *Hitler: Legend, Myth and Reality,* pp. 194-208; and Glenn B. Infield, *Eva and Adolf* (New York, 1974).

11. For studies of Hitler's mental and physical health, see the works listed in Note 3, Chapter VII.

Chapter 14

1. For discussions on society and culture under Hitler, see Richard Grunberger, *The 12-Year Reich: A Social History of Nazi Germany 1933-1945* (New York, 1971); George L. Mosse, *Nazi Culture* (New York, 1966); and Wheaton, *The Nazi Revolution.* For documents relating to Nazi culture, see Hofer, *Der Nationalsozialismus;* Noakes and Pridham, *Documents on Nazism;* International Military Tribunal, *The Nuremberg Documents;* and Michaelis, *Ursachen und Folgen,* 9: 478-512.

2. Speer, *Inside the Third Reich,* pp. 92-100; Shirer, *Berlin Diary,* pp. 16-23.

3. For a discussion of the role of women in the Third Reich, see Grunberger, *The 12 Year Reich,* pp. 275-92; Schoenbaum, *Hitler's Social Revolution,* pp. 178-92; and Hans Peter Bluel, *Sex and Society in Nazi Germany* trans. by J. Maxwell Brownjohn (New York, 1974).

4. For a discussion of the Hitler Youth, see H. W. Kock, *The Hitler Youth* (London, 1976).

5. For discussions of the churches in the Third Reich, see Arthur C. Cochrane, *The Church's Confession under Hitler* (Philadelphia, 1962); Grunberger, *The 12 Year Reich,* pp. 481-501; and Wheaton, *The Nazi Revolution,* pp. 387-410. For documents relating to the churches, see Hofer, *Der Nationalsozialismus,* pp. 127-66; International Military Tribunal, *The Nuremberg Documents;* and Michaelis, *Ursachen und Folgen,* 9: 537-618.

Chapter 15

1. For information on Hitler's aims in foreign policy, see the works listed in Notes 1 and 6, Chapter VII, especially Adolf Hitler, *Mein Kampf,* pp. 605-67.

2. For discussions on Nazi foreign policy, see the works listed in Note 1, Chapter VII, Note 1, Chapter VIII, and Note 2, Chapter XIII; and William Carr, *Arms, Autarky, and Aggression: A Study in German Foreign Policy, 1933-1939* (New York, 1973); Klaus Hildebrand, *The Foreign Policy of the*

Third Reich, trans. by Anthony Fothergill (Berkeley, 1973); David Hoggan, *Der Erzwungene Krieg* (Tübingen, 1970); Warren B. Morris, Jr., *The Revisionist Historians and German War Guilt* (New York, 1977); Rich, Norman, *Hitler's War Aims: Ideology, the Nazi State and the Course of Expansion,* 2 vols. (New York, 1973); A. J. P. Taylor, *The Origins of the Second World War* (Greenwich, Conn., 1968). For documents see Alexander Cadogan, *The Diaries of Sir Alexander Cadogan, 1938–1945* (New York, 1972); Galeazzo Ciano, *The Ciano Diaries, 1939–1943: The Complete Unabridged Diaries of Count Galeazzo Ciano: Italian Minister for Foreign Affairs, 1936–1943* (Garden City, N.Y., 1946); Galeazzo Ciano, *Ciano's Diplomatic Papers* (London, 1948); Anthony Eden, *The Memoirs of Anthony Eden* (Boston, 1965); Nevile Henderson, *Failure of a Mission: Berlin 1937–1939* (New York, 1940); Fritz Hesse, *Hitler and the English* trans. by F.A. Vogt (London, 1954); Office of the U.S. Prosecution, *Nazi Conspiracy and Aggression;* International Military Tribunal, *The Nuremberg Documents;* Nuremberg Military Tribunal, *Trial of the War Criminals;* E. P. Perkins, ed., *Foreign Relations of The United States: Diplomatic Papers, 1938* and *Foreign Relations of the United States: Diplomatic Papers, 1939* (Washington, D.C., 1955); Joachim von Ribbentrop, *The Ribbentrop Memoirs* trans. by Oliver Watson (London, 1954); Raymond James Sontag et al., eds., *Documents on German Foreign Policy from the Archives of the German Foreign Ministry, Series D* (Washington D.C., 1948); Paul Schmidt, *Hitler's Interpreter* trans. by R.H.C. Steed, (London, 1950); Edward Frederick L. Wood, *The Earl of Halifax: Fullness of Days* (London, 1957); E. L. Woodward and Rohan Butler, eds., *Documents on British Foreign Policy, Third Series* (London, 1950); and Michaelis, *Ursachen und Folgen,* vol. 10.

3. For a discussion of Nazi propaganda in Austria, see Zeman, *Nazi Propaganda,* pp. 111–33.

CHAPTER 16

1. For discussions and documents on Nazi foreign policy, see the works listed in Note 2, Chapter XV.

2. Stanley G. Payne, *A History of Spain and Portugal* (Madison, Wis.: University of Wisconsin Press, 1973), 2: 645–62.

3. Noakes and Pridham, *Documents on Nazism,* pp. 522–28.

4. For discussions of the army under Hitler, see the works listed in Note 2, Chapter XIII.

5. For a study of the life and work of Canaris, see Andre Brissaud, *Canaris* (London, 1970).

6. For a discussion on the relationship between the anti-Nazi forces in Germany and British intelligence see Anthony Cave Brown, *Bodyguard of Lies* (New York, 1975).

7. Kurt von Schuschnigg, *Austrian Requiem,* trans. by Franz von Hildebrand (New York, 1946) pp. 11–27.

8. Hugh Seton-Watson, *Eastern Europe Between the Wars, 1918–1941* (New York, n.p., 1967), pp. 278–82.

9. For studies of the Beck-Halder plot, see the works listed in Note 2, Chap-

ter XIII; and Ernst von Weizsäcker, *The Memoirs of Ernst von Weizsäcker* trans. by John Andrews (London, 1951), pp. 141–49.

10. For a discussion of the Munich agreement, see Henri Nogueres, *Munich "Peace in Our Time"* trans. by Patrick O'Brian (New York, 1965).

11. For documents relating to the negotiations between Germany and Poland, see the works listed in Note 2, Chapter XV; and Josef Lipski, *Papers and Memoirs of Josef Lipski, Ambassador of Poland, Diplomat in Berlin 1933–1939* ed. by Waclaw Jedrzejewicz (New York, 1968).

Chapter 17

1. For secondary and primary works dealing with the war, see the works listed in Note 1, Chapter VII, and Note 2, Chapter XIII; Winston S. Churchill, *The Second World War*, 6 vols. (New York, 1961); John Lukacs, *The Last European War* (Garden City, N.Y., 1976); George H. Stein, *The Waffen S. S. Hitler's Elite Guard at War 1939–1945* (Ithaca, N.Y., 1966); Hans-Adolf Jacobsen, ed., *Kriegstagbuch der Oberkommando der Wehrmacht*, 4 vols. (Frankfurt, 1961–65); William Keitel, *The Memoirs of Field Marshal Keitel*, ed. by Walter Gorlits and trans. by David Irving (New York, 1965); and H. R. Trevor-Roper, ed., *Blitzkrieg to Defeat: Hitler's War Directives 1939–1945* (New York, n.p., 1965).

2. For documents on Hitler's conduct of the war and relations with his generals, see the works listed above; Franz Halder, *Kriegstagbuch*, 3 vols., ed. by Hans-Adolf Jacobsen (Stuttgart, 1962–64); Helmut Heiber, ed., *Hitlers Lagebesprechungen: Die Protokollefragmente seiner militärischen Konferenzen 1942–1945* (Stuttgart, n.p., 1962); Joseph Goebbels, *The Goebbels Diaries 1942–1943* (Garden City, N.Y., 1948); and Speer, *Inside the Third Reich*.

3. For studies on intelligence during the war, see Brown, *Bodyguard of Lies;* and Walter Schellenberg, *Hitler's Secret Service*, trans. by Louis Hagen (New York, 1974).

4. For a discussion of the role of Project Ultra in the war, see F. W. Winterbotham, *The Ultra Secret* (New York, 1974); and Brown, *Bodyguard of Lies*.

5. For a study of the Battle of Britain, see Richard Collier, *Eagle Day, The Battle of Britain, August 6–September 15, 1940* (New York, 1966).

Chapter 18

1. For histories and documents on the war, see the works listed in notes 1 and 2, Chapter XVII.

2. Seton-Watson, *Eastern Europe Between the Wars,* pp. 397–402: and L. S. Stavrianos, *The Balkans Since 1453* (New York, 1966), pp. 699–749.

3. Brown, *Bodyguard of Lies,* pp. 213–214.

4. Stavrianos, *The Balkans Since 1453,* pp. 755–99.

5. For studies of Stalin and the war in Russia, see Trumbull Higgins, *Hitler and Russia: The Third Reich in a Two Front War 1937–1943* (New York, 1966); Albert Seaton, *The Russo-German War 1941–1945* (New York; 1970); Alexander Werth, *Russia at War, 1941–1945* (New York, 1964); Georgi K. Zhukov, *Marshal Zhukov's Greatest Battles* trans. by Theodore Shabab (New York, 1969); and Adam B. Ulam, *Stalin: The Man and His Era* (New York, 1973).

6. For a discussion of Stalingrad, see Vasili I, Chuikov, *The Battle for Stalingrad*, trans. by Harold Silver (New York, 1964).
7. For an account of Popov's work during the war, see Dusko Popov, *Spy Counter Spy* (New York, 1974).
8. Brown, *Bodyguard of Lies,* pp. 92–133.
9. For a discussion of the American role in Africa and Europe, see Dwight D. Eisenhower, *Crusade in Europe* (Garden City, N.Y., 1948).
10. For a discussion of the battle of Leningrad, see Harrison E. Salisbury, *The 900 Days: The Siege of Leningrad* (New York, 1969).
11. For a complete discussion of Allied deception in preparation for D-Day, see Brown, *Bodyguard of Lies.*

CHAPTER 19

1. For documents and information on the occupied countries, see Raphäel Lewkin, *Axis Rule in Occupied Europe, Laws of Occupation Analysis of Government, Proposals for Redress* (Washington D.C., 1944); Jacobsen, *Der Zweite Weltkrieg,* pp. 180–203; International Military Tribunal, *The Nuremberg Documents;* Office of the U.S. Prosecution, *Nazi Conspiracy and Aggression;* Shirer, *The Rise and Fall of the Third Reich,* pp. 937–94.
2. For accounts of life in the concentration camps, see Kogan, *The Theory and Practice of Hell;* Jean Francois Steiner, *Treblinka* trans. by Helen Weaver (New York, 1967); and Tillion, *Ravensbrück.*
3. For studies of the fate of the Jews during the war, see the works listed in Note 6, Chapter XIII, and Morris, *The Revisionist Historians and German War Guilt,* pp. 78–94. For documents and an eyewitness account of the gas chambers, see Rudolf Höss, *Commandant of Auschwitz* trans. by Constantine Fitzgibbon (London, 1959), pp. 148–52; and Noakes and Pridham, *Documents on Nazism,* pp. 485–93.
4. For discussions and documents concerning the German opposition to Hitler, see the works listed in Note 2, Chapter XIII; Bundeszentrale für politische Bildung, *Germans Against Hitler* (Bonn, 1964); Peter Hoffmann, *Wiederstand Staatstreich Attentat* (Munich, n.p., 1959); Hans Rothfels, *The German Opposition to Hitler* (Hinsdale, Ill., 1948); Hofer, *Der Nationalsozialismus,* pp. 322–59; and Eberhard Zeller, *The Flame of Freedom: The German Struggle Against Hitler* (Coral Gables, Fla., 1969).
5. Manvell and Fraenkel, *Hess,* pp. 94–134.
6. Ger von Roon, *German Resistance to Hitler: Count von Moltke and the Kreisau Circle* (London, 1971).
7. For discussions of the plot to assassinate Hitler, see Constantine Fitzgibbon, *20 July* (New York, 1956); Joachim Kramarz, *Stauffenberg,* trans. by R. H. Barry (New York, 1967); and Fabian von Schlabrendorff, *The Secret War Against Hitler* trans. by Hilde Simon (New York, 1965).
8. Speer, *Inside the Third Reich,* pp. 484–504; Zeller, *The Flame of Freedom,* p. 318.
9. For a discussion of July 20 in Paris, see Wilhelm von Schramm, *Der 20 Juli in Paris* (Bad Wörishofen, 1953).

Chapter 20

1. For discussions and documents relating to the war, see notes 1 and 2, Chapter XVII.
2. For information on the mental and physical health of Hitler, see the works listed in note 3, Chapter VII.
3. Goebbels, *Diaries,* pp. 266, 287; and Speer, *Inside the Third Reich,* pp. 595–617.
4. For a detailed account of the Allied air war against Germany, see Charles Webster and Noble Frankland, *The Strategic Air Offensive Against Germany 1939–1945,* 4 vols. (London, 1961).
5. Noakes and Pridham, *Documents on Nazism,* pp. 631–53.
6. Shirer, *Berlin Diary,* pp. 142–77 passim, 418–19; and Speer, *Inside the Third Reich,* pp. 229–30, 383.
7. Brown, *Bodyguard of Lies,* pp. 370–77.
8. For a discussion of the liberation of Paris and Hitler's order for its destruction, see Larry Collins and Dominique Lapierre, *Is Paris Burning?* (New York, 1965).
9. For a discussion of the Battle of the Bulge, see Peter Elstob, *Hitler's Last Offensive: The Full Story of the Battle of the Ardennes* (New York, 1971).
10. For accounts of the fall of Nazi Germany, see Vasili Chuikov, *The Fall of Berlin,* trans. by Ruth Kisch (New York, 1967); Cornelius Ryan, *The Last Battle,* (New York, 1966); and John Toland, *The Last 100 Days* (New York, 1966).
11. For an account of the last days of Hitler, see H. R. Trevor-Roper, ed., *The Last Days of Hitler* (New York, 1962).
12. For an account of the Russian autopsy of Hitler's body, see Lev Bezymenski, *The Death of Adolf Hitler: Unknown Documents From The Soviet Archives* (New York, 1968).
13. Reinhard Gehlen, *The Service,* trans. by David Irving (New York, 1972), p. 70.

Selected Bibliography

1. Primary Sources

Absolon, Rudolf F., ed. *Die Wehrmacht im Dritten Reich.* 3 vols. Poppard am Rhein: Harold Boldt Verlag, 1969.
Auswärtigen Amtes und Reichsministerum des Innern. *Amtliche Urkunde zur Vorgeschichte des Waffenstillstandes 1919.* Berlin: Deutsche Verlagsgesellschaft für Politik und Geschichte, 1924.
Bartlett, Ruhl F., ed. *The Record of American Diplomacy: Documents and Readings in the History of American Foreign Relations.* New York: Alfred A. Knopf, 1964.
Bezymenski, Lev. *The Death of Adolf Hitler: Unknown Documents from Soviet Archives.* New York: Harcourt, Brace and World, 1968.
Bismarck, Otto von. *Reflections and Reminiscences.* Edited by Theodore S. Hamerow. New York: Harper Torchbooks, 1968.
Cadogan, Alexander. *The Diaries of Sir Alexander Cadogan, 1938–1945.* Edited by David Dilks. New York: G.P. Putnam's Sons, 1972.
Calic, Edouard, ed. *Unmasked: Two Confidential Interviews with Hitler in 1931.* Translated by Richard Barry. London: Chatto and Windus, 1971.
Ciano, Galeazzo. *The Ciano Diaries, 1939–1943: The Complete Unabridged Diaries of Count Galeazzo Ciano: Italian Minister for Foreign Affairs, 1936–1943.* Garden City, N.Y.: Doubleday and Co., 1946.
———. *Ciano's Diplomatic Papers.* Edited by Malcolm Muggeridge. Translated by Stuart Hood. London: Oldhams Press, 1948.
Eden, Anthony. *The Memoirs of Anthony Eden.* Boston: Houghton Mifflin, 1965.
Eisenhower, Dwight D. *Crusade in Europe.* Garden City, N.Y.: Doubleday and Co., 1948.
Fromm, Bella. *Blood and Banquets: A Berlin Social Diary.* New York: Harper and Brothers, 1942.
Goebbels, Joseph. *The Goebbels Diaries, 1942–1943.* Translated by Louis Lochner. Garden City, N.Y.: Doubleday and Co., 1948.

Göring, Hermann. *Germany Reborn.* London: Elkin Mathews and Marrot, 1934.
Halder, Franz. *Kriegstagbuch.* 3 vols. Edited by Hans-Adolf Jacobsen. Stuttgart: W. Kohlhammer Verlag, 1962–64.
Henderson, Nevile. *Failure of a Mission: Berlin 1937–1939.* New York: G. P. Putnam's Sons, 1940.
Hesse, Fritz. *Hitler and the English.* Translated by F. A. Vogt. London: Allan Wingate, 1954.
Hilberg, Raul, ed. *Documents of Destruction: Germany and Jewry 1933–1945.* Chicago: Quadrangle Books, 1971.
Himmler, Heinrich. *Reichsführer! . . . Briefe an und von Himmler.* Edited by Helmut Heiber. Stuttgart: Deutsche Verlag, 1968.
Hitler, Adolf. *Blitzkrieg to Defeat: Hitler's War Directives 1939–1944.* Edited by H. R. Trevor Roper. New York: Holt, Rinehart and Winston, 1971.
———. *Hitlers Lagebesprechung: Die Protokollfragmente seiner militärischen Konferenzen 1942–1945.* Edited by Helmut Heiber. Stuttgart: Deutsche Verlag, 1962.
———. *Hitler's Letters and Notes.* Edited by Werner Maser. Translated by Arnold Pommenans. London: Heinemann, 1972.
———. *Hitlers Rede und Proklamationen 1932–1945.* 2 vols. Edited by Max Domarus. Würzburg: Verlagsdruckerei Schmidt, 1962.
———. *Hitler's Secret Book.* Translated by Salvator Attansio. New York: Grove Press, 1961.
———. *Hitler's Secret Conversations 1941–1944.* Translated by Norman Cameron and R. H. Stevens. New York: Farrar, Straus, 1953.
———. *Mein Kampf.* Translated by Ralph Nanheim. Boston: Houghton Mifflin, 1943.
———. *The Speeches of Adolf Hitler, April 1922–August 1939.* 2 vols. Edited by Norman H. Baynes. London: Oxford University Press, 1942.
———. *Hitlers Tischgespräche im Führerhauptquartier 1941–1942,* Edited by Henry Picker. Stuttgart: Seewald Verlag, 1965.
Hofer, Walter, ed. *Der Nationalsozialismus: Dokuments 1933–1945.* Frankfurt: Fischer Bücherei, 1965.
Höss, Rudolf. *Commandant of Auschwitz.* Translated by Constantine Fitzgibbon. London: Weiden Feld and Nicolson, 1959.
International Military Tribunal. *Trial of the Major War Criminals Before the International Military Tribunal, Nuremberg, 14 November 1945–1 October 1946.* 42 vols. Nuremberg: International Military Tribunal, 1949.
Jacobsen, Hans-Adolf, ed. *Kriegstagbuch der Oberkommando der Wehrmacht.* 4 vols. Frankfurt: Bernard Graefe Verlag, 1961–65.
———. *Der Zweite Weltkrieg.* Frankfurt: Fischer Bucherei, 1965.
Keitel, Wilhelm. *The Memoirs of Field Marshal Keitel.* Edited by Walter Gorlits. Translated by David Irving. New York: Stein and Day, 1965.
Kersten, Felix. *The Kersten Memoirs, 1940–1945.* Translated by Constantine Fitzgibbon and James Oliver. New York: The Macmillan Co., 1957.
Kogan, Eugen. *The Theory and Practice of Hell.* Translated by Heinz Norden. New York: Berkley Windhover, 1975.
Kolb, Eberhard, ed. *Der Zentralrat der deutschen sozialistischen Republic 9. 12. 1918–8. 4. 1919.* Leiden: E. J. Brill, 1968.

Kubizek, August. *Young Hitler: The Story of Our Friendship.* Translated by E. V. Anderson. London: Allan Wingate, 1954.

Lewkin, Raphäel, *Axis Rule in Occupied Europe. Laws of Occupation, Analysis of Government, Proposals for Redress.* Washington, D.C.: Carnegie Endowment for International Peace, 1944.

Lipski, Josef. *Papers and Memoirs of Josef Lipski, Ambassador of Poland, Diplomat in Berlin 1933–1939.* Edited by Waclaw Jedrzejewicz. New York: Columbia University Press, 1968.

Luckau, Alma, ed. *The German Delegation at the Paris Peace Conference.* New York: Columbia University Press, 1941.

Ludecke, Kurt. *I Knew Hitler.* London: Jarrolds, 1938.

Marx, Karl, and Engels, Frederick. *Selected Works.* New York: International Publishers, 1974.

Michaelis, Herbert et al., eds. *Ursachen und Folgen von deutschen Zusammenbruch 1918 und 1945 bis zur staatlichen Neuordnung Deutschlands in der Gagenwart.* Berlin: Dokumente Verlag Dr. Herbert Wendler and Col, 1962.

Nicolson, Harold. *Peace Making, 1919.* New York: Grosset and Dunlap, 1965.

Nietzsche, Friedrich. *The Portable Nietzsche,* Edited and translated by Walter Kaufmann. New York: The Viking Press, 1968.

Noakes, Jeremy, and Pridham, Geoffrey, eds. *Documents on Nazism 1919–1945.* London: Jonathan Cape, 1974.

Nuremberg Military Tribunal. *Trials of the War Criminals Before the Nuremberg Tribunal Under Control Council Law no. 10 Nuremberg, October 1946–April 1949,* 15 vols. Washington, D.C.: U.S. Government Printing Office, 1950.

Office of Reparation Payments. *The Execution of the Expert's Plan.* Berlin: Office of Reparation Payments; annual reports issued 1924–30.

Office of the United States Chief Counsel for Prosecution of Axis Criminality. *Nazi Conspiracy and Aggression.* 8 vols. 2 supplements. Washington D.C.: U.S. Government Printing Office, 1946–48.

Papen, Franz von. *Memoirs.* Translated by Brian Corell. New York: E. P. Dutton and Co., 1953.

Perkins, E. P., ed. *Foreign Relations of the United States: Diplomatic Papers, 1938.* 5 vols. Washington, D.C.: U.S. Government Printing Office, 1955.

———. *Foreign Relations of the United States: Diplomatic Papers, 1939.* 5 vols. Washington, D.C.: U.S. Government Printing Office, 1956.

Ribbentrop, Joachim von. *The Ribbentrop Memoirs.* Translated by Oliver Watson. London: Weidenfeld and Nicolson, 1954.

Scheidemann, Philip. *Memoirs of a Social Democrat.* 2 vols. Translated by J.E. Michell. London: Hodder and Stoughton, 1929.

Schellenberg, Walter. *Hitler's Secret Service.* Translated by Louis Hagen. New York: Pyramid Books, 1974.

Schmidt, Paul. *Hitler's Interpreter.* Translated by R. H.C. Steed. London: William Heinemann, 1950.

Schuschnigg, Kurt von. *Austrian Requiem.* Translated by Franz von Hildebrand. New York: G.P. Putnam's Sons, 1946.

Seeckt, Hans von. *Aus seinem Leben.* Berlin: Hase and Koehler, 1940.

Shirer, William L. *Berlin Diary: The Journal of a Foreign Correspondent 1934–1941.* New York: Popular Library, 1961.

Sontag, Raymond James et al., eds. *Documents on German Foreign Policy from the Archives of the German Foreign Ministry, Series D.* 7 vols. Washington, D.C.: U.S. Government Printing Office, 1948.

Speer, Albert. *Inside the Third Reich,* Translated by Richard and Clara Winston, New York: Avon Books, 1973.

———. Spandau, *The Secret Diaries.* Translated by Richard and Clara Winston. New York: Pocket Books, 1977.

Stresemann, Gustav. *His Diaries, Letters, and Papers.* 3 vols. Edited and translated by Erich Sutton. New York: Macmillan Co., 1935.

Weizsäcker, Ernst von. *The Memoirs of Ernst von Weizsäcker.* Translated by John Andrews. London: Victor Gollancz, 1951.

Wood, Edward Frederick L. *The Earl of Halifax: Fullness of Days.* London: Collins, 1957.

Woodward, E.L., and Butler, Rohan, eds. *Documents on British Foreign Policy, Third Series.* 9 vols. London: His Majesty's Stationery Office, 1950.

Zhukov, Georgi K. *Marshal Zhukov's Greatest Battles.* Translated by Theodore Shabab. New York: Harper and Row, 1969.

2. SECONDARY SOURCES

Albertini, Luigi. *The Origins of the War of 1914.* 3 vols. London: Oxford University Press, 1953.

Austin, William W. *Music in the 20th Century.* New York: W. W. Norton, 1966.

Bailey, Thomas A. *Woodrow Wilson and the Lost Peace.* Chicago: Quadrangle Paperbacks, 1963.

Bauer, Heinrich. *Stresemann, Ein deutscher Staatsmann.* Berlin: Verlag von George Stilke, 1930.

Belfour, Michael. *The Kaiser and His Times.* New York: W. W. Norton, 1972.

Bewley, Charles. *Hermann Göring and the Third Reich.* New York: Devon-Adair, 1962.

Bluel, Hans Peter. *Sex and Society in Nazi Germany.* Translated by J. Maxwell Brownjohn. New York: Bantam Books, 1974.

Bracher, Karl Dietrich. *The German Dictatorship.* Translated by Jean Steinberg. New York: Praeger Publishers, 1970.

Bresciani-Turroni, Constantino. *The Economics of Inflation: A Study of Currency Depreciation in Post-War Germany.* Translated by Millicent E. Sayers. London: George Allen and Unwin, 1937.

Brissaud, Andre. *Canaris.* London: Weiden Field and Nicolson, 1970.

Brown, Anthony Cave. *Bodyguard of Lies.* New York: Harper and Row, 1975.

Bullock, Alan. *Hitler: A Study in Tyranny.* New York: Harper and Row, 1962.

Bundeszentrale für politische Bildung. *Germans Against Hitler. July 20, 1944.* Bonn: Press and Information Office of the Federal Government of Germany, 1964.

Bibliography

Carr, William. *Arms, Autarky, and Aggression: A Study in German Foreign Policy, 1933–1939.* New York: W. W. Norton, 1973.

Carsten, F. L. *The Reichswehr and Politics 1918–1933.* Berkeley: The University of California Press, 1973.

Chuikov, Vasili I. *The Battle for Stalingrad.* Translated by Harold Silver. New York: Holt, Rinehart and Winston, 1964.

———. *The Fall of Berlin.* Translated by Ruth Kisch. New York: Holt, Rinehart and Winston, 1967.

Churchill, Winston S. *The Second World War.* 6 vols. New York: Bantam Books, 1961.

Cochrane. Arthur C. *The Church's Confession under Hitler.* Philadelphia: Westminister Press, 1962.

Collier, Richard. *Eagle Day: The Battle of Britain, August 6–September 15, 1940.* New York: E. P. Dutton and Co., 1966.

Collins, Larry, and Lapierre, Dominique. *Is Paris Burning?* New York: Pocket Books, 1965.

Cowles, Virginia, *The Kaiser.* New York: Harper and Row, 1963.

Craig, Gordon A. *The Politics of the Prussian Army, 1640–1945.* London: Oxford University Press, 1955.

Davidson, Eugene. *The Trial of the Germans.* New York: Collier Books, 1972.

Dawidowicz, Lucy S. *The War Against the Jews, 1933–1945.* New York: Holt, Rinehart and Winston, 1975.

Dedijer, Vladimir. *The Road to Sarajevo.* New York: Simon and Schuster, 1966.

Deri, Otto. *Exploring Twentieth Century Music.* New York: Holt, Rinehart and Winston, 1968.

Dorpalen, Andreas. *Hindenburg and the Weimar Republic.* Princeton: Princeton University Press, 1964.

Elstob, Peter. *Hitler's Last Offensive: The Full Story of the Battle of the Ardennes.* New York: Macmillan Co., 1971.

Eyck, Erich. *Bismarck and the German Empire.* New York: W. W. Norton, 1968.

———. *A History of the Weimar Republic.* 2 vols. Cambridge, Mass.: Harvard University Press, 1962.

Fainson, Merle. *International Socialism and the World War.* Garden City, N.Y.: Doubleday and Co., 1961.

Fay, Sidney B. *The Origins of the World War.* 2 vols. London: Macmillan Co., 1930.

Fest, Joachim C. *The Face of the Third Reich: Portraits of The Nazi Leadership.* Translated by Michael Bullock. New York: Ace Books, 1970.

———. *Hitler.* Translated by Richard and Clara Winston. New York: W. W. Norton, 1967.

Fischer, Louis. *The Life of Lenin.* New York: Harper and Row, 1964.

Fitzgibbon, Constantine. *20 July.* New York: W. W. Norton, 1956.

Friedrich, Otto. *Before the Deluge: A Portrait of Berlin in the 1920s.* New York: Avon Books, 1973.

Friedrich, Werner P. *History of German Literature.* New York: Barnes and Noble, 1948.

Gay, Peter. *Weimar Culture: The Outsider as Insider.* New York: Harper Torchbooks, 1968.

Gehlen, Reinhard. *The Service.* Translated by David Irving. New York: World Publishers, 1972.

Graham, Frank D. *Exchange Prices and Production in Hyper-Inflation Germany, 1920–1923.* Princeton: Princeton University Press, 1930.

Grunberger, Richard. *The 12 Year Reich: A Social History of Nazi Germany 1933–1945.* New York: Ballantine Books, 1971.

Halperin, S. William. *Germany Tried Democracy: A Political History of the Reich from 1918 to 1933.* New York: W. W. Norton, 1965.

Hart, B. H. Liddell. *History of the Second World War.* New York: G. P. Putnam's Sons, 1971.

Heiber, Helmut. *Joseph Goebbels.* Berlin: Colloquium Verlag, 1962.

Heiden, Konrad. *Der Fuehrer.* Boston: Houghton Mifflin, 1944.

Herre, Paul. *Kronprinz Wilhelm: Seine Rolle in der deutschen Politik.* Munich: Verlag C. H. Beck, 1954.

Higgins, Trumbull. *Hitler and Russia: The Third Reich in a Two Front War 1937–1943.* New York: Macmillan Co., 1966.

Hilberg, Raul. *The Destruction of the European Jews.* Chicago: Quadrangle Books, 1961.

Hildebrand, Klaus. *The Foreign Policy of the Third Reich.* Translated by Anthony Fothergill. Berkeley: The University of California Press, 1973.

Hoffmann, Hans Hubert. *Der Hitler Putsch.* Munich: Nymphenburger Verlagshandlung, 1961.

Hoggan, David. *Der Erzwungene Krieg.* Tübingen: Verlag der deutschen Hochschullerer Zeitung, 1970.

Höhne, Heinz. *The Order of the Death's Head: The Story of Hitler's S.S.* Translated by Richard Barry. New York: Coward-McCann, 1967.

Holborn, Hajo. *A History of Modern Germany,* 3 vols. New York: Alfred A. Knopf, 1959. Vol. 1: *The Reformation.* Vol. 2: *1648–1840.* Vol. 3: *1840–1945.*

Infield, Glenn B. *Eva and Adolf.* New York: Ballantine Books, 1974.

Janson, H. W., and Janson, Dora Jane. *The Story of Painting for Young People.* New York: Abrams, 1962.

Jenks, William S. *Vienna and the Young Hitler.* New York: Columbia University Press, 1960.

Jetzinger, Franz. *Hitlers Jugend: Phantasien Lügen und die Wahrheit.* Vienna: Europa Verlag, 1956.

Keynes, John Maynard. *The Economic Consequences of the Peace.* New York: Harcourt, Brace and How, 1920.

Knight-Patterson, W. M. *Germany from Defeat to Conquest.* London: George Allen and Unwin, 1945.

Kock, H.W. *The Hitler Youth.* London: McDonald and Jones, 1976.

Kohn, Hans. *The Mind of Germany: The Education of a Nation.* New York: Harper Torchbooks, 1965.

Kracauer, Siegfried. *From Caligari to Hitler: A Psychological History of German Film.* Princeton: Princeton University Press, 1966.

Kramarz, Joachim. *Stauffenberg.* Translated by R. H. Barry. New York: Macmillan Co., 1967.

Krausnick, Helmut. *Anatomy of the S.S. State.* Translated by Richard Barry. London: Collins, 1968.
Langer, Walter, *The Mind of Adolf Hitler.* New York: Basic Books, 1972.
Levin, Nora. *The Holocaust: The Destruction of European Jewry 1933–1945.* New York: Thomas Y. Crowell Co., 1968.
Lukacs, John. *The Last European War.* Garden City, N.Y.: Anchor Press, 1976.
Machlis, Joseph. *The Enjoyment of Music.* New York: W. W. Norton, 1963.
Manvell, Roger, and Fraenkel, Heinrich. *Hess: A Biography.* London: McGibbon and Kee, 1971.
———. *Himmler.* New York: G. P. Putnam's Sons, 1964.
Maser, Werner. *Der Frühgeschichte der NSDAP: Hitlers Weg bis 1924.* Frankfurt: Anthenäum Verlag, 1966.
———. *Hitler: Legend, Myth and Reality.* Translated by Peter and Betty Ross. New York: Harper Torchbooks, 1971.
Mitchell, Allan. *Revolution in Bavaria 1918–1919: The Eisner Regime and the Soviet Republic.* Princeton: Princeton University Press, 1965.
Morris, Warren B., Jr. *The Revisionist Historians and German War Guilt.* New York: The Revisionist Press, 1977.
———. *The Road to Olmütz: The Career of Joseph Maria von Radowitz.* New York: The Revisionist Press, 1976.
Mosley, Leonard. *The Reich Marshal: A Biography of Hermann Göring.* New York: Dell, 1974.
Mosse, George L. *The Crisis of German Ideology, Intellectual Origins of the Third Reich.* New York: The Universal Library, 1964.
———. *Nazi Culture.* New York: The Universal Library, 1966.
Nettle, J. P. *Rosa Luxemburg.* New York: Oxford University Press, 1969.
Neumann, Franz. *Behemoth: The Structure and Practice of National Socialism 1933–1944.* New York: Harper Torchbooks, 1944.
Nogueres, Henri. *Munich "Peace in Our Time."* Translated by Patrick O'Brian. New York: McGraw Hill, 1965.
Payne, Robert. *The Life and Death of Adolf Hitler.* New York: Popular Library, 1973.
Pinson, Koppels. *Modern Germany: Its History and Civilization.* New York: The Macmillan Co., 1966.
Popov, Dusko. *Spy Counter Spy.* New York: Grosset and Dunlap, 1974.
Post, Gaines, Jr. *The Civil Military Fabric of Weimar Foreign Policy.* Princeton: Princeton University Press, 1973.
Pridham, Geoffrey. *Hitler's Rise to Power: The Nazi Movement in Bavaria, 1923–1933.* New York: Harper and Row, 1973.
Reinmann, Viktor. *Dr. Joseph Goebbels.* Vienna: Verlag Fritz Molden, 1971.
Reitlinger, Gerald. *The Final Solution: The Attempt to Exterminate the Jews of Europe 1939–1945.* New York: A.S. Barnes and Co., 1961.
Rich, Norman. *Hitler's War Aims: Ideology, the Nazi State, and the Course of Expansion.* 2 vols. New York: W. W. Norton, 1973.
Robertson, J. G. et al. *A History of German Literature.* London: British Book Center, 1966.
Robertson, Priscilla. *The Revolutions of 1848: A Social History.* Princeton: Princeton University Press, 1967.

Rodes, John E. *Germany: A History.* New York: Holt, Rinehart and Winston, 1964.
Roh, Franz. *German Art in the 20th Century.* Greenwich, Conn.: New York Graphic Society, 1968.
Röhrs, Hans-Dietrich. *Hitlers Krankheit.* Neckargemünd: Kurt Vowinckei Verlag, 1966.
Roon, Ger von. *German Resistance to Hitler: Count von Moltke and The Kreisau Circle.* London: Van Nostrand Reinhold Co., 1971.
Rose, Ernst. *A History of German Literature.* New York: The Gotham Library, 1960.
Rothfels, Hans. *The German Opposition to Hitler.* Hinsdale, Ill.: Henry Regnery Co., 1948.
Ryan, Cornelius. *The Last Battle.* New York: Simon and Schuster, 1966.
———. *The Longest Day, June 6, 1944.* New York: Simon and Schuster, 1959.
Ryder, Arthur John. *The German Revolution of 1918: A Study of German Socialism in War and Revolt.* Cambridge: Cambridge University Press, 1967.
Salisbury, Harrison E. *The 900 Days: The Siege of Leningrad.* New York: Harper and Row, 1969.
Schlabrendorff, Fabian von. *The Secret War Against Hitler.* Translated by Hilde Simon. New York: Pitman, 1965.
Schmitt, Bernadotte E. *The Coming of the War, 1914.* New York: Charles Scribner and Sons, 1930.
Schoenbaum, David. *Hitler's Social Revolution: Class and Society in Nazi Germany 1933–1939.* Garden City, N.Y.: Doubleday and Co., 1966.
Schramm, Wilhelm von. *Der 20 Juli in Paris.* Bad Wörishofen: Kindler and Schiermeyer Verlag, 1953.
Seaton, Albert. *The Russo-German War 1941–1945.* New York: Praeger Publishers, 1970.
Shirer, William L. *The Rise and Fall of the Third Reich.* New York: Simon and Schuster, 1960.
Smith, Bradley F. *Adolf Hitler, His Family, Childhood, and Youth.* Stanford: The Hoover Institution on War, Revolution, and Peace, 1967.
Stavrianos, L.S. *The Balkans Since 1453.* New York: Holt, Rinehart and Winston, 1966.
Stein, George H. *The Waffen S.S. Hitler's Elite Guard at War 1939–1945.* Ithaca, N.Y.: Cornell University Press, 1966.
Steiner, Jean Francois. *Treblinka.* Translated by Helen Weaver. New York: Simon and Schuster, 1967.
Stern, Fritz. *The Politics of Cultural Despair: A Study in The Rise of the Germanic Ideology.* Berkeley: The University of California Press, 1974.
Sybel, Heinrich von. *The Founding of the German Empire by William I.* 6 vols. Translated by Marschall Livingston Perrin and Gamalied Bradford. New York: Thomas Y. Crowell and Co., 1890.

Taylor, A.J.P. *Bismarck: The Man and the Statesman.* New York: Vintage Books, 1955.
———. *The Origins of the Second World War.* Greenwich, Conn.: Fawcett Books, 1968.
Taylor, Telford. *Sword and Swastika, Generals and Nazis in The Third Reich.* Chicago: Quadrangle Paperbooks, 1969.
Tillion, Germaine. *Ravensbrück.* Translated by Gerald Satterwhite. Garden City, N.Y.: Anchor Books, 1975.
Tobias, Fritz. *The Reichstag Fire.* New York: G. P. Putnam's Sons, 1964.
Toland, John. *The Last 100 Days.* New York: Random House, 1966.
Trevor-Roper, H. R., ed. *The Last Days of Hitler.* New York: Collier Books, 1962.
Ulam, Adam B. *Stalin: The Man and His Era.* New York: The Viking Press, 1973.
Valentine, Veit. *Geschichte der deutschen Revolution von 1848–1849.* 2 vols. Aalen: Scientia Verlag, 1968.
Vogt, Hannah. *The Burden of Guilt.* Translated by Herbert Strauss. New York: Oxford University Press, 1964.
Waite, Robert G.L. *Vanguard of Nazism: The Free Corps Movement in Postwar Germany 1918–1923.* New York: W. W. Norton, 1969.
Waldman, Erich. *The Spartacist Uprising of 1919.* Milwaukee: The Marquette University Press, 1956.
Watt, Richard M. *The Kings Depart: The Tragedy of Germany, Versailles and the German Revolution.* New York: Clarion Books, 1968.
Webster, Charles, and Frankland, Noble. *The Strategic Air Offensive Against Germany 1939–1945.* 4 vols. London: Her Majesty's Stationery Office, 1961.
Weinberg, Gerald. *The Foreign Policy of Hitler's Germany: Diplomatic Revolution in Europe, 1933–1936.* Chicago: The University of Chicago Press, 1970.
Welcker, Hans Meir. *Seeckt.* Frankfurt: Bernard and Graefe Verlag, 1967.
Werth, Alexander. *Russia at War 1941–1945.* New York: E. P. Dutton and Co., 1964.
Wheaton, Elliot Barculo. *The Nazi Revolution 1933–1935: Prelude to Calamity.* Garden City, N.Y.: Doubleday and Co., 1969.
Wheeler-Bennett, John W. *The Nemesis of Power: The German Army in Politics 1918–1945.* London: Macmillan Co., 1964.
Winterbotham, F. W. *The Ultra Secret.* New York: Harper and Row, 1974.
Zeller, Eberhard. *The Flame of Freedom: The German Struggle Against Hitler.* Coral Gables Fla.: University of Miami Press, 1969.
Zeman, A. A. B. *Nazi Propaganda.* New York: Oxford University Press, 1973.

Index

Abraham, Karl, 150
Adermann, Paul, 183
Ahlwardt, Hermann, 14
Alfonso XIII (king of Spain), 250
Altelt, Karl, 48, 50
Alvensleben, Werner von, 180–81
Amann, Max, 107
Ame, Cesare, 315
Anti-Comintern Pact, 252–53
Anti-Semitism, 17, 100, 103–4, 152, 160–61, 207, 210, 220, 221, 223, 226, 331–35
Antonescu, Ion, 298
Anzio, Battle of, 317–18
Arco-Valley, Anton von, 58–59
Arnim, Achim von, 7
Arnold, Karl, 143
Asquith, Herbert, 24
Atlantic Charter, 309
Auchinleck, Claude, 310
Auer, Erhard, 59, 115
Auerbach, Berthold, 12
Auschwitz, 329, 334–35
Austria, 3, 4, 10; German nationalism in, 236–37; Nazi movement in, 237–40, 246–47; Nazi occupation, 258–63
Axis, 251–52
Azana, Manuel, 250

Badoglio, Pietro, 315
Baldwin, Stanley, 132
Balkan Wars, 21
Barbarossa, Operation, 298, 300, 301, 303–6
Bauer, Max, 73–74
Bauhaus, 146–47
Bavaria, 58–60
Bebel, August, 17, 51
Beck, Josef, 272
Beck, Ludwig, 256–57, 264–65, 340, 343–44
Becker, Nicholas, 8
Beckmann, Max, 147
Belgium, 22–23, 286
Bell, G. K. A., 227
Belzec, 334
Beneš, 132, 264–66, 268
Benn, Gottfried, 145
Berchtold, Leopold, 21
Bergmann, Karl, 83
Berlin: culture in the 1920s, 148; Revolution of 1918–1919, 50, 54–57
Berlin, Trade Union Council of, 50–51
Berlin, Treaty of, 134, 236
Berlin, University of, 221–22
Bernadotte, Folke, 358
Bernhardt, Johannes, 250
Bernstein, Eduard, 17, 30
Bernstorff, Johann von, 35

Bertram, Ernst, 144
Bethmann-Hollweg, Theobald von, 21, 22, 29, 32, 35
Bismarck, Otto von, 9–12, 19–20, 184
Black Band, 256, 266, 281, 336
Blitzkrieg, 279
Blomberg, Werner von, 179, 180–81, 200, 202, 241, 245, 255, 256, 257–58
Blue Rider, 146
Blumentritt, Günther, 272–73
Blunck, Hans Friedrich, 219
Bock, Fedor von, 304, 305
Böckel, Otto, 14
Bockelberg, Vollard, 242
Bodenschats, Karl, 242
Bodyguard, Operation, 320–21
Bonhöffer, Dietrich, 227–28, 336, 340
Boris III (tsar of Bulgaria), 302
Bormann, Martin, 211, 337, 357, 358, 359
Bosch, Carl, 242
Bradley, Omar, 322, 354
Brauchitsch, Walter von, 264, 265, 281, 298
Braun, Eva, 214, 349, 358, 359
Braun, Otto, 82, 131
Brecht, Bertolt, 149–50
Brentano, Clemens, 7
Brest-Litovsk, Treaty of, 36–37
Briand, Aristide, 83, 132–33
"The Bridge," 146
Broadcasting, Reich Chamber of, 221
Brockdorff-Ahlenfeldt, Walter von, 266
Brooke, Alan, 309
Bruck, Moeller van den, 151–52
Brüning, Heinrich, 159–60, 161–62, 163–65, 166–69, 172, 188, 192
Buchenwald, 330
Bulge, Battle of the, 355–56
Bülow, Bernhard Wilhelm von, 161
Bülow, Hans von, 143
Burschenschaft, 7

Canaris, Wilhelm Franz, 255–56, 281, 300, 315, 336, 340, 353
Carol (king of Rumania), 298
Cassirer, Ernst, 150
Catholic Youth, 224, 229
Center Party, 62, 77, 81, 82, 128, 130, 131, 160, 174, 183, 185, 192
Central Cooperative Union, 53
Central Council of the Workers' and Soldiers' Councils, 64
Chamberlain, Austen, 132
Chamberlain, Houston Stewart, 14, 117
Chamberlain, Neville, 253, 267–70, 272
Charlemagne, 2
Charles I (Emperor of Austria), 31

385

INDEX

Charles IV (Holy Roman Emperor), 3
Chateau Thierry, 39
Chelmo, 332
Chicherin, Gregory, 134
Choltitz, Dietrich von, 354–55
Churchill, Winston, 266, 288, 291, 294, 309, 313
Ciano, Galeazzo, 251–52, 274, 280
Class, Heinrich, 28–29, 137
Classicism, 4
Clemenceau, Georges, 64–66
Confessing Church, 227–28
Communist Party of Germany, 54, 57, 63, 81, 82, 128, 131, 135, 160, 166, 174, 187
Communist Revolt of 1920, 77–78
Communists, international, 326–27
Concentration camps, 182, 205–6, 329–31, 334–35
Congress of Workers' and Soldiers' Councils, 53
Corinth, Louis, 143
Credit Anstalt, 162
Cult of the folk, 12–15, 114, 117, 217, 223
Culture, Reich Chamber of, 219
Czechoslovakia, 263–70, 270–71
Czerin, Ottokar, 31

Dachau, 205, 329, 330
Dahlerus, Birger, 275
Daladier, Edouard, 267–68, 269
Danzig, 66, 235–36, 271–72, 274–76
Darlan, Jean-Francois, 312
Darmstädter Bank, 163
Darwin, Charles, 14
Däuming, Ernst, 82
Dawes, Charles G., 129
Dawes Plan, 129–30, 136
De Gaulle, Charles, 312
Delp, Alfred, 337
Democratic Party, German, 62, 80, 81, 82, 128, 131, 174, 192
Denmark, 10, 284, 327
Depression, 158–69
Derres, Alfred, 194
De Wiart, Carton, 285
Diedrichs, Eugene, 13
Dietrich, Marlene, 145
Dimitrijevich, Dragutin, 21
Dittmann, Wilhelm, 82
Döblin, Alfred, 145
Dohnayi, Hans von, 266, 336, 340
Dolfuss, Engelbert, 237, 238, 240, 246, 260
Dönitz, Karl von, 319–20, 358
Dorten, Adam, 127–28
Doumer, Paul, 83
Dowding, Hugh, 292
Dresden, 351
Drews, Wilhelm, 44
Drexler, Anton, 110–11, 113
Dreyfus, Alfred, 17

Duisberg, Carl, 242
Dunkirk, 289
Düsterberg, Theodor, 166–67
Dynamo, Operation, 289

Eagle, Operation, 292
Eben Emael, 287
Ebert, Friedrich, 77, 121, 128, 186; death, 131; early life, 50–51; formation of government, 51–53; formation of Weimar Republic, 63–64; Kapp Putsch, 74–77; Treaty of Versailles, 68–69
Eden, Anthony, 243
Ehrhardt, Hermann, 74–75
Ehrhardt Brigade, 74
Eichhorn, Emil, 54–55
Eichmann, Adolf, 333
Eicke, Theodor, 205
Eisenhower, Dwight D., 312–13, 314; Normandy Invasion, 320–22
Eisenlohr, Ernst, 263
Eisner, Kurt, 51, 57–59
Eitingon, Max, 150
Enabling Act, 185–86
Enigma Machine, 282
Enlightenment, 4
Epenstein, Hermann von, 119
Epp, Franz von, 118
Eppler, John, 311
Ernst, Max, 146
Erzberger, Matthias, 31–32, 45, 85
Esser, Hermann, 116
Ethiopia, 244–45
Experiments, medical, 329–31
Expressionism, 145–48

Falkhayn, Erich von, 26
Fallersleben, Heinrich von, 8
Farben, I.G., 205, 242–43
Faulhaber, Michael von, 229–30
Feder, Gottfried, 111
Fedyunisky, I.I., 318
Fehrenbach, Konstantin, 82
Fellgiebel, Erich, 281–82
Felix, Undertaking, 299
Ferdinand, Franz, 21, 106, 303
Fichte, Johann Gottlieb, 6
Film Credit Bank, 221
Final Solution, 333–35
Finland, 242, 274, 283
Foch, Ferdinand, 38–39, 45
Foley, Francis, 256
Forster, Albert, 271
Fourteen Points, 37–38
Four Year Plan, 199
France, 25, 235, 242, 243, 244, 246, 251, 263, 267–69, 275–76; German invasion, 288–90; liberation, 320–22, 353–55; occupation of the Ruhr, 86–87, 126–28
Franco, Francisco, 250–51, 256, 299

Index

Franco-Prussian War, 11
Frank, Hans, 92, 219, 251, 326
Frankfurt National Assembly, 8
Frauendorfer, Max, 195
Frederick I (king of Prussia), 4
Frederick II (king of Prussia), 4, 184, 220
Frederick IX (king of Denmark), 327
Frederick William the Great Elector, 3
Frederick William I (king of Prussia), 3, 184
Frederick William IV (king of Prussia), 8–9
Free Corps, 56, 59–60
Freud, Sigmund, 140, 150
Frick, Wilhelm, 124, 160, 167, 192, 208, 227, 359
Friedman, William F., 308
Fritsch, Werner von, 178, 201, 241, 255, 257–58
Fromm, Friedrich, 341, 344
Frontier Guard Units, 79–80
Funk, Walter, 195–96

Gabeik, Josef, 327
Geneva Protocol, 132
George V (king of Great Britain), 24
George, Stefan, 144–45
German Christianity, 225–26, 229
Gersdorf, Rudolf von, 339–40
Gessler, Otto, 78
Gilbert, Parker, 130, 136
Giraud, Henri, 312
Glassl, Anna, 90, 92–93
Gleichschaltung, 191–210
Gneisenau, August von, 241
Gobineau, Arthur de, 14
Goebbels, Paul Josef, 177, 210, 211, 213, 235, 236, 238, 344, 357, 358; early life, 156–57; as propaganda minister, 219–25
Goethe, Johann Wolfgang von, 4, 222
Golz, Rüdiger von der, 258
Gördeler, Carl Friedrich, 336, 340
Göring, Hermann, 121, 175, 177, 179, 183, 185–86, 195, 204, 211, 227, 257, 258, 262, 266, 268, 271, 275, 282, 283, 289, 292–94, 297, 333, 357, 358, 359; Beer Hall Putsch, 122; early life, 119–20; formation of Luftwaffe, 241–42; Four Year Plan, 199–200
Gort, John, 280
Graf, Ulrich, 124
Graf, Willi, 338
Great Britain, 235, 242–46, 263, 266–69, 275–76
Greece, 300, 303
Green, Case, 264, 265, 266
Green Front, 136
Grimm, Jacob, 7
Grimm, Wilhelm, 7
Gröber, Conrad, 230
Gröner, Wilhelm, 27, 45, 52, 54, 68, 167–68, 171, 172
Gropius, Walter, 146

Grosz, George, 146
Grünberg, Carl, 150
Grynspan, Herschell, 209
Guderian, Heinz, 305
Gustav Line, 317

Haakon VII (king of Norway), 284
Habicht, Theodor, 237–38
Habsburg, Otto von, 261
Habsburg, Rudolf of, 2
Hacha, Emil, 271
Häften, Werner von, 342, 343
Hagen, Louis, 127
Halder, Franz, 265, 269
Halifax, Edward Frederick Wood, Earl of, 253
Hamburg, 350
Hammerstein, Kurt von, 168–78, 180
Hanfstängl, Ernst, 124
Hanisch, Reinhold, 104–5
Hardenberg, Friedrich von, 6
Harding, Warren G., 83–84
Harrer, Karl, 110
Harriman, Averell, 309
Harris, Arthur, 350
Haukelid, Knut, 353
Hauptmann, Gerhardt, 16
Haushofer, Karl, 118, 234
Hausmann, Raul, 146
Hecker, Erich, 146
Heerman, Augustus, 282
Heine, Heinrich, 8, 16, 221, 222
Heine, Th.Th., 143
Heines, Edmund, 202
Heisenberg, Werner, 353
Helldorf, Wolf Heinrich von, 257
Helfferich, Karl, 27
Henderson, Nevile, 275, 276
Henlein, Konrad, 263–64, 267
Herber, Franz, 344
Herder, Johann Gottfried von, 6
Hermann, Curt, 143
Herriot, Edouard, 129
Herwegen, Ildefons, 230
Hess, Rudolf, 107, 118–21, 155, 177, 211, 227, 234, 336–37
Hesse, Hermann, 142
Heyde, Werner, 205
Heydrich, Reinhard, 327, 331, 332
Heyne, Wilhelm, 76
Hiedler, Georg Johann, 90, 91
Hiedler, Johann Nepomuk, 90, 92
Hilfdering, Rudolf, 82
Himmler, Heinrich, 203–7, 255, 257, 263, 266, 326, 340, 345–346, 358
Hindemith, Paul, 150
Hindenburg, Oskar von, 171, 180
Hindenburg, Paul von, 25–26, 40, 44, 131–32, 159, 160, 166–67, 172, 174, 175, 177–81, 183, 184, 186, 201, 203

Hindenburg Program, 27–28
Hirt, August, 330
Hitler, Adolf, 113–15, 137, 155–58, 165–66, 211, 212, 217–28; acquisition of power by, 166–81, 183–86; anti-Semitism of, 160–61, 209, 331–35; attempted assassination of, 338–46; attitude toward homosexuality, 101; Beer Hall Putsch, 121–24; beginnings of Nazi movement, 109–21; domestic policy of, 191–203; early years in Vienna, 98–105; foreign policy of, 233–71; last days of, 357–59; life-style of, 212–13, 349; mental health of, 348; Officers Corps, 255–58; physical health of, 95, 214–15, 347–48; rearmament, 240–43; and women, 95, 98, 101, 213–14; and World War I, 106–8; and World War II, 271–359; youth of, 89–98
Hitler, Alois. *See* Schicklgruber, Alois
Hitler, Klara Pölzl, 90, 93–94
Hitler Youth, 224–25
Hobbs, Leland S., 354
Hoffman, Heinrich, 214
Hoffman, Johannes, 59
Hoffmann, Max von, 36–37
Hoffmannsthal, Hugo von, 143
Hohenzollerns, 5, 9–11, 17
Holy Roman Empire, 2–5
Hölz, Max, 78
Hoover, Herbert, 162–63
Höpner, Erich, 266
Hörl, Heinrich, 146
Horlacher, Michael, 110
Horthy, Nikolaus, 270
Höss, Rudolf, 205, 329, 334–35
Hossbach, Friedrich, 254
Hossbach Memorandum, 254–55
House, Edward M., 34
Hoyer, Hermann Otto, 220
Huber, Kurt, 338
Huch, Ricarda, 143
Hugenberg, Alfred, 137, 166, 179, 192, 194
Hughes, Charles Evans, 129
Hungary, 220–21, 298
Huntzinger, Charles, 290
Husky, Operation, 313

Impressionism, 139–45
Independent Socialists, 30, 52, 63, 64, 81–82
Inflation, 87–88, 126–27
Iron Guard, 298
Italy (see also Benito Mussolini) 316–18

Jacop, Frank, 341
Janowitz, Hans, 148
Japan, 252–53, 307–8
Jarres, Karl, 131
Jawlensky, Alexi von, 146
Jodl, Alfred, 264, 302
Joffe, Adolf, 36
Joseph II (Holy Roman Emperor), 4

Jünger, Ernst, 149
Jutland, Battle of, 47

Kaas, Ludwig, 173, 185–86, 192, 229
Kafka, Franz, 145–46, 222
Kahr, Gustav von, 85, 121–23, 203
Kaltenbrunner, Ernst, 333, 359
Kant, Immanuel, 5
Kantorowicz, Ernst, 144–45
Kantzow, Carin von, 119
Kantzow, Nils von, 119
Kapp Putsch, 73–77
Kapp, Wolfgang, 74–77
Karlsbad Decrees, 7
Karlsbad Demands, 264–66
Kautsky, Karl, 30
Keitel, Wilhelm, 258–60, 343–45
Keller, Gottfried, 16
Kellermann, Bernhard, 105, 115
Kellogg-Briand Pact, 133
Kellogg, Frank B., 133
Kemnits, Mathilde, 122
Kerensky, Alexander, 36
Kerrl, Hans, 168, 226, 228
Kesselring, Albert, 316–18
Keudell, Walter von, 135
Kiel Mutiny, 48–50
Kirchner, Ernst Ludwig, 146
Kirsch, Wilhelm, 219
Kjellen, Rudolf, 234
Klagge, Dietrich, 165, 167
Klee, Paul, 146
Kleist, Heinrich von, 7
Kleist-Schmenzin, Ewald von, 266
Klintzsch, Johann Ulrich, 120
Kluge, Gunther von, 339, 341, 345, 354
Koch, Ilsa, 330–31
Kommerell, Max, 144
Königgrätz, Battle of, 10
Korfanty, Wojciech, 79–80
Korsun, Battle of, 319
Koryzes, Alexander, 303
Kotzebue, August von, 7
Krauch, Carl, 242
Krause, Reinhardt, 226
Kreisau Circle, 337, 340
Krüger, Gerhard, 223
Krupp, Friedrich, 242
Krupp, Gustaf, 196, 242
Krupp Works, 242
Kryha, Alexander von, 308
Kubis, Jan, 327
Kubizek, August, 97, 100–102
Küchler, Georg von, 319
Kühlmann, Richard von, 36
Kulmhof, 334

Labor Front, 193–94
Labor Service, 223, 225
Lagarde, Paul de, 13

L'Allemand, Siegmund, 99
Langbehn, Carl, 340
Langbehn, Julius, 13
Lansing, Robert, 35
Lanz, Adolf Josef, 104
Lanzinger, Hubert, 220
Large Germany Party, 8, 28
Layton Report, 164–65
League of Nations, 66, 132, 133, 234–35, 243, 252
League of Three Emperors, 20
Lebensborn, 206–7
Leber, Julius, 341
Leeb, Wilhelm von, 303
Leiber, Robert, 281
Leitz, Hermann, 14–15
Lenin, Vladimir Ilyich, 30, 36–37
Leningrad, 318–19
Leopold of Hohenzollern-Sigmaringen, 11
Leopold III (king of Belgium), 288
Lessing, Gotthold, 4, 221
Ley, Robert, 193, 223
Libski, Josef, 271–72, 276
Lidice, 327–28
Lidner, Alois, 59
Liebenfels, Lanz von, 104
Liebermann, Max, 142–43
Liebknecht, Karl, 24–25, 30, 50, 54, 56
Liebknecht, Wilhelm, 17
Lightfoot, Operation, 311
List, Guido von, 13
List, Wilhelm von, 107
Literature, German: before World War I, 4–5, 6–7, 8, 12, 16; during the Weimar Era, 140–53; in the Third Reich, 221–22
Literature, Reich Chamber of, 221–22
Lloyd George, David, 64–66, 83
Lloyd of Dolbran, 266
Locarno, Treaty of, 133
Löns, Hermann, 12–13
Lossow, Otto von, 120, 121, 122–23
Lotter, Michael, 110
Louis XVI (king of France), 5
Louis Philippe (king of France), 8
Lubbe, Martinus van der, 182–83
Lucas, John Porter, 317–18
Ludendorff, Erich von, 25–26, 29, 35, 38–40, 41, 44, 122–23, 158
Ludwig, Emil, 144
Lüger, Karl, 102, 115
Luther, Hans, 126, 131, 132, 163
Luther, Martin, 2, 226
Lüttwitz, Walter von, 74
Luxembourg, 287, 294
Luxemburg, Rosa, 30, 53–54, 56

McAuliffe, Anthony C., 353
MacDonald, Ramsay, 129, 132, 162, 235

Mackensen, Fritz, 143
Mackesy, P. J., 285
Magic, Project, 308
Maginot Line, 246, 280, 289
Maidens, Society of German, 225
Mann, Heinrich, 145
Mann, Thomas, 141–42, 145, 221–22
Manstein, Erich von, 286
Marc, Franz, 146
March, Don Juan, 256
Märcker, Ludwig, 56
Maria Theresa (Holy Roman Empress), 3, 4
Marita, Operation, 302
Markovich, Tsintsar, 302
Marne, First Battle of, 25
Marne, Second Battle of, 39
Marshall, George, 309
Marx, Wilhelm, 128, 131, 134, 135
Marxism, 16–17
Matzelberger, Franziska, 90, 92, 93
Maurice, Emil, 155
Max, Prince of Baden, 40–45, 51
May, Karl, 94
Mayer, Carl, 148
Mayer, Conrad Ferdinand, 12
Mayr, Karl, 110
Meinecke, Friedrich, 151
Meiser, Hans, 226–27
Menzies, Stewart Graham, 256, 266, 282
Metternich, Klemens von, 7
Michael (king of Rumania), 298
Michaelis, George, 32
Miklas, Wilhelm, 261
Milch, Erhard, 242
Modersohn-Becker, Paula, 146
Molotov, Viachaslav, 273, 301
Moltke, Helmuth von, 22, 26
Moltke, Helmut James von, 337, 340
Monet, Claude, 139, 142
Monkaster, Peter, 311
Monte Cassino, Battle of, 317
Montgomery, Bernard Law, 311–13, 314–15, 355
Morell, Theodor, 214, 347, 349
Morocco Incident, 20–21
Mukden Incident, 252
Müller, Hermann, 77, 135, 137, 159
Müller, Josef, 281, 336, 340
Müller, Karl Alexander von, 110
Müller, Ludwig, 226–27
Müller, Richard, 50, 52
Munich Agreement, 269–70, 276–77
Music, Reich Chamber of, 220–21
Mussolini, Benito, 116, 121, 237–40, 261, 262, 269, 274, 279, 280, 300, 301; Axis formation, 251–52; Balkan invasion, 300–301; Ethiopian invasion, 244–45; North African invasion, 30; overthrow of, 315; rescue of, 315; and Spanish Civil War, 250; and Tripartite Pact, 253

Naples, 317
Napoleon Bonaparte (emperor of France), 5–6
Napoleon III (emperor of France), 10–11
National Redoubt, Operation, 351
National Service Law, 27
Nationalism, 6–8. *See also* Cult of the Folk
Nationalist Party, German, 63, 81, 128, 130, 131, 135, 166, 177, 192
National Socialist German Worker's Party, 128, 131, 135, 160; in Beer Hall Putsch, 121–24; consolidation of power within, 184–86, 191–210; founding of, 110–21; growth of, 165–66, 174; platform of, 112–13; reorganization of, 157–58
National Socialist Student Union, 223
Neoclassicism, 144–45
Netherlands, 286, 288
Neurath, Constantin von, 245–46, 255–56
New Matter of Factness, the 148–50
New Fatherland, Society of The, 24–25
Nicholas II (tsar of Russia), 22, 23, 31, 36
Nicolson, Harold, 69
Niemöller, Martin, 227
Nietzsche, Friedrich, 15–16, 106, 149
Night of the Long Knives, 202–3
Normandy Invasion, 320–22
North Africa, World War II in, 301, 310–13
Noske, Gustav, 49–50, 55–56, 74–77, 78
Nuremberg Party Rallies, 217–19

Officers corps, German, 186, 257, 338, Kapp Putsch, 73–77; leadership by Hitler, 200–201, 257–58, opposition to Hitler, 255, 264; origins of, 3
Olbricht, Friedrich, 338, 342–44
Omaha Beach, Battle of, 322
Oradour-sur-Glane, 328
Orbis, Heinz, 127–28
Orlando, Vittorio, 64–66
Oshima, Hiroshi, 252, 308
Oster, Hans von, 266, 281
Ott, Eugene, 176
Otto, Operation, 261
Otto I (Holy Roman Emperor), 2
Overbeck, Fritz, 143
Overlord, Operation, 320–22

Papen, Franz von: chancellorship, 173–76; early life, 172; as German ambassador to Austria, 240, 245, 259; negotiations with Hitler, 174–75, 176–77, 178–81
Papst, Waldemar, 73–74
Paris, 354–55
Paris Peace Conference, 64–66, 69
Pashich, Nikola, 22
Pastor's Emergency League, 227
Patton, George S., 314, 321, 354, 355
Paul (prince of Yugoslavia), 302
Paulus, Friedrich von, 306

Payer, Friedrich von, 44
Peace Resolution of July 19, 1917, 31, 38
Pearl Harbor, 307–8
People's Party, German, 62–63, 81, 82, 128, 130, 131
Petain, Henri-Philippe, 289, 312
Peter II (king of Yugoslavia), 302
Philip of Hesse, 261, 262
Pilsudski, Joseph, 236
Pius XI (pope), 223, 229
Poincaré, Raymond, 22, 86
Poland, 271–72, 274–76, 279–80, 326, 356
Pölchau, Harald, 337
Pölzl, Klara, 90, 93
Pommer, Erich, 148
Poncet, Andre Francois, 202
Popitz, Johannes, 340
Popov, Dusko, 308
Popp, Arthur, 48
Pötsch, Leopold, 96
Preuss, Hugo, 61–62
Princip, Gavrilo, 21
Protestantism, 2, 226–28
Prussia, 3–4, 8, 9, 82, 174
Prussian Customs Union, 8
Prussian Plan of Union, 9
Psychoanalytical Institute of Berlin, 150
Punishment, Operation, 302–3
Puttkammer, Karl von, 322

Quisling, Vidkun, 283, 326

Racism, 13–14, 206–7. *See also* Anti-Semitism
Radek, Karl, 30
Räder, Erich, 241, 292, 299
Radowitz, Joseph Maria von, 9
Ranke, Leopold von, 144
Rapallo, Treaty of, 85–86, 236
Rath, Ernst von, 209
Rathenau, Walter, 27, 41, 84–85
Raubal, Angela, 213–14
Raubal, Geli, 214
Ravensbrück, 330
Realism, 16
Rearmament, 240–43
Reichenau, Walter von, 200, 258, 291
Reichsbanner, Black, Red, and Gold, 80, 168
Reichskrstall Nacht, 209–10
Reichstag fire, 182–83
Reichwein, Adolf, 337, 341
Reifenstahl, Lini, 218
Reinhardt, Walter, 75
Reinsurance Treaty, 20
Reitsch, Hanna, 358
Remarque, Erich Maria, 149
Remer, Otto, 344
Renoir, Auguste, 139, 142
Rentenmarks, 126–27

Index

Reparations, 67–68, 83–84, 128–30, 136–37, 162, 164–65, 173–74
Ribbentrop, Joachim von, 244, 253, 259–63, 271, 272, 273–74, 275–76, 298, 301, 357, 359
Riehl, Walter, 236
Riehl, Wilhelm Heinrich, 12
Rilke, Ranier Maria, 140–41
Rivera, Jose Antonio Primo de, 250
Rivera, Miguel Primo de, 250
Rodin, Auguste, 140
Röhm, Ernst, 118–19, 120, 123, 161, 201–2
Roman Catholicism, 17, 228–30
Romanticism, 5, 6–8
Rommel, Erwin, 309–13, 321, 341, 345, 346
Roosevelt, Franklin D., 289, 307, 308, 309, 313–14
Rosenberg, Alfred, 117–18, 359
Rostock, Max, 327–28
Royal Air Force, 292, 294, 350–51, 352
Rudolf of Habsburg, 2
Ruhr, French occupation of, 86–87, 126–28
Rumania, 298–99
Rundstedt, Gerd von, 291, 321–22, 355
Rundstedt, Karl von, 303–4
Runciman, Walter, 267
Rupprecht, Prince, 123
Rust, Bernhard, 223

Sachs, Hans, 150
Säkow, Anton, 341
Salerno, Battle of, 316
Salmon, Pfeffer von, 157–58
Samsonov, Alexander, 26
Sand, Karl, 7
Saxl, Fritz, 150
Sazanov, Serge, 22
Schacht, Hjalmar, 126–27, 195, 198–99, 242
Scharnhorst, Gerhard von, 241
Scheidemann, Philip, 50, 51–52, 64
Schellenberg, Walter, 340
Scherbius, Arthur, 281, 308
Schicklgruber, Alois (Hitler), 89–96
Schicklgruber, Maria Anna, 89–90, 91, 100
Schiller, Friedrich, 4, 222
Schindler, Oskar, 336
Schirach, Baldur von, 224
Schlabrendorff, Fabian von, 339
Schlageter, Albert Leo, 87, 220
Schlegel, August Wilhelm, 6
Schlegel, Friedrich, 6
Schleicher, Kurt von, 168, 172–73, 176, 256; chancellorship, 177–78; death, 203; early life, 171–72; negotiations with Hitler, 178–81
Schlieffen, Alfred von, 22
Schlieffen Plan, 22, 25, 286
Schmalkaldic League, War of the, 2

Schmorell, Alexander, 338
Schneckenburger, Max, 8
Schnitzler, Arthur, 140
Schnurre, Julius, 273
Scholl, Hans, 337–38
Scholl, Sophie, 337–38
Schönberg, Arnold, 147–48
Schuler, Alfred, 13
Schulte, Karl Joseph, 229
Schultze, Walter, 223
Schuschnigg, Kurt von, 240, 246, 251, 258–61
Schwarzenburg, Felix von, 9
Schwerin, Gerhard von, 281
Schweyer, Franz, 115
Sea Lion, Operation, 291–92
Sebottendorff, Rudolf von (Alfred Rudolf Glauer), 110
Seeckt, Hans von, 29, 75, 77–80, 86, 123, 130, 132, 172
Seisser, Hans von, 122
Seldte, Franz, 79, 137, 179, 181
Seven Weeks War, 10
Seven Years War, 4
Severing, Carl, 77
Seyss-Inquart, Arthur, 259, 359
Sicily, 314–15
Silesia, Upper, 84
Simon, John, 243
Simovich, Dushan, 302
Sinclair, Upton, 221
Skinnerland, Einar, 353
Skorzeny, Otto, 316
Slevogt, Max, 142
Slovakia, 270
Sobobir, 334
Social Democratic Party of Germany, 16–17, 19–20, 24–25, 29–30, 63, 64, 77, 80, 82, 88, 128, 130–31, 135, 160, 168, 174, 177, 183, 186, 192
Souchon, Wilhelm, 48
Soviet Union, 85–86, 236, 251, 253, 256, 273–74, 283; German invasion, 302–6; liberation, 306–7, 318–19
Spain, 250–51, 299–300
Spartacists, 50, 53–54, 57
Speer, Albert, 212, 218, 352, 357, 358
Speidel, Hans, 354
Spengler, Oswald, 151
S.S., 203–7, 219, 255, 263, 276, 326, 328, 335; Death's Head units, 329–31, 334–35; Einsatzgruppen, 332–33
Stahlein, 79, 179, 201
Stalin, Joseph, 236, 251, 273–74, 280, 283, 304, 309
Stalingrad, Battle of, 306
Stauffenberg, Claus von, 338–44
Stehlin, Paul, 268
Steiner, Felix, 357
Stimson, Henry L., 162

Stolz, Adam von Trott zu, 336
Storm Troopers, 120, 122–23, 157–58, 161, 167–68, 174, 182, 193, 197, 201–3, 219, 235, 237
Strasser, Gregor, 156–57, 177, 203
Strauss, Adolf, 291
Strauss, Richard, 143–44, 219
Streicher, Julius, 116–17, 121, 359
Strength Through Joy, 193–94
Stresemann, Gustav, 125–30, 132–34, 136–37
Stülpnagel, Heinrich von, 345
Stumme, George, 311
Sudetenland, 263–70
Suez Canal, 301
Suñer, Serrano, 299
Swastika, 114–15

Tannenberg, Battle of, 25–26
Tarnhari, 13
Thälmann, Ernst, 131, 166–67
Theresienstadt, 333
Thirty Years War, 2
Thomas, Ferdinand, 341
Thule Society, 59, 110
Tieck, Ludwig, 6
Tiso, Joseph, 270–71
Todt, Fritz, 220
Torgler, Ernst, 182
Treblinka, 334
Treeck, Robert, 256
Tresckow, Henning von, 339–40
Tripartite Pact, 253
Trotsky, Leon, 36–37
Trummelschlager, Johann, 89, 92
Tsoderos, Emmanuel, 303
Tsolakgou, George, 303
Tsvetkovich, Dragisha, 302
Tuka, Vojtech, 270

Udet, Ernst, 242
Uhde, Fritz von, 143
Ukraine, 319
Ultra, Project, 281–82, 288, 293, 294, 304, 312, 319, 320
United States, 34–36, 307–9
University Lecturers, National Socialist Association of, 223

V-1 Rocket Bomb, 352
V-2 Rocket Bomb, 352–53
Valkyrie, Operation, 338–44
Vasittart, Robert, 266
Veitinghoff, Heinrich von, 316

Versailles, Treaty of, 66–70, 233, 234, 235, 240, 241, 242, 245, 246, 271
Vienna, Congress of, 7

Wackenroder, Wilhelm, 6
Wagener, Otto Wilhelm, 195
Wagner, Richard, 15, 97, 100, 143, 217–21
Wagner, Walter, 358
Wandervögel, 15
Wannsee Conference, 333
War aims, World War I, 28–29, 34
Warburg, Aby, 150
Warsaw ghetto uprising, 335
Wartenburg, Yorck von, 337
Weber, Carl Maria von, 15
Wedekind, Frank, 145
Weill, Kurt, 149
Weimar Republic, 63–189; constitution, 70–71; founding of, 63–64; reasons for failure of, 186–89
Wels, Otto, 186
Werfkin, Marianne von, 146
Weser, Operation, 283
Westphalia, Peace of, 2–3
Weygand, Maxime, 288–89
White, Plan, 272–73
White Rose, Society of the, 338
Wiene, Robert, 148
Wietersheim, Gustav von, 265
Wilhelmina (queen of the Netherlands), 287
William I (emperor of Germany), 9, 11–12, 26
William II (emperor of Germany), 19–23, 32, 40, 44–45, 166
Wilson, Woodrow, 32, 33–36, 37–38, 40–45, 64–66, 187
Wincklemann, Johann, 4
Winterbotham, Frederick W., 282
Wirt, Christian, 331–32
Wirt, Joseph, 33, 84
Witzleben, Edwin von, 341

Yellow, Case, 280–81
Young Folk, 224
Young Maidens, 225
Young, Owen D., 137
Young Plan, 136–37, 162, 173
Youth Associations, Reich Committee of German, 224
Yugoslavia, 302–3

Zhukov, Georgi K., 306–7
Zimmermann Note, 35–36
Zog (king of Albania), 300